D1610891

The EU General Data Protection Regulation (GDPR): A Commentary

Lukas Feiler
Nikolaus Forgó
Michaela Weigl

Globe Law
and Business

German Law Publishers

Authors
Lukas Feiler
Nikolaus Forgó
Michaela Weigl

Managing director
Sian O'Neill

The EU General Data Protection Regulation (GDPR): A Commentary
is published by

Globe Law and Business Ltd
3 Mylor Close
Horsell
Woking
Surrey GU21 4DD
United Kingdom
Tel: +44 20 3745 4770
www.globelawandbusiness.com

Printed by CPI Group (UK) Ltd, Croydon CR0 4YY

The EU General Data Protection Regulation (GDPR): A Commentary
ISBN 9781787421363
EPUB ISBN 9781787421370
Adobe PDF ISBN 9781787421387
Mobi ISBN 9781787421394

DISCLAIMER
This publication is intended as a general guide only. The information and opinions which it contains
are not intended to be a comprehensive study, nor to provide legal advice, and should not be treated
as a substitute for legal advice concerning particular situations. Legal advice should always be sought
before taking any action based on the information provided. The publishers bear no responsibility for
any errors or omissions contained herein.

Contents

List of abbreviations

Art.	article
Board	European Data Protection Board (as defined in Recital 72 and Art. 68 GDPR)
Brussels Ia-Regulation	Regulation (EU) No 1215/2012 of the European Parliament and of the Council of 12 December 2012 on jurisdiction and the recognition and enforcement of judgments in civil and commercial matters
cf.	confer/compare
C.F.R.	Code of Federal Regulations
CJEU	Court of Justice of the European Union
cmt.	comment
Charter	Charter of Fundamental Rights of the European Union
Data Protection Directive	Directive 95/46/EC of the European Parliament and of the Council of 24 October 1995 on the protection of individuals with regard to the processing of personal data and on the free movement of such data
E-Commerce Directive	Directive 2000/31/EC of the European Parliament and of the Council of 8 June 2000 on certain legal aspects of information society services, in particular electronic commerce, in the Internal Market
ECHR	European Convention for the Protection of Human Rights and Fundamental Freedoms
ECtHR	European Court of Human Rights
EEA	European Economic Area
eg	exempli gratia/for example
ePrivacy Directive	Directive 2002/58/EC of the European Parliament and of the Council of 12 July 2002 concerning the processing of personal data and the protection of privacy in the electronic communications sector (as amended by Directive 2009/136/EC)
et seq.	et sequens/and the following thing
et seqq.	et sequentia/and the following things
etc	et cetera/and the other things
EU	European Union

GDPR	General Data Protection Regulation (Regulation (EU) 2016/679 of the European Parliament and of the Council of 27 April 2016 on the protection of natural persons with regard to the processing of personal data and on the free movement of such data, and repealing Directive 95/46/EC
HR	Human Resources
ie	id est/that means
IP	Internet Protocol
lit.	litera
NGO	non-government organisation
No.	number
para.	paragraph
Rome I Regulation	Regulation (EC) No 593/2008 of the European Parliament and of the Council of 17 June 2008 on the law applicable to contractual obligations
Rome II Regulation	Regulation (EC) No 864/2007 of the European Parliament and of the Council of 11 July 2007 on the law applicable to non-contractual obligations
Sec.	Section
subpara.	subparagraph
TFEU	Treaty on the Functioning of the European Union
TEU	Treaty of the European Union

List of Recitals of the General Data Protection Regulation

Introduction to the General Data Protection Regulation

1. Introduction

The General Data Protection Regulation (GDPR) is one of the most ambitious legal projects of the European Union in the last years. From 25 May 2018 the GDPR will replace the Data Protection Directive and the data protection laws in 28 Member States will become obsolete to a large extent. Only those companies that start adapting their contracts, business processes and IT solutions pursuant to the GDPR in a timely manner will achieve a prudent level of compliance when the GDPR applies from 25 May 2018.

Not only the high fines of up to EUR 20 million or 4% of the total worldwide annual turnover illustrate that companies must take the GDPR seriously. Data protection has become one of the largest compliance risk areas and therefore necessarily a priority for the management of every company.

The below introduction allows the reader to quickly get an overview of the GDPR or certain parts of the GDPR. For certain details, the introduction refers to specific articles of the GDPR or specific comments of articles of the GDPR in the commentary section of this book.

2. The most important compliance steps to be implemented before the GDPR applies from 25 May 2018

The GDPR will apply from **25 May 2018** (Art. 99 para. 2). To achieve minimum compliance with the GDPR by then, controllers and processors must begin with compliance steps sooner rather than later.

For controllers the most important compliance steps to be implemented by 25 May 2018 can be summarised as follows:

1) implementation of a basic **data protection compliance programme** (see chapter 11 below) including the appointment of a **data protection officer**, to the extent reasonable or required in the particular case (see chapter 14 below);
2) preparation of a **record of processing activities** (see chapter 12 below);
3) review of the legal basis of the respective data processing operation (see chapter 7 below), in particular the new requirements regarding valid consent (see chapter 7.2 below);
4) development of GDPR compliant **privacy notices** (see chapter 8 below); and
5) review of the legal basis for **international data transfers** (see chapter 18 below).

For processors the most important compliance steps to be implemented by 25 May 2018 can be summarised as follows:

1) appointment of a **data protection officer** to the extent required or reasonable in the particular case (see chapter 14 below);
2) preparation of **records of processing activities** (see chapter 12 below);
3) implementation of **appropriate security measures** (see chapter 15.1);
4) ensuring that **subprocessors** are engaged only with prior specific or general written authorisation of the controller (Art. 28 para. 2); and
5) assurance that **international data transfers** take place only if compliant with the requirements of the GDPR (see chapter 18 below).

The above-mentioned measures will not produce full compliance with the GDPR but they help to focus the personnel and financial resources of a controller or processor on central compliance aspects.

For larger organisations it will also be required to assess generally in advance the regulatory risks resulting from the GDPR to allow for an efficient deployment of resources.

3.   Basic terms of the GDPR

The GDPR exclusively applies to **personal data** (see chapter 4.1 below). Personal data are defined as any information relating to an identified or identifiable **natural** person, who is referred to as the **data subject** (Art. 4 No. 1).

A subset of personal data is **sensitive data** (also 'special categories of personal data'). Sensitive data are defined in Art. 9 para. 1 as personal data revealing racial or ethnic origin, political opinions, religious or philosophical beliefs, trade union membership, data concerning a natural person's sex life or sexual orientation, data concerning health within the meaning of Art. 4 No. 15, genetic data within the meaning of Art. 4 No. 13 and biometric data (eg, fingerprints or facial images) if processed for the purpose of uniquely identifying a natural person (Art. 9 cmt. 3). Furthermore, social security numbers might be regarded as sensitive data (cf. Art. 4 cmt. 35).

The GPDR applies to controllers and processors (cf. Art. 3 cmt. 4). The GDPR defines the term **controller** as the natural or legal person which, alone or jointly with others, determines the purposes and means of the processing of personal data (Art. 4 No. 7).

Processor means a natural or legal person which processes personal data on behalf of the controller, that is, that it does not determine the purposes and means of the processing of personal data (Art. 4 No. 8). For example, if a company outsources the operation of its customer database to an IT service provider, the company still acts as a controller, whereas the IT service provider acts as a processor.

Processing is defined broadly as any operation which is performed on personal data such as the collection, recording, structuring, alteration, retrieval, use, disclosure by transmission, erasure or destruction (Art. 4 No. 2).

The term **transfer** is used quite frequently throughout the GDPR. However, it is not defined. Transfer includes the disclosure vis-à-vis another controller or processor, respectively a subprocessor (see Art. 44 cmt. 1).

The term **supervisory authority** means the data protection authority respectively established by each Member State.

4. The scope of the GDPR

The following provides an outline concerning: (i) the processing activities that are covered by the GDPR (see chapter 4.1 below), (ii) those to whom the GDPR applies (see chapter 4.2 below), and (iii) where the GDPR applies (see chapter 4.3 below).

4.1 Material scope – what processing activities are covered?

The GDPR generally applies to any processing of personal data. As set out above under chapter 3, personal data means any information relating to an **identified or identifiable natural person**. Whether a natural person is identifiable must be assessed **objectively**, not only taking into consideration the legal and factual possibilities of the controller, but also the possibilities of third parties (Art. 4 cmt. 3). For example, the IP address of a user constitutes personal data for the operator of a website, even if the operator of the website cannot identify the person but only the Internet access provider can identify the user (see decision of the CJEU, C-582/14 – Breye/Germany regarding the interpretation under the Data Protection Directive; see also the statement of the advocate general).

If data relate to **legal persons**, they only constitute personal data pursuant to the GDPR if the name of the legal person contains the name of a natural person (Art. 4 cmt. 1). Moreover, data that relate to deceased persons do not constitute personal data within the meaning of the GDPR (Art. 4 cmt. 2).

The GDPR basically only applies to **data processed by automatic means**. For data that is processed manually (generally on paper) the GDPR applies only if the personal data form part of a filing system or if they are intended to form part of a filing system (Art. 2 para. 1). 'Filing system' means any structured set of personal data which are accessible according to specific criteria (Art. 4 No. 6) such as HR files organised pursuant to names. Individual paper-based files are not subject to the GDPR (Art. 2 cmt. 4).

As an act of law of the Union, the GDPR does not apply to matters which fall outside the scope of Union law (eg, national security; see Art. 2 para. 2 lit. a). Furthermore, the GDPR does not apply to common foreign and security policy (Art. 2 para. 2 lit. d) or to the areas of the prevention, investigation, detection or prosecution of criminal offences and the execution of criminal penalties, including the safeguarding against and the prevention of threats to public security (Art. 2 para. 2 lit. d; in these areas, Directive (EU) 2016/680 applies which will have to be implemented separately into national laws).

Furthermore, the GDPR does not apply to the processing of personal data by natural persons in the course of a purely personal or household activity ('**household exemption**'; Art. 2 para. 2 lit. c). This covers in particular the use of social networks for private purposes (Art. 2 cmt. 7).

4.2 Personal scope – who does the GDPR apply to?

The GDPR applies to controllers and processors (see chapter 3 above regarding the definition of these terms).

Under the Data Protection Directive the role of the processor was advantageous because the processor was subject to only a few regulatory obligations. The commercial disadvantage was – and still is – the obligation to not use personal data for one's own purposes and to not commercially exploit them. If a company wants to use personal data for its own purposes and wants to commercially exploit the data (ie, is aiming for '**data ownership**'), the company has to be qualified as a controller which results in substantial additional obligations.

This has been changed by the GDPR because the GDPR applies to processors as it does to controllers and therefore makes processors subject to substantial regulatory obligations (see chapter 2 above) and subject to the same administrative fines (see chapter 20 below). Due to the alignment of obligations of controllers and processors, the commercial advantages of being a controller will become more attractive. Many companies that have so far limited themselves to being a processor, will likely try to move into a controller role. This would not only result in the applicability of regulatory obligations regarding the legal basis of the data processing such as consent of the data subject (see chapter 7 below) and transparency requirements (see chapter 8 below), but also in the requirement to revise existing contracts with customers, vendors and data subjects to reflect the new regulatory reality.

4.3 Territorial scope – where does the GDPR apply?

The GDPR applies to controllers and processors that are **established in the EU or the EEA** (see Art. 3 cmt. 5). Processors in the EU are subject to the GDPR even if they process data for controllers that are not subject to the GDPR (Art. 3 cmt. 4).

Furthermore, the GDPR applies if the controller, respectively the processor, is not established in the EU or the EEA, but has an establishment (eg, an affiliate) in the EU or in the EEA and the processing of personal data takes place **in the context of the activities of this establishment**. This applies, for example, if the US parent company processes personal data of customers of a German or Austrian affiliate to support the sales activities of that affiliate (see Art. 3 cmt. 2).

To ensure that companies that do not have an establishment in the EU/EEA but are active in the European market are subject to the same conditions of competition as European companies, the GDPR also applies to controllers and processors that are not established in the Union if they are **offering their goods or services, irrespective of whether a payment is required, in the Union, respectively the EEA** (Art. 3 para. 2 lit. b).

Furthermore, the GDPR applies to controllers and processors that are not established in the Union, but monitor the behaviour of data subjects in the Union (Art. 3 para. 2 lit. b). This applies in particular to online advertising networks which log the web browsing activities of Internet users to deliver personal online advertisement.

5. The relationship with national data protection laws

Like any EU regulation, the GDPR in general applies directly and may not be implemented by national law. The previously existing national data protection laws will therefore be largely superseded by the GDPR as of 25 May 2018.

Outside the scope of the GDPR (see chapter 4 above) national legislatures may enact additional data protection provisions. For example, this applies to data protection laws regarding legal persons where it remains to be seen whether Member States will make use of this possibility. In any case, taking into account the protection under the national laws transposing the Trade Secrets Directive (2016/943/EU), a blanket regulation of personal data relating to legal persons does not seem warranted.

Notwithstanding the above, there are numerous topics within the scope of the GDPR for which the GDPR does not (or not comprehensively) provide an answer but expressly authorises Member States through **opening clauses** to enact national laws. The GDPR therefore allows for deviations among Member States. This applies in particular to the following topics (cf. Art. 92 cmt. 4):

1) How old must a minor be to validly consent to the processing of his/her personal data? (Art. 8 para. 1 subpara. 2)
2) When is it not possible to validly consent to the processing of sensitive data? (Art. 9 para. 2 lit. a)
3) Is the processing of genetic data, biometric data or health data subject to additional limitations? (Art. 9 para. 5)
4) Is it permitted at all to process personal data on criminal convictions and offences? (eg, in connection with a whistleblower hotline; Art. 10)
5) Are automated individual decisions and profiling that are not necessary for the performance of the contract with the data subject permitted without consent of the data subject? (Art. 22 para. 2 lit. b)
6) Are the rights of data subjects subject to additional limitations? (Art. 23)
7) Do all controllers and processors have to appoint a data protection officer or only certain controllers and processors? (Art. 37 para. 4)
8) Is it possible to impose administrative fines on public authorities and bodies? (Art. 83 para. 7)
9) May data protection NGOs claim damages on behalf of data subjects? (Art. 80 para. 1)
10) May data protection NGOs initiate legal proceedings against a controller or a processor without a data subject's mandate? (Art. 80 para. 2)

Additionally, the GDPR grants the Member States a very far-reaching legislative competence for the processing of employees' personal data in the **employment context** (Art. 88) and allows the Member States to regulate the processing of personal data for journalistic purposes and the purposes of academic, artistic or literary expression (Art. 85) and to find reconciliation between the right to public access to official documents and the right to the protection of personal data (Art. 86).

As a result, the GDPR must always be read together with the respectively applicable national 'GDPR implementation act'. Therefore, the GDPR is also called a **'limping regulation'**. It is problematic that the GDPR does not contain any **'conflict of law'** provisions. Therefore, it remains unclear when to apply the law of which Member State.

In our opinion, this is an unintended gap which must be solved by analogy to the rules of competence under the GDPR (see chapter 19 above). If there is a lead competence of a certain supervisory authority for a controller or processor pursuant to Art. 56, the 'GDPR implementation act' of such Member State applies (see in detail Art. 92 cmt. 5).

6.   **The principles relating to the processing of personal data**

The GDPR stipulates the following principles that must be complied with whenever personal data is processed (Art. 5 para. 1):

1) **Lawfulness** (Art. 5 para. 1 lit. a): Personal data must be processed lawfully, that is, a legal basis for the processing is required (see chapter 7 below).

2) Fairness (Art. 5 para. 1 lit. a): Personal data must be processed fairly which is of relevance in particular when conducting a balancing of interests test (see, eg, Art. 6 para. 1 lit. f).

3) **Transparency** (Art. 5 para. 1 lit. a): Personal data must be processed in a transparent manner in relation to the data subject. This principle is further specified by the information obligations contained in the GDPR (see chapter 8 below).

4) **Purpose limitation** (Art. 5 para. 1 lit. b): The first element of the purpose limitation principle is that personal data may only be collected if an explicit and legitimate purpose was specified no later than at the time of the collection (principle of **purpose specification**). This may, for example, be done by documenting the processing purposes in the record of processing activities (see chapter 12 below). Since the processing purposes must be legitimate, other laws (eg, consumer protection law) must indirectly also be taken into consideration in data protection assessments. The second element of the purpose limitation principle requires that collected data may not be further processed in a manner that is incompatible with the purposes originally specified (**purpose limitation in a strict sense**) unless the data subject consented (Art. 6 cmt. 12). Whether the purposes are compatible must be assessed by applying certain criteria stipulated in Art. 6 para. 4. If the new purpose is compatible with the former (original) purpose, the processing is permitted without the need for a new legal basis (eg, new consent) (cf. Art. 6 cmt. 14). However, data subjects must be informed about the new processing purpose (Art. 13 para. 3 and Art. 14 para. 4).

5) **Data minimisation** (Art. 5 para. 1 lit. c): The type and scope of the processed data must be adequate, relevant, and limited to what is necessary in relation to the purposes for which they are processed. This principle is a specification of the general principle of proportionality. It would be regarded excessive and therefore a violation of the data minimisation principle if, for example, in order to document the used data volume of each employee, a company does not only log the size of the downloaded files but also the file name and the time of a download.

6) **Accuracy** (Art. 5 para. 1 lit. d): Personal data must be accurate and, where necessary for the processing purpose, kept up to date.

7) **Storage limitation** (Art. 5 para. 1 lit. e): Personal data may be stored no longer than necessary for the specified purposes for which the personal data

are processed. Upon expiration of that period, data must be deleted or anonymised. For example, due to the principle of storage limitation, the storage of documents regarding a contractual relationship to defend against potential claims of a customer would violate the GDPR after the statutory limitation period expired.

8) **Integrity and confidentiality** (Art. 5 para. 1 lit. f): Contrary to its name, this principle does not only require appropriate measures to protect the integrity and confidentiality of personal data, but also measures to protect availability and lawfulness of the processing. 'Security and lawfulness' would therefore be the more appropriate name for the principle in Art. 5 para. 1 lit. f (see Art. 5 cmt. 11).

The principles relating to processing of personal data are complemented by the principle of **accountability** which requires that the controller implements compliance measures to ensure compliance with the above-mentioned principles and that the controller is able to demonstrate compliance with these principles (Art. 5 para. 2). The second element of the accountability principle does not shift the burden of proof (which would not be compliant with the presumption of innocence), but results in a material obligation to demonstrate compliance. A violation of this material obligation is not subject to any administrative fines but only to the enforcement powers of the competent data protection authority (Art. 5 cmt. 13).

7. Legal basis requirement for any data processing activity

Due to the structure of the GDPR, any processing of personal data is prohibited unless Arts. 6, 9, or 10 (which list statutory permissions conclusively) provide for a respective legal basis for the processing. If a specific legal basis cannot be identified when assessing the compliance of a certain processing activity with the GDPR, the respective processing is prohibited.

7.1 Available legal bases

To identify a potentially applicable legal basis, a differentiation between the different types of personal data is necessary first.

If the processing operation covers personal data relating to **criminal convictions and offences** or related security measures (eg, in case of a whistleblowing hotline), Art. 10 applies and the legal basis must be identified under national law.

In case of **sensitive data** (see chapter 3 above for a definition), the potential legal bases are exhaustively listed in Art. 9; in the case of **any other personal data**, the legal bases are exhaustively listed in Art. 6.

Art. 6 provides the following legal bases for the processing of personal data:

1) implied or explicit **consent** of the data subject (Art. 6 para. 1 lit. a);
2) necessity to perform a **contract** to which the data subject is party or in order to take steps at the request of the data subject prior to entering into a contract (Art. 6 para. 1 lit. b);
3) necessity to comply with a **legal obligation** to which the controller is subject (Art. 6 para. 1 lit. c);

4) necessity to protect the **vital interests** of the data subject or of another natural person (Art. 6 para. 1 lit. d);

5) necessity to perform a task carried out in the **public interest** or in the exercise of official authority vested in the controller (Art. 6 para. 1 lit. e); or

6) **prevailing legitimate interests** pursued by the controller (Art. 6 para. 1 lit. f).

For the processing of sensitive data Art. 9 provides the following limited catalogue of potential legal bases:

1) **explicit consent** of the data subject (Art. 9 para. 2 lit. a);

2) necessity for the purposes of carrying out the obligations and exercising specific rights of the controller or of the data subject in the field of **employment and social security and social protection law** which also includes rights and obligations pursuant to collective agreements or works council agreements (Art. 9 para. 2 lit. b; Art. 9 cmt. 11);

3) necessity to protect the **vital interests** of the data subject or of another natural person where the data subject is physically or legally incapable of giving consent (Art. 9 para. 2 lit. c);

4) processing of personal data of members by a foundation, association or any other **not-for-profit body** with a political, philosophical, religious, or trade union aim (Art. 9 para. 2 lit. d);

5) the processing relates to personal data which are manifestly **made public** by the data subject (Art. 9 para. 2 lit. e);

6) necessity for the **establishment, exercise or defense of legal claims** or whenever courts are acting in their judicial capacity (Art. 9 para. 2 lit. f);

7) necessity for reasons of **substantial public interest** on the basis of Union or Member State law (Art. 9 para. 2 lit. g);

8) necessity for the purposes of **health or social care systems** on the basis of Union or Member State law or pursuant to contract with a health professional (Art. 9 para. 2 lit. h);

9) necessity for reasons of public interest in the area of **public health** on the basis of Union or Member State law (Art. 9 para. 2 lit. i); and

10) necessity for **archiving purposes** in the public interest, scientific or historical **research purposes** or **statistical purposes** based on Union or Member State law (Art. 9 para. 2 lit. j).

In practice, the data subject's consent is particularly relevant. The legal basis of consent is regulated in a detailed manner in the GDPR. Therefore, the following paragraph will focus on consent in more detail.

7.2 Requirements for valid consent

Valid consent requires that consent must be freely given, specific, informed and unambiguous (cf. Art. 4 No. 11). The GDPR further clarifies that consent can be withdrawn at any time with future effect (Art. 7 para. 3).

Consent is **freely** given if the data subject has a real and free choice and therefore may reject or withdraw his or her consent without suffering any disadvantages (Art. 4 cmt. 23). This does, for example, not apply if an employee is threatened with dismissal in case the employee does not provide consent or withdraws his or her consent.

A freely given consent further requires that consent can be provided or rejected **separately for individual processing operations** – to the extent appropriate considering the situation (see Art. 4 cmt. 23; principle of separate consents). In practice, this means that when drafting consent declarations for more than one processing operation there should be a checkbox for each processing operation (eg, a checkbox for the processing of contact data for direct marketing purposes and another checkbox for the processing of creditworthiness data to decide on the contract conditions).

Additionally, a freely given consent requires that the performance of a contract or the provision of a service is not conditional on consent to the processing of personal data if that consent is not necessary for the performance of the contract or the provision of the service (cf. Art. 4 cmt. 23 and Art. 7 para. 4). This **consent-related tying-in prohibition** seems to question the business model of services that is offered for free on the Internet and financed through the analysis of user data. However, in our opinion, consent is (commercially) necessary in situations where only consent creates commercial conditions for a provision of the goods and services for free and, therefore, the tying-in prohibition regarding consent does not make consent invalid (see Art. 7 cmt. 11). If consent is, indeed, not necessary for technical, economic or legal reasons in order to perform the contract or provide the services, consent can, in our opinion, be given freely by offering two options for the provision of goods or services: first, conditional on consent, and secondly in exchange for adequate remuneration. In such a case, the performance of the contract and the provision of the services are not conditional on consent because the customer is free to choose the second option.

The requirement that consent must be given **for a specific case** means that a general consent without specification of the particular purpose of the processing is invalid (Art. 4 cmt. 24).

Informed consent means that the data subject must be acting in awareness of the facts, that is, that the data subject should be aware at least of the identity of the controller and the processing purposes and was informed about his or her right to withdraw consent at any time (cf. Art. 7 para. 3). Compliance with the information obligations (see chapter 8 below) is not required for consent to be valid (see Art. 4 cmt. 25).

The consent declaration can also be part of general **terms and conditions.** However, the request for consent must be presented in a manner which is clearly distinguishable from the other matters, in an intelligible and easily accessible form, using clear and plain language (Art. 7 para. 2).

The GDPR contains a special provision for the consent capacity of **children** regarding online services (information society service within the meaning of Art. 4 No. 25) that are offered to them directly (Art. 8 para. 1). The age of consent capacity is generally set at 16. It can, however, be lowered by Member State law to any age not below 13 years (regarding the lack of a conflict of laws regime, see chapter 5 above). If an online service is offered directly to a child but the child has not yet reached the age of consent capacity, the service provider must make reasonable efforts to verify that consent is given or authorised by the holder of parental responsibility (Art. 8

para. 2). If the online service is not directly offered to children – which could in particular be documented by asking for the age during the registration process – such measures do not have to be implemented (cf. Art. 8 cmt. 10).

Consents that were given before the **applicability of the GDPR on 25 May 2018** will only be considered a valid basis for the processing if the consent has been given in line with the requirements of the GDPR (Recital 171 sentence 3). In Austria, for example, the requirements regarding valid consent under the Austrian Data Protection Act 2000 as interpreted by the courts were already very strict so that most consents should continue to be valid (Art. 4 cmt. 29).

Finally, it must be noted that the controller bears the burden of proof that the data subject has consented to the processing (Art. 7 para. 1). From a practical standpoint, every data subject consent should therefore be documented.

8. Information obligations and privacy notices

The GDPR provides comprehensive information obligations for controllers to transparently disclose to the data subject which of his or her personal data is processed by whom and under which conditions.

If personal data are collected from the data subject (cf. Art. 13 cmt. 2), the data subject must be informed no later than at the time when the personal data is collected (Art. 13 para. 1). If, on the other hand, the personal data have not been obtained from the data subject, the information must be provided at the latest within one month after obtaining the personal data, respectively if a disclosure to another recipient is envisaged, at the latest when the personal data are first disclosed (Art. 14 para. 3).

Irrespective of whether the personal data were obtained from the data subject, the controller must inform the data subject about the following:

1) name, respectively company name and legal form, and contact details of the **controller** (Art. 13 para. 1 lit. a; Art. 14 para. 1 lit. a);
2) contract details of the **data protection officer** (Art. 13 para. 1 lit. b; Art. 14 para. 1 lit. b);
3) **purposes of the processing and legal basis** for the processing (Art. 13 para. 1 lit. c; Art. 14 para. 1 lit. c);
4) the **recipients** or categories of recipients (controllers as well as processors; Art. 13 para. 1 lit. e; Art. 14 para. 1 lit. e);
5) in case of transfers to controllers or processors located in a country **outside the EU/EEA** (Art. 13 para. 1 lit. f; Art. 14 para. 1 lit. f): whether an adequacy decision by the Commission exists for the third country and, if such adequacy decision does not exist, reference to the appropriate or suitable safeguards (eg, concluded standard contractual clauses) and the means by which to obtain a copy of them (eg, an email address or a URL);
6) the **storage period** or, if that is not possible, the criteria used to determine that period (Art. 13 para. 2 lit. a; Art. 14 para. 2 lit. a);
7) to the extent the processing is based on prevailing legitimate interests pursuant to Art. 6 para. 1 lit. f: the **legitimate interests** pursued by the controller or by the third party (Art. 13 para. 1 lit. d; Art. 14 para. 2 lit. b);

8) the existence of **data subject rights**, that is, the right to request access, rectification, erasure, restriction of the processing and to object as well as the right to data portability (Art. 13 para. 2 lit. b; Art. 14 para. 2 lit. c);
9) to the extent the processing is based on consent of the data subject, the existence of the right to **withdraw** consent at any time (Art. 13 para. 2 lit. c; Art. 14 para. 2 lit. d);
10) the right to **lodge a complaint** with a supervisory authority (Art. 13 para. 2 lit. d; Art. 14 para. 2 lit. e); and
11) to the extent there is an **automated decision-making, including profiling** pursuant to Art. 22, the fact that such processing takes place and meaningful information about the logic that is involved as well as the significance and the envisaged consequences of such a decision (Art. 13 para. 2 lit. f; Art. 14 para. 2 lit. g).

If personal data are collected from the data subject, the controller must additionally inform about the following (cf. Art. 13 cmt. 2):

1) whether the provision of personal data by the data subject is **necessary or obligatory** and the possible consequences of failing to provide such data (Art. 13 para. 2 lit. e).

If personal data are not obtained from the data subject, the controller must additionally inform about the following:

1) the **categories of personal data concerned** (Art. 14 para. 1 lit. d); and
2) to the extent available (cf. Art. 14 cmt. 25): the **source** from which the personal data originates as well as whether it came from publicly accessible sources (Art. 14 para. 2 lit. f).

The above-mentioned information must be provided to data subjects in a concise, transparent, intelligible and easily accessible form, using clear and plain language (Art. 12 para. 1). For example, the information obligations regarding the processing operations conducted on a public website can be fulfilled by a privacy statement that is accessible through a link at the bottom of each page of the website.

In light of the scope of information that must be provided, it is questionable how such a privacy statement – also called a privacy notice – can be created in a clearly and easy to understand manner. In practice, it is common to use a **'layered privacy notice'** (cf. Art. 12 cmt. 1):

1) Layer 1 – The Short Notice: The data subject receives a short notice about the processing of his or her personal data together with the possibility to obtain more detailed information (eg, via a link).
2) Layer 2 – The Condensed Notice: If the data subject would like to receive more detailed information, the data subject is provided a summary of the privacy statement which contains the most important aspects of the privacy statement, taking into consideration the particular circumstances. The summary also refers to the possibility of receiving the entire privacy statement (eg, again via a link).
3) Layer 3 – The Full Notice: Only in this layer does the data subject receive the entire information.

9.   Rights of the data subject

Besides the information rights (see chapter 8 above) and the rights against automatic decision-making and profiling (see chapter 10 below), the GDPR provides the following rights of data subjects vis-à-vis controllers:

1) the right of **access** (Art. 15): The data subject is entitled to obtain, within a period of one month which can be extended by a further two months (Art. 12 para. 3): (i) a confirmation as to whether or not personal data concerning him or her are being processed (Art. 15 para. 1 half sentence 1); (ii) a subset of the information that must be disclosed in a privacy statement anyway (for details see Art. 15 para. 1 lit. a–h and para. 2); and (iii) a copy of the processed personal data (Art. 15 para. 3 and para. 4);

2) the right to **data portability** (Art. 20): The data subject has the right to receive personal data concerning him or her from the controller – but not from the processor (see Art. 20 cmt. 4) – in a structured, commonly used and machine-readable format and to have the personal data transmitted directly from the controller to another controller (Art. 20 para. 1 and 2). This right to data portability only exists to the extent:

   (i) the data subject has provided the respective data to the controller;

   (ii) the processing is based on the data subject's consent (Art. 6 para. 1 lit. a or Art. 9 para. 2 lit. a) or on the necessity to perform a contract concluded with the data subject (Art. 6 para. 1 lit. b); and

   (iii) the processing is carried out by automated means (ie, electronically).

   Furthermore, exercising the right to data portability may not adversely affect the rights and freedoms of others (Art. 20 para. 4). This will likely result in difficulties with data that is shared on social networking sites.

3) the right to **rectification** (Art. 16): If personal data is inaccurate or incomplete, the data subject has the right to rectification, and/or completion, of the personal data;

4) the right to **erasure** (Art. 17): The data subject has the right to erasure of personal data concerning him or her without undue delay if the processing violates the GDPR, in particular because the data subject withdraws a prior given consent or lawfully objects to the processing. If the controller has made the personal data public, it must also take reasonable steps to inform other controllers that the data subject has requested the erasure of such data (including links that lead to that data), to the extent that is technically and organisationally possible ('right to be forgotten', Art. 17 para. 2);

5) the right to **restriction of processing** (Art. 18): The data subject has the right to exclusion of the personal data concerning him or her from any further processing if the data subject has exercised his or her right to rectification or objection but the controller has not decided on that yet;

6) the right to **object** (Art. 21): The data subject has the right to object vis-à-vis the controller if:

   (i) the processing is based on **prevailing legitimate interests** (Art. 6 para. 1 lit. f) and the controller cannot demonstrate that in the particular situation of the data subject: (a) the interests of the controller or of a third party prevail; or (b) the processing is performed for the establishment, exercise or defense of legal claims. If the controller fails to demonstrate the above, the objection leads to the unlawfulness of any further processing of the data relating to the data subject;

(ii) personal data are processed for **direct marketing** purposes (eg, by profiling); here, a balancing of interests is not relevant (Art. 21 para. 2), giving the objection an 'opt-out' effect that makes any further use of the data for direct marketing purposes unlawful (Art. 21 para. 3); or

(iii) personal data are processed for scientific or historical **research purposes or statistical purposes** unless the processing is necessary for the performance of a task carried out for reasons of public interest (Art. 21 para. 6).

10. Profiling and automated individual decision-making

Automated decisions that are made concerning an individual (cf. Art. 22 cmt. 1) and produce legal effects concerning him or her or similarly significantly affect him or her (see Art. 22 cmt. 4) are only permitted to a very limited extent pursuant to Art. 22. An example of a regulated automated decision would be the automatic termination of an insurance contract based on risky driving behaviour identified by the on-board computer of the insured vehicle.

Under the GDPR, these decisions also include **profiling** which means any form of automated processing of personal data to analyse or predict certain personal aspects relating to a natural person (eg, performance at work, economic situation, health, personal preferences, interests, reliability, behaviour or location) (see Art. 4 No. 4).

Automated individual decision-making as described above – including profiling – is permitted only if the following cumulative requirements have been met:

1) the data subject **consented explicitly** to it (Art. 22 para. 2 lit. c), it is authorised by **statutory law** (Art. 22 para. 2 lit. b), or the decision is necessary for entering into or performing a **contract** between the data subject and the controller (Art. 22 para. 2 lit. a);

2) at least the right of the data subject to obtain human intervention on the part of the controller, to express his or her point of view, and to contest the decision must be implemented by the controller (Art. 22 para. 3) – except if the automated decision is authorised by statutory law (Art. 22 para. 2 lit. b);

3) the decision must **not be based on special categories of personal data** unless the data subject has explicitly consented to the processing of his or her sensitive data for this purpose or a statutory authorisation applies (Art. 22 para. 4);

4) the data subject is provided with **information** (see chapter 8 above) in due time on the automated decision-making, the decision logic involved as well as the significance and the envisaged consequences of such processing (Art. 13 para. 2 lit. f and Art. 14 para. 2 lit. g).

Since an automated decision-making will in many cases neither be required for contract conclusion or contract performance, nor covered by a statutory authorisation, explicit consent of the data subject will be particularly important in practice.

11.   Data protection compliance programme

As part of the **accountability obligation** pursuant to Art. 5 para. 2 ('Accountability'), every controller is obligated pursuant to Art. 24 to implement appropriate technical and organisational measures to **ensure compliance with the GDPR** and to also **demonstrate compliance** (see chapter 6 above).

11.1   Organisational measures including data protection strategies

Organisational measures include at least (see Art. 24 para. 2) the implementation of **data protection policies.**

From a practical perspective, data protection policies must first determine the objectives pursued by the controller as well as the internal roles and responsibilities. Whether a data protection officer must be appointed or is appointed voluntarily (see chapter 14 below) should be considered when developing the organisational data protection compliance structure.

Based on that, detailed data protection policies addressing certain types of personal data (eg, employee data, customer data or vendor data) or addressing certain topics (eg, the period of storage through a 'Data Retention Policy' or the procedure in case of a security breach through an 'Incident Response Policy') should be implemented.

11.2   Technical measures including privacy by design and by default

In addition to the above-mentioned organisational measures, controllers must also implement technical compliance measures. In contrast to the measures that must be implemented to ensure data security (see chapter 15.1 below), technical compliance measures pursue the objective of ensuring the lawfulness of the data processing and to proactively prevent data protection risks.

The GDPR provides for two technical measures that must be implemented as a minimum requirement: privacy by design and privacy by default.

Privacy by design (Art. 25 para. 1) requires the implementation of technical measures that reflect the data protection principles (see chapter 6 above). An example of privacy by design would be to minimise the categories and amount of personal data collected and to pseudonymise it as soon as possible (see Art. 25 cmt. 3). Privacy by design can also be realised by implementing technical measures that prevent types of access that would be incompatible with the specified processing purposes (eg, by implementing a role-based access control system that prevents the HR manager who is responsible for dismissals to access data on the religious beliefs of employees).

Privacy by default (Art. 25 para. 2) means that the controller must implement default settings that ensure that personal data is processed only to the extent necessary for the particular processing purpose. In particular, it must be ensured that by default personal data are not made accessible to an indefinite number of natural persons without the data subject's intervention (Art. 25 para. 2 last sentence). This obligation will be relevant in particular for developing websites that allow for a private as well as a public communication with other users.

12. Maintaining a record of processing activities

In principle, every controller and every processor must maintain a record of processing activities in writing or in electronic form (Art. 30 para. 3) and make it available to the supervisory authority upon request (Art. 30 para. 4). Data subjects do not have a right to access the records of processing activities (Art. 30 cmt. 10).

Companies are exempted from the obligation to maintain a record of processing activities only if cumulatively: (i) they are employing **less than 250 employees**; (ii) the processing does not result in risks for the data subjects (cf. chapter 13 below); (iii) the processing is only occasional (eg, only once a month); and (iv) the processing does not include sensitive data or personal data relating to criminal convictions or offences (Art. 30 para. 5).

A processing activity is the sum of all processing operations that are conducted for a certain purpose or for several connected purposes (eg, customer relationship management on the one hand and human capital management on the other hand).

The **record of processing to be maintained by a controller** must include the following information (Art. 30 para. 1):

1) the name and the contact details of the controller and, where applicable, the joint controller (see Art. 26);
2) if the controller is not established in the EU: name and contact details of the **controller's representative** (see Art. 27);
3) name and contact details of the **data protection officer**, where applicable (see chapter 14 below);
4) the purposes of the processing;
5) a description of the **categories of data subjects**;
6) a description of the **categories of personal data**;
7) the **categories of recipients**, including recipients in third countries or international organisations;
8) in the case of **transfers of personal data to a third country** (non-EU/EEA country) or to an international organisation: name of the third country, respectively the international organisation and in case of transfers that must be registered (see chapter 18.2 below), the documentation of the assessment conducted pursuant to Art. 49 para. 1 subpara. 2 as well as suitable safeguards (Art. 49 para. 6);
9) the envisaged **time limits for erasure** of the different categories of personal data; and
10) a general description of the technical and organisational **security measures** (see chapter 15.1 below).

To improve the internal documentation, controllers could add the following in addition to the minimum content: a copy of the privacy statement (see chapter 8 above), a template of the used consent declarations, if any (see chapter 7.2 above), a link to the data protection impact assessment performed, if any (see chapter 13 below), and a link to the documentation of personal data breaches (see chapter 15.2 below).

The **record of processing activities to be maintained by a processor** must contain the following information (Art. 30 para. 2):

1) name and contact details of the **processor** and, where applicable, of the data protection officer and, if the processor is not established in the EU, of the processor's representative;

2) name and contact details of each **controller** on behalf of which the processor is acting and, where applicable, of their respective data protection officers and, if the controllers are not established in the EU, of their respective representatives;

3) the **categories of processing** carried out on behalf of the controller (eg, hosting of a customer relationship management system);

4) in case of **transfers of personal data to recipients in third countries** (non-EU/EEA countries) or to an international organisation: name of the third country, respectively of the international organisation and in case of transfers that must be notified to the supervisory authority (see chapter 18.2 below), the documentation of the assessment pursuant to Art. 49 para. 1 subpara. 2 and of the suitable safeguards (Art. 49 para. 6); and

5) a general description of the technical and organisational **security measures** (see chapter 15.1 below).

13.   **Data protection impact assessment and consultation obligation with supervisory authority**

A controller must, prior to the processing (cf. Art. 35 cmt. 4), carry out a data protection impact assessment (also called 'privacy impact assessment'), if the processing is likely to result in a high risk to the rights and freedoms of natural persons (Art. 35 para. 1). Such a risk is likely at least in the following cases:

1) systematic and extensive evaluation of personal aspects relating to natural persons on which decisions are based that produce legal effects concerning the natural person or similarly significantly affect the natural person (Art. 35 para. 3 lit. a);

2) processing on a large scale of special categories of data or of personal data relating to criminal convictions and offences (Art. 35 para. 3 lit. b);

3) systematic monitoring of a publicly accessible area on a large scale (Art. 35 para. 3 lit. c), for example by using a large amount of electronic CCTV cameras (see Art. 35 cmt. 9); or

4) any processing operation contained on a 'black list' published by the supervisory authority (Art. 35 para. 4).

If a data protection impact assessment is required the controller must seek the advice of the data protection officer – if one has been appointed – when carrying out the data protection impact assessment (Art. 35 para. 2). The data protection impact assessment must contain at least the following information (Art. 35 para. 7):

1) a systematic **description of the envisaged processing operations and the purposes** of the processing, including, where applicable, the legitimate interest pursued by the controller;

2) an assessment of the **necessity and proportionality** of the processing operations in relation to the purpose;

3) the **measures** envisaged to mitigate the risks for the rights and freedoms of the data subjects;

4) an **assessment of the risks** to the rights and freedoms of data subjects taking into consideration the envisaged measures – the risk assessment must indicate, whether there is a high risk (cf. Art. 35 cmt. 17).

If the data protection impact assessment indicates that the processing would result in a high risk, the controller must consult the supervisory authority (Art. 36 para. 1). However, given that this is not an approval process, the controller is not required to wait for the reaction of the supervisory authority (Art. 36 cmt. 1).

As part of the consultation process, the controller must provide the following information to the supervisory authority:

1) in particular in the case of a processing within a group of undertakings: the respective **responsibilities** of the controller (cf. Art. 26), joint controllers, and processors involved in the processing;
2) the **purposes and means** of the intended processing;
3) the **measures and safeguards** provided to protect the rights and freedoms of data subjects;
4) where applicable, the contact details of the **data protection officer**;
5) the **data protection impact assessment**; and
6) any other **information requested** by the supervisory authority.

Where the supervisory authority is of the opinion that the intended processing would infringe the GDPR, the supervisory authority must, within a period of up to eight weeks which can be extended by an additional six weeks, provide advice or an instruction. If the supervisory authority is of the opinion that the intended processing complies with the GDPR, a formal decision of the supervisory authority is not foreseen.

14. Data protection officer

A controller or a processor must appoint a data protection officer if:

1) such appointment is required by Member State law (Art. 37 para. 4; this will likely be the case in Germany but not in Austria);
2) the controller is a public authority or body (see Art. 37 cmt. 2; Art. 37 para. 1 lit. a);
3) the core activities of the controller or the processor consist of processing operations which require regular and systematic monitoring of data subjects on a large scale (Art. 37 para. 1 lit. b; eg, online advertising networks that are logging the online activities of users to present tailored advertising); or
4) the core activities of the controller or the processor consist of processing on a large scale of special categories of data or personal data relating to criminal convictions and offences (Art. 37 para. 1 lit. c; eg, a company that specialises in criminal background checks or a processor specialised in the health area).

Since the latter two cases require 'core activities' which consist in the processing of personal data, the requirement to appoint a data protection officer will primarily have to be met by companies that pursue a **data-driven business model**. For example, a law firm is not required to appoint a data protection officer because its core activity consists in the provision of legal advice and the representation before courts and public authorities – the processing of sensitive data or data relating to criminal convictions or offences is only an ancillary activity (cf. Art. 37 cmt. 3).

A single data protection officer may be appointed for a group of undertakings (Art. 37 para. 2) as well as for several public authorities or bodies (Art. 37 para. 3).

For the person appointed as a data protection officer, the following **requirements** apply:

1) the data protection officer must have professional qualities and expert knowledge of data protection law (Art. 37 para. 5) and
2) the data protection officer may be a staff member of the controller or processor or fulfil the tasks on the basis of a service contract (Art. 37 para. 6); therefore also the appointment of an external data protection officer is possible (eg, of an attorney; see Art. 38 cmt. 7).

Regarding the **position** of the data protection officer the GDPR provides that the data protection officer:

1) **does not receive any instructions** (Art. 38 para. 3 sentence 1);
2) is granted **protection against dismissal** (Art. 38 para. 3 sentence 2);
3) must directly **report to the highest management level** of the controller or the processor (Art. 38 para. 3 sentence 3);
4) is **involved** properly and in a timely manner in all issues which relate to the protection of personal data (Art. 38 para. 1);
5) has all **resources** necessary to carry out his or her tasks (Art. 38 para. 2);
6) has **access** to personal data and processing operations (Art. 38 para. 2);
7) serves as a **contact person** for data subjects (Art. 38 para. 4); and
8) is bound by **secrecy or confidentiality** (Art. 38 para. 5).

Pursuant to the GDPR, the data protection officer has the task to **advise** the controller or the processor and its employees of their obligations pursuant to the GDPR (Art. 39 para. 1 lit. a and c), to **monitor** compliance with the GDPR and internal privacy policies in particular regarding the data protection impact assessment (Art. 39 para. 1 lit. b and c), and to **cooperate** with the supervisory authority (Art. 39 para. 1 lit. d and e).

Pursuant to the GDPR, the data protection officer is not obligated to maintain the record of processing activities (see chapter 12 above) or to conduct the data protection impact assessment (see chapter 13 above). Furthermore, the GDPR does not provide any personal liability of the data protection officer in case of violations of any of the above requirements or the GDPR in general (Art. 39 cmt. 1).

15.   Data security

Controllers and processors are obligated to implement appropriate data security measures on the one hand (see chapter 15.1 below) and to notify certain security breaches on the other (see chapter 15.2 below).

15.1   Mandatory data security measures

Every controller and every processor must implement technical and organisational security measures pursuant to Art. 32 in order to ensure a **level of security appropriate to the risk**. Thus, primarily, the risks for the rights and freedoms of the data subjects have to be taken into account which, in effect, requires a quantitative or qualitative risk assessment (cf. Art. 32 cmt. 2).

When selecting the security measures, (i) the state of the art, (ii) the costs of implementation, and (iii) the nature, scope, context and purposes of processing have to be considered (Art. 32 para. 1).

The security that must be provided consist of the three components: **confidentiality, integrity and availability** of personal data (see Art. 32 cmt. 6).

The GDPR provides that in particular the following measures should be considered: (i) pseudonymisation and encryption of personal data (Art. 32 para. 1 lit. a); (ii) measures to ensure the security of IT systems that are used for the data processing (Art. 32 para. 1 lit. b); (iii) incident response capabilities including data recovery processes to react to incidents (Art. 32 para. 1 lit. c); and (iv) a regular evaluation of the effectiveness of the implemented security measures (Art. 32 para. 1 lit. d).

In practice, the following **standards** have gained international recognition **in the area of information security** which could be considered as a guidance in addition to the measures mentioned above:

1) ISO/IEC 27001 ('Information technology – Security techniques – Information security management systems – Requirements') describes the requirements regarding an information security management system. In particular for processors, a certification pursuant to ISO/IEC 27001 is a proven means to demonstrate an appropriate level of data security vis-à-vis their customers.

2) ISO/IEC 27002 ('Information technology – Security techniques – Code of practice for information security controls') contains a catalogue of technical and organisational security measures which can be implemented based on ISO/IEC 27001. However, a certification pursuant to ISO/IEC 27002 is not possible.

3) The 'Critical Security Controls for Effective Cyber Defense' of the Center for Internet Security (CIS) were originally developed by US defense contractors and US authorities including the National Security Agency and provide a prioritised list of the 20 most important security measures (see www.cisecurity.org/critical-controls).

4) The 'IT-Grundschutz' of the German Federal Office for Information Security ('BSI') offers comprehensive catalogues and standards (see www.bsi.bund.de/DE/Themen/ITGrundschutz/itgrundschutz_node.html).

15.2   Obligation to notify personal data breaches

Subject to the conditions set out below, the GDPR establishes a requirement for controllers to notify personal data breaches to: (i) the supervisory authority (Art. 33 para. 1); and (ii) the data subjects (Art. 34 para. 1). Furthermore, the GDPR establishes a notification obligation for processors vis-à-vis the controller (Art. 33 para. 2).

The notification obligation is triggered by a violation of the protection of personal data, that is: (i) a permanent violation of the availability (a temporary server outage would be irrelevant); (ii) a violation of the integrity; or (iii) a violation of the confidentiality of personal data (see Art. 4 No. 12).

Pursuant to Art. 33 para. 1, the controller must, as a general rule, notify every personal data breach to the **supervisory authority**, unless the personal data breach is unlikely to result in a risk to the rights and freedoms of natural persons (eg, because personal data was encrypted in a secure manner). The notification must be made without undue delay but no later than **within 72 hours** after the controller has become aware of the personal data breach (Art. 33 para. 1) and must contain the following information (Art. 33 para. 3):

1) a description of the nature of the personal data breach including, where possible, the categories and approximate number of data subjects concerned and the categories and approximate number of personal data records concerned;

2) the name and contact details of the data protection officer or another contact point where more information can be obtained;

3) a description of the likely consequences of the personal data breach; and

4) a description of the measures taken or proposed to be taken by the controller to address the personal data breach including, where appropriate, measures to mitigate its possible adverse effects.

Where the notification to the supervisory authority is not made within 72 hours, the notification must be accompanied by reasons for the delay (Art. 33 para. 1 sentence 2). To the extent all the necessary information cannot be provided at the same time, the information may be provided in phases without undue further delay (Art. 33 para. 4).

In addition, the controller must notify the **data subjects** without undue delay if the personal data breach is likely to result in a **high risk** to the rights and freedoms of natural persons (Art. 34 para. 1). In our opinion, such risk can be assumed to exist if the security of a data processing activity that requires a data protection impact assessment has been compromised (cf. chapter 13 above). On the other hand, such risk should not be assumed to exist if the data were securely encrypted (Art. 34 para. 3 lit. a). In order to obtain legal certainty in case of doubt, there is a possibility to seek a decision on the matter from the supervisory authority (Art. 34 para. 4).

The notification to the data subjects must describe in clear and plain language the nature of the personal data breach and contain at least the following information (Art. 34 para. 2):

1) the name and the contact details of the data protection officer or another contact point where more information can be obtained;

2) a description of the likely consequences of the personal data breach; and

3) a description of the measures taken or proposed to be taken by the controller to address the personal data breach including, where appropriate, measures to mitigate its possible adverse effects.

The controller does not have to inform the data subjects of the categories or the number of data subjects or the affected personal data records (cf. Art. 34 cmt. 6).

If an individual notification of each data subject would involve a disproportionate effort, the controller may alternatively make a public communication or take other measure if it is ensured that the data subjects are informed in an equally effective manner (see Art. 34 para. 3 lit. c). This could be done by advertisements in the mass media or, in our opinion, also on the website of the company.

Finally, it must be noted that all personal data breaches must be **documented** by the controller, irrespective of a potential notification obligation (Art. 33 para. 5).

16. Mandatory arrangements between joint controllers

If two or more controllers jointly determine the purposes and means of the data processing, they are joint controllers within the meaning of Art. 26. In such cases both are obligated to conclude an arrangement that fulfills the following requirements (Art. 26 para. 1 and 2):

1) it determines in a transparent manner the controllers' respective responsibilities for compliance with the obligations under the GDPR, in particular as regards the exercising of the rights of the data subject (cf. chapter 9 above);
2) it determines which controller fulfills the information requirements vis-à-vis data subjects (cf. chapter 8 above);
3) it duly reflects the respective roles and relationships of the joint controllers vis-à-vis the data subjects.

The essence of the arrangement must be made available to the data subjects (Art. 26 para. 2 sentence 2) and it seems appropriate to include the respective information in the privacy statement (cf. Art. 26 cmt. 2). Irrespective of the arrangement, the data subjects may exercise their rights under the GDPR in respect of and against each of the controllers, that is, the controllers are jointly liable (Art. 26 para. 3).

In practice, it is difficult to **differentiate** between: (i) the concept of joint controllers; and (ii) a transfer from one controller to another controller (eg, if several companies in a group of companies store their customer data in a customer relationship management system and mutually access their data). It will be decisive, whether they determine the purposes of the respective processing by themselves or jointly (regarding the superiority of the decision on the purposes, cf. Art. 4 cmt. 12).

17. Obligations in case of outsourcing

In principle, a controller is free to decide whether to outsource its data processing to one or more processors. However, the controller is required to ensure that the selected processors provide sufficient guarantees that the processing can be performed in compliance with the GDPR (Art. 28 para. 1).

The controller and the processor are both required to conclude a **data processing agreement** in written or electronic form (cf. Art. 28 para. 9) before the processor starts to process any personal data on behalf of the controller. Such a data processing agreement has to set out at least: (i) the **subject matter and duration** of the processing; (ii) **the nature and purpose of the processing**; (iii) the **type of personal data**; (iv) the **categories of data subjects**; and (v) the **obligations and rights** of the controller which include the following obligations of the processor (Art. 28 para. 3):

1) to process the personal data only on documented **instructions** from the controller unless the processor is required to perform the respective

processing operation by law (eg, to disclose personal data to a public authority); in such cases, the processor must inform the controller, to the extent permitted under applicable law (Art. 28 para. 3 subpara. 1 lit. a);

2) to immediately inform the controller if, in the processor's opinion, an **instruction infringes the GDPR** or other applicable law (Art. 28 para. 3 subpara. 2)

3) to ensure that persons authorised to process the personal data have committed themselves to **confidentiality** if they are not under an appropriate statutory obligation of confidentiality (Art. 28 para. 3 subpara. 1 lit. b);

4) to take all required **data security measures** (Art. 28 para. 3 subpara. 1 lit. c; cf. chapter 15.1 above);

5) to engage a **subprocessor** only if (Art. 28 para. 3 subpara. 1 lit. d):
   (i) the processor concludes with the subprocessor a subprocessing agreement which imposes the same data protection obligations as set out in the data processing agreement (Art. 28 para. 4 sentence 1);
   (ii) the processor is fully liable for the subprocessor (liability of a vicarious agent; Art. 28 para. 4 last sentence); and
   (iii) the controller provided its approval of the particular subprocessor in advance in writing or electronically (see Art. 28 cmt. 3) or, in case of a general written authorisation, the processor informs the controller of the addition of the particular subprocessor, thereby giving the controller the opportunity to object (Art. 28 para. 2);

6) to assist the controller with the fulfilment of its obligations regarding **data subject rights** (Art. 28 para. 3 subpara. 1 lit. e; see chapter 9 above);

7) **to assist** the controller in ensuring compliance with the following obligations (Art. 28 para. 3 subpara. 1 lit. f): (i) ensuring data security (Art. 32; cf. chapter 15.1 above), (ii) data breach notification (Arts. 33 and 34; cf. paragraph 15.2 above), and (iii) conducting data protection impact assessments and prior consultations (Arts. 35 and 36; cf. chapter 13 above);

8) **after the end** of the provision of the services to delete or return all personal data at the choice of the controller (unless a statutory retention period applies; Art. 28 para. 3 subpara. 1 lit. g); and

9) to make available to the controller all information necessary to demonstrate compliance with the obligations mentioned above as well as to allow for and contribute to **audits** of the controller or a third-party auditor mandated by the controller (Art. 28 para. 3 subpara. 1 lit. h).

The European Commission and any supervisory authority may lay down standard contractual clauses ('Standard Contractual Clauses') which fulfill the above-mentioned requirements (Art. 28 paras. 7 and 8).

18. International data transfers

The GDPR contains detailed provisions governing transfers to controllers or processors established in a third country, that is, a country outside the EU/EEA, or to an international organisation (Arts. 44 to 50). In accordance with the purpose of the GDPR – to enable a free data flow within the single market – transfers within the

EU/EEA are not subject to any specific requirements (notwithstanding the general rules on outsourcing; see chapter 17 above).

When assessing the GDPR compliance of an international data transfer to a third country or an international organisation, it should be determined first whether the transfer can be based on a provision that neither requires a notification nor an approval (see chapter 18.1 below). Secondly, it should be assessed whether the transfer can be based on a provision that requires a notification of a supervisory authority (see chapter 18.2 below). If neither of the first two options apply, it should be determined whether the international transfer could be based a provision that requires the supervisory authority's approval (see chapter 18.3 below). If none of these apply, the transfer will be unlawful (cf. Art. 44).

For the sake of completeness, it must be noted that also the onward transfer (the transfer from an original recipient to a third party; eg, from a processor to a subprocessor) is generally subject to the requirements discussed in this paragraph (cf. Art. 44 cmt. 6).

18.1 Transfers not subject to notification or approval

International data transfers are neither subject to a notification nor an approval requirement if one of the following conditions are met:

1) there is an **adequacy decision** of the European Commission which states that the third country, respectively the international organisation, ensures an adequate level of data protection (Art. 45 para. 1) – this applies to Andorra, Argentina, the Faroe Islands, Guernsey, Israel, the Isle of Man, Jersey, Canada (to the extent the recipient is subject to the Canadian Personal Information Protection and Electronic Documents Act), New Zealand, Uruguay, the United States of America (to the extent the recipient is self-certified under the Privacy Shield), and Switzerland;

2) the transferring controller or processor and the recipient concluded **standard data protection clauses** which were adopted by the European Commission (Art. 46 para. 2 lit. c) or by a supervisory authority (Art. 46 para. 2 lit. d) – at the moment there are standard contractual clauses for data transfers from a controller to another controller (European Commission Decision 2004/915/EC), as well as from a controller to a processor (European Commission Decision 2010/87/EC), but not for transfers from a processor to a subprocessor;

3) in case of intra-group data transfers: **binding corporate rules** that have been approved by the supervisory authority are concluded (see Art. 46 para. 2 lit. b in conjunction with Art. 47);

4) in case of data transfers between public authorities or bodies: a legally binding and enforceable instrument is created (Art. 46 para. 2 lit. a);

5) approved codes of conduct (see Art. 40) or an approved certification mechanism (see Art. 42) are implemented, each together with binding and enforceable commitments of the recipient (Art. 46 para. 2 lit. e and f); or

6) one of the following special derogations applies (Art. 49 para. 1 subpara. 1):

   (i) **explicit consent** of the data subject after having been informed of the possible risks of such transfers (Art. 49 para. 1 subpara. 1 lit. a);

(ii) necessity of the transfer for the **conclusion or the performance of a contract** between: (i) the data subject and the controller; or (ii) the controller and another natural or legal person if the conclusion is in the interest of the data subject (Art. 49 para. 1 subpara. 1 lit. b and c);

(iii) necessity of the transfer for **important reasons of public interest** (Art. 49 para. 1 subpara. 1 lit. d; eg, to control epidemics);

(iv) necessity of the transfer for the **establishment, exercise or defense of legal claims** (Art. 49 para. 1 subpara. 1 lit. e);

(v) necessity of the transfer in order to protect the **vital interests** of the data subject or of other persons where the data subject is physically or legally incapable of giving consent (Art. 49 para. 1 subpara. 1 lit. f); or

(vi) transfer from a **public register** (eg, the commercial register; Art. 49 para. 1 subpara. 1 lit. g).

18.2 Transfers subject to notification

The GDPR provides for a notification of the transfer to a supervisory authority only in rare cases. If none of the provisions outlined in chapter 18.1 above apply, an international transfer is not subject to an approval (but must only be notified to the supervisory authority) if all of the following conditions are met (Art. 49 para. 1 subpara. 2):

1) the transfer is **not repetitive**;
2) the **number of data subjects is limited**;
3) the transfer is necessary for the purposes of **compelling legitimate interests** pursued by the controller which are not overridden by the interests or rights and freedoms of the data subject; and
4) the controller has assessed all the circumstances surrounding the data transfer and has, on the basis of that assessment, provided **suitable safeguards** with regard to the protection of personal data.

A transfer based on that legal basis will be rather rare in practice but could, for example, be relevant in internal investigations.

18.3 Transfers subject to approval

If none of the provisions outlined above in chapters 18.1 and 18.2 apply, an international transfer may be performed **only with the supervisory authority's approval** (Art. 46 para. 3). The issuance of such approval requires appropriate safeguards which may be provided by contractual clauses concluded between the controller or processor and the recipient (Art. 46 para. 3 lit. a) or, in the case of two public authorities or bodies, provisions to be included into administrative arrangements (Art. 46 para. 3 lit. b).

19. International jurisdiction of supervisory authorities

The GDPR provides for a broadly defined general competence (ie, jurisdiction) of a supervisory authority on the territory of its own Member State (Art. 55 para. 1) and for a special competence ('lead competence') for certain cross-border processing (Art. 56 para. 1).

In addition, Art. 55 para. 2 contains an **exception** for: (i) public authorities; and (ii) private bodies processing personal data on the legal basis of a legal obligation (Art. 6 para. 1 lit. c) or the necessity for the performance of a task carried out in the public interest or in the exercise of official authority (Art. 6 para. 1 lit. e). In such cases, the competence of the supervisory authority is exclusively determined by the seat of the public authority, or of the private body (see Art. 55 cmt. 7).

Due to the interaction of the general competence pursuant to Art. 55 para. 1 and the lead competence pursuant to Art. 56 para. 1, the rules determining the competent supervisory authority (or authorities) are rather complex.

The **general competence** pursuant to Art. 55 para. 1 applies in particular if the controller or processor is established on the territory of the supervisory authority or the data processing operation affects data subjects on the territory of the supervisory authority (cf. Art. 55 cmt. 5). Due to the broad wording of Art. 55 para. 1, the requirements for a 'general competence' will, in many cases, be fulfilled at the same time for multiple supervisory authorities in different Member States.

In contrast, there will be a concentration of competence if a **lead competence** applies pursuant to Art. 56. This may be strategically meaningful for controllers or processors because otherwise there will be multiple administrative proceedings as well as an increased likelihood of a parallel applicability of the different national laws implementing the GDPR's opening clauses (see chapter 5 above regarding applicable national law).

Pursuant to Art. 56 para. 1, a concentration of competence at the lead authority is subject to various requirements:

If the controller or the processor has only a **single establishment** in the EU (where legally dependent branches and affiliates constitute an establishment; see Art. 3 cmt. 3), a lead competence applies only if the processing substantially affects or may substantially affect data subjects in multiple Member States, making it a **cross-border processing** (Art. 4 No. 23 lit. b).

If the controller or the processor has **establishments in multiple Member States**, there is only a lead competence if

1) the **main establishment** within the meaning of Art. 4 No. 16 is located in the EU – this means:
   (i) in case of a controller: one establishment in the Union decides on the purposes and means of the processing and has the power to have its decisions implemented (Art. 4 No. 16 lit. a) – the location of the central administration is only of secondary relevance (see Art. 4 cmt. 41); or
   (ii) in case of a processor: the place of central administration is located in the EU or, if that is not the case, the (main) processing activities take place in the context of the activities of an establishment in the EU (Art. 4 No. 16 lit. b), and

2) there is a **cross-border processing** pursuant to Art. 4 No 23, that is, the processing takes place in the context of the activities of several establishments in different Member States (Art. 4 No. 23 lit. a) or the processing substantially affects data subjects in more than one Member State (Art. 4 No. 23 lit. b).

If the above-mentioned requirements for a lead competence are fulfilled, the **lead competence** will rest with the supervisory authority of the Member State where the single establishment, respectively the main establishment of the controller or the processor, is located (Art. 65 para. 1). Such a supervisory authority will also be the **sole interlocutor** of the controller, or the processor (Art. 56 para. 6). All other concerned supervisory authorities within the meaning of Art. 4 No. 22 must cooperate with the lead authority (Art. 60 para. 1) and the lead authority must align its draft decisions with the other concerned supervisory authorities (Art. 60 paras. 3 to 9). If the supervisory authorities cannot agree on a common position, a dispute resolution mechanism is provided by the **European Data Protection Board** (Art. 60 para. 4 in conjunction with Art. 65 para. 1 lit. a). The decisions of the European Data Protection Board are binding for the supervisory authorities (Art. 65 para. 2 last sentence) and – in case of a direct and individual concern – for the complainant and the controller or the processor (Art. 65 cmt. 11).

By derogation from the above, the lead authority may decide to not handle the case and to leave it with another supervisory authority (Art. 56 paras. 2 to 5) if: (i) the subject matter of the case relates only to an establishment in the Member State of the other supervisory authority; or (ii) the subject matter of the case substantially affects data subjects only in the Member State of the other supervisory authority. This will apply in particular in the area of **employee data protection** (Art. 56 cmt. 11).

In addition, it must be noted that in the case of **conflicting views among supervisory authorities** regarding the competence for a main establishment of a particular controller or processor, the European Data Protection Board may adopt a binding decision (Art. 65 para. 1 lit. b). The right to request such a decision is, in our opinion, not limited to the supervisory authorities but also applies to the controller or the processor (Art. 65 cmt. 2).

Based on the definition of the term 'main establishment' it is possible to create a **group-wide competence** with a single lead authority (a real '**One-Stop-Shop**') for processors (cf. Art. 4 cmt. 44) but not for controllers (cf. Art. 4 cmt. 42) because the place of central administration is the primary decisive factor only for processors.

In conclusion, it must be noted that the GDPR rules concerning the competence of supervisory authorities are quite complex. Nevertheless, it will still be possible for internationally operating controllers and processors to determine the competent supervisory authority via **forum shopping** by strategically locating their main establishment in a certain Member State. As a result, this might also effectively lead to a **choice of law** (cf. chapter 5 above regarding applicable law).

20.   Administrative fines and other sanctions

The GDPR provides high administrative fines for violations of obligations of a controller or processor.

A violation of one of the following provisions is subject to administrative fines up to **10 million Euro** or, in the case of an undertaking, up to **2% of the total worldwide annual turnover** of the preceding financial year, whichever is higher (Art. 83 para. 4):

1) conditions for consent of a child (Art. 8);

2) obligations in connection with data which the controller cannot relate to a data subject (Art. 11);

3) privacy by design and by default (Art. 25);

4) obligation to contractually determine the responsibilities between joint controllers (Art. 26);

5) obligation for controllers or processors not established in the EU to designate a representative (Art. 27);

6) obligations when engaging processors (Art. 28);

7) prohibition for processors or any person acting under the authority of a controller or processor to process data except on instructions (Art. 29);

8) maintaining a record of processing activities (Art. 30);

9) cooperation with the supervisory authority (Art. 31);

10) data security and data breach notification (Arts. 32 to 34);

11) data protection impact assessment and prior consultation (Arts. 35 and 36);

12) provisions regarding the data protection officer (Arts. 37 to 39); and

13) provisions regarding approved codes of conduct and certifications (Arts. 41 to 43).

Infringements of the following provisions are subject to administrative fines of up to **20 million Euro** or, in the case of an undertaking, up to **4% of the total worldwide annual turnover** of the preceding financial year, whichever is higher (Art. 83 paras. 5 and 6):

1) obligation to comply with the basic principles for processing and the requirements for a legal basis of the processing, except the conditions for consent of a child (Arts. 5 to 7 and Art. 9);

2) rights of the data subjects including information obligations of the controller as well as limitations of automated decision-making and profiling (Arts. 12 to 22);

3) provisions on international data transfers (Arts. 44 to 49);

4) obligation to grant access to the supervisory authority (Art. 58 para. 1 lit. e and f);

5) obligation to comply with the instructions of the supervisory authority (Art. 58 para. 2); and

6) Member State law which has been enacted based on Arts. 85 to 91 (provisions regarding special processing situations, including the employment context).

Since the term 'undertaking' in the GDPR must be understood in accordance with the term 'undertaking' under EU competition law, the **worldwide annual turnover of the entire group of companies** has to be considered for the calculation of fines and such fines may also be **imposed on the parent company of the controller or the processor** (Art. 83 cmt. 11). When deciding on the amount of the administrative fine, the criteria listed in Art. 83 para. 2 must be taken into consideration. If a controller or processor infringes several provisions of the GDPR, several administrative fines within the applicable range of fines may be imposed (**principle of cumulation**), unless the infringements concern the same or linked processing operations (Art. 83 para. 3).

Finally, it must be noted that only two of the obligations listed in the GDPR are not listed in Art. 83 and their infringement is therefore not subject to any sanctions under the GDPR:

1) the prohibition to process personal data relating to criminal convictions and offences (subject to Member State law) (Art. 10); and
2) the obligation to implement technical and organisational compliance measures (Art. 24).

However, the Member States may lay down rules in national law on penalties applicable to infringements of these provision (Art. 84).

21.   Civil liability and private enforcement

In addition to the right to lodge a complaint with a supervisory authority (Art. 77), every data subject has the right to an effective judicial remedy to enforce his/her **rights pursuant to Arts. 12 to 23** (cf. Art. 79 cmt. 1) against a controller or processor.

Furthermore, a data subject is entitled to **claim compensation** if the following elements can be established: (i) material or non-material damages (Art. 82 para. 1); (ii) unlawfulness (Art. 82 para. 2); (iii) causation (Art. 82 para. 2); and (iv) fault, where, in principle, the defendant bears the burden of proof that it acted without fault (Art. 82 para. 3).

Not-for-profit data protection organisations have the right to exercise the rights of the data subjects in court (and in front of a supervisory authority) in the name and on behalf of the data subject (Art. 80 para. 1). The right to claim damages in the name of a data subject requires that national law provides such a right (regarding the applicable law see chapter 5 above). Additionally, Member States may provide that not-for-profit data protection organisations may exercise the rights of data subjects (except for the right to claim damages) also via a **representative action**, that is, independently of a data subject's mandate (Art. 80 para. 2).

To facilitate the enforcement of judicial remedies of the GDPR, the GDPR provides that controllers, and/or processors, may be sued where: (i) the defendant has an establishment (including affiliates); or (ii) the claimant has his or her habitual residence (Art. 79 para. 2). This makes it possible for claimants to engage in **forum shopping**.

Text of the General Data Protection Regulation and commentary*

REGULATION (EU) 2016/679 OF THE EUROPEAN PARLIAMENT AND OF THE COUNCIL

of 27 April 2016

on the protection of natural persons with regard to the processing of personal data and on the free movement of such data, and repealing Directive 95/46/EC (General Data Protection Regulation)

(Text with EEA relevance)

THE EUROPEAN PARLIAMENT AND THE COUNCIL OF THE EUROPEAN UNION,

Having regard to the Treaty on the Functioning of the European Union, and in particular Article 16 thereof,

Having regard to the proposal from the European Commission,

After transmission of the draft legislative act to the national parliaments,

Having regard to the opinion of the European Economic and Social Committee,[1]

Having regard to the opinion of the Committee of the Regions,[2]

Acting in accordance with the ordinary legislative procedure,[3]

Whereas:

---

*   The text of the EU General Data Protection Regulation, http://eur-lex.europa.eu © European Union, 1998–2017
1   OJ C 229, 31.7.2012, p90.
2   OJ C 391, 18.12.2012, p127.
3   Position of the European Parliament of 12 March 2014 (not yet published in the Official Journal) and position of the Council at first reading of 8 April 2016 (not yet published in the Official Journal). Position of the European Parliament of 14 April 2016.

Chapter I – General provisions

Article 1

Subject-matter and objectives

1. This Regulation lays down rules relating to the protection of natural persons[1] with regard to the processing[2] of personal data[3] and rules relating to the free movement of personal data.

2. This Regulation protects fundamental rights and freedoms of natural persons and in particular their right to the protection of personal data.[4]

3. The free movement of personal data within the Union shall be neither restricted nor prohibited for reasons connected with the protection of natural persons with regard to the processing of personal data.[5]

Recitals:

(1) *The protection of natural persons in relation to the processing of personal data is a fundamental right. Article 8(1) of the Charter of Fundamental Rights of the European Union (the 'Charter') and Article 16(1) of the Treaty on the Functioning of the European Union (TFEU) provide that everyone has the right to the protection of personal data concerning him or her.*

(2) *The principles of, and rules on the protection of natural persons with regard to the processing of their personal data should, whatever their nationality or residence, respect their fundamental rights and freedoms, in particular their right to the protection of personal data. This Regulation is intended to contribute to the accomplishment of an area of freedom, security and justice and of an economic union, to economic and social progress, to the strengthening and the convergence of the economies within the internal market, and to the well-being of natural persons.*

(3) *Directive 95/46/EC of the European Parliament and of the Council seeks to harmonise the protection of fundamental rights and freedoms of natural persons in respect of processing activities and to ensure the free flow of personal data between Member States.*

(4) *The processing of personal data should be designed to serve mankind. The right to the protection of personal data is not an absolute right; it must be considered in relation to its function in society and be balanced against other fundamental rights, in accordance with the principle of proportionality. This Regulation respects all fundamental rights and observes the freedoms and principles recognised in the Charter as enshrined in the Treaties, in particular the respect for private and family life, home and communications,*

the protection of personal data, freedom of thought, conscience and religion, freedom of expression and information, freedom to conduct a business, the right to an effective remedy and to a fair trial, and cultural, religious and linguistic diversity.

(5)   *The economic and social integration resulting from the functioning of the internal market has led to a substantial increase in cross-border flows of personal data. The exchange of personal data between public and private actors, including natural persons, associations and undertakings across the Union has increased. National authorities in the Member States are being called upon by Union law to cooperate and exchange personal data so as to be able to perform their duties or carry out tasks on behalf of an authority in another Member State.*

(6)   *Rapid technological developments and globalisation have brought new challenges for the protection of personal data. The scale of the collection and sharing of personal data has increased significantly. Technology allows both private companies and public authorities to make use of personal data on an unprecedented scale in order to pursue their activities. Natural persons increasingly make personal information available publicly and globally. Technology has transformed both the economy and social life, and should further facilitate the free flow of personal data within the Union and the transfer to third countries and international organisations, while ensuring a high level of the protection of personal data.*

(7)   *Those developments require a strong and more coherent data protection framework in the Union, backed by strong enforcement, given the importance of creating the trust that will allow the digital economy to develop across the internal market. Natural persons should have control of their own personal data. Legal and practical certainty for natural persons, economic operators and public authorities should be enhanced.*

(8)   *Where this Regulation provides for specifications or restrictions of its rules by Member State law, Member States may, as far as necessary for coherence and for making the national provisions comprehensible to the persons to whom they apply, incorporate elements of this Regulation into their national law.*

(9)   *The objectives and principles of Directive 95/46/EC remain sound, but it has not prevented fragmentation in the implementation of data protection across the Union, legal uncertainty or a widespread public perception that there are significant risks to the protection of natural persons, in particular with regard to online activity. Differences in the level of protection of the rights and freedoms of natural persons, in particular the right to the protection of personal data, with regard to the processing of personal data in the Member States may prevent the free flow of personal data throughout the Union. Those differences may therefore constitute an obstacle to the pursuit of economic activities at the level of the Union, distort competition and impede authorities in the discharge of their responsibilities under Union law. Such a difference in levels of protection is due to the existence of differences in the implementation and application of Directive 95/46/EC.*

(10) *In order to ensure a consistent and high level of protection of natural persons and to remove the obstacles to flows of personal data within the Union, the level of protection of the rights and freedoms of natural persons with regard to the processing of such data should be equivalent in all Member States. Consistent and homogenous application of the rules for the protection of the fundamental rights and freedoms of natural persons*

with regard to the processing of personal data should be ensured throughout the Union. Regarding the processing of personal data for compliance with a legal obligation, for the performance of a task carried out in the public interest or in the exercise of official authority vested in the controller, Member States should be allowed to maintain or introduce national provisions to further specify the application of the rules of this Regulation. In conjunction with the general and horizontal law on data protection implementing Directive 95/46/EC, Member States have several sector-specific laws in areas that need more specific provisions. This Regulation also provides a margin of manoeuvre for Member States to specify its rules, including for the processing of special categories of personal data ('sensitive data'). To that extent, this Regulation does not exclude Member State law that sets out the circumstances for specific processing situations, including determining more precisely the conditions under which the processing of personal data is lawful.

(11) Effective protection of personal data throughout the Union requires the strengthening and setting out in detail of the rights of data subjects and the obligations of those who process and determine the processing of personal data, as well as equivalent powers for monitoring and ensuring compliance with the rules for the protection of personal data and equivalent sanctions for infringements in the Member States.

(12) Article 16(2) TFEU mandates the European Parliament and the Council to lay down the rules relating to the protection of natural persons with regard to the processing of personal data and the rules relating to the free movement of personal data.

(13) In order to ensure a consistent level of protection for natural persons throughout the Union and to prevent divergences hampering the free movement of personal data within the internal market, a Regulation is necessary to provide legal certainty and transparency for economic operators, including micro, small and medium-sized enterprises, and to provide natural persons in all Member States with the same level of legally enforceable rights and obligations and responsibilities for controllers and processors, to ensure consistent monitoring of the processing of personal data, and equivalent sanctions in all Member States as well as effective cooperation between the supervisory authorities of different Member States. The proper functioning of the internal market requires that the free movement of personal data within the Union is not restricted or prohibited for reasons connected with the protection of natural persons with regard to the processing of personal data. To take account of the specific situation of micro, small and medium-sized enterprises, this Regulation includes a derogation for organisations with fewer than 250 employees with regard to record-keeping. In addition, the Union institutions and bodies, and Member States and their supervisory authorities, are encouraged to take account of the specific needs of micro, small and medium-sized enterprises in the application of this Regulation. The notion of micro, small and medium-sized enterprises should draw from Article 2 of the Annex to Commission Recommendation 2003/361/EC.

(14) The protection afforded by this Regulation should apply to natural persons, whatever their nationality or place of residence, in relation to the processing of their personal data. This Regulation does not cover the processing of personal data which concerns legal persons and in particular undertakings established as legal persons, including the name and the form of the legal person and the contact details of the legal person.

Commentary:

1   See Art. 4 cmt. 1.

2   See Art. 4 No. 2 regarding the definition of the term "processing".

3   See Art. 4 No. 1 regarding the definition of the term "personal data". Cf. also Recital 14 sentence 2. The GDPR does not provide data protection for legal entities, as provided, for example, by the data protection law of Austria. On this topic, please see CJEU 9 November 2010, C92/09 and C93/09 – *Schecke*.

4   Cf. Art. 8 Charter ("Protection of personal data") and Art. 16 TFEU; cf. Recital 1.

5   As before under the Data Protection Directive, the GDPR does not only protect the **fundamental right of data protection**, but equally serves the purpose of implementing the **fundamental freedoms**. Therefore, exceeding the level of data protection set out in the GDPR by national laws continues to be problematic. Cf. in this regard CJEU 6 November 2003, C101/01 – *Lindqvist* and CJEU 24 November 2011, C468/10, C-469/10 – *ASNEF.*

Article 2

Material scope

1. This Regulation applies to the processing[1] of personal data[2] wholly or partly by automated means and to the processing other than by automated means of personal data which form part of a filing system[3,4] or are intended to form part of a filing system.

2. This Regulation does not apply to the processing of personal data:

(a) in the course of an activity which falls outside the scope of Union law;[5]

(b) by the Member States when carrying out activities which fall within the scope of Chapter 2 of Title V of the TEU;[6]

(c) by a natural person in the course of a purely personal or household activity;[7]

(d) by competent authorities for the purposes of the prevention, investigation, detection or prosecution of criminal offences, the execution of criminal penalties, including the safeguarding against and the prevention of threats to public security.[8]

3. For the processing of personal data by the Union institutions, bodies, offices and agencies, Regulation (EC) No 45/2001 applies. Regulation (EC) No 45/2001 and other Union legal acts applicable to such processing of personal data shall be adapted to the principles and rules of this Regulation in accordance with Article 98.[9]

4. This Regulation shall be without prejudice to the application of Directive 2000/31/EC, in particular of the liability rules of intermediary service providers in Articles 12 to 15 of that Directive.[10]

Recitals:

(15) In order to prevent creating a serious risk of circumvention, the protection of natural persons should be technologically neutral and should not depend on the techniques used. The protection of natural persons should apply to the processing of personal data by automated means, as well as to manual processing, if the personal data are contained or are intended to be contained in a filing system. Files or sets of files, as well as their cover pages, which are not structured according to specific criteria should not fall within the scope of this Regulation.

(16) This Regulation does not apply to issues of protection of fundamental rights and freedoms or the free flow of personal data related to activities which fall outside the scope of Union law, such as activities concerning national security. This Regulation does not apply to the processing of personal data by the Member States when carrying out activities in relation to the common foreign and security policy of the Union.

(17) Regulation (EC) No 45/2001 of the European Parliament and of the Council applies to the processing of personal data by the Union institutions, bodies, offices and agencies. Regulation (EC) No 45/2001 and other Union legal acts applicable to such processing of personal data should be adapted to the principles and rules established in this Regulation and applied in the light of this Regulation. In order to provide a strong and coherent data protection framework in the Union, the necessary

adaptations of Regulation (EC) No 45/2001 should follow after the adoption of this Regulation, in order to allow application at the same time as this Regulation.

(18) *This Regulation does not apply to the processing of personal data by a natural person in the course of a purely personal or household activity and thus with no connection to a professional or commercial activity. Personal or household activities could include correspondence and the holding of addresses, or social networking and online activity undertaken within the context of such activities. However, this Regulation applies to controllers or processors which provide the means for processing personal data for such personal or household activities.*

(19) *The protection of natural persons with regard to the processing of personal data by competent authorities for the purposes of the prevention, investigation, detection or prosecution of criminal offences or the execution of criminal penalties, including the safeguarding against and the prevention of threats to public security and the free movement of such data, is the subject of a specific Union legal act. This Regulation should not, therefore, apply to processing activities for those purposes. However, personal data processed by public authorities under this Regulation should, when used for those purposes, be governed by a more specific Union legal act, namely Directive (EU) 2016/680 of the European Parliament and of the Council. Member States may entrust competent authorities within the meaning of Directive (EU) 2016/680 with tasks which are not necessarily carried out for the purposes of the prevention, investigation, detection or prosecution of criminal offences or the execution of criminal penalties, including the safeguarding against and prevention of threats to public security, so that the processing of personal data for those other purposes, in so far as it is within the scope of Union law, falls within the scope of this Regulation. With regard to the processing of personal data by those competent authorities for purposes falling within scope of this Regulation, Member States should be able to maintain or introduce more specific provisions to adapt the application of the rules of this Regulation. Such provisions may determine more precisely specific requirements for the processing of personal data by those competent authorities for those other purposes, taking into account the constitutional, organisational and administrative structure of the respective Member State. When the processing of personal data by private bodies falls within the scope of this Regulation, this Regulation should provide for the possibility for Member States under specific conditions to restrict by law certain obligations and rights when such a restriction constitutes a necessary and proportionate measure in a democratic society to safeguard specific important interests including public security and the prevention, investigation, detection or prosecution of criminal offences or the execution of criminal penalties, including the safeguarding against and the prevention of threats to public security. This is relevant for instance in the framework of anti-money laundering or the activities of forensic laboratories.*

(20) *While this Regulation applies, inter alia, to the activities of courts and other judicial authorities, Union or Member State law could specify the processing operations and processing procedures in relation to the processing of personal data by courts and other judicial authorities. The competence of the supervisory authorities should not cover the processing of personal data when courts are acting in their judicial capacity, in order to safeguard the independence of the judiciary in the performance of its judicial tasks,*

including decision-making. It should be possible to entrust supervision of such data processing operations to specific bodies within the judicial system of the Member State, which should, in particular ensure compliance with the rules of this Regulation, enhance awareness among members of the judiciary of their obligations under this Regulation and handle complaints in relation to such data processing operations.

(21) This Regulation is without prejudice to the application of Directive 2000/31/EC of the European Parliament and of the Council, in particular of the liability rules of intermediary service providers in Articles 12 to 15 of that Directive. That Directive seeks to contribute to the proper functioning of the internal market by ensuring the free movement of information society services between Member States.

Commentary:

1 Cf. Art. 4 No. 2 regarding the definition of the term "processing".

2 Cf. Art. 4 No. 1 regarding the definition of the term "personal data".

3 Cf. Art. 4 No. 6 regarding the definition of the term "filing system".

4 **Paper files** are not covered by the material scope of the GDPR. Recital 15 last sentence stipulates that "[f]iles or sets of files, as well as their cover pages, which are not structured according to specific criteria should not fall within the scope of this Regulation" (cf. Recital 27 last sentence of the Data Protection Directive).

5 In particular, activities concerning **national security** are outside the scope of European Union law and, pursuant to Art. 2 para. 2 lit. a, therefore are not covered by the GDPR (see Recital 16; Art. 4 No. 2 TEU).

6 Chapter 2 of Title V of the TEU mentioned in para. 2 lit. b refers to the **common foreign and security policy of the Union** (cf. Recital 16 sentence 2).

7 The "household exemption" in para. 2 lit. c corresponds to Art. 3 para. 2 indent 2 Data Protection Directive. Recital 18 clarifies that "professional or commercial activity" is not covered by the term "personal activity". Recital 18 mentions further examples for "purely personal or household activities": (1) maintaining correspondence, (2) holding of address directories, or (3) the use of social networking and online activity undertaken within the context of such personal or household activities. On the basis of the examples in Recital 18, the disclosure of personal data, as it is typically the case in social networks, may be out of scope of the GDPR. However, the exemption must be interpreted narrowly (cf. in particular CJEU 6 November 2003, C-101/01 – *Lindqvist*). As an example, the operation of a camera system, as a result of which a video recording of people is stored on a continuous recording device such as a hard disk drive, installed by an individual on his family home for the purposes of protecting the property, health and life of the home owners, but which also monitors a public space does not qualify as a "purely personal or household activity" (CJEU 11 December 2014, C-212/13 – *Ryneš*). The publication of personal data on a privately motivated but publicly available website is also not covered by the "household exemption" (cf. CJEU 11 November 2003, C101/01 – *Lindqvist*).

8 Data processing activities mentioned in para. 2 lit. d which are in particular stipulated in criminal procedure codes, criminal codes and police laws of the Member States are subject to Directive (EU) 2016/680 (cf. Recital 19).

9   See Recital 17. The reform of Regulation 45/2001 has not been implemented yet (as of August 2017), but is currently pending with the European Parliament (2017/0002/COD).

10   Since the GDPR is "without prejudice to" the **safe harbours** of Art. 12 to 15 E-Commerce-Directive, the provision of Internet access services (Art. 12), of caching services (Art. 13) or hosting services (Art. 14) will only be subject to criminal liability and/or liability for damages if the respective requirements are fulfilled. This applies in particular to damages pursuant to Art. 82, fines pursuant to Art. 83, and other penalties pursuant to Art. 84. Cf. also Recital 21.

Article 3

Territorial scope[1]

1. This Regulation applies to the processing of personal data in the context of the activities[2] of an establishment[3] of a controller or a processor[4] in the Union, regardless of whether the processing takes place in the Union or not.[5]

2. This Regulation applies to the processing of personal data of data subjects who are in the Union by a controller or processor[6] not established in the Union,[7] where the processing activities are related to:

   (a) the offering of goods or services,[8] irrespective of whether a payment of the data subject is required, to such data subjects in the Union; or

   (b) the monitoring of their behaviour as far as their behaviour takes place within the Union.[9]

3. This Regulation applies to the processing of personal data by a controller not established in the Union, but in a place where Member State law applies by virtue of public international law.[10]

Recitals:

(22) Any processing of personal data in the context of the activities of an establishment of a controller or a processor in the Union should be carried out in accordance with this Regulation, regardless of whether the processing itself takes place within the Union. Establishment implies the effective and real exercise of activity through stable arrangements. The legal form of such arrangements, whether through a branch or a subsidiary with a legal personality, is not the determining factor in that respect.

(23) In order to ensure that natural persons are not deprived of the protection to which they are entitled under this Regulation, the processing of personal data of data subjects who are in the Union by a controller or a processor not established in the Union should be subject to this Regulation where the processing activities are related to offering goods or services to such data subjects irrespective of whether connected to a payment. In order to determine whether such a controller or processor is offering goods or services to data subjects who are in the Union, it should be ascertained whether it is apparent that the controller or processor envisages offering services to data subjects in one or more Member States in the Union. Whereas the mere accessibility of the controller's, processor's or an intermediary's website in the Union, of an email address or of other contact details, or the use of a language generally used in the third country where the controller is established, is insufficient to ascertain such intention, factors such as the use of a language or a currency generally used in one or more Member States with the possibility of ordering goods and services in that other language, or the mentioning of customers or users who are in the Union, may make it apparent that the controller envisages offering goods or services to data subjects in the Union.

(24) The processing of personal data of data subjects who are in the Union by a controller or processor not established in the Union should also be subject to this Regulation when it is related to the monitoring of the behaviour of such data subjects in so far as their behaviour takes place within the Union. In order to determine whether a processing activity can be considered to monitor the behaviour of data subjects, it

should be ascertained whether natural persons are tracked on the internet including potential subsequent use of personal data processing techniques which consist of profiling a natural person, particularly in order to take decisions concerning her or him or for analysing or predicting her or his personal preferences, behaviours and attitudes.

(25) Where Member State law applies by virtue of public international law, this Regulation should also apply to a controller not established in the Union, such as in a Member State's diplomatic mission or consular post.

Commentary:

1   Pursuant to Art. 4 Data Protection Directive (respectively pursuant to the data protection laws of the Member States), the Data Protection Directive generally applies to controllers if the data processing: (1) is carried out in the context of the activities of an establishment of the controller on the territory of the Member State (cf. Art. 4 No. 1 lit. a Data Protection Directive); or (2) is carried out by using equipment situated in the territory of a Member State (cf. Art. 4 No. 1 lit. c Data Protection Directive). The alternative triggers for the applicability of European data protection law provided by the Data Protection Directive are therefore the establishment of a controller and the place of data processing. As provided in the Commission's proposal for the GDPR (see COM (2012) 11/4), the GDPR maintains the first trigger to a large extent (cf. Art. 3 para. 1) but replaces the second trigger (place of data processing) with the location of the data subject. Pursuant to Art. 3 para. 2, the GDPR also applies to controllers without an establishment in the EU if the data processing is related to: (a) the offering of goods or services to data subjects in the Union, irrespective of whether a payment of the data subject is required; or (b) the monitoring of their behaviour as far as their behaviour takes place within the EU (Art. 3 para. 2). These provisions are supposed to ensure that non-EU internet companies that compete with EU-companies in the European market comply with the same data protection laws.

2   A processing takes place **"in the context of the activities"** of an establishment if the establishment itself performs the processing or if there is at least a close connection between the data processing and the activities of the establishment. This applies if the processing takes place for the purposes of the establishment. In its judgment *Google Spain* the CJEU decided that the processing takes place **"in the context of the activities"** of an establishment, "when the operator of a search engine [established in the US] sets up in a Member State a branch or subsidiary which is intended to promote and sell advertising space offered by that engine and which orientates its activity towards the inhabitants of that Member State" (CJEU 13 May 2014, C-131/12, para. 60). Pursuant to this broad interpretation, it might be sufficient if the activities of an establishment commercially promote the parent company's data processing.

3   Pursuant to Recital 22, the term **"establishment"** requires "the effective and real exercise of activity through stable arrangements", where the legal form of the establishment – "whether through a branch or a subsidiary with legal personality" – is not decisive. This is the same wording used in Recital 19 of the

Data Protection Directive. Therefore, the previous case law of the CJEU applies pursuant to which also subsidiaries with legal personality constitute an establishment (CJEU 13 May 2014, C-131/12 – *Google Spain*) even if the establishment with legal personality does not operate in the core business of the parent company (but merely sells advertisement, as in *Google Spain*). In its *Weltimmo* judgment dated 1 October 2015, the CJEU interpreted the term "establishment" under the Data Protection Directive broadly and stated that "the presence of only one representative can, in some circumstances, suffice to constitute a stable arrangement if that representative acts with a sufficient degree of stability through the presence of the necessary equipment for provision of the specific services concerned in the Member State in question" (CJEU 1 October 2015, C-230/14 – *Weltimmo*, para. 31). Pursuant to the CJEU, a "real and effective activity" might already apply if it is a "minimal one" (CJEU 1 October 2015, C-230/14 – *Weltimmo*, para. 31). This is true for "the running of one or several property dealing websites concerning properties situated in Hungary, which are written in Hungarian and whose advertisements are subject to a fee after a period of one month" (CJEU 1 October 2015, C-230/14 – *Weltimmo*, para. 32). A website's accessibility in a Member State does not constitute an establishment (CJEU 28 July 2016, C-191/15 – *VKI v Amazon*, para. 76).

4   The **personal scope** of the GDPR is significantly extended compared to the Data Protection Directive because the GDPR not only obligates the controller but **also the processor**. The territorial scope does not only focus on the establishment of the controller, but also on the establishment of the processor. That means that the obligations of the processor pursuant to the GDPR – in particular to not engage a subprocessor without prior separate or general consent of the controller (Art. 28 para. 2), to maintain records of each category of processing activity (Art. 30 para. 2), to appoint a data protection officer (Art. 37), and to transfer personal data to third countries only in compliance with Chapter V – also apply to a processor located in the EU, even if the processor processes personal data for a controller that is not subject to the GDPR (which again, cf. cmt. 1 above, requires that the controller neither has an establishment in the EU nor addresses the European market). This makes little practical sense because the data usually are subject to less data protection at the controller's location anyway. This will limit the competitiveness of European processors which offer their services for example in the US because competing US-based processors and the controller itself are not subject to such obligations.

5   Upon incorporation into the **EEA Agreement**, the GDPR will also apply in Iceland, Liechtenstein and Norway. For the current status regarding the incorporation into the EEA Agreement cf. www.efta.int/eea-lex/32016R0679.

6   Since para. 2 addresses controllers and processors, the GDPR also applies to processors without an establishment in the EU that offer services (eg, cloud services) to controllers in the EU (see also cmt. 8 below). In our opinion, notwithstanding this, transfers to such processors must comply with the provisions regarding the transfer of personal data to third countries pursuant to Art. 44 et seq. (cf. Art. 44 cmt. 3).

7   Due to the wording in para. 2, there is the following **gap** in relation to para. 1: A controller, or a processor established outside the Union which monitors the behaviour of data subjects in the Union (or offers goods or services to data subjects in the Union, whose data it is processing) may, at least pursuant to the clear language of para. 2, avoid the applicability of the GDPR by establishing a subsidiary (or other establishment; cf. cmt. 3) in the Union, without processing data in the context of the activities of such an establishment. In such a case the wording of para. 2 does not apply because the controller, or processor, is not "established in the Union". Para. 1 does not apply either because the processing would not take place "in the context of the activities of the establishment" of the controller in the Union. However, it might be argued that para. 2 must be extended to controllers and processors that have an establishment in the Union because, in such a case, the connection to the laws of the Union are even stronger than in the situation explicitly described in para. 2. It also has to be considered that the CJEU's requirements regarding the existence of an establishment that processes personal data in the context of its activities are very low (cf. above cmt. 3).

8   Pursuant to Recital 23 sentence 2, it is of relevance when answering the question whether a controller or processor is offering goods or services to data subjects in the Union, "**whether it is apparent that the controller or processor envisages offering services to data subjects in one or more Member States in the Union**". Recital 23 sentence 3 furthermore states that the following circumstances would not be sufficient to ascertain such intent: (1) the mere accessibility of the controller's, processor's or an intermediary's website in the EU; (2) the mere accessibility of an email address or of other contact details; or (3) the use of a language generally used in the third country where the controller is established. However, such intent can be derived from Recital 23 sentence 3 for the following circumstances: (1) the use of a language or currency that is generally used in one or more Member States (but not at the place of establishment of the operator) in connection with the possibility to order goods and services in such other language; or (2) the mentioning of customers or users that are in the Union.

9   Recital 24 sentence 2 clarifies that in particular the tracking (ie, logging) of internet activities of data subjects – for example to generate personalised advertisement – constitutes a "**monitoring**" within the meaning of para. 2 lit. b. The use of cookies might therefore result in such monitoring if they are used for personalising content.

10   Recital 25 mentions a Member State's diplomatic mission or consular post in a third country as an example.

Article 4

Definitions

For the purposes of this Regulation:

(1) 'personal data' means any information relating to an identified or identifiable natural person[1,2] ('data subject');[3] an identifiable natural person is one who can be identified, directly or indirectly, in particular by reference to an identifier such as a name, an identification number, location data, an online identifier or to one or more factors specific to the physical, physiological, genetic, mental, economic, cultural or social identity of that natural person;[4]

(2) 'processing' means any operation or set of operations which is performed on personal data or on sets of personal data, whether or not by automated means, such as collection, recording, organisation, structuring, storage, adaptation or alteration, retrieval, consultation, use, disclosure by transmission, dissemination or otherwise making available, alignment or combination, restriction, erasure or destruction;

(3) 'restriction of processing' means the marking of stored personal data with the aim of limiting their processing in the future;[5]

(4) 'profiling' means any form of automated processing of personal data consisting of the use of personal data to evaluate certain personal aspects relating to a natural person, in particular to analyse or predict aspects concerning that natural person's performance at work, economic situation, health, personal preferences, interests, reliability, behaviour, location or movements;[6]

(5) 'pseudonymisation' means the processing of personal data in such a manner that the personal data can no longer be attributed to a specific data subject without the use of additional information, provided that such additional information is kept separately and is subject to technical and organisational measures to ensure that the personal data are not attributed to an identified or identifiable natural person;[7,8]

(6) 'filing system'[9] means any structured set of personal data which are accessible according to specific criteria, whether centralised, decentralised or dispersed on a functional or geographical basis;[10]

(7) 'controller'[11] means the natural or legal person, public authority, agency or other body which, alone or jointly with others, determines the purposes and means of the processing of personal data;[12,13] where the purposes and means of such processing are determined by Union or Member State law, the controller or the specific criteria for its nomination may be provided for by Union or Member State law;[14]

(8) 'processor'[15] means a natural or legal person, public authority, agency or other body which processes personal data on behalf of the controller;[16]

(9) 'recipient' means a natural or legal person, public authority, agency or another body, to which the personal data are disclosed, whether a third party[17] or not.[18] However, public authorities which may receive personal data in the framework of a particular inquiry in accordance with Union or Member State

law shall not be regarded as recipients;[19] the processing of those data by those public authorities shall be in compliance with the applicable data protection rules according to the purposes of the processing;[20]

(10) 'third party' means a natural or legal person, public authority, agency or body other than the data subject, controller, processor and persons who, under the direct authority of the controller or processor, are authorised to process personal data;[21]

(11) 'consent'[22] of the data subject means any freely[23] given, specific,[24] informed[25] and unambiguous indication of the data subject's wishes[26,27] by which he or she, by a statement or by a clear affirmative action, signifies agreement to the processing of personal data relating to him or her;[28,29]

(12) 'personal data breach' means a breach of security leading to the accidental or unlawful destruction, loss, alteration, unauthorised disclosure of, or access to,[30] personal data transmitted, stored or otherwise processed;

(13) 'genetic data' means personal data relating to the inherited or acquired genetic characteristics of a natural person which give unique information about the physiology or the health of that natural person and which result, in particular, from an analysis of a biological sample from the natural person in question;[31]

(14) 'biometric data' means personal data resulting from specific technical processing relating to the physical, physiological or behavioural characteristics of a natural person, which allow or confirm the unique identification of that natural person,[32] such as facial images[33] or dactyloscopic data;[34]

(15) 'data concerning health' means personal data related to the physical or mental health of a natural person, including the provision of health care services, which reveal information about his or her health status;[35]

(16) 'main establishment'[36] means:

(a) as regards a controller with establishments[37] in more than one Member State,[38] the place of its central administration[39] in the Union,[40] unless the decisions on the purposes and means of the processing of personal data are taken in another establishment of the controller in the Union[41] and the latter establishment has the power to have such decisions implemented,[42] in which case the establishment having taken such decisions is to be considered to be the main establishment;

(b) as regards a processor with establishments[43] in more than one Member State, the place of its central administration in the Union,[44] or, if the processor has no central administration in the Union, the establishment of the processor in the Union where the main processing activities in the context of the activities of an establishment of the processor take place[45] to the extent that the processor is subject to specific obligations under this Regulation;

(17) 'representative' means a natural or legal person established in the Union who, designated by the controller or processor in writing pursuant to Article 27, represents the controller or processor with regard to their respective obligations under this Regulation;

(18) 'enterprise' means a natural or legal person engaged in an economic activity, irrespective of its legal form, including partnerships or associations regularly engaged in an economic activity;[46]

(19) 'group of undertakings' means a controlling[47] undertaking[48] and its controlled undertakings;[49]

(20) 'binding corporate rules'[50] means personal data protection policies which are adhered to by a controller or processor established on the territory of a Member State for transfers or a set of transfers of personal data to a controller or processor in one or more third countries within a group of undertakings,[51] or group of enterprises engaged in a joint economic activity;[52]

(21) 'supervisory authority' means an independent public authority which is established by a Member State pursuant to Article 51;

(22) 'supervisory authority concerned' means a supervisory authority which is concerned by the processing of personal data because:[53]

    (a) the controller or processor is established on the territory of the Member State of that supervisory authority;

    (b) data subjects residing in the Member State of that supervisory authority are substantially affected or likely to be substantially affected by the processing; or

    (c) a complaint has been lodged with that supervisory authority;[54]

(23) 'cross-border processing'[55] means either:

    (a) processing of personal data which takes place in the context of the activities of establishments[56] in more than one Member State[57] of a controller or processor in the Union where the controller or processor is established in more than one Member State; or

    (b) processing of personal data which takes place in the context of the activities of a single establishment of a controller or processor in the Union[58] but which substantially affects or is likely to substantially affect data subjects in more than one Member State.

(24) 'relevant and reasoned objection' means an objection to a draft decision as to whether there is an infringement of this Regulation, or whether envisaged action in relation to the controller or processor complies with this Regulation, which clearly demonstrates the significance of the risks posed by the draft decision as regards the fundamental rights and freedoms of data subjects and, where applicable, the free flow of personal data within the Union;

(25) 'information society service' means a service as defined in point (b) of Article 1(1) of Directive (EU) 2015/1535[59] of the European Parliament and of the Council;

(26) 'international organisation' means an organisation and its subordinate bodies governed by public international law, or any other body which is set up by, or on the basis of, an agreement between two or more countries.

Recitals:

Regarding para. 1 ("personal data"):

(26) The principles of data protection should apply to any information concerning an

identified or identifiable natural person. Personal data which have undergone pseudonymisation, which could be attributed to a natural person by the use of additional information should be considered to be information on an identifiable natural person. To determine whether a natural person is identifiable, account should be taken of all the means reasonably likely to be used, such as singling out, either by the controller or by another person to identify the natural person directly or indirectly. To ascertain whether means are reasonably likely to be used to identify the natural person, account should be taken of all objective factors, such as the costs of and the amount of time required for identification, taking into consideration the available technology at the time of the processing and technological developments. The principles of data protection should therefore not apply to anonymous information, namely information which does not relate to an identified or identifiable natural person or to personal data rendered anonymous in such a manner that the data subject is not or no longer identifiable. This Regulation does not therefore concern the processing of such anonymous information, including for statistical or research purposes.

(27) This Regulation does not apply to the personal data of deceased persons. Member States may provide for rules regarding the processing of personal data of deceased persons.

Regarding para. 5 ("Pseudonymisation"):

(28) The application of pseudonymisation to personal data can reduce the risks to the data subjects concerned and help controllers and processors to meet their data-protection obligations. The explicit introduction of 'pseudonymisation' in this Regulation is not intended to preclude any other measures of data protection.

(29) In order to create incentives to apply pseudonymisation when processing personal data, measures of pseudonymisation should, whilst allowing general analysis, be possible within the same controller when that controller has taken technical and organisational measures necessary to ensure, for the processing concerned, that this Regulation is implemented, and that additional information for attributing the personal data to a specific data subject is kept separately. The controller processing the personal data should indicate the authorised persons within the same controller.

Regarding para. 4 ("Profiling")

(30) Natural persons may be associated with online identifiers provided by their devices, applications, tools and protocols, such as internet protocol addresses, cookie identifiers or other identifiers such as radio frequency identification tags. This may leave traces which, in particular when combined with unique identifiers and other information received by the servers, may be used to create profiles of the natural persons and identify them.

Regarding para. 9 ("Recipient"):

(31) Public authorities to which personal data are disclosed in accordance with a legal obligation for the exercise of their official mission, such as tax and customs authorities, financial investigation units, independent administrative authorities, or

financial market authorities responsible for the regulation and supervision of securities markets should not be regarded as recipients if they receive personal data which are necessary to carry out a particular inquiry in the general interest, in accordance with Union or Member State law. The requests for disclosure sent by the public authorities should always be in writing, reasoned and occasional and should not concern the entirety of a filing system or lead to the interconnection of filing systems. The processing of personal data by those public authorities should comply with the applicable data-protection rules according to the purposes of the processing.

Regarding para. 11 ("Consent"):

(32) Consent should be given by a clear affirmative act establishing a freely given, specific, informed and unambiguous indication of the data subject's agreement to the processing of personal data relating to him or her, such as by a written statement, including by electronic means, or an oral statement. This could include ticking a box when visiting an internet website, choosing technical settings for information society services or another statement or conduct which clearly indicates in this context the data subject's acceptance of the proposed processing of his or her personal data. Silence, pre-ticked boxes or inactivity should not therefore constitute consent. Consent should cover all processing activities carried out for the same purpose or purposes. When the processing has multiple purposes, consent should be given for all of them. If the data subject's consent is to be given following a request by electronic means, the request must be clear, concise and not unnecessarily disruptive to the use of the service for which it is provided.

(33) It is often not possible to fully identify the purpose of personal data processing for scientific research purposes at the time of data collection. Therefore, data subjects should be allowed to give their consent to certain areas of scientific research when in keeping with recognised ethical standards for scientific research. Data subjects should have the opportunity to give their consent only to certain areas of research or parts of research projects to the extent allowed by the intended purpose.

Regarding para. 13 ("genetic data"):

(34) Genetic data should be defined as personal data relating to the inherited or acquired genetic characteristics of a natural person which result from the analysis of a biological sample from the natural person in question, in particular chromosomal, deoxyribonucleic acid (DNA) or ribonucleic acid (RNA) analysis, or from the analysis of another element enabling equivalent information to be obtained.

Regarding para. 15 ("data concerning health"):

(35) Personal data concerning health should include all data pertaining to the health status of a data subject which reveal information relating to the past, current or future physical or mental health status of the data subject. This includes information about the natural person collected in the course of the registration for, or the provision of, health care services as referred to in Directive 2011/24/EU of the European Parliament and of the Council to that natural person; a number, symbol or particular assigned to a natural person to uniquely identify the natural person for health purposes;

information derived from the testing or examination of a body part or bodily substance, including from genetic data and biological samples; and any information on, for example, a disease, disability, disease risk, medical history, clinical treatment or the physiological or biomedical state of the data subject independent of its source, for example from a physician or other health professional, a hospital, a medical device or an in vitro diagnostic test.

Regarding para. 16 ("main establishment"):

(36) The main establishment of a controller in the Union should be the place of its central administration in the Union, unless the decisions on the purposes and means of the processing of personal data are taken in another establishment of the controller in the Union, in which case that other establishment should be considered to be the main establishment. The main establishment of a controller in the Union should be determined according to objective criteria and should imply the effective and real exercise of management activities determining the main decisions as to the purposes and means of processing through stable arrangements. That criterion should not depend on whether the processing of personal data is carried out at that location. The presence and use of technical means and technologies for processing personal data or processing activities do not, in themselves, constitute a main establishment and are therefore not determining criteria for a main establishment. The main establishment of the processor should be the place of its central administration in the Union or, if it has no central administration in the Union, the place where the main processing activities take place in the Union. In cases involving both the controller and the processor, the competent lead supervisory authority should remain the supervisory authority of the Member State where the controller has its main establishment, but the supervisory authority of the processor should be considered to be a supervisory authority concerned and that supervisory authority should participate in the cooperation procedure provided for by this Regulation. In any case, the supervisory authorities of the Member State or Member States where the processor has one or more establishments should not be considered to be supervisory authorities concerned where the draft decision concerns only the controller. Where the processing is carried out by a group of undertakings, the main establishment of the controlling undertaking should be considered to be the main establishment of the group of undertakings, except where the purposes and means of processing are determined by another undertaking.

Regarding para. 19 ("group of undertakings"):

(37) A group of undertakings should cover a controlling undertaking and its controlled undertakings, whereby the controlling undertaking should be the undertaking which can exert a dominant influence over the other undertakings by virtue, for example, of ownership, financial participation or the rules which govern it or the power to have personal data protection rules implemented. An undertaking which controls the processing of personal data in undertakings affiliated to it should be regarded, together with those undertakings, as a group of undertakings.

[Recital 38 can be found with Art. 8.]

Commentary:

1   Data referring to **legal entities** are not covered by the GDPR. This does not apply if the official title of the legal person identifies one or more natural persons (CJEU 9 November 2010, C-92/09 and C-93/09 – *Schecke*, para. 53; cf. also Recital 14 sentence 2: "This Regulation does not cover the processing of personal data which concerns legal persons and in particular undertakings established as legal persons, including the name and the form of the legal person and the contact details of the legal person.").

2   The term natural person only covers living natural persons, but not **deceased persons** (see Recital 27 sentence 1 and Recital 158 sentence 1) and (likely) also not **unborn children**. Whether and to what extent data of deceased persons are protected has to be determined pursuant to national law (Recital 27 sentence 2).

3   Recital 26 sentence 3 provides that in order to determine whether a natural person is identifiable and therefore the data qualifies as personal data, account should be taken of "all the means reasonably likely to be used, such as singling out, either by the controller or by another person to identify the natural person directly or indirectly". The wording corresponds to the principles developed by the Art. 29 Working Party in 2014 regarding **anonymisation** (Art. 29 Working Party, Opinion 5/2014 on Anonymisation Techniques, WP 216 (2014), at 3). The opinion points out that not only the knowledge and means of the controller are relevant, but also the knowledge and means of third parties ("objective" approach).

It can be concluded from Recital 26 sentence 4 that the qualification as personal data could also develop retrospectively since the "time of the processing" and not the time of the collection is relevant in order to determine whether means are reasonably likely to be used to identify the natural person. Moreover, "technological developments" that are foreseeable in the future must be taken into consideration which leads to a further expansion of the term "personal data". Anonymous data are not covered by the scope of the GDPR (as under the Data Protection Directive).

4   The addition that the identifiable person is one who can be identified "by reference to an identifier such as a name, an identification number, location data, an online identifier or to one or more factors specific to the physical, physiological, genetic, mental, economic, cultural or social identity of that natural person" does not extend the material scope compared to the Data Protection Directive (cf. Art. 29 Working Party, Opinion 9/2014 on the application of Directive 2002/58/EC to device fingerprinting, WP 224 (2014), at 4, which states that a device fingerprint generally qualifies as personal data under the Data Protection Directive).

5   See Art. 18 regarding the **restriction of processing** in general and in particular Art. 18 cmt. 2 regarding the interpretation of the term "restriction of processing". The definition in Art. 4 No. 3 is of little help because it equates: (i) the restriction; with (ii) the marking of personal data with the aim of limiting their processing. This is not helpful from a linguistic perspective and, furthermore, leaves it unclear who has to pursue the aim, when and for how long.

6   Recital 30 makes clear that with Art. 4 No. 4, the legislature of the Union
     intended to cover **profiling** which uses the IP address or device identifier of the
     user and is therefore in general based on pseudonymous data. The concepts of
     profiling and pseudonymisation therefore do not exclude each either, neither
     from a technical nor from a legal perspective.

7   Pseudonymisation pursuant to Art. 4 No. 5 requires "technical and
     organisational measures to ensure that the personal data are not attributed to
     an identified or identifiable natural person". If such pseudonymisation is
     applied within the same controller, Recital 29 sentence 2 requires as one
     measure that "the controller processing the personal data should indicate the
     authorized persons within the same controller". This means that the controller
     must implement access control measures and, as a first step, define which
     employee is authorised to **remove the pseudonymisation by connecting the
     data with non-pseudonymous data**. A role-based access control system should
     be considered sufficient for this purpose.

8   Cf. Recital 29 sentence 1 which states that "incentives to apply
     pseudonymisation" should be created.

9   The term "**filing system**" remains the same as under the Data Protection
     Directive (although, eg, the German translation of "filing system" used in the
     Data Protection Directive differs from the German translation of "filing system"
     used in the GDPR).

10   Cf. Recital 15 which points out the principle of technological neutrality but
     clarifies that "**Files** or **sets of files**, as well as their cover pages, which are not
     structured according to specific criteria should not fall within the scope of this
     Regulation" (cf. also Art. 2 cmt. 4).

11   The term "controller" remains the same as under the Data Protection Directive
     (although, eg, the German translation of "controller" used in the Data
     Protection Directive differs from the German translation of "controller" used in
     the GDPR).

12   Controller can only be the one who decides on the "purpose" of the processing.
     The decision regarding the "means" of the processing, that is, questions
     regarding technical and organisational measures can be delegated by the
     controller. Substantive issues that concern the compliance of the processing
     with the GDPR, for example the data categories to be processed, retention
     periods, access rights, etc, must be decided by the controller. For details
     regarding the distinction between controllers and processors, see Art. 29
     Working Party, Opinion 1/2010 on the concepts of "controller" and
     "processor", WP 169 (2010), available at http://ec.europa.eu/justice/policies/
     privacy/docs/wpdocs/2010/wp169_en.pdf.

13   The definition of the term "controller" makes it possible that a **natural person
     is the controller of his or her own personal data**. That is of relevance in the
     following scenario: If a data subject entrusts a third party (eg, a host provider)
     with his or her own personal data in a manner that the third party may process
     the personal data only according to the data subject's instructions and only for
     the data subject's purposes, the third party will be obligated to ensure data

security only if the third party is qualified as a processor. The qualification as a processor (Art. 4 No. 8) requires that the data subject is qualified as a controller. If the data subject is qualified as a controller of his or her own data the third party will be qualified as a processor and will be subject to the GDPR. The data subject (ie, controller) however, may rely on the exception of Art. 2 para. 2 lit. c to the extent that only his or her own personal data is processed and is therefore not subject to the GDPR because interests of third parties are not concerned.

14 Cf. Recital 45 sentence 5 which provides that for cases based on Art. 6 para. 1 subpara. 1 lit. c and e Union or Member State law may "establish specifications for determining the controller".

15 The definition of "processor" remains the same as in Art. 2 lit. e Data Protection Directive. See cmt. 12 regarding the distinction between processors and controllers.

16 A processor that infringes its obligations and determines the purposes and means of processing will be qualified as a controller (see Art. 28 para. 10).

17 See Art. 4 No. 10 regarding the definition of the term "third party".

18 The clarification in Art. 4 No. 9 "whether a third party or not" means that a processor, a controller and even the data subject itself can be a **"recipient"**.

19 See also Recital 31 sentence 1 that mentions "tax and customs authorities, financial investigation units, independent administrative authorities, or financial market authorities responsible for the regulation and supervision of securities markets" as examples for **public authorities** within the meaning of Art. 4 No. 9 sentence 2. The disclosure vis-à-vis intelligence services of a Member State (Art. 2 para. 2 lit. a) or law enforcement agencies of a Member State (Art. 2 para. 2 lit. d) is not subject to the GDPR and remains subject to national laws.

20 Recital 31 sentence 2 requires the following for **requests for disclosure sent by the public authorities** (eg, by tax authorities): They should be: (1) always in writing; (2) reasoned; (3) occasional; and (4) not concern the entirety of a filing system or lead to the interconnection of filing systems. These requirements, of course, only apply within the scope of the GDPR (see cmt. 19 above).

21 Therefore, if a controller discloses personal data to its subsidiary which subsequently determines the means and purposes of the processing of the received data by itself, the subsidiary will be qualified as a "third party". This applies notwithstanding the wording of recital 47 sentence 1.

22 Additional requirements for the validity of consent are stipulated in Art. 7 et seq.

23 Consent will only be regarded as **freely** given if the data subject has a "genuine and free choice and is able to refuse or withdraw consent without detriment" (Recital 42 last sentence). It is not relevant whether this reaches the level of "significant negative consequences" for the data subject (as was required for "without coercion" in Art. 2 lit. h Data Protection Directive; cf. Art. 29 Working Party, Opinion 15/2011 on the definition of consent, WP 187 (2011), at 12, available at http://ec.europa.eu/justice/data-protection/article-29/documentation/opinion-recommendation/files/2011/wp187_en.pdf).

Recital 43 further states that consent will not be deemed freely given if "there is a **clear imbalance** between the data subject and the controller, in particular where the controller is a public authority and it is therefore unlikely that consent was freely given in all the circumstances of that specific situation". Whether the imbalance that usually exists in an employment relationship renders employee consent unfree has to be determined under national law pursuant to Art. 88 (Art. 88 cmt. 2).

Pursuant to Recital 43 last sentence, consent is presumed not to be freely given "if it **does not allow separate consent to be given to different personal data processing operations** despite it being appropriate in the individual case". Furthermore, consent is presumed not to be freely given pursuant to Recital 43 last sentence, "if the performance of a contract, including the provision of a service, is dependent on the consent despite such **consent not being necessary for such performance**" (see also Art. 7 para. 4).

24   The requirement "**specific**" appear to remain unchanged in relation to Art. 2 lit. h Data Protection Directive. This means that "blanket consent without specifying the exact purpose of the processing is not acceptable" (Art. 29 Working Party, Opinion 15/2011 on the definition of consent, WP 187 (2011), at 17, available at http://ec.europa.eu/justice/data-protection/article-29/ documentation/opinion-recommendation/files/2011/wp187_en.pdf. It is not required to describe the specific use case; rather, it is sufficient to describe the specific purpose which applies to one or more use cases. This is of relevance for consents provided for the purposes of "follow-up studies" in the area of (medical) research.

25   Pursuant to Recital 42 sentence 4, for a consent to be "**informed**", "the data subject should be aware at least of the identity of the controller and the purposes of the processing for which the personal data are intended". Art. 7 para. 3 sentence 2 furthermore requires that the data subject must be informed about his or her right to withdraw his or her consent at any time prior to giving consent.

The Art. 29 Working Party is of the opinion that "there must always be information [pursuant to Art. 10 et seq. Data Protection Directive] before there can be consent" (Art. 29 Working Party, Opinion 15/2011 on the definition of consent, WP 187 (2011), at 19, available at http://ec.europa.eu/justice/data-protection/article-29/documentation/opinion-recommendation/files/2011/ wp187_en.pdf). The information obligations in Art. 10 et seq. Data Protection Directive are, of course, significantly easier to comply with than the information obligations under Art. 12 et seqq. GDPR and require as a minimum – like Recital 42 sentence 4 – only the identity of the controller (Art. 10 lit. a and Art. 11 para. 1 lit. a Data Protection Directive) and the purposes of the processing (Art. 10 lit. b and Art. 11 para. 1 lit. b Data Protection Directive). Therefore, the opinion of the Art. 29 Working Party that valid consent requires compliance with all information obligations, will not necessarily apply to the GDPR in particular because this would in practice exclude implied and oral consent.

Since Recital 42 sentence 4 indicates that the provision of information on the identity of the controller and the purposes of the processing is only a minimum ("at least"), it might be advisable for controllers to also inform data subjects about the right to withdraw consent at any time pursuant to Art. 7 para. 3 sentence 2 and the data categories and the recipients, if any.

With regard to the determination of the purposes, Recital 33 stipulates that "it is often not possible to fully identify the purpose of personal data processing for scientific research purposes at the time of data collection". Therefore, data subjects should be allowed "to give their consent to certain areas of scientific research when in keeping with recognised ethical standards for scientific research".

26 **Implied consent** is generally sufficient. However, silence or pre-ticked checkboxes on a website do constitute consent pursuant to Recital 32. This is stricter than the German Federal Court of Justice's interpretation of the German data protection law under the Data Protection Directive (German Federal Court of Justice 11 November 2009, VIII ZR 12/08 – *Happy Digits*; German Federal Court of Justice 16 July 2008, VIII ZR 348/06 – *Payback*).

27 There is no **formal requirement** for consent; it can be given by a written statement, electronic means or by an oral statement (see Recital 32).

28 The controller has the **burden of proof** for demonstrating that the data subject consented (Art. 7 para. 1; Recital 42 sentence 1). Controllers should therefore keep appropriate records.

29 Regarding the **continued validity of consent obtained under the Data Protection Directive**, Recital 171 sentence 3 states: "Where processing is based on consent pursuant to Directive 95/46/EC, it is not necessary for the data subject to give his or her consent again if the manner in which the consent has been given is in line with the conditions of this Regulation, so as to allow the controller to continue such processing after the date of application of this Regulation."

Therefore, a consent declaration obtained before 25 May 2018 will only continue to be valid under the GDPR if it complies with the requirements of the GDPR. In Austria, for example, where the requirements for consent are already very strict under the Data Protection Directive, consents will in most cases continue to be valid (subject to Art. 7 para. 4 and the conditions applicable to a child's consent).

30 A **personal data breach** within the meaning of Art. 4 No. 12 exists only if there is a permanent breach of availability ("destruction" or "loss"), a breach of integrity ("alteration") or a breach of confidentiality ("unauthorized disclosure" or "unauthorized access". A violation of lawfulness or an "unauthorized or unlawful processing" (see Art. 5 para. 1 lit. f) does not constitute a personal data breach. The same applies to temporary impairments of availability of personal data because there is neither a "destruction" nor a "loss".

31 See Recital 34.

32 **Biometric data** within the meaning of Art. 4 No. 14 will only be regarded as sensitive data within the meaning of Art. 9 if the data do not only potentially

allow the identification of a natural personal but are also processed for that purpose. See Art. 9 cmt. 3.

33 **Facial images** mentioned in Art. 4 No. 14 will only constitute sensitive data within the meaning of Art. 9 if they are processed for the purpose of uniquely identifying a natural person (see Recital 51 sentence 3 and Art. 9 cmt. 3).

34 The term "dactyloscopic data" in Art. 4 No. 14 means **fingerprint data**.

35 Pursuant to Recital 35, data concerning health include also "a number, symbol, or particular assigned to a natural person to uniquely identify the natural person for health purposes". Therefore, in countries that have a social security number, such a **social security number** might constitute health data and therefore sensitive data pursuant to Art. 9 (at least, if it can be assumed that the social security number serves the purpose to uniquely identify the data subject as it is for example the case in Austria).

36 The term "main establishment" is defined differently for controllers and for processors in Art. 4 No. 16. However, both definitions provide that: (1) a controller, respectively a processor, can **conceptually only have a main establishment if it has at least one establishment in the Union** (see cmt. 38 and 45); and (2) the term "main establishment" is relative to the respective processing activity, that is, a controller or processor might have not only one main establishment but, depending on the respective processing activity, can have different main establishments (see also Art. 29 Working Party, Guidelines for identifying a controller or processor's lead supervisory authority, WP 244 rev. 1 (2017), at 5, available at http://ec.europa.eu/newsroom/just/item-detail.cfm?item_id=50083). This follows from lit. a which focuses on the establishment that determines the purposes and means of the processing and lit. b which focuses on the establishment, in the context of the activities of which the data is processed (see cmt. 45). Furthermore, it must be noted that pursuant to lit. a, there is **no group-wide main establishment for controllers**, whereas pursuant to lit. b, there might very well be a **group-wide main establishment for processors** (see cmt. 44).

37 See Art. 3 cmt. 3 regarding the definition of the term "establishment".

38 A controller without establishments in the Union cannot have a "main establishment" by definition. This applies also to processors (see cmt. 45).

39 The term **central administration** is not defined in the GDPR. The Art. 29 Working Party states that the "central administration in the EU is the place where decisions about the purposes and means of the processing of personal data are taken and this place has the power to have such decisions implemented" (Art. 29 Working Party, Guidelines for identifying a controller or processor's lead supervisory authority, WP 244 rev. 1 (2017), at 5, available at http://ec.europa.eu/newsroom/just/item-detail.cfm?item_id=50083).

40 Art. 4 No. 16 lit. a refers to the place of the "main establishment in the Union". Therefore, a **main establishment not located in the Union** cannot be a main establishment. In such a case, the Art. 29 Working Party recommends that the "company should designate the establishment that has the authority to implement decisions about the processing activity and liability for the

processing, including having sufficient assets, as its main establishment". They further state that if "the company does not designate a main establishment in this way, it will not be possible to designate a lead authority" (Art. 29 Working Party, Guidelines for identifying a controller or processor's lead supervisory authority, WP 244 rev. 1 (2017), at 8, available at http://ec.europa.eu/ newsroom/just/item-detail.cfm?item_id=50083). However, the Art. 29 Working Party also states that "the GDPR does not permit 'forum shopping'". The Art. 29 Working Party further states that "if a company claims to have its main establishment in one Member State, but no effective and real exercise of management activity or decision making over the processing of personal data takes place there, the relevant supervisory authorities (or ultimately the [European Data Protection Board]) will decide which supervisory authority is the 'lead', using objective criteria and looking at the evidence". The Art. 29 Working Party emphasises that "conclusions cannot be based solely on statements by the organisation under review", but that "the burden of proof ultimately falls in the controllers and processors to demonstrate to the relevant supervisory authorities where the relevant processing decisions are taken and where there is the power to implement such decisions" (Art. 29 Working Party, Guidelines for identifying a controller or processor's lead supervisory authority, WP 244 rev. 1 (2017), at 8, available at http://ec.europa.eu/newsroom/ just/item-detail.cfm?item_id=50083). Recital 36 sentence 2 states that "the main establishment of a controller in the Union should be determined according to objective criteria". One criteria should be the "effective and real exercise of management activities determining the main decisions as to the purposes and means of processing through stable arrangements".

In order to determine the location of a controller's main establishment, in cases where it is not the location of its central administration, the Art. 29 Working Party outlines the following factors: "(i) where are decisions about the purposes and means of the processing given final 'sign off'?; (ii) where are decisions about business activities that involve data processing made?; (iii) where does the power to have decisions implemented effectively lie?; (iv) where is the director (or directors) with overall management responsibility for the cross border processing located?, (v) where is the controller or processor registered as a company in a single territory?" (Art. 29 Working Party, Guidelines for identifying a controller or processor's lead supervisory authority, WP 244 rev. 1 (2017), at 7, available at http://ec.europa.eu/newsroom/ just/item-detail.cfm?item_id=50083).

41   An establishment, where the decisions regarding purposes and means of the processing are taken, can only be a main establishment within the meaning of Art. 4 No. 16 lit. a if this establishment is located within the Union. If the controller takes its decisions regarding the purposes and means of the processing in an establishment located in a third country – and if the central administration of the controller, too, is located in a third country (see above cmt. 40) – the controller cannot have a main establishment within the meaning of Art. 4 No. 16 lit. a.

42   Due to the addition in Art. 4 No. 16 lit. a "unless the decisions on the purposes and means of the processing [...] are taken in another establishment [...]", **there is no group-wide main establishment for controllers** – if an affiliate is the controller, the parent company can generally not be the main establishment of the controller. Focusing on the parent company when determining the main establishment of an affiliate seems to be the right way because the term "establishment" includes establishments without legal personality and establishments with legal personality such as affiliates (Art. 3 cmt. 3). Moreover, Recital 36 sentence 8 states: "Where the processing is carried out by a group of undertakings, the main establishment of the controlling undertaking should be considered to be the main establishment of the group of undertakings." Pursuant to Art. 4 No. 16, the place of the central administration of the group of undertakings should not be relevant, if "decisions on the purposes and means of the processing of personal data are taken in another establishment of the controller in the Union and the latter establishment has the power to have such decisions implemented" (see also Recital 36 sentence 8 second half-sentence).

The main establishment is determined primarily by **the place where the decisions concerning the purposes and means of the processing are made and only secondarily by the place of central administration**. As a result, local establishments (rather than the place of central administration of the parent company) will in practice often be qualified as the "main establishment" for particular data processing operations – contrary to the apparently clear wording. In particular if an affiliate in a group of undertakings decides on the means and purposes of the processing of its customer data or employee data (and has the power to implement its decisions), the establishment of the affiliate instead of the place of the central administration of the group of undertakings will be the "main establishment". The place of the central administration of the group of companies will indeed only be relevant in borderline cases, in particular if the means and purposes of the data processing are determined jointly by at the place of central administration of the parent company and a local establishment with legal personality or if the local establishment with legal personality is not entitled to implement decisions by itself. In such cases the local establishment with legal personality would "not have the power to have such decisions implemented". Therefore, the place of the central administration would be relevant.

As a result, the main establishment of the controller in a group of undertakings **must be determined as follows:** (1) identify the group company in the Union that acts as a controller, that is, determine on means and purposes (see Art. 4 No. 7); and (2) identify the place of the central administration of this group company (and not the place of the central administration of the parent company) primarily by asking which establishment of the group company decides on the means and purposes of the processing.

For an internationally operating enterprise there are in particular the following practical scenarios:

a) The parent company determines the means and purposes of the data processing by itself: even if the data processing takes place within the activities of the establishments (with or without legal personality) of the parent company, only the place of the central administration of the parent company will be relevant.

b) The company determines the means and purposes of the data processing jointly with its establishments with legal personality: generally the place of the central administration of the company will be the main establishment because despite the fact that the establishments without legal personality also decide on the means and purposes they do not have the power "to have such decisions implemented" (by themselves) (see Art. 4 No. 16 lit. a GDPR). According to the Art. 29 Working Party, joint controllers can benefit from the one-stop-shop principle if they "designate (among the establishments where decisions are taken) which establishment of the joint controllers will have the power to implement decisions about the processing with respect to all joint controllers". They further state that "this establishment will then be considered to be the main establishment for the processing carried out in the joint controller situation" (Art. 29 Working Party, Guidelines for identifying a controller or processor's lead supervisory authority, WP 244 rev. 1 (2017), at 8, available at http://ec.europa.eu/newsroom/just/item-detail.cfm?item_id=50083).

c) The company's establishments which do not have separate legal personality determine the means and purposes by themselves (and have the power to have such decisions implemented): each establishment qualifies as a main establishment for its processing operations. Since they are only establishments without separate legal personality, the main establishment will always be the same legal entity.

d) The parent company's establishments which have legal personality determine the means and purposes respectively by themselves: Each of the establishments with legal personality (affiliates) constitutes a controller and for each of these companies the main establishment has to be analysed separately.

e) The parent company's establishments which have legal personality determine the means and purposes of the data processing jointly with the parent company (joint controllers within the meaning of Art. 26): Each of the companies is a controller and the main establishment must be analysed for each of the companies separately.

In comparison to the provision of Art. 4 Data Protection Directive which focuses on the data processing operations of the respective establishment, there will only be a change in the above scenarios a) and b), that is., only in scenarios where the data processing operation takes place within the activities of an establishment but such establishment: (a) does not determine the means and purposes of the data processing; or (b) is an establishment without legal personality and cannot implement such decision by itself.

43 See Art. 3 cmt. 3 regarding the definition of the term "establishment".

44   In our opinion there is, in principle, a **group-wide main establishment for processors** – the main establishment (in the Union) of the controlling company constitutes the main establishment of the group of undertakings: Since the term establishment includes establishments without legal personality and establishments with legal personality such as affiliates (Art. 3 cmt. 3), main establishment can be the place of the central administration. This interpretation is supported by Recital 36 sentence 8 half sentence 1 which states: "Where the processing is carried out by a group of undertakings, the main establishment of the controlling undertaking should be considered to be the main establishment of the group of undertakings." This principle does not apply pursuant to the wording of Recital 36 sentence 8 half sentence 2 "where the purposes and means of processing are determined by another undertaking". The provision of half sentence 2 could be interpreted in two ways regarding processors: first it could be argued that half sentence 2 always refers to the controller and therefore half sentence 1 never applies to processors which would lead to the consequence that there was no privilege for a group of undertakings for processors. Secondly, Recital 36 in connection with the wording of Art. 4 No. 16 lit. a (relating to controllers) and lit. b (relating to processors) could be read in a manner that – pursuant to the wording of lit. a – the provision of half sentence 2 of Recital 36 sentence 8 applies only to controllers and, therefore, processors are only subject to the principle of half sentence 1. The latter interpretation is supported by the fact that the exception in half sentence 2 of the Recital 36 sentence 8 can only be found in Art. 4 No. 16 lit. a, but not in lit. b.

45   The rather imprecise wording in Art. 4 No. 16 lit. b ("the establishment of the processor in the Union where the main processing activities in the context of the activities of an establishment of the processor take place") is clarified by Recital 36 sentence 5, according to which the main establishment is "the place where the main processing activities take place in the Union" if the processor has no central administration in the Union. Despite this wording that apparently focuses on the place of the processing activities, the clear wording of Art. 4 No. 16 lit. b requires and focuses on an establishment in the Union.

46   For purposes of Art. 83, the definition of "enterprise" pursuant to Art. 4 No. 18 does not apply but the definition of undertakings pursuant to antitrust law does apply – Art. 101 lit. f TFEU (see Art. 83 cmt. 11).

47   See Recital 37 sentence 1 according to which a **controlling** undertaking within the meaning of Art. 4 No. 19 exists in particular if an undertaking can "exert a dominant influence over the other undertakings by virtue, for example, of ownership, financial participation or the rules which govern it or the power to have personal data protection rules implemented". Recital 37 sentence 2, however, seems to suggest that the mere control over the processing of personal data is not sufficient; there will only be such control if exercised among "undertakings affiliated to it". Due to the only exemplary list in Recital 37 sentence 1 ("for example") other forms of control might also be relevant.

48   See Art. 4 No. 18 regarding the definition of the term "**enterprise**". Art. 4 No. 19

does not use the term "enterprise" defined in Art. 4 No. 18 but rather the term "undertaking". However, the German, French and Spanish versions use the same term as defined in Art. 4 No. 18 ("Unternehmen", "entreprise", and "empresa", respectively). Against the background that provisions should be interpreted and applied uniformly in the light of the versions existing in all European Union languages (see CJEU 3 April 2008, C?187/07 – Endendijk, para. 22 with further citations) it must be assumed that the term "enterprise" defined in Art. 4 No. 18 is identical with the term "undertaking" used in Art. 4 No. 19.

49   The term **"group of enterprises engaged in a joint economic activity"** which is not defined in the GDPR does (in contrast to the term "group of undertakings") not require that one undertaking controls the other undertakings of the group. In particular, all enterprises that are part of a single franchise system could constitute a "group of enterprises engaged in a joint economic activity".

50   "Binding corporate rules" are also referred to as **"BCR"** in practice.

51   See Art. 4 No. 19 regarding the definition of the term "group of undertakings".

52   The scope of application of "binding corporate rules" was extended from a "group of undertakings" pursuant to Art. 4 No. 19 to a "group of enterprises engaged in a joint economic activity" by the Council within the legislative process. Regarding the term **"group of enterprises engaged in a joint economic activity"** see cmt. 49 above.

53   Regarding the three alternative requirements of a "supervisory authority concerned" within the meaning of Art. 4 No. 22, see also Recital 124 sentence 2.

54   Recital 124 sentence 3 clarifies regarding Art. 4 No. 22 lit. c that "the supervisory authority with which such complaint has been lodged should also be a supervisory authority concerned", "where a data subject not residing in that Member State has lodged a complaint".

55   A **cross-border processing** requires that: (1) the controller or the processor has establishments in more than one Member State (lit. a); or (2) the processing substantially affects data subjects in more than one Member State (lit. b). Therefore, not every cross-border situation constitutes a "cross-border processing". According to the Art. 29 Working Party, "substantially affects" requires that "the substantial effect must be more likely than not", however, it does not require "to be actually affected". The Art. 29 Working Party states that the term "substantially affects" will be interpreted on a case-by-case basis by the supervisory authorities, taking "into account the context of the processing, the type of data, the purpose of the processing and factors as to whether the processing (i) causes, or is likely to cause damage, loss or distress to individuals; (ii) has, or is likely to have, an actual effect in terms of limiting rights or denying an opportunity; (iii) affects, or is likely to affect, individual's health, well-being or peace of mind; (iv) affects, or is likely to affect, individuals' financial or economic status or circumstances; (v) leaves the individuals open to discrimination or unfair treatment; (vi) involves the analysis of the special categories of personal or other intrusive data, particularily the personal data of

children; (vii) causes, or is likely to cause individuals to change their behaviour in a significant way; (viii) has unlikely, unanticipated or unwanted consequences for individuals; (ix) creates embarrassment or other negative outcomes, including reputational damage; or (x) involves the processing of a wide range of personal data" (Art. 29 Working Party, Guidelines for identifying a controller or processor's lead supervisory authority, WP 244 rev. 1 (2017), at 4, available at http://ec.europa.eu/newsroom/just/item-detail.cfm?item _id=50083).

56 See Art. 3 cmt. 3 regarding the definition of the term "establishment".

57 If the controller, respectively the processor, does not have an establishment in the Union, a "cross-border processing" pursuant to Art. 4 No. 23 lit. a is excluded.

58 A "cross-border processing" pursuant to Art. 4 No. 23 lit. b, requires that the controller, or the processor, also has an establishment in the Union.

59 Art. 1 No. 1 lit. b of Directive (EU) 2015/1535 defines the term **Information Society service** as "any service normally provided for remuneration, at a distance, by electronic means and at the individual request of a recipient of services", where the individual components are defined as follows:
  – a service provided "at a distance": "the service is provided without the parties being simultaneously present";
  – a service provided by "electronic means": "the service is sent initially and received at its destination by means of electronic equipment for the processing (including digital compression) and storage of data, and entirely transmitted, conveyed and received by wire, by radio, by optical means or by other electromagnetic means";
  – a service provided "at the individual request of a recipient of services": "the service is provided through the transmission of data on individual request";
  – a service normally provided "for remuneration": "a service that does not require remuneration in the individual case".
Therefore, an Information Society service is in particular a website that is operated for commercial purposes and not for mere private interests.

Chapter II – Principles

Article 5

Principles relating to processing of personal data

1. Personal data shall be:
   (a) processed lawfully,[1] fairly[2] and in a transparent manner in relation to the data subject ('lawfulness, fairness and transparency');[3]
   (b) collected for specified,[4] explicit[5] and legitimate[6] purposes[7] and not further processed in a manner that is incompatible with those purposes;[8] further processing for archiving purposes in the public interest, scientific or historical research purposes or statistical purposes shall, in accordance with Article 89(1), not be considered to be incompatible with the initial purposes ('purpose limitation');
   (c) adequate, relevant and limited to what is necessary in relation to the purposes for which they are processed ('data minimisation');
   (d) accurate and, where necessary, kept up to date;[9] every reasonable step must be taken to ensure that personal data that are inaccurate, having regard to the purposes for which they are processed, are erased or rectified without delay ('accuracy');
   (e) kept in a form which permits identification of data subjects for no longer than is necessary for the purposes for which the personal data are processed;[10] personal data may be stored for longer periods insofar as the personal data will be processed solely for archiving purposes in the public interest, scientific or historical research purposes or statistical purposes in accordance with Article 89(1) subject to implementation of the appropriate technical and organisational measures required by this Regulation in order to safeguard the rights and freedoms of the data subject ('storage limitation');
   (f) processed in a manner that ensures appropriate security of the personal data, including protection against unauthorised or unlawful processing and against accidental loss, destruction or damage, using appropriate technical or organisational measures ('integrity and confidentiality').[11]
2. The controller[12] shall be responsible for, and be able to demonstrate compliance with, paragraph 1 ('accountability').[13,14]

Recital:

(39) Any processing of personal data should be lawful and fair. It should be transparent to natural persons that personal data concerning them are collected, used, consulted or otherwise processed and to what extent the personal data are or will be processed. The principle of transparency requires that any information and communication relating to the processing of those personal data be easily accessible and easy to understand, and that clear and plain language be used. That principle concerns, in particular, information to the data subjects on the identity of the controller and the purposes of the processing and further information to ensure fair and transparent processing in respect of the natural persons concerned and their right to obtain confirmation and communication of personal data concerning them which are being processed. Natural persons should be made aware of risks, rules, safeguards and rights in relation to the processing of personal data and how to exercise their rights in relation to such processing. In particular, the specific purposes for which personal data are processed should be explicit and legitimate and determined at the time of the collection of the personal data. The personal data should be adequate, relevant and limited to what is necessary for the purposes for which they are processed. This requires, in particular, ensuring that the period for which the personal data are stored is limited to a strict minimum. Personal data should be processed only if the purpose of the processing could not reasonably be fulfilled by other means. In order to ensure that the personal data are not kept longer than necessary, time limits should be established by the controller for erasure or for a periodic review. Every reasonable step should be taken to ensure that personal data which are inaccurate are rectified or deleted. Personal data should be processed in a manner that ensures appropriate security and confidentiality of the personal data, including for preventing unauthorised access to or use of personal data and the equipment used for the processing.

Commentary:

1   The principle of **lawfulness** pursuant to para. 1 lit. a primarily means that personal data may only be processed if there is a legal basis pursuant to Arts. 6, 9 or 10. Furthermore, the principle can be seen as a reference to the necessity to have lawful processing purposes (cf. cmt. 6 below).

2   The principle of **fairness and transparency** constitutes – as before in Art. 6 para. 1 lit. a Data Protection Directive – a kind of a "catch-all" clause which must be considered in particular when conducting a balancing of interests test (cf., eg, Art. 6 para. 1 lit. f).

3   The requirements resulting from the principle of **transparency** in para. 1 lit. a are stipulated in Art. 12 et seqq.

4   The requirement of **purpose specification** in para. 1 lit. b (resulting from the requirement to determine the purpose) constitutes a material aspect of the principle of "purpose limitation". The purposes must be specified sufficiently precise so that: (i) it can be assessed which types of processing are covered; and (ii) it is possible to assess the lawfulness of the purposes as well as the lawfulness of the processing in general. Processing purposes like "marketing purposes" or "IT-security purposes" are, in principle, not sufficient (see the explicit statement of the Art. 29 Working Party, Opinion 03/2012 on purpose limitation WP 203

(2013), at 16, available at http://ec.europa.eu/justice/data-protection/article-29/documentation/opinion-recommendation/files/2013/wp203_en.pdf).

5 Purposes will be **explicit** within the meaning of para. 1 lit. b only if the purposes are documented in an intelligible manner and if they are expressed in a manner so that they are not only understood by the controller and the engaged processor but also by the supervisory authorities and the data subjects in the same manner (Art. 29 Working Party, Opinion 03/2012 on purpose limitation, WP 203 (2013), at 17, available at http://ec.europa.eu/justice/data-protection/article-29/documentation/opinion-recommendation/files/2013/wp203_en.pdf).

6 The **legitimacy** of the purposes within the meaning of para. 1 lit. b does not only require that the data processing can be based on one of the statutory permissions of Art. 6 para. 1 subpara. 1 lit. a to f, respectively Art. 9 para. 2 lit. a to j, but also that the data processing is in compliance with other legal obligations which may result from employment law, contract law or consumer protection law (cf. Art. 29 Working Party, Opinion 03/2012 on purpose limitation, WP 203 (2013), at 19 et seq., available at http://ec.europa.eu/justice/data-protection/article-29/documentation/opinion-recommendation/files/2013/wp203_en.pdf).

7 Since the data collection is the decisive moment, the **purposes must be specified no later than at the time when the collection** of personal data occurs (Art. 29 Working Party, Opinion 03/2012 on purpose limitation, WP 203 (2013), at 15, available at http://ec.europa.eu/justice/data-protection/article-29/documentation/opinion-recommendation/files/2013/wp203_en.pdf).

8 See Art. 6 para. 4 regarding the criteria of **compatibility of new purposes** with the purposes for which the personal data were initially collected. Regarding the relationship between the **purpose limitation principle** in para. 1 lit. b and the principle of lawfulness of the processing, see Art. 6 cmt. 14. Regarding the relationship to the transparency principle and the information obligations in case of processing for another purpose, see Art. 13 para. 3 and Art. 14 para. 4.

9 Whether it is necessary to keep the data up to date, should depend on the respective processing purpose.

10 Para. 1 lit. e addresses in particular a pseudonymisation or subsequent anonymisation of the data.

11 The definition of the **principle of integrity and confidentialit**y in para. 1 lit. f can be criticised for several reasons: First of all, the exemplary list of protection objectives is incomplete in light of the name of the principle. In contrast to Art. 17 para. 1 Data Protection Directive and Art. 32 para. 2 GDPR, para. 1 lit. f does not explicitly state that personal data must be secured against unlawful disclosure or unauthorised access which would address the confidentiality of data. Since the legislature of the Union designated the principle in para. 1 lit. f "integrity and confidentiality", there is no doubt that pursuant to this principle personal data must also be protected against unlawful access.

Secondly, the term "integrity and confidentiality" is not broad enough since personal data must, pursuant the protection objectives, also be protected against unintended loss, respectively the unintended destruction, that is, against loss of availability of the data.

Finally, para. 1 lit. f uses the term "security" inconsistently in comparison to Art. 32 et seq.: Pursuant to para. 1 lit. f, the security of personal data also covers the "protection of unauthorized or unlawful processing" which addresses the lawfulness of the processing. Pursuant to Art. 32, only the confidentiality, integrity and availability of data, but not the lawfulness of its processing constitutes a protection objective (cf. Art. 32 para. 2). The obligation regarding data breach notifications (Art. 33 et seqq.), too, is limited to infringements of the confidentiality, integrity and availability of the data (see Art. 4 cmt. 30). The understanding of Art. 32 et seq. is also reflected in Recital 83 sentence 1 which requires measures to "maintain security" on the one hand and to "prevent processing in infringement of this Regulation" on the other hand. The latter one is not subject to Art. 32 et seq. but to Art. 24.

The principle codified in para. 1 lit. f should therefore have been name "security and lawfulness" where "security" refers to Art. 32 et seq. and "lawfulness" to Art. 24.

12 The **accountability** principle of para. 2 therefore does not apply to processors (cf. also Art. 24 cmt. 3).

13 Regarding the term **accountability** of para. 2, the Art. 29 Working Party states that it "comes from the Anglo-Saxon world where it is in common use and where there is a broadly shared understanding of its meaning – even though defining what exactly 'accountability' means in practice is complex". The Art. 29 Working Party further provides that "[i]n general terms though its emphasis is on showing how responsibility is exercised and making this verifiable" and that "[r]esponsibility and accountability are two sides of the same coin and both essential elements of good governance" because "[o]nly when responsibility is demonstrated as working effectively in practice can sufficient trust be developed" (Art. 29 Working Party, Opinion 3/2010 on the principle of accountability, WP 173 (2010), recital 21).

Accountability pursuant to para. 2 contains two elements: First, the controller "shall be responsible for [...] compliance with, paragraph 1" and secondly "shall [...] be able to demonstrate compliance with [...] paragraph 1".

The first element of accountability in essence means that the controller must implement **compliance measures** which ensure that the principles pursuant to para. 1 are complied with (cf. Art. 29 Working Party, Opinion 3/2010 on the principle of accountability, WP 173 (2010), recital 39). This obligation is outlined in more detail in Art. 24.

The second element of accountability in essence provides a **material obligation to demonstrate compliance** (cf. Art. 29 Working Party, Opinion 3/2010 on the principle of accountability, WP 173 (2010), recital 39) which does not result in a shifting of the burden of proof – which would violate the assumption of innocence pursuant to Art. 48 para. 1 Charter. Since a violation of accountability is not subject to fines (cf. Art. 83 and Art. 24 cmt. 1) and accountability is not a right of the data subject (cf. the catalogue of data subject's rights pursuant to Art. 12 et seqq.; this is in line with the OECD Privacy Guidelines from 2013, see cmt. 14 below), the obligation to demonstrate compliance may only be enforced by the supervisory authorities by enforcement actions (see the investigative powers pursuant to Art. 58 para. 1). As a result, the obligation to demonstrate compliance only exists vis-à-vis the competent supervisory authorities. Vis-à-vis a data subject, the ability to demonstrate compliance is not a legal obligation but may help to fulfill the burden of proof (see Art. 82 cmt. 5).

According to the Art. 29 Working Party, the internal analysis carried out to determine whether or not a data protection officer is to be appointed is part of the documentation under the accountability principle. The Art. 29 Working Party therefore recommends that controllers and processors document the internal analysis. The same applies according to the Art. 29 Working Party if the controller disagrees with the advice provided by a data protection officer in connection with a data protection impact assessment (see Art. 29 Working Party, Guidelines on Data Protection Officers, WP 243 rev. 01 (2017), at 5, available at http://ec.europa.eu/newsroom/just/item-detail.cfm?item_id= 50083) or if the controller does not seek the views of data subjects in connection with a data protection impact assessment because it decides that this is not appropriate or if the controller's final decision differs from the views of the data subjects (see Art. 29 Working Party, Guidelines on Data Protection Impact Assessment (DPIA) and determining whether processing is "likely to result in a high risk" for the purposes of Regulation 2016/679, WP 248 (2016), at 13, available at http://ec.europa.eu/newsroom/just/item-detail.cfm? item_id=50083).

14 **Background of accountability:** The concept of accountability was already contained in the OECD Guidelines on the Protection of Privacy and Transborder Flows of Personal Data from 1980. It was, however, limited to the first element set out in para. 2, responsibility (see Sec. 14 of the OECD Guidelines: "A data controller should be accountable for complying with measures which give effect to the principles stated above").

The International Standards on the Protection of Personal Data and Privacy of the International Conference of Data Protection and Privacy Commissioners dated 5 November 2009 (available at https://icdppc.org/wp-content/uploads/2015/02/The-Madrid-Resolution.pdf), also known as "The Madrid Resolution", already provided for an accountability principle which contained elements of responsibility and an obligation to demonstrate compliance ("The responsible person shall: a) Take all the necessary measures to observe the principles and obligations set out in this Document and in the applicable national legislation, and b) have the necessary internal mechanisms in place for demonstrating such observance both to data subjects and to the supervisory authorities in the exercise of their powers, as established in section 23.")

In 2010, the Art. 29 Working Party proposed the introduction of the principle of accountability in its Opinion 3/2010 (Art. 29 Working Party, Opinion 3/2010 on the principle of accountability, WP 173 (2010)).

The international standard ISO/IEC 29100 ("Information technology – Security techniques – Privacy framework") from 2011 also provides for a principle of accountability.

Finally, the OECD Privacy Guidelines from 2013 (available at www.oecd.org/sti/ieconomy/oecd_privacy_framework.pdf) provide that the principle of accountability must be implemented, *inter alia*, by a privacy management programme and an obligation to demonstrate compliance (cf. Sec. 15 lit. b of the OECD Privacy Guidelines: "Be prepared to demonstrate its privacy management programme as appropriate, in particular at the request of a competent privacy enforcement authority or another entity responsible for promoting adherence to a code of conduct or similar arrangement giving binding effect to these Guidelines").

Article 6

Lawfulness of processing

1. Processing shall be lawful only if and to the extent that at least one of the following applies:[1]

    (a) the data subject has given consent[2] to the processing of his or her personal data for one or more specific purposes;

    (b) processing is necessary for the performance of a contract to which the data subject is party or in order to take steps at the request of the data subject prior to entering into a contract;

    (c) processing is necessary for compliance with a legal obligation[3] to which the controller is subject;[4]

    (d) processing is necessary in order to protect the vital interests of the data subject or of another[5] natural person;

    (e) processing is necessary for the performance of a task carried out in the public interest or in the exercise of official authority vested in the controller;[6]

    (f) processing is necessary for the purposes of the legitimate interests[7] pursued by the controller or by a third party, except where such interests are overridden by the interests or fundamental rights and freedoms of the data subject which require protection of personal data,[8] in particular where the data subject is a child.[9]

Point (f) of the first subparagraph shall not apply to processing carried out by public authorities in the performance of their tasks.[10]

2. Member States may maintain or introduce more specific provisions to adapt the application of the rules of this Regulation with regard to processing for compliance with points (c) and (e) of paragraph 1 by determining more precisely specific requirements for the processing and other measures to ensure lawful and fair processing including for other specific processing situations as provided for in Chapter IX.

3. The basis for the processing referred to in point (c) and (e) of paragraph 1 shall be laid down by:[11]

    (a) Union law; or

    (b) Member State law to which the controller is subject.

The purpose of the processing shall be determined in that legal basis or, as regards the processing referred to in point (e) of paragraph 1, shall be necessary for the performance of a task carried out in the public interest or in the exercise of official authority vested in the controller. That legal basis may contain specific provisions to adapt the application of rules of this Regulation, inter alia: the general conditions governing the lawfulness of processing by the controller; the types of data which are subject to the processing; the data subjects concerned; the entities to, and the purposes for which, the personal data may be disclosed; the purpose limitation; storage periods; and processing operations and processing procedures, including measures to ensure lawful and fair processing such as those for other specific processing situations as provided for in Chapter IX. The Union or the Member State law shall meet an objective of public interest and be proportionate to the legitimate aim pursued.

4. Where the processing for a purpose other than that for which the personal data have been collected is not based on the data subject's[12] consent or on a Union or Member State law which constitutes a necessary and proportionate measure in a democratic society to safeguard the objectives referred to in Article 23(1), the controller shall, in order to ascertain whether processing for another purpose is compatible with the purpose for which the personal data are initially collected, take into account, inter alia:[13,14,15]

(a) any link between the purposes for which the personal data have been collected and the purposes of the intended further processing;

(b) the context in which the personal data have been collected, in particular regarding the relationship between data subjects and the controller;[16]

(c) the nature of the personal data, in particular whether special categories of personal data are processed, pursuant to Article 9, or whether personal data related to criminal convictions and offences are processed,[17] pursuant to Article 10;

(d) the possible consequences of the intended further processing for data subjects;

(e) the existence of appropriate safeguards, which may include encryption or pseudonymisation.[18]

Recitals:

Regarding para. 1:

(40) In order for processing to be lawful, personal data should be processed on the basis of the consent of the data subject concerned or some other legitimate basis, laid down by law, either in this Regulation or in other Union or Member State law as referred to in this Regulation, including the necessity for compliance with the legal obligation to which the controller is subject or the necessity for the performance of a contract to which the data subject is party or in order to take steps at the request of the data subject prior to entering into a contract.

Regarding para. 1 lit. c and lit. e as well as para. 3:

(41) Where this Regulation refers to a legal basis or a legislative measure, this does not necessarily require a legislative act adopted by a parliament, without prejudice to requirements pursuant to the constitutional order of the Member State concerned. However, such a legal basis or legislative measure should be clear and precise and its application should be foreseeable to persons subject to it, in accordance with the case-law of the Court of Justice of the European Union (the 'Court of Justice') and the European Court of Human Rights.

Regarding para. 1 lit. a:

(42) *Where processing is based on the data subject's consent, the controller should be able to demonstrate that the data subject has given consent to the processing operation. In particular in the context of a written declaration on another matter, safeguards should ensure that the data subject is aware of the fact that and the extent to which consent is given. In accordance with Council Directive 93/13/EEC a declaration of consent pre-formulated by the controller should be provided in an intelligible and easily accessible form, using clear and plain language and it should not contain unfair terms. For consent to be informed, the data subject should be aware at least of the identity of the controller and the purposes of the processing for which the personal data are intended. Consent should not be regarded as freely given if the data subject has no genuine or free choice or is unable to refuse or withdraw consent without detriment.*

(43) *In order to ensure that consent is freely given, consent should not provide a valid legal ground for the processing of personal data in a specific case where there is a clear imbalance between the data subject and the controller, in particular where the controller is a public authority and it is therefore unlikely that consent was freely given in all the circumstances of that specific situation. Consent is presumed not to be freely given if it does not allow separate consent to be given to different personal data processing operations despite it being appropriate in the individual case, or if the performance of a contract, including the provision of a service, is dependent on the consent despite such consent not being necessary for such performance.*

Regarding para. 1 lit. b:

(44) *Processing should be lawful where it is necessary in the context of a contract or the intention to enter into a contract.*

Regarding para. 1 lit. c and lit. e as well as para. 3:

(45) *Where processing is carried out in accordance with a legal obligation to which the controller is subject or where processing is necessary for the performance of a task carried out in the public interest or in the exercise of official authority, the processing should have a basis in Union or Member State law. This Regulation does not require a specific law for each individual processing. A law as a basis for several processing operations based on a legal obligation to which the controller is subject or where processing is necessary for the performance of a task carried out in the public interest or in the exercise of an official authority may be sufficient. It should also be for Union or Member State law to determine the purpose of processing. Furthermore, that law could specify the general conditions of this Regulation governing the lawfulness of personal data processing, establish specifications for determining the controller, the type of personal data which are subject to the processing, the data subjects concerned, the entities to which the personal data may be disclosed, the purpose limitations, the storage period and other measures to ensure lawful and fair processing. It should also be for Union or Member State law to determine whether the controller performing a task carried out in the public interest or in the exercise of official authority should be a public authority or another natural or legal person governed by public law, or, where it is in the public interest to do so, including for health purposes such as public health*

and social protection and the management of health care services, by private law, such as a professional association.

Regarding para. 1 lit. d:

(46) The processing of personal data should also be regarded to be lawful where it is necessary to protect an interest which is essential for the life of the data subject or that of another natural person. Processing of personal data based on the vital interest of another natural person should in principle take place only where the processing cannot be manifestly based on another legal basis. Some types of processing may serve both important grounds of public interest and the vital interests of the data subject as for instance when processing is necessary for humanitarian purposes, including for monitoring epidemics and their spread or in situations of humanitarian emergencies, in particular in situations of natural and man-made disasters.

Regarding para. 1 lit. f:

(47) The legitimate interests of a controller, including those of a controller to which the personal data may be disclosed, or of a third party, may provide a legal basis for processing, provided that the interests or the fundamental rights and freedoms of the data subject are not overriding, taking into consideration the reasonable expectations of data subjects based on their relationship with the controller. Such legitimate interest could exist for example where there is a relevant and appropriate relationship between the data subject and the controller in situations such as where the data subject is a client or in the service of the controller. At any rate the existence of a legitimate interest would need careful assessment including whether a data subject can reasonably expect at the time and in the context of the collection of the personal data that processing for that purpose may take place. The interests and fundamental rights of the data subject could in particular override the interest of the data controller where personal data are processed in circumstances where data subjects do not reasonably expect further processing. Given that it is for the legislator to provide by law for the legal basis for public authorities to process personal data, that legal basis should not apply to the processing by public authorities in the performance of their tasks. The processing of personal data strictly necessary for the purposes of preventing fraud also constitutes a legitimate interest of the data controller concerned. The processing of personal data for direct marketing purposes may be regarded as carried out for a legitimate interest.

(48) Controllers that are part of a group of undertakings or institutions affiliated to a central body may have a legitimate interest in transmitting personal data within the group of undertakings for internal administrative purposes, including the processing of clients' or employees' personal data. The general principles for the transfer of personal data, within a group of undertakings, to an undertaking located in a third country remain unaffected.

(49) The processing of personal data to the extent strictly necessary and proportionate for the purposes of ensuring network and information security, i.e. the ability of a network or an information system to resist, at a given level of confidence, accidental events or unlawful or malicious actions that compromise the availability, authenticity, integrity and confidentiality of stored or transmitted personal data, and the security of the

related services offered by, or accessible via, those networks and systems, by public authorities, by computer emergency response teams (CERTs), computer security incident response teams (CSIRTs), by providers of electronic communications networks and services and by providers of security technologies and services, constitutes a legitimate interest of the data controller concerned. This could, for example, include preventing unauthorised access to electronic communications networks and malicious code distribution and stopping 'denial of service' attacks and damage to computer and electronic communication systems.

Regarding para. 4:

(50) The processing of personal data for purposes other than those for which the personal data were initially collected should be allowed only where the processing is compatible with the purposes for which the personal data were initially collected. In such a case, no legal basis separate from that which allowed the collection of the personal data is required. If the processing is necessary for the performance of a task carried out in the public interest or in the exercise of official authority vested in the controller, Union or Member State law may determine and specify the tasks and purposes for which the further processing should be regarded as compatible and lawful. Further processing for archiving purposes in the public interest, scientific or historical research purposes or statistical purposes should be considered to be compatible lawful processing operations. The legal basis provided by Union or Member State law for the processing of personal data may also provide a legal basis for further processing. In order to ascertain whether a purpose of further processing is compatible with the purpose for which the personal data are initially collected, the controller, after having met all the requirements for the lawfulness of the original processing, should take into account, inter alia: any link between those purposes and the purposes of the intended further processing; the context in which the personal data have been collected, in particular the reasonable expectations of data subjects based on their relationship with the controller as to their further use; the nature of the personal data; the consequences of the intended further processing for data subjects; and the existence of appropriate safeguards in both the original and intended further processing operations.

Where the data subject has given consent or the processing is based on Union or Member State law which constitutes a necessary and proportionate measure in a democratic society to safeguard, in particular, important objectives of general public interest, the controller should be allowed to further process the personal data irrespective of the compatibility of the purposes. In any case, the application of the principles set out in this Regulation and in particular the information of the data subject on those other purposes and on his or her rights including the right to object, should be ensured. Indicating possible criminal acts or threats to public security by the controller and transmitting the relevant personal data in individual cases or in several cases relating to the same criminal act or threats to public security to a competent authority should be regarded as being in the legitimate interest pursued by the controller. However, such transmission in the legitimate interest of the controller or further processing of personal data should be prohibited if the processing is not compatible with a legal, professional or other binding obligation of secrecy.

Commentary:

1   Art. 6 maintains the **regulatory framework** of Art. 7 Data Protection Directive: Any processing of personal data is prohibited, unless it can be based on a statutory permission (cf. also Recital 40).

2   See Art. 4 No. 11 regarding the definition of the term **"consent"** as well as Arts. 7 and 8 regarding the conditions for consent. Cf. also Recital 42 and 43.

3   The **obligation** within the meaning of para. 1 subpara. 1 lit. c must stem from Union law or from statutory law of one or more Member States (cf. also Recital 41) to which the controller is subject. An obligation stemming from a contract or an obligation stemming from a state that is not a Member State is not taken into account in para. 1 subpara. 1 lit. c.

4   Processing based on para. 1 lit. c is subject to the competence of the supervisory authority of Art. 55 para. 2.

5   To the extent processing is necessary in order to protect the **vital interests** of another natural person, the legal basis of para. 1 subpara. 1 lit. d is subsidiary to the other legal bases in para. 1 (cf. Recital 46 sentence 2 according to which lit. d applies "only where the processing cannot be manifestly based on another legal basis").

6   Processing based on para. 1 lit. e is subject to the competence of supervisory authorities of Art. 55 para. 2.

7   A **legitimate interest** within the meaning of para. 1 subpara. 1 lit. f can be seen in direct marketing and the prevention of fraud (Recital 47 sentences 6 and 7) and in ensuring network and information security (Recital 49). Furthermore, controllers that are part of a group of undertakings may have a legitimate interest to transfer personal data within the group of undertakings for internal administrative purposes, including the processing of clients' or employees' personal data (Recital 48). Further examples are: (i) exercise of the right to freedom of expression or information, including in the media and the arts; (ii) conventional direct marketing and other forms of marketing or advertisement; (iii) enforcement of legal claims including debt collection via out-of-court procedures; (iv) prevention of fraud, misuse of services, or money laundering; (v) employee monitoring for safety or management purposes; (vi) whistle-blowing schemes; (vii) physical security, IT and network security; (viii) processing for historical, scientific or statistical purposes; (ix) processing for research purposes (including marketing research) (cf. Art. 29 Working Party, Opinion 06/2014 on the notion of legitimate interests of the controller under Article 7 of Directive 95/46/EC, WP 217 (2014) 25).

However, an authority that considers the processing necessary to fulfill its statutory tasks, does not have a legitimate interest – this must be based on the legal basis of para. 1 subpara. 1 lit. e (para. 1 subpara. 2). Regarding the obligation to inform about the prevailing legitimate interests, cf. Art. 13 para. 1 lit. d.

8   To determine whether the interests or fundamental rights and freedoms of the data subjects prevail, one should in particular consider **"reasonable expectations** of data subjects based on their relationship with the controller",

that is, "whether a data subject can reasonably expect at the time and in the context of the collection of the personal data that processing for that purpose may take place" (Recital 47). This reflects the well-known concept of a "**reasonable expectation of privacy**" as developed by the US Supreme Court concerning the Fourth Amendment to the US Constitution. Under the case law of the US Supreme Court, "there is a twofold requirement, first that a person have exhibited an actual (subjective) expectation of privacy and, second, that the expectation be one that society is prepared to recognize as 'reasonable'" (*Katz v United States*, 389 U.S. 347, 361 (1967). The reasonable subjective expectation of privacy of the data subject could be problematic in our view if such expectations are understood as empirical (rather than normative) because revelations like those of Edward Snowden might result in generally lowered expectations of the data subjects which should, however, not result in lower protection under the law. The concept of "reasonable expectation of privacy" comes dangerously close to a naturalistic fallacy where the reality could determine the legal interpretation. To prevent that, balancing tests to determine whether the interests or fundamental rights of the data subjects prevail should be performed without regard for whether the controller has informed the data subject prior to the data collection about the scope and purposes of the data collection because this is, anyhow, a legal obligation of the controller pursuant to Art. 13 et seq. Rather, it is decisive whether the data subject had the subjective expectation that he or she *should* be protected. In a second step, it must be assessed objectively whether such an expectation was legitimate.

9   Art. 8 para. 1 states that "the processing of the personal data of a child shall be lawful where the child is at least 16 years old". From this it follows that the term "child" also includes individuals who have already reached the age of 16. Thus, there are good arguments to interpret the term "**child**" as defined in Art. 1 of the UN Convention on the Rights of the Child as a "person below the age of 18, unless the laws of a particular country set the legal age for adulthood younger".

10   Cf. Recital 47 sentence 5.

11   The **material requirements for a provision in Union or Member State law mentioned in para. 3** are further detailed in Recital 45: First, the law must "determine the purpose of processing" (Recital 45 sentence 4). Secondly, the law must in the case of para. 1 subpara. 1 lit. e stipulate "whether the controller [...] should be a public authority or another natural or legal person governed by public law, or, where it is in the public interest to do so, including for health purposes such as public health and social protection and the management of health care services, by private law, such as a professional association" (Recital 45 last sentence). Pursuant to Recital 45 sentence 5 such law could further: (1) specify the general conditions of the GDPR governing the lawfulness of personal data processing; (2) establish specifications for determining the controller; (3) define the type of personal data which are subject to the processing; (4) define the data subjects concerned; (5) define the

entities to which the personal data may be disclosed; (6) provide the purpose limitations or the storage period; and (7) define other measures to ensure lawful and fair processing.

12 Para. 4 contains a clarification that a **change of the purpose with the data subject's consent** does not interfere with the principle of purpose limitation.

13 According to the prevailing opinion under the Data Protection Directive, various factors also had to be considered to determine the **compatibility of the new purpose** with the purpose determined at the time of the data collection (cf. Art. 29 Working Party, Opinion 03/2012 on purpose limitation, WP 203 (2013), at 23 et seq., available at http://ec.europa.eu/justice/data-protection/article-29/documentation/opinion-recommendation/files/2013/wp203_en.pdf).

14 Pursuant to Recital 50 sentence 2, "no legal basis separate from that which allowed the collection of the personal data is required" for the compatibility of the purposes. If interpreted literally, that means that the **compatibility of purposes** would undermine the principle of lawfulness. Therefore, the fact whether the new purpose is covered by the current legal basis of the processing must be considered as a further aspect when assessing the compatibility of the purposes pursuant to para. 4.

15 If the purposes are compatible, a processing for the new purpose is only in compliance with the GDPR if the data subject has been **informed** "on those other purposes and on his or her rights, including the right to object" (Recital 50 sentence 8). Such information must be provided prior to commencing the further processing (Art. 13 para. 3).

16 In connection with para. 4 lit. b, "in particular the **reasonable expectations** of data subjects based on their relationship with the controller as to their further use" must be considered. Regarding the problems in connection with "reasonable expectations of the data subject" which must be understood as a normative rather than empirical expectations, cf. cmt. 8.

17 In connection with para. 4 lit. c, Recital 50 sentence 9 and 10 must be considered which state that the controller – notwithstanding any binding, in particular professional obligations of secrecy – has a legitimate interest in indicating possible criminal acts or threats to public security and **transmitting the relevant personal data to a competent authority**.

18 See Art. 4 No. 5 regarding the definition of the term "**pseudonymisation**". See also Recital 28 which states that "pseudonymisation [...] can reduce the risks to the data subjects concerned and help controllers and processors to meet their data-protection obligations". Recital 29 additionally outlines that "in order to create incentives to apply pseudonymisation when processing personal data, measures of pseudonymisation should, whilst allowing general analysis, be possible within the same controller".

Article 7

Conditions for consent

1. Where processing is based on consent,[1] the controller shall be able to demonstrate that the data subject has consented to processing of his or her personal data.[2]

2. If the data subject's consent is given in the context of a written declaration which also concerns other matters, the request for consent shall be presented in a manner which is clearly distinguishable from the other matters, in an intelligible and easily accessible form, using clear and plain language.[3] Any part of such a declaration which constitutes an infringement of this Regulation shall not be binding.[4]

3. The data subject shall have the right to withdraw his or her consent at any time. The withdrawal of consent shall not affect the lawfulness of processing based on consent before its withdrawal. Prior to giving consent, the data subject shall be informed thereof.[5] It shall be as easy to withdraw as to give consent.[6]

4. When assessing whether consent is freely given, utmost account shall be taken[7] of whether, inter alia, the performance[8] of a contract, including the provision of a service, is conditional on consent to the processing of personal data[9] that is not necessary for the performance of that contract.[10,11]

Commentary:

1   See Art. 4 No. 11 regarding the definition of the term "consent" which contains further requirements for consent. See in particular Art. 4 cmt. 29 regarding the question whether consent pursuant to the Data Protection Directive continues to be valid.

2   Since pursuant to para. 1 the controller bears the **burden of proof** for the issuance of consent and its scope (cf. also Recital 42 sentence 1), it is advisable (but not required) to obtain consent in writing.

3   Compliance with the requirement that consent must be **clearly distinguishable** from other matters as set out in para. 2 sentence 1 can in a long contract be achieved by placing the consent wording under the heading "consent to the processing of personal data" and thereby highlighting it appropriately.

4   A severability clause is therefore basically not required in privacy statements.

5   To inform the data subject about his or her right to **withdraw consent** at any time it is necessary for the consent to be "informed" (see Art. 4 cmt. 25). This has been the case under Austrian law before the GDPR (Austrian Supreme Court, 19 November 2002, case no. 4 Ob 179/02f), however, not necessarily under German law. The information does not only have to contain the information that consent may be withdrawn at any time but also has to include the information that "the lawfulness of the processing based on consent until the withdrawal remains unaffected", that is, that a subsequent change of the data processing activities cannot be expected (eg, in the context of research projects). This follows from Art. 13 para. 2 lit. c which requires informing data

subjects about "the existence of the right to withdraw consent at any time, without affecting the lawfulness of processing based on consent before its withdrawal".

6   Para. 3 sentence 3 makes it necessary to enable the withdrawal of consent via a website if the consent was obtained during the registration on a website.

7   Pursuant to Art. 7 para. 4, when assessing whether consent is freely given **"utmost account** shall be taken of whether, inter alia, the performance of a contract [...] is conditional on consent to the processing of personal data that is not necessary for the performance of that contract". Pursuant to Recital 43, not only "utmost account shall be taken" but consent "is presumed not to be freely given" if the performance of a contract is dependent on the consent despite such consent not being necessary for such performance. Therefore, it is likely that the existence of such a fact results in a statutory presumption that consent is not freely given and is therefore invalid.

8   The same applies if not the performance but the **conclusion of a contract is conditional on consent** ("inter alia, the performance").

9   Performance (respectively conclusion) of a contract would in our opinion not be "conditional" on consent within the meaning of para. 4 if the provider offers the same goods or services in **two versions:** Once without consent **for the regular price** and once **with the requirement to consent and a reduced price.** In such a case, the data subject can choose freely – at least from a commercial perspective – whether he/she wants to pay for the receipt of the goods, respectively services, with his/her personal data.

10   This half sentence does not refer to the "personal data" mentioned in the previous half sentence but to consent. It is not decisive whether the personal data are necessary for the performance of the contract but **whether consent is necessary for the performance of the contract.** This can also be concluded from Recital 43 last sentence which states that consent is presumed not to be freely given "if the performance of a contract, including the provision of a service, is conditional on consent to the processing of personal data that is not necessary for the performance of that contract". Whereas this is stated quite clearly in the English language version, this is not quite clear in the German version due to a translation error.

11   The provision of para. 4 jeopardises the business models of providers that are based on the provisioning of goods or services free of charge to users that consent to the collection and processing of their personal data for marketing purposes (eg, a free online service that is financed by advertisements). However, it must be considered that consent to the processing of personal data and the provision of services are not necessarily in a legal but in a commercial relationship: The issuance of **consent provides the commercial conditions for the provisioning of the goods and services free of charge.** Therefore, in these cases it can be argued that consent is (commercially) required for the fulfillment of the contract and therefore consent is valid. This might not apply where the data subject indeed paid a reasonable price and consent is therefore not a commercial condition for the provision of the service. If in such a case the

performance of the contract is conditioned on consent (see also cmt. 9 above) which is not necessary for any other reasons, consent would likely be deemed not freely given. However, in a well-functioning market, an appropriate "price" – consisting of the sum of the monetary consideration and the economic value of any consent to the data processing – can be expected to develop, making "unnecessary consents" disappear from the market.

Article 8

Conditions applicable to child's consent in relation to information society services[1]

1. Where point (a) of Article 6(1) applies, in relation to the offer of information society services,[2] directly[3] to a child[4] the processing of the personal data of a child shall be lawful where the child is at least 16 years old. Where the child is below the age of 16 years, such processing shall be lawful only if and to the extent that consent[5] is given or authorised by the holder of parental responsibility[6] over the child.[7]

Member States may provide by law for a lower age for those purposes provided that such lower age is not below 13 years.[8]

2. The controller shall make reasonable efforts[9] to verify in such cases[10] that consent is given or authorised by the holder of parental responsibility over the child, taking into consideration available technology.

3. Paragraph 1 shall not affect the general contract law of Member States such as the rules on the validity, formation or effect of a contract in relation to a child.[11]

Recital:

(38) Children merit specific protection with regard to their personal data, as they may be less aware of the risks, consequences and safeguards concerned and their rights in relation to the processing of personal data. Such specific protection should, in particular, apply to the use of personal data of children for the purposes of marketing or creating personality or user profiles and the collection of personal data with regard to children when using services offered directly to a child. The consent of the holder of parental responsibility should not be necessary in the context of preventive or counselling services offered directly to a child.

Commentary:

1   Since Art. 8 applies to information society services only, there is a gap regarding the capability to consent in the **"offline world"**. Since it cannot be assumed that such a gap arose unintentionally, Art. 8 does not apply analogously. Notwithstanding the aforementioned, in our opinion: (1) the cognitive faculty of the data subject will be relevant to determine whether consent was provided in an "informed" manner within the meaning of Art. 4 No. 11; and (2) the ability to judge will be relevant for the question whether consent was provided "freely". Taking into consideration the assessments of the Union legislature in Art. 8, it can be assumed that on reaching the age of 16, an individual has sufficient cognitive faculty and ability to judge.

2   See Art. 4 No. 25 regarding the definition of the term "information society service".

3   In our opinion an offer will be made "directly to a child" only if the service is addressed to children or the controller is aware that the user to whom the services are offered is a child. See cmt. 10 below.

4   See Art. 6 cmt. 9 regarding the definition of the term "child".

5   See Art. 4 No. 11 regarding the definition of the term "consent" and Art. 7 regarding the requirements for consent.

6   This means a **legal representative**, for example, in Austria pursuant to Sec. 167 Austrian Civil Code or in Germany pursuant to Sec. 107, 1629 German Civil Code.

7   Therefore, consent can be provided (1) **by the holder of parental responsibility** for the child and (2) **by the child itself with the authorisation of the holder of parental responsibility over the child**. Consent of the holder of parental responsibility is not necessary in the context of **preventive or counselling services** offered directly to a child (Recital 38 last sentence).

8   The GDPR does not state which Member State law applies. Regarding the conflict of laws in general, see in detail Art. 92 cmt. 5.

9   Since there is no public register that indicates which person is the holder of parental responsibility of a particular child, the requirements regarding "reasonable efforts" should not be interpreted in an overly strict manner. In particular, it cannot be concluded from Art. 7 para. 1 that the controller must prove the parental responsibility in case of a dispute.

10   According to para. 2, the obligation to make "reasonable efforts" applies only "to such cases", that is, if the information society service is offered directly to a child. It remains to be seen which "reasonable efforts" the controller must make to verify whether the user of the service is a child at all. As a result, it will be relevant whether: (1) the information society service is addressed to persons that do not yet have the capacity to consent; or (2) the controller is aware that the user is a person that does not yet have the capacity to consent. Similarly, the US Children's Online Privacy Protection Act, Pub.L. 105–277, 112 Stat. 2681-728 ("COPPA") and the COPPA Rule, 16 C.F.R. Part 312, apply only if the online service is "directed to children" or the provider "has actual knowledge that it is collecting or maintaining personal information from a child"; see 16 C.F.R. § 312.3). This applies in particular if in the course of the data collection the birth date is collected. There is no particular obligation to verify the correctness of the information provided.

11   Cf., for example, in Austria Sec. 167 et seqq., 865 of the Austrian Civil Code and in Germany Sec. 104 et seqq. of the German Civil Code.

Article 9

Processing of special categories of personal data

1. Processing of personal data revealing racial or ethnic origin, political opinions, religious or philosophical beliefs,[1] or trade union membership, and the processing of genetic data,[2] biometric data[3] for the purpose of uniquely identifying a natural person, data concerning health[4] or data concerning a natural person's sex life or sexual orientation[5] shall be prohibited.[6]

2. Paragraph 1 shall not apply if one of the following applies:

   (a) the data subject has given explicit consent to the processing of those personal data for one or more specified purposes,[7] except where Union or Member State law provide that the prohibition referred to in paragraph 1 may not be lifted by the data subject;[8]

   (b) processing is necessary for the purposes of carrying out the obligations and exercising specific rights of the controller or of the data subject in the field of employment[9] and social security and social protection law in so far as it is authorised by Union or Member State law[10] or a collective agreement[11] pursuant to Member State law providing for appropriate safeguards for the fundamental rights and the interests of the data subject;

   (c) processing is necessary to protect the vital interests of the data subject or of another natural person where the data subject is physically or legally incapable of giving consent;

   (d) processing is carried out in the course of its legitimate activities with appropriate safeguards by a foundation, association or any other not-for-profit body with a political, philosophical, religious or trade union aim and on condition that the processing relates solely to the members or to former members of the body or to persons who have regular contact with it in connection with its purposes and that the personal data are not disclosed outside that body without the consent of the data subjects;[12]

   (e) processing relates to personal data which are manifestly made public by the data subject;[13]

   (f) processing is necessary for the establishment, exercise or defence of legal claims[14] or whenever courts are acting in their judicial capacity;[15]

   (g) processing is necessary for reasons of substantial public interest, on the basis of Union or Member State law which shall be proportionate to the aim pursued, respect the essence of the right to data protection and provide for suitable and specific measures to safeguard the fundamental rights and the interests of the data subject;

   (h) processing is necessary for the purposes of preventive or occupational medicine, for the assessment of the working capacity of the employee, medical diagnosis, the provision of health or social care or treatment or the management of health or social care systems and services[16] on the basis of Union or Member State law or pursuant to contract with a health professional and subject to the conditions and safeguards referred to in paragraph 3;

(i) processing is necessary for reasons of public interest in the area of public health,[17] such as protecting against serious cross-border threats to health or ensuring high standards of quality and safety of health care and of medicinal products or medical devices, on the basis of Union or Member State law which provides for suitable and specific measures to safeguard the rights and freedoms of the data subject, in particular professional secrecy;

(j) processing is necessary for archiving purposes in the public interest, scientific or historical research purposes or statistical purposes in accordance with Article 89(1) based on Union or Member State law which shall be proportionate to the aim pursued, respect the essence of the right to data protection and provide for suitable and specific measures to safeguard the fundamental rights and the interests of the data subject.

3. Personal data referred to in paragraph 1 may be processed for the purposes referred to in point (h) of paragraph 2 when those data are processed by or under the responsibility of a professional subject to the obligation of professional secrecy under Union or Member State law or rules established by national competent bodies or by another person also subject to an obligation of secrecy under Union or Member State law or rules established by national competent bodies.

4. Member States may maintain or introduce further conditions, including limitations, with regard to the processing of genetic data, biometric data[18] or data concerning health.

Recitals:

Regarding para. 1:

(51) Personal data which are, by their nature, particularly sensitive in relation to fundamental rights and freedoms merit specific protection as the context of their processing could create significant risks to the fundamental rights and freedoms. Those personal data should include personal data revealing racial or ethnic origin, whereby the use of the term 'racial origin' in this Regulation does not imply an acceptance by the Union of theories which attempt to determine the existence of separate human races. The processing of photographs should not systematically be considered to be processing of special categories of personal data as they are covered by the definition of biometric data only when processed through a specific technical means allowing the unique identification or authentication of a natural person. Such personal data should not be processed, unless processing is allowed in specific cases set out in this Regulation, taking into account that Member States law may lay down specific provisions on data protection in order to adapt the application of the rules of this Regulation for compliance with a legal obligation or for the performance of a task carried out in the public interest or in the exercise of official authority vested in the controller. In addition to the specific requirements for such processing, the general principles and other rules of this Regulation should apply, in particular as regards the conditions for lawful processing. Derogations from the general prohibition for processing such special categories of personal data should be explicitly provided, inter

alia, where the data subject gives his or her explicit consent or in respect of specific needs in particular where the processing is carried out in the course of legitimate activities by certain associations or foundations the purpose of which is to permit the exercise of fundamental freedoms.

Regarding para. 2:

(52) Derogating from the prohibition on processing special categories of personal data should also be allowed when provided for in Union or Member State law and subject to suitable safeguards, so as to protect personal data and other fundamental rights, where it is in the public interest to do so, in particular processing personal data in the field of employment law, social protection law including pensions and for health security, monitoring and alert purposes, the prevention or control of communicable diseases and other serious threats to health. Such a derogation may be made for health purposes, including public health and the management of health-care services, especially in order to ensure the quality and cost-effectiveness of the procedures used for settling claims for benefits and services in the health insurance system, or for archiving purposes in the public interest, scientific or historical research purposes or statistical purposes. A derogation should also allow the processing of such personal data where necessary for the establishment, exercise or defence of legal claims, whether in court proceedings or in an administrative or out-of-court procedure.

Regarding para. 2 lit. h:

(53) Special categories of personal data which merit higher protection should be processed for health-related purposes only where necessary to achieve those purposes for the benefit of natural persons and society as a whole, in particular in the context of the management of health or social care services and systems, including processing by the management and central national health authorities of such data for the purpose of quality control, management information and the general national and local supervision of the health or social care system, and ensuring continuity of health or social care and cross-border healthcare or health security, monitoring and alert purposes, or for archiving purposes in the public interest, scientific or historical research purposes or statistical purposes, based on Union or Member State law which has to meet an objective of public interest, as well as for studies conducted in the public interest in the area of public health. Therefore, this Regulation should provide for harmonised conditions for the processing of special categories of personal data concerning health, in respect of specific needs, in particular where the processing of such data is carried out for certain health-related purposes by persons subject to a legal obligation of professional secrecy. Union or Member State law should provide for specific and suitable measures so as to protect the fundamental rights and the personal data of natural persons. Member States should be allowed to maintain or introduce further conditions, including limitations, with regard to the processing of genetic data, biometric data or data concerning health. However, this should not hamper the free flow of personal data within the Union when those conditions apply to cross-border processing of such data.

Regarding para. 2 lit. i:

(54) The processing of special categories of personal data may be necessary for reasons of public interest in the areas of public health without consent of the data subject. Such processing should be subject to suitable and specific measures so as to protect the rights and freedoms of natural persons. In that context, 'public health' should be interpreted as defined in Regulation (EC) No 1338/2008 of the European Parliament and of the Council, namely all elements related to health, namely health status, including morbidity and disability, the determinants having an effect on that health status, health care needs, resources allocated to health care, the provision of, and universal access to, health care as well as health care expenditure and financing, and the causes of mortality. Such processing of data concerning health for reasons of public interest should not result in personal data being processed for other purposes by third parties such as employers or insurance and banking companies.

Regarding para. 2 lit. g:

(55) Moreover, the processing of personal data by official authorities for the purpose of achieving the aims, laid down by constitutional law or by international public law, of officially recognised religious associations, is carried out on grounds of public interest.

(56) Where in the course of electoral activities, the operation of the democratic system in a Member State requires that political parties compile personal data on people's political opinions, the processing of such data may be permitted for reasons of public interest, provided that appropriate safeguards are established.

Commentary:

1   Although the German version of the term "philosophical beliefs" ("weltanschauliche Überzeugung") is different than it was in Art. 8 para. 1 Data Protection Directive ("philosophische Überzeugung") there is no change of the term from a substantive perspective (the English versions of the Data Protection Directive and the GDPR are identical – "philosophical beliefs").

2   See Art. 4 No. 13 regarding the definition of the term "genetic data".

3   See Art. 4 No. 14 regarding the definition of the term "biometric data". Pursuant to Art. 4 No. 14, biometric data means personal data "which allow or confirm the unique identification of that natural person". Pursuant to Art. 9 para. 1, biometric data are only regarded as sensitive data if they are actually processed "for the purpose of uniquely identifying a natural person". **Whether biometric data constitute sensitive data must therefore be assessed on the basis of the particular processing purpose.**

4   See Art. 4 No. 15 regarding the definition of the term "health data" which may also cover social security numbers (cf. Art. 4 cmt. 35).

5   This is a clarification that data regarding the "sexual orientation" of a person also constitute sensitive data.

6   To describe these data categories, the GDPR uses the term **"sensitive data"** as well as the term **"special categories of personal data"** (see Recital 10). In contrast to Art. 8 Data Protection Directive, the definition of special categories of personal data in particular also covers: (1) genetic data (cf. cmt. 2 above); and

(2) biometric data (cf. cmt. 3 above), processed for the purpose of uniquely identifying a natural person.

7   See Art. 4 No. 11 regarding the definition of the term "consent" as well as Art. 7 regarding further requirements for consent. In addition to the requirements mentioned there, consent regarding the processing of sensitive data must be explicit. For example, ticking a respective **checkbox** in the course of an online registration process is considered explicit consent.

8   For example, according to the Austrian data protection authority, the purpose of the social security number is stipulated in Sec. 31 para. 4 no. 1 General Social Insurance Code – that is, the administration of personal data for social insurance purposes – and requires an additional statutory permission for every use of the social security number for other purposes (Austrian Data Protection Commission, 2 November 2004, case no. K120.941/0012-DSK/2004; 7 September 2006, case no. K211.623/0005-DSK/2006).

9   See also Art. 88.

10   See Recital 10 last sentence which states that the GDPR "provides a margin of manoeuvre for Member States to specify its rules, including for the processing of special categories of personal data" and that the GDPR "does not exclude Member State law that sets out the circumstances for specific processing situations, including determining more precisely the conditions under which the processing of personal data is lawful".

11   The term "**collective agreement**" includes works council agreements in addition to collective bargaining agreements (see Recital 155 sentence 1).

12   Para. 2 lit. d provides the necessary legal basis for the administration of member lists, for example, for religious or political associations, trade unions or civil rights organisations (cf. Recital 51 last sentence which refers in particular to "associations or foundations the purpose of which is to permit the exercise of fundamental freedoms").

13   In particular the processing of data of public social media services, such as Twitter, can be based on the legal basis of para. 2 lit. e.

14   Recital 52 last sentence clarifies that the derogation necessary for the **establishment, exercise or defense of legal claims** is not limited to court proceedings, but also includes an "administrative or out-of-court procedure".

15   "Courts acting in their **judicial capacity**" exclusively refers to processing operations that courts perform as controllers. Regarding the competence of the supervisory authorities in these cases, see Art. 55 para. 3.

16   Pursuant to Recital 53, the processing of sensitive data for health-related purposes should be performed only "where necessary to achieve those purposes for the benefit of natural persons and society as a whole". Examples thereof can be found in Recital 53.

17   Pursuant to Recital 54 the term "public health" must be interpreted as defined in Regulation (EC) No. 1338/2008 and therefore means "all elements related to health, namely health status, including morbidity and disability, the determinants having an effect on that health status, health care needs, resources allocated to health care, the provision of, and universal access to,

health care as well as health care expenditure and financing, and the causes of mortality" (Art. 3 lit. c Regulation (EC) No. 1338/2008).

18   Although para. 4, in contrast to para. 1, does not refer to "biometric data for the purpose of uniquely identifying a natural person" but to "biometric data" in general, the wording "further conditions" indicates that biometric data are covered by para. 4 only if covered by para. 1, that is, if they are actually used for the purpose of uniquely identifying a natural person (see cmt. 3 above). Therefore, national legislatures may in particular not provide general conditions and limitations for the processing of facial images.

Article 10

Processing of personal data relating to criminal convictions and offences

Processing of personal data relating to criminal convictions and offences[1] or related security measures based on Article 6(1) shall be carried out only under the control of official authority or when the processing is authorised by Union or Member State law[2] providing for appropriate safeguards for the rights and freedoms of data subjects.[3] Any comprehensive register of criminal convictions shall be kept only under the control of official authority.

Commentary:

1   It remains unclear whether Art. 10 also covers data regarding the suspicion of an offence (eg, a notification in the context of a whistleblower hotline, in connection with background checks, in connection with sanction lists or data collected in the context of internal compliance investigations). If Art. 10 was interpreted in a manner also covering the suspicion of an offence, the implementation of a whistleblowing hotline or internal investigations into potential criminal offences would only be permissible if authorised by Union or Member State law. Since Art. 10 does not only cover "criminal convictions" but explicitly also "offences", Art. 10 does, in our opinion, likely cover cases where there is a **specific reasonable suspicion** against a particular person and therefore a specific statutory basis will be required, unless the processing is carried out under the control of an official authority.

2   The GDPR does not state which Member State law will be applicable. Regarding the conflict of laws in general see Art. 92 cmt. 5.

3   Due to the requirement of appropriate safeguards, it can be concluded that it is not sufficient that Member State law (or Union law) does not prohibit the processing of data relating to offences. A **statutory authorisation** will be required.

Article 11

Processing which does not require identification

1. If the purposes for which a controller processes personal data do not or do no longer require the identification of a data subject by the controller, the controller shall not be obliged to maintain, acquire or process additional information in order to identify the data subject for the sole purpose of complying with this Regulation.[1]

2. Where, in cases referred to in paragraph 1 of this Article, the controller is able to demonstrate that it is not in a position to identify the data subject, the controller shall inform the data subject accordingly, if possible.[2] In such cases, Articles 15 to 20 shall not apply[3] except where the data subject, for the purpose of exercising his or her rights under those articles, provides additional information enabling his or her identification.[4]

Recital:

(57) If the personal data processed by a controller do not permit the controller to identify a natural person, the data controller should not be obliged to acquire additional information in order to identify the data subject for the sole purpose of complying with any provision of this Regulation. However, the controller should not refuse to take additional information provided by the data subject in order to support the exercise of his or her rights. Identification should include the digital identification of a data subject, for example through authentication mechanism such as the same credentials, used by the data subject to log-in to the on-line service offered by the data controller.

Commentary:

1   Para. 1 clarifies that the principle of **data minimisation** (Art. 5 para. 1 lit. c) is **not put into question by the rights of the data subject or other obligations included in the GDPR** (cf. Recital 64 sentence 2 which states that "a controller should not retain personal data for the sole purpose of being able to react to potential requests").

2   The wording of para. 2 sentence 1 is unfortunate. It should read: Not in a position to identify which data refer to the person that exercises his rights (eg, the right of access pursuant to Art. 15) (cf. Art. 12 para. 2).

3   Cf. Art. 12 para. 2 sentence 2.

4   For example, if the username and password that the data subject used in the past are still available to the controller, the data subject may be identified by using this data (cf. Recital 57 sentence 2).

Chapter III – Rights of the data subject

Section 1 – Transparency and modalities

Article 12

Transparent information, communication and modalities for the exercise of the rights of the data subject
1. The controller shall take appropriate measures to provide any information referred to in Articles 13 and 14 and any communication under Articles 15 to 22 and 34 relating to processing to the data subject in a concise, transparent, intelligible and easily accessible form,[1] using clear and plain language,[2] in particular for any information addressed specifically to a child.[3] The information shall be provided in writing, or by other means, including, where appropriate, by electronic means. When requested by the data subject, the information may be provided orally, provided that the identity of the data subject is proven by other means.
2. The controller shall facilitate the exercise of data subject rights under Articles 15 to 22.[4] In the cases referred to in Article 11(2), the controller shall not refuse to act on the request of the data subject for exercising his or her rights under Articles 15 to 22, unless the controller demonstrates that it is not in a position to identify the data subject.[5]
3. The controller shall provide information on action taken on a request under Articles 15 to 22 to the data subject without undue delay and in any event within one month of receipt of the request. That period may be extended by two further months where necessary, taking into account the complexity and number of the requests. The controller shall inform the data subject of any such extension within one month of receipt of the request, together with the reasons for the delay. Where the data subject makes the request by electronic form means, the information shall be provided by electronic means where possible, unless otherwise requested by the data subject.
4. If the controller does not take action on the request of the data subject, the controller shall inform the data subject without delay and at the latest within one month[6] of receipt of the request of the reasons for not taking action and on the possibility of lodging a complaint[7] with a supervisory authority and seeking a judicial remedy.[8]
5. Information provided under Articles 13 and 14 and any communication and

any actions taken under Articles 15 to 22 and 34 shall be provided free of charge. Where requests from a data subject are manifestly unfounded or excessive, in particular because of their repetitive character, the controller may either:

(a) charge a reasonable fee taking into account the administrative costs of providing the information or communication or taking the action requested; or

(b) refuse to act on the request.[9]

The controller shall bear the burden of demonstrating the manifestly unfounded or excessive character of the request.

6. Without prejudice to Article 11, where the controller has reasonable doubts concerning the identity of the natural person making the request referred to in Articles 15 to 21, the controller may request the provision of additional information necessary to confirm the identity of the data subject.[10]

7. The information to be provided to data subjects pursuant to Articles 13 and 14 may[11] be provided in combination[12] with standardised icons in order to give in an easily visible, intelligible and clearly legible manner a meaningful overview of the intended processing. Where the icons are presented electronically they shall be machine-readable.

8. The Commission shall be empowered to adopt delegated acts in accordance with Article 92 for the purpose of determining the information to be presented by the icons[13] and the procedures for providing standardised icons.

Recitals:

(58) *The principle of transparency requires that any information addressed to the public or to the data subject be concise, easily accessible and easy to understand, and that clear and plain language and, additionally, where appropriate, visualisation be used. Such information could be provided in electronic form, for example, when addressed to the public, through a website. This is of particular relevance in situations where the proliferation of actors and the technological complexity of practice make it difficult for the data subject to know and understand whether, by whom and for what purpose personal data relating to him or her are being collected, such as in the case of online advertising. Given that children merit specific protection, any information and communication, where processing is addressed to a child, should be in such a clear and plain language that the child can easily understand.*

(59) *Modalities should be provided for facilitating the exercise of the data subject's rights under this Regulation, including mechanisms to request and, if applicable, obtain, free of charge, in particular, access to and rectification or erasure of personal data and the exercise of the right to object. The controller should also provide means for requests to be made electronically, especially where personal data are processed by electronic means. The controller should be obliged to respond to requests from the data subject without undue delay and at the latest within one month and to give reasons where the controller does not intend to comply with any such requests.*

Commentary:

1   The information is "easily accessible" on a website if made available via a linked "privacy statement" in the footer of every page.

The requirement to provide information in a concise, transparent, intelligible and easily accessible form can be easily complied with by using a "**layered privacy notice**" which enables the data subject to access a short notice, a condensed notice and the full notice depending on the data subject's need for information (cf. Art. 29 Working Party, Opinion 10/2004 on More Harmonised Information Provisions, WP 100 (2004), available at http://ec.europa.eu/justice/data-protection/article-29/documentation/opinion-recommendation/files/2004/wp100_en.pdf and Annex 1 of the opinion available at http://ec.europa.eu/justice/data-protection/article-29/documentation/opinion-recommendation/files/2004/wp100a_en.pdf).

2   The GDPR does not explicitly set out in **which language** the information must be provided. In our opinion, it is likely that an information society service must make available the information in the same language(s) as the service itself. Privacy statements provided to an employee must likely be provided in the same language(s) as the other agreements (eg, employment agreement).

3   See Art. 6 cmt. 9 regarding the definition of the term "child". Recital 58 last sentence states that "**where processing is addressed to a child**", "any information and communication [...] should be in such a clear and plain language that the child can easily understand", "given that children merit specific protection". In our opinion, this does not apply if the child does not yet have the capacity to consent pursuant to Art. 8 (and therefore usually does not have sufficient cognitive faculty). In such a case, the type of information must be provided in accordance with the cognitive faculty of an adult (the holder of parental responsibility).

4   To facilitate exercising the rights, Recital 59 sentence 2 provides that "the controller should also provide means for **requests to be made electronically**, especially where personal data are processed by electronic means". Therefore, an electronic request (eg, via email) may not per se trigger reasonable doubts concerning the identity of the natural person making the request which would allow the controller to request the provision of additional information necessary to confirm the identity of the data subject (cf. para. 6).

5   The wording of para. 2 sentence 2 is unfortunate. It should read: Not in a position to identify the person to which the data relate. In such cases the controller must inform the data subject accordingly that the controller can no longer attribute any data to the respective person (Art. 11 para. 2 sentence 1).

6   The time period for rejecting a data subject request cannot be extended – in contrast to the time period for complying with a data subject request (see para. 3). In practice this means that at least the information obligation must be assessed and decided on within the first month. In this regard, the Art. 29 Working Party emphasises "the obligation to respond within the given terms, even if it concerns a refusal" and states that the controller "cannot remain silent when it is asked to answer a data portability request" (see Art. 29 Working

Party, Guidelines on the right to data portability, WP 242 rev. 01 (2017), at 15, available at http://ec.europa.eu/newsroom/just/item-detail.cfm?item_id=50083).

7   Cf. Art. 77.

8   Cf. Art. 78.

9   Due to this provision, the data subject will lose his or her right if **requests are excessive (ie, abusive)**. However, the burden of demonstrating the excessive character of the request rests with the controller (para. 5 subpara. 2). With regard to the costs, the Art. 29 Working Party clarifies that "the overall system implementation costs should neither be charged to the data subjects, nor be used to justify a refusal to answer portability requests" (see Art. 29 Working Party, Guidelines on the right to data portability, WP 242 rev. 01 (2017), at 15, available at http://ec.europa.eu/newsroom/just/item-detail.cfm?item_id= 50083).

10   According to the Art. 29 Working Party, this requires that controllers "must implement an authentication procedure in order to strongly ascertain the identity of the data subject requesting his or her personal data or more generally exercising the rights granted by the GDPR". The Art. 29 Working Party also states that "in many cases such authentication procedures are already in place", for example, usernames and passwords for accessing their data in their email accounts, social networking accounts, and accounts used for various other services (see Art. 29 Working Party, Guidelines on the right to data portability, WP 242 rev. 01 (2017), at 14, available at http://ec.europa.eu/ newsroom/just/item-detail.cfm?item_id=50083). With regard to the right to data portability, the Art. 29 Working Party outlines that risk mitigation measures to securely deliver personal data to the right person include "if the data subject already needs to be authenticated, using additional authentication information, such as a shared secret, or another factor of authentication, such as a onetime password; suspending or freezing the transmission if there is suspicion that the account has been compromised; in cases of a direct transmission from a data controller to another data controller, authentication by mandate, such as token-based authentications" (see Art. 29 Working Party, Guidelines on the right to data portability, WP 242 rev. 01 (2017), at 19, available at http://ec.europa.eu/newsroom/just/item-detail.cfm?item_id= 50083).

11   To the extent a delegated act pursuant to para. 8 does not stipulate anything to the contrary (cf. cmt. 13 below), the (additional; cf. cmt. 12 below) display of information with standardised **icons** is voluntary.

12   Recital 60 sentence 5, too, provides that the information "may be provided in combination with standardised **icons**". The provision of information in the form of standardised icons does not replace the provision of text-based information.

13   The wording "to be provided by the icons" indicates that the (additional; cf. cmt. 12 above) display of icons might become mandatory by a delegated act of the Commission.

Section 2 – Information and access to personal data

Article 13

Information to be provided where personal data are collected from the data subject[1]

1. Where personal data relating to a data subject[2] are collected from the data subject, the controller shall, at the time when personal data are obtained,[3] provide the data subject with all of the following information:[4,5]

   (a) the identity[6] and the contact details[7] of the controller and, where applicable, of the controller's representative;[8]

   (b) the contact details[9] of the data protection officer, where applicable;[10]

   (c) the purposes of the processing for which the personal data are intended as well as the legal basis[11] for the processing;

   (d) where the processing is based on point (f) of Article 6(1), the legitimate interests pursued by the controller or by a third party;[12]

   (e) the recipients[13] or categories of recipients of the personal data, if any;

   (f) where applicable, the fact that the controller intends to transfer[14] personal data to a third country[15] or international organisation[16] and the existence[17] or absence of an adequacy decision by the Commission, or in the case of transfers referred to in Article 46 or 47, or the second subparagraph of Article 49(1), reference to the appropriate or suitable safeguards and the means by which to obtain a copy of them[18] or where they have been made available.

2. In addition to the information referred to in paragraph 1, the controller shall, at the time when personal data are obtained,[19] provide the data subject with the following further information necessary to ensure fair and transparent processing:

   (a) the period for which the personal data will be stored, or if that is not possible, the criteria used to determine that period;[20]

   (b) the existence of the right to request from the controller access to[21] and rectification[22] or erasure[23] of personal data or restriction of processing[24] concerning the data subject or to object[25] to processing as well as the right to data portability;[26]

   (c) where the processing is based on point (a) of Article 6(1) or point (a) of Article 9(2), the existence of the right to withdraw[27] consent[28] at any time, without affecting the lawfulness of processing based on consent before its withdrawal;

   (d) the right to lodge a complaint with a supervisory authority;[29]

   (e) whether the provision of personal data is a statutory or contractual requirement, or a requirement necessary to enter into a contract, as well as whether the data subject is obliged to provide the personal data and of the possible consequences of failure to provide such data;

   (f) the existence of automated decision-making, including profiling, referred to in Article 22(1) and (4) and, at least in those cases,[30] meaningful information about the logic involved, as well as the significance and the envisaged consequences of such processing for the data subject.

3. Where the controller intends to further process the personal data for a purpose other than that for which the personal data were collected,[31] the controller shall provide the data subject prior to that further processing with information on that other purpose and with any relevant[32] further information as referred to in paragraph 2.

4. Paragraphs 1, 2 and 3 shall not apply where and insofar as the data subject already has the information.

Recital:

(60) The principles of fair and transparent processing require that the data subject be informed of the existence of the processing operation and its purposes. The controller should provide the data subject with any further information necessary to ensure fair and transparent processing taking into account the specific circumstances and context in which the personal data are processed. Furthermore, the data subject should be informed of the existence of profiling and the consequences of such profiling. Where the personal data are collected from the data subject, the data subject should also be informed whether he or she is obliged to provide the personal data and of the consequences, where he or she does not provide such data. That information may be provided in combination with standardised icons in order to give in an easily visible, intelligible and clearly legible manner, a meaningful overview of the intended processing. Where the icons are presented electronically, they should be machine-readable.

Commentary:

1   The subdivision of the information obligations in para. 1 and para. 2 is irrelevant in particular because the information obligations must be fulfilled at the same time (see cmt. 19 below). The lists with information obligations in Art. 13 and Art. 14, which are identical to a large extent, could also have been drafted in a more approachable manner. Regarding the deviations between Art. 14 and Art. 13, see Art. 14 cmt. 1.

In addition to Art. 13 (and Art. 14), the following information obligation applies: Joint controllers must make available to the data subject the essence of the arrangement concluded pursuant to Art. 26 para. 1 (Art. 26 para. 2 sentence 2).

2   Since Art. 13, in contrast to Art. 14, does not require information on the categories of personal data concerned and on the other hand only Art. 13 requires that the controller informs the data subject about the obligation or necessity to provide data, it can be concluded that personal data are collected "from the data subject" only where the data subject had actual knowledge of the specific collected data, in particular where the subject provides the data him or herself (eg, by entering it into a form).

3   In our opinion, there are good arguments for the opinion that the information obligation of Art. 13 does **not apply to data collections that were completed before the applicability of the GDPR** because the obligation to inform the

data subject "at the time when personal data are obtained" cannot be fulfilled if the collection took place before the applicability of the GDPR on 25 May 2018 (see Art. 35 cmt. 4 regarding the same problem concerning data protection impact assessments and Art. 36 cmt. 3 regarding the same problem concerning the obligation of prior consultation).

4   This information as well as the information in para. 2 may also be displayed in combination with standardised icons (see Art. 12 para. 7 and 8; cf. also Recital 60 sentence 5).

5   It is not required to inform about the categories of personal data. Such an obligation applies only if personal data have not been obtained from the data subject (see Art. 14 para. 1 lit. d).

6   In the case of a legal entity, the name consists of the full corporate name including its legal form.

7   The term "**contact details**" is not defined in the GDPR. In our opinion, this means a summonable address of the controller, respectively its representative, because such an address is required: (i) to sufficiently identify the controller, respectively the representative, and (ii) to efficiently exercise the rights of the data subjects. Since Recital 23 uses the wording "of an email address or of other contact details" (although in a different context), it can be concluded that "contact details" encompasses an email address. Additionally, pursuant to Art. 12 para. 2 sentence 1, the controller is generally obligated to "facilitate" the exercise of the data subject's rights under Arts. 15 to 22. Pursuant to Recital 59 sentence 2, this could in particular be achieved by providing "means for requests to be made electronically". Therefore, there are good arguments that the term "contact details" means **summonable address and email address**. The obligation to provide further contact details, in particular the telephone number, could stem from other provisions (eg, the national implementations of the E-Commerce Directive).

8   See Art. 4 No. 17 regarding the definition of the term "representative".

9   See cmt. 7 regarding the definition of the term "contact details". It should be noted that the name of the data protection officer does not have to be disclosed. In practice, it will therefore not be necessary to amend a privacy statement every time a new data protection officer is appointed – assuming that the contact details remain the same which can be achieved by using a functional email address.

10   Cf. Art. 37 et seqq.

11   The obligation to provide **information on the legal basis** for the processing pursuant to para. 1 lit. c constitutes a significant deviation from Art. 10 Data Protection Directive. The controller must disclose which legal basis under Art. 6 para. 1 subpara. 1 lit. a to f, Art. 9 para. 2 lit. a to j or Art. 10 the processing is based on. To the extent the data processing is based on a provision stemming from national law, the information obligation very likely covers information on such a provision. Based on the mere wording of para. 1 lit. c, "information on the legal basis" might include citing the exact law. However, since this might be extremely challenging (in particular in the employment context) controllers

may be able to rely on the "disproportionate effort" exception in Art. 14 para. 5 lit. b (although it is unclear whether Art. 14 para. 5 can be applied to the obligations stemming from Art. 13). Moreover, Art. 12 para. 1 sentence 1 provides that the information must be made available "using clear and plain language". There are good arguments that citing laws and using legal verbiage does not comply with this requirement.

12 Para. 1 lit. d requires the controller to externally document the balancing of interests.

13 See Art. 4 No. 9 regarding the definition of the term "recipient" which: (i) covers **controllers and processors** (cf. Art. 4 cmt. 18); but (ii) does not cover public authorities which may receive personal data in the framework of a particular inquiry in accordance with Union or Member state law. Therefore, it is not required to disclose the lawful transfer of personal data to law enforcement authorities of a Member State.

14 Therefore, the information obligation pursuant to para. 1 lit. f applies with regard to third party controllers and processors in **third countries** (cf. Art. 44 cmt. 1 regarding the definition of the term "transfer").

15 See Art. 44 cmt. 2 regarding the definition of the term "third country".

16 See Art. 4 No. 26 regarding the definition of the term "international organisation".

17 The requirement to also inform about **the existence of an adequacy decision** by the Commission in case of data transfers to the respective third country results from the fact that adequacy decisions do not have to exist permanently (cf. CJEU 10 October 2015, C-362/14 – *Schrems*).

18 "The means by which to obtain a copy of them" means the ways to receive a copy of the safeguards. This constitutes a substantial innovation in comparison to the Data Protection Directive because controllers might need to provide copies of their standard contractual clauses.

19 The information pursuant to para. 2 must therefore be provided at the same time as the information pursuant to para. 1.

20 It will likely not be sufficient to just disclose that personal data is stored "no longer than is necessary for the purposes for which the personal data are processed" since this would only repeat the principle of storage limitation (cf. Art. 5 para. 1 lit. e). However, it will be difficult to state precise time periods since retention obligations and retention periods depend on various criteria (eg, tax relevance).

21 See Art. 15 regarding the right of access.

22 See Art. 16 regarding the right to rectification.

23 See Art. 17 regarding the right to erasure.

24 See Art. 18 regarding the right to restriction of processing.

25 See Art. 21 regarding the right to object. Pursuant to Art. 21 para. 4, the right to object must, in cases of Art. 21 paras. 1 and 2, be brought to the attention of the data subject "at the latest at the time of the first communication with the data subject".

26 See Art. 20 regarding the right to data portability. According to the Art. 29

Working Party, controllers "must ensure that they distinguish the right to data portability from other rights". Therefore, the Art. 29 Working Party "recommends in particular that data controllers clearly explain the difference between the types of data that a data subject can receive through the rights of subject access and data portability" (see Art. 29 Working Party, Guidelines on the right to data portability, WP 242 rev. 01 (2017), at 13, available at http://ec.europa.eu/newsroom/just/item-detail.cfm?item_id=50083).

27   Regarding the right of withdrawal of consent cf. Art. 7 para. 3.

28   See Art. 4 No. 11 regarding the definition of the term "consent". Regarding the further requirements for consent see Art. 7 et seq.

29   See Art. 77 regarding the right to lodge a complaint with a supervisory authority.

30   **"Meaningful information about the logic involved**, as well as the significance and the envisaged consequences of such processing for the data subject" mentioned in para. 2 lit. f must also be provided in cases other than automated decision-making to the extent such information is "necessary to ensure fair and transparent processing taking into account the specific circumstances and context in which the personal data are processed" (Recital 60 sentence 2).

31   Cf. Art. 6 para. 4.

32   "Relevant" within the meaning of para. 3 is in particular the information on the right of withdrawal (cf. Recital 50 sentence 8).

Article 14

Information to be provided where personal data have not been obtained from the data subject[1]

1. Where personal data have not been obtained from the data subject,[2] the controller shall provide the data subject with the following information:[3]

(a) the identity and the contact details[4] of the controller and, where applicable, of the controller's representative;[5]

(b) the contact details[6] of the data protection officer, where applicable;[7]

(c) the purposes of the processing for which the personal data are intended as well as the legal basis[8] for the processing;

(d) the categories of personal data concerned;

(e) the recipients or categories of recipients[9] of the personal data, if any;

(f) where applicable, that the controller intends to transfer[10] personal data to a recipient in a third country[11] or international organisation,[12] and the existence[13] or absence of an adequacy decision by the Commission, or in the case of transfers referred to in Article 46 or 47, or the second subparagraph of Article 49(1), reference to the appropriate or suitable safeguards and the means to obtain a copy of them or where they have been made available.

2. In addition to the information referred to in paragraph 1, the controller shall provide the data subject with the following information necessary to ensure fair and transparent processing in respect of the data subject:

(a) the period for which the personal data will be stored, or if that is not possible, the criteria used to determine that period;[14]

(b) where the processing is based on point (f) of Article 6(1), the legitimate interests pursued by the controller or by a third party;[15]

(c) the existence of the right to request from the controller access to[16] and rectification[17] or erasure[18] of personal data or restriction[19] of processing concerning the data subject and to object[20] to processing as well as the right to data portability;[21]

(d) where processing is based on point (a) of Article 6(1) or point (a) of Article 9(2), the existence of the right to withdraw[22] consent[23] at any time, without affecting the lawfulness of processing based on consent before its withdrawal;

(e) the right to lodge a complaint with a supervisory authority;[24]

(f) from which source the personal data originate, and if applicable, whether it came from publicly accessible sources;[25]

(g) the existence of automated decision-making, including profiling, referred to in Article 22(1) and (4) and, at least in those cases,[26] meaningful information about the logic involved, as well as the significance and the envisaged consequences of such processing for the data subject.

3. The controller shall provide the information referred to in paragraphs 1 and 2:[27]

(a) within a reasonable period after obtaining the personal data, but at the latest within one month, having regard to the specific circumstances in which the personal data are processed;

(b) if the personal data are to be used for communication with the data subject, at the latest at the time of the first communication to that data subject; or

(c) if a disclosure to another recipient[28] is envisaged, at the latest when the personal data are first disclosed.

4. Where the controller intends to further process the personal data for a purpose other than that for which the personal data were obtained,[29] the controller shall provide the data subject prior to that further processing with information on that other purpose and with any relevant further information as referred to in paragraph 2.

5. Paragraphs 1 to 4 shall not apply where and insofar as:

(a) the data subject already has the information;

(b) the provision of such information proves impossible or would involve a disproportionate effort,[30] in particular for processing for archiving purposes in the public interest, scientific or historical research purposes or statistical purposes, subject to the conditions and safeguards referred to in Article 89(1) or in so far as the obligation referred to in paragraph 1 of this Article is likely to render impossible or seriously impair the achievement of the objectives of that processing. In such cases the controller shall take appropriate measures to protect the data subject's rights and freedoms and legitimate interests, including making the information publicly available;

(c) obtaining or disclosure is expressly laid down by Union or Member State law to which the controller is subject and which provides appropriate measures to protect the data subject's legitimate interests; or

(d) where the personal data must remain confidential subject to an obligation of professional secrecy regulated by Union or Member State law, including a statutory obligation of secrecy.

Recitals:

(61) The information in relation to the processing of personal data relating to the data subject should be given to him or her at the time of collection from the data subject, or, where the personal data are obtained from another source, within a reasonable period, depending on the circumstances of the case. Where personal data can be legitimately disclosed to another recipient, the data subject should be informed when the personal data are first disclosed to the recipient. Where the controller intends to process the personal data for a purpose other than that for which they were collected, the controller should provide the data subject prior to that further processing with information on that other purpose and other necessary information. Where the origin of the personal data cannot be provided to the data subject because various sources have been used, general information should be provided.

(62) However, it is not necessary to impose the obligation to provide information where the data subject already possesses the information, where the recording or disclosure of the personal data is expressly laid down by law or where the provision of information to

*the data subject proves to be impossible or would involve a disproportionate effort. The
latter could in particular be the case where processing is carried out for archiving
purposes in the public interest, scientific or historical research purposes or statistical
purposes. In that regard, the number of data subjects, the age of the data and any
appropriate safeguards adopted should be taken into consideration.*

Commentary:

1   Apart from minor deviations not changing the meaning of the provision
(cmt. 11), **the information obligations in Art. 14 deviate from the
information obligations in Art. 13** only concerning the following aspects: (a)
only Art. 14 requires the disclosure of the data categories (Art. 14 para. 1 lit. d)
and the sources from which the personal data originate (Art. 14 para. 2 lit. f);
and (b) only Art. 13 requires the disclosure of whether the provision of personal
data is a requirement or a necessity for contract conclusion (Art. 13 para. 2
lit. e). Therefore, the information obligations pursuant to Art. 14 paras. 1 and 2
correspond with those pursuant to Art. 13 paras. 1 and 2 as follows:

Subject matter of the information	Art. 14	Art. 13
Controller	para. 1 lit. a	para. 1 lit. a
Data protection officer	para. 1 lit. b	para. 1 lit. b
Processing purposes and legal basis	para. 1 lit. c	para. 1 lit. c
Data categories	para. 1 lit. d	*no corresponding provision*
Recipients	para. 1 lit. e	para. 1 lit. e
Third country transfer	para. 1 lit. f	para. 1 lit. f
Storage period	para. 2 lit. a	para. 2 lit. a
Prevailing legitimate interests	para. 2 lit. b	para. 1 lit. d
Rights of the data subject	para. 2 lit. c	para. 2 lit. b
Withdrawal of consent	para. 2 lit. d	para. 2 lit. c
Right to lodge a complaint	para. 2 lit. e	para. 2 lit. d
Obligation/necessity to provide data	*no corresponding provision*	para. 2 lit. e
Data sources	para. 2 lit. f	*no corresponding provision*
Decision-making logic	para. 2 lit. g	para. 2 lit. f
Further processing for compatible purpose	para. 4	para. 3

2   See Art. 13 cmt. 2 regarding the meaning of collecting data "**from the data
subject**".

3   This information as well as the information in para. 2 may also be provided in
combination with standardised icons (see Art. 12 para. 7 and 8; cf. also
Recital 60 sentence 5).

4   See Art. 13 cmt. 7 regarding the definition of the term "contact details".

5   See Art. 4 No. 17 regarding the definition of the term "representative".

6   See Art. 13 cmt. 7 regarding the definition of the term "contact details". It should be noted that **the name of the data protection officer does not have to be disclosed**. In practice, it will therefore not be necessary to amend the privacy statement every time a new data protection officer is appointed.

7   Cf. Art. 37 et seqq.

8   See Art. 13 cmt. 11.

9   See Art. 13 cmt. 13.

10 The information obligation pursuant to para. 1 lit. f applies regarding third party controllers and processors in third countries (cf. Art. 44 cmt. 1 regarding the definition of the term "transfer").

11 Apart from the minor deviation from the wording of Art. 13 para. 1 lit. f ("to a recipient in a third country" instead of "to a third country") the meaning is the same as in Art. 13 para. 1 lit. f. See Art. 44 cmt. 2 regarding the definition of the term "third country".

12 See Art. 4 No. 26 regarding the definition of the term "international organisation".

13 See Art. 13 cmt. 17.

14 See Art. 13 cmt. 20.

15 Para. 2 lit. b requires the controller to **externally document the balancing of interests**.

16 See Art. 15 regarding the right of access.

17 See Art. 16 regarding the right to rectification.

18 See Art. 17 regarding the right to erasure.

19 See Art. 18 regarding the right to restriction of processing.

20 See Art. 21 regarding the right to object. Pursuant to Art. 21 para. 4, the **right to object** must, in cases of Art. 21 para. 1 and 2, be brought to the attention of the data subject "**at the latest at the time of the first communication with the data subject**".

21 See Art. 20 regarding the right to data portability. Cf. Art. 13 cmt. 26.

22 Regarding the right of withdrawal of consent cf. Art. 7 para. 3.

23 See Art. 4 No. 11 regarding the definition of the term "consent". Regarding the further requirements for consent see Art. 7 et seq.

24 See Art. 77 regarding the right to lodge a complaint with a supervisory authority.

25 There is no obligation to document the data sources in order to comply with this information obligation. This follows from Recital 61 last sentence which states that "where the origin of the personal data cannot be provided to the data subject because various sources have been used, general information should be provided". Cf. also Art. 15 para. 1 lit. g which states that only "any available information as to the source" must be provided.

26 "Meaningful information about the logic involved, as well as the significance and the envisaged consequences of such processing for the data subject" mentioned in para. 2 lit. f must also be provided in cases other than automated decision-making to the extent such information is "necessary to ensure fair and

transparent processing taking into account the specific circumstances and context in which the personal data are processed" (Recital 60 sentence 2).

27   Para. 3 does not clarify whether lit. b and lit. c respectively constitute a *lex specialis* compared to lit. a. In such case, the **one-month period** of lit. a would not apply if lit. b and c applied. At least where the data processing is performed exclusively for communication with the data subject (lit. b) or exclusively for the disclosure to another recipient (lit. c) the one-month period in lit. a should not apply.

28   See Art. 4 No. 9 regarding the definition of the term "recipient".

29   Cf. Art. 6 para. 4.

30   Pursuant to Recital 62 last sentence, "in that regard, the number of data subjects, the age of the data and any appropriate safeguards adopted should be taken into consideration".

Article 15

Right of access by the data subject

1. The data subject shall have the right to obtain from the controller confirmation[1] as to whether or not personal data concerning him or her are being processed, and, where that is the case, access to the personal data and the following information:[2,3]

(a) the purposes of the processing;

(b) the categories of personal data concerned;

(c) the recipients[4] or categories of recipient[5] to whom the personal data have been or will be disclosed, in particular recipients in third countries[6] or international organisations;[7]

(d) where possible, the envisaged period for which the personal data will be stored, or, if not possible, the criteria used to determine that period;[8]

(e) the existence of the right to request from the controller rectification[9] or erasure[10] of personal data or restriction of processing[11] of personal data concerning the data subject or to object to[12] such processing;

(f) the right to lodge a complaint with a supervisory authority;[13]

(g) where the personal data are not collected from the data subject, any available[14] information as to their source;

(h) the existence of automated decision-making, including profiling, referred to in Article 22(1) and (4) and, at least in those cases, meaningful information about the logic involved, as well as the significance and the envisaged consequences of such processing for the data subject.

2. Where personal data are transferred to a third country or to an international organisation, the data subject shall have the right to be informed of the appropriate safeguards pursuant to Article 46 relating to the transfer.

3. The controller shall provide a copy of the personal data undergoing processing.[15] For any further copies requested by the data subject, the controller may charge a reasonable fee based on administrative costs.[16] Where the data subject makes the request by electronic means, and unless otherwise requested by the data subject,[17] the information shall be provided in a commonly used electronic form.

4. The right to obtain a copy referred to in paragraph 3 shall not adversely affect the rights and freedoms of others[18,19]

Recitals:

(63) A data subject should have the right of access to personal data which have been collected concerning him or her, and to exercise that right easily and at reasonable intervals, in order to be aware of, and verify, the lawfulness of the processing. This includes the right for data subjects to have access to data concerning their health, for example the data in their medical records containing information such as diagnoses, examination results, assessments by treating physicians and any treatment or interventions provided. Every data subject should therefore have the right to know and obtain communication in particular with regard to the purposes for which the personal

data are processed, where possible the period for which the personal data are processed, the recipients of the personal data, the logic involved in any automatic personal data processing and, at least when based on profiling, the consequences of such processing. Where possible, the controller should be able to provide remote access to a secure system which would provide the data subject with direct access to his or her personal data. That right should not adversely affect the rights or freedoms of others, including trade secrets or intellectual property and in particular the copyright protecting the software. However, the result of those considerations should not be a refusal to provide all information to the data subject. Where the controller processes a large quantity of information concerning the data subject, the controller should be able to request that, before the information is delivered, the data subject specify the information or processing activities to which the request relates.

(64) *The controller should use all reasonable measures to verify the identity of a data subject who requests access, in particular in the context of online services and online identifiers. A controller should not retain personal data for the sole purpose of being able to react to potential requests.*

Commentary:

1   Recital 63 last sentence states that "where the controller processes a large quantity of information concerning the data subject, the controller should be able to request that, before the information is delivered, the data subject specify the information or processing activities to which the request relates". In such a case the data subject is **obligated to specify** the request.

2   Access to personal data must be granted without undue delay and in any event within a **one-month period** which can be **extended by two further months** (Art. 12 para. 3).

3   Where the data subject makes the request by electronic form means, **information must also be provided by electronic means** (Art. 12 para. 3 last sentence).

4   See Art. 4 No. 9 regarding the definition of the term "recipient".

5   In connection with the rectification or erasure of personal data or the restriction of processing, Art. 19 sentence 2 contains a specific right of access which cannot be fulfilled by disclosing the categories of recipients.

6   See Art. 44 cmt. 2 regarding the definition of the term "third country".

7   See Art. 4 No. 26 regarding the term "international organisation".

8   It will likely not be sufficient to only disclose that personal data is stored "no longer than is necessary for the purposes for which the personal data are processed" because this would only repeat the principle of storage limitation (cf. Art. 5 para. 1 lit. e).

9   See Art. 16 regarding the right to rectification.

10   See Art. 17 regarding the right to erasure.

11   See Art. 18 regarding the right to restriction of processing.

12   See Art. 21 regarding the right to object.

13   See Art. 77 regarding the right to lodge a complaint with a supervisory authority.

14   There is no obligation to document the **data sources** in order to comply with this information obligation. See also Art. 14 cmt. 25.

15   Before providing personal data, "the controller should use all reasonable measures to **verify the identity of a data subject who requests access**, in particular in the context of online services and online identifiers" (Recital 64 sentence 1).

16   The possibility to charge a reasonable **fee** for further copies applies only in the case of manifestly unfounded or excessive requests (see Art. 12 para. 5). Cf. also Recital 63 sentence 1 which states that the data subject should have the right of access "easily and at reasonable intervals".

17   Cf. Recital 63 sentence 4 which states that "where possible, the controller should be able to provide **remote access** to a secure system which would provide the data subject with direct access to his or her personal data".

18   "Of others" within the meaning of para. 4 covers all persons other than the data subject (eg, the controller). Therefore, a company may likely deny access requests of the suspect regarding preliminary investigation results during internal compliance investigations.

19   Pursuant to para. 4 (in conjunction with Art. 23 para. 1 lit. j), the right of access may be restricted by way of legislative measures of the Member States.

Section 3 – Rectification and erasure

Article 16

Right to rectification

The data subject shall have the right to obtain from the controller without undue delay the rectification of inaccurate personal data concerning him or her. Taking into account the purposes of the processing, the data subject shall have the right to have incomplete personal data completed, including by means of providing a supplementary statement.[1]

Commentary:

1   A right to provide a "supplementary statement" (referred to as a "corrective statement" in the draft of the Commission), will apply in our opinion only if a regular completion of personal data is impossible or unfeasible.

Article 17

Right to erasure ('right to be forgotten')[1]

1. The data subject shall have the right to obtain from the controller the erasure of personal data concerning him or her without undue delay and the controller shall have the obligation to erase personal data without undue delay where one of the following grounds applies:

   (a) the personal data are no longer necessary[2] in relation to the purposes for which they were collected or otherwise processed;[3]

   (b) the data subject withdraws consent[4] on which the processing is based according to point (a) of Article 6(1), or point (a) of Article 9(2), and where there is no other legal ground for the processing;

   (c) the data subject objects to the processing pursuant to Article 21(1) and there are no overriding legitimate grounds for the processing, or the data subject objects to the processing pursuant to Article 21(2);

   (d) the personal data have been[5] unlawfully processed;

   (e) the personal data have to be erased for compliance with a legal obligation in Union or Member State law to which the controller is subject;

   (f) the personal data have been collected in relation to the offer of information society services referred to in Article 8(1).[6]

2. Where the controller has made the personal data public and is obliged pursuant to paragraph 1 to erase the personal data, the controller, taking account of available technology and the cost of implementation, shall take reasonable steps, including technical measures, to inform controllers which are processing the personal data that the data subject has requested the erasure by such controllers of any links to, or copy or replication of, those personal data.[7]

3. Paragraphs 1 and 2 shall not apply to the extent that processing is necessary:[8]

   (a) for exercising the right of freedom of expression and information;[9]

   (b) for compliance with a legal obligation which requires processing by Union or Member State law to which the controller is subject or for the performance of a task carried out in the public interest or in the exercise of official authority vested in the controller;

   (c) for reasons of public interest in the area of public health in accordance with points (h) and (i) of Article 9(2) as well as Article 9(3);

   (d) for archiving purposes in the public interest, scientific or historical research purposes or statistical purposes in accordance with Article 89(1) in so far as the right referred to in paragraph 1 is likely to render impossible or seriously impair the achievement of the objectives of that processing; or

   (e) for the establishment, exercise or defence of legal claims.

Recitals:

Regarding para. 1 and para. 3:

(65)   A data subject should have the right to have personal data concerning him or her rectified and a 'right to be forgotten' where the retention of such data infringes this Regulation or Union or Member State law to which the controller is subject. In particular, a data subject should have the right to have his or her personal data erased and no longer processed where the personal data are no longer necessary in relation to the purposes for which they are collected or otherwise processed, where a data subject has withdrawn his or her consent or objects to the processing of personal data concerning him or her, or where the processing of his or her personal data does not otherwise comply with this Regulation. That right is relevant in particular where the data subject has given his or her consent as a child and is not fully aware of the risks involved by the processing, and later wants to remove such personal data, especially on the internet. The data subject should be able to exercise that right notwithstanding the fact that he or she is no longer a child. However, the further retention of the personal data should be lawful where it is necessary, for exercising the right of freedom of expression and information, for compliance with a legal obligation, for the performance of a task carried out in the public interest or in the exercise of official authority vested in the controller, on the grounds of public interest in the area of public health, for archiving purposes in the public interest, scientific or historical research purposes or statistical purposes, or for the establishment, exercise or defence of legal claims.

Regarding para. 2:

(66)   To strengthen the right to be forgotten in the online environment, the right to erasure should also be extended in such a way that a controller who has made the personal data public should be obliged to inform the controllers which are processing such personal data to erase any links to, or copies or replications of those personal data. In doing so, that controller should take reasonable steps, taking into account available technology and the means available to the controller, including technical measures, to inform the controllers which are processing the personal data of the data subject's request.

Commentary:

1   The term "right to be forgotten" is misleading since the GDPR does not provide for an expiry date for personal data but only provides for a right to erasure, provided that the requirements of Art. 17 are fulfilled. Also, the term seems to only refer to the procedure in para. 2. Additionally, the term is mentioned in quotation marks, which seems to refer to the underlying political discussion.

2   Para. 1 lit. a refers to the principle of data minimisation (see Art. 5 para. 1 lit. c).

3   The wording "the purposes for which they were collected or otherwise processed" means those purposes which are compatible with the purposes the data was collected for (cf. Art. 5 para. 1 lit. b in conjunction with Art. 6 para. 4).

4   See Art. 4 No. 11 regarding the definition of the term "consent". See Art. 7 para. 3 regarding the right of withdrawal.

5   Due to the use of the tense present perfect continuous (ie, the tense used for actions that commenced in the past but continue until the present time; "have been unlawfully processed"), it can be concluded that para. 1 applies only if the **state of unlawfulness continues**. If the originally unlawful state became lawful in the meantime, there is no need to grant for a right to erasure.

6   Para. 1 lit. f grants the right to erasure where "the data subject has given his or her **consent as a child** and is not fully aware of the risks involved by the processing, and later wants to remove such personal data, especially on the internet" (Recital 65 sentence 3). Since consent can be withdrawn at any time anyway (see Art. 7 para. 3) and the right to erasure pursuant to para. 1 lit. b already applies, para. 1 lit. f seems to constitute a clarification only. The wording contained in Recital 65 sentence 4 that the data subject should be able "to exercise that right notwithstanding the fact that he or she is no longer a child" only underlines that the right of withdrawal of a consent that was provided as a child cannot be forfeited.

7   Pursuant to the information obligation in para. 2 (which is somewhat contrary to the overall regulatory concept of the information obligations), the controller must **inform other controllers** where a data subject has requested the erasure by such controllers. Therefore, the information obligation requires that the data subject informs a controller which has disclosed personal data that he or she also requests erasure by the other controllers (without having contacted these yet).

The Board may publish guidance, recommendations and procedures in this regard (Art. 70 para. 1 lit. d).

However, there is only an obligation to take reasonable steps. The reasonableness is to be determined taking into account available technology and the costs of implementation. As a result, the actual consequences that have to be expected remain unclear. The legislature of the GDPR probably had in mind the "sharing" of content in social networks which remains accessible by third parties after it was deleted at the source. Even if the operator of a social network could be obligated to inform third parties about the request for erasure, this does not (necessarily) lead to an erasure because third parties might not be subject to European data protection law. Additionally, the limitations of para. 3 apply (see below).

8   The provision in para. 3 is contrary to the regulatory concept. If para. 3 applies, there is already a legal basis for the processing of personal data and therefore para. 1 does not apply. **Thus, if para. 3 applies**, there will be no claim for erasure and **the processing will not be unlawful**. Indeed, para. 3 lit. a refers to those cases where a legal basis exists in the form of Art. 6 para. 1 subpara. 1 lit. f or Art. 85. Accordingly: (i) lit. b corresponds with Art. 6 para. 1 subpara. 1 lit. f respectively Art. 9 para. 2 lit. g; (ii) lit. c corresponds with Art. 6 para. 1 subpara. 1 lit. e respectively Art. 9 para. 2 lit. h and lit. i as well as Art. 9 para. 3; (iii) lit. d corresponds with Art. 6 para. 1 subpara. 1 lit. f and Art. 89 respectively Art. 9 para. 2 lit. j; and (iv) lit. e corresponds with Art. 6 para. 1 subpara. 1 lit. f respectively Art. 9 para. 2 lit. f.

9   Cf. Art. 11 Charter. The rules governing such a conflict of fundamental rights are subject to the competence of the national legislature pursuant to Art. 85. The provision is so general and vague that divergences in the interpretation of the right to be forgotten are to be expected.

Article 18

Right to restriction of processing[1]

1. The data subject shall have the right to obtain from the controller restriction of processing[2] where one of the following applies:
   (a) the accuracy of the personal data is contested by the data subject, for a period enabling the controller to verify the accuracy of the personal data;[3]
   (b) the processing is unlawful and the data subject opposes the erasure of the personal data and requests the restriction of their use instead;[4]
   (c) the controller no longer needs the personal data for the purposes of the processing, but they are required by the data subject for the establishment, exercise or defence of legal claims;[5]
   (d) the data subject has objected to processing pursuant to Article 21(1) pending the verification[6] whether the legitimate grounds of the controller override those of the data subject.

2. Where processing has been restricted under paragraph 1, such personal data shall, with the exception of storage, only be processed with the data subject's consent[7] or for the establishment, exercise or defence of legal claims or for the protection of the rights of another natural or legal person or for reasons of important public interest of the Union or of a Member State.

3. A data subject who has obtained restriction of processing pursuant to paragraph 1 shall be informed by the controller before the restriction of processing is lifted.

Recital:

(67) Methods by which to restrict the processing of personal data could include, inter alia, temporarily moving the selected data to another processing system, making the selected personal data unavailable to users, or temporarily removing published data from a website. In automated filing systems, the restriction of processing should in principle be ensured by technical means in such a manner that the personal data are not subject to further processing operations and cannot be changed. The fact that the processing of personal data is restricted should be clearly indicated in the system.

Commentary:

1   The right to restriction of processing exceeds the right of blocking of the data under Art. 12 lit. b Data Protection Directive. However, the chosen regulatory concept results in significant legal uncertainty regarding the question whether a data subject may force the controller to restrict the processing instead of erasing the data – see in particular cmts. 4 and 5 regarding para. 1 lit. c and lit. d.

2   Art. 4 No. 3 defines the term "restriction of processing" as "the marking of stored personal data with the aim of limiting their processing in the future". This definition is not very helpful but is clarified by para. 3 and Recital 67. Therefore, the exercise of the right of restriction of processing triggers the **following obligations of the controller:**

First, the **restriction of processing** stipulated in para. 2 applies. Pursuant to Recital 67 sentence 1, this can be implemented by: (i) temporarily moving the selected data to another processing system; or (ii) making the selected personal data unavailable to users; or (iii) temporarily removing published data from a website. Recital 67 sentence 2 further states that the restriction of processing pursuant to para. 2 should be implemented in such a manner that personal data cannot be changed.

Second, Recital 67 last sentence provides that "the fact that the processing of personal data is restricted should be **clearly indicated in the system**".

3   As soon as the controller comes to the conclusion that personal data are correct, contrary to the claim of the data subject, the right of restriction of processing pursuant to **para. 1 lit. a** does not apply. This is an incentive for controllers to handle rectification claims pursuant to Art. 16 in a timely manner.

4   The provision of **para. 1 lit. b** appears problematic because in case the processing is unlawful, the controller may not process personal data any longer (for its own purposes) and therefore may not determine the purposes of the processing any longer. If the controller can be forced – against its will – to restrict the processing instead of erasing the data, the further storage would only be for the purposes of the data subject and the controller would lose his position as a controller (cf. Art. 4 No. 7). Moreover, the controller would be exposed to a significant risk of evidence and litigation – for example, if the supervisory authority conducts an inspection *ex officio*. Therefore, and despite the wording to the contrary, the controller is likely to be entitled to erase the data instead of restricting their processing, also against the will of the data subject, if it is ensured that the evidence available to the data subject is not reduced. This applies, for example, if the processing has been ruled unlawful in a legally binding decision or the controller has conceded the unlawfulness without reservations.

5   The legal claims mentioned in **para. 1 lit. c** are those between the data subject and the controller only. Otherwise, the data subject would have the legal possibility to force the controller to store the data due to a reason unrelated to the controller (eg, a lawsuit with a third party). To that extent, lit. c facilitates the **preservation of evidence** as relevant for the relationship between the controller and the data subject. However, as is also the case for lit. b (see cmt. 4), it must be considered that an obligation of the controller to restrict the processing (ie, to retain it) instead of erasing it, would have the result that the controller loses its position as a controller because the controller would no longer determine the purposes of the processing. Therefore, there are good arguments that the controller **may also transfer a copy of the respective data to the data subject and subsequently erase the data** instead of restricting the processing as requested by the data subject under para. 1 lit. c.

6   It is questionable whether the wording "pending the verification" in **para. 1 lit. d** refers to a verification by the controller or a verification by the supervisory authority. Since para. 1 lit. a also refers to a verification, ie, review, by the controller, it can be concluded that para. 1 lit. d, too, refers to the controller.

Thus, para. 1 lit. d provides a significant incentive for the controller to handle objections in a timely manner.

7   See Art. 4 No. 11 regarding the definition of the term "consent".

Article 19

Notification obligation regarding rectification or erasure of personal data or restriction of processing

The controller shall communicate any rectification[1] or erasure[2] of personal data or restriction of processing[3] carried out in accordance with Article 16, Article 17(1) and Article 18 to each recipient[4] to whom the personal data have been disclosed, unless this proves impossible or involves disproportionate effort. The controller shall inform the data subject about those recipients if the data subject requests it.[5]

Commentary:

1   See Art. 16 regarding the right to rectification.
2   See Art. 17 regarding the right to erasure.
3   See Art. 18 regarding the right to restriction of processing.
4   See Art. 4 No. 9 regarding the definition of the term "recipient".
5   Since the individual recipients and not only the categories of recipients must be disclosed, this notification obligation exceeds Art. 15 para. 1 lit. c (cf. also Art. 15 cmt. 5).

Article 20

Right to data portability[1]

1. The data subject shall have the right to receive the personal data concerning him or her, which he or she[2] has provided to[3] a controller,[4] in a structured, commonly used and machine-readable format[5] and have the right to transmit those data to another controller without hindrance[6] from the controller to which the personal data have been provided, where:

   (a) the processing is based on consent pursuant to point (a) of Article 6(1) or point (a) of Article 9(2) or on a contract pursuant to point (b) of Article 6(1);[7] and

   (b) the processing is carried out by automated means.

2. In exercising his or her right to data portability pursuant to paragraph 1, the data subject shall have the right to have the personal data transmitted directly from one controller to another, where technically feasible.[8]

3. The exercise of the right referred to in paragraph 1 of this Article shall be without prejudice to Article 17. That right shall not apply to processing necessary for the performance of a task carried out in the public interest or in the exercise of official authority vested in the controller.

4. The right referred to in paragraph 1 shall not adversely affect the rights and freedoms of others[9]

Recital:

(68) *To further strengthen the control over his or her own data, where the processing of personal data is carried out by automated means, the data subject should also be allowed to receive personal data concerning him or her which he or she has provided to a controller in a structured, commonly used, machine-readable and interoperable format, and to transmit it to another controller. Data controllers should be encouraged to develop interoperable formats that enable data portability. That right should apply where the data subject provided the personal data on the basis of his or her consent or the processing is necessary for the performance of a contract. It should not apply where processing is based on a legal ground other than consent or contract. By its very nature, that right should not be exercised against controllers processing personal data in the exercise of their public duties. It should therefore not apply where the processing of the personal data is necessary for compliance with a legal obligation to which the controller is subject or for the performance of a task carried out in the public interest or in the exercise of an official authority vested in the controller. The data subject's right to transmit or receive personal data concerning him or her should not create an obligation for the controllers to adopt or maintain processing systems which are technically compatible. Where, in a certain set of personal data, more than one data subject is concerned, the right to receive the personal data should be without prejudice to the rights and freedoms of other data subjects in accordance with this Regulation. Furthermore, that right should not prejudice the right of the data subject to obtain the erasure of personal data and the limitations of that right as set out in this Regulation and should, in particular, not imply the erasure of personal data concerning the data*

subject which have been provided by him or her for the performance of a contract to the extent that and for as long as the personal data are necessary for the performance of that contract. Where technically feasible, the data subject should have the right to have the personal data transmitted directly from one controller to another.

Commentary:

1   The purpose of the right to data portability is mainly to make it easier for users to change from one service provider to another service provider or, from an economic perspective, **to reduce switching costs and, thus, prevent a lock-in effect**. This is designed to foster the competition between the service providers, in particular between cloud providers. Given that the right to data portability is limited to the data subject-controller relationship (cf. cmt. 4), this objective will be realised only in a limited manner.

2   Under the plain language of para. 1, the **right to data portability does not apply** to the extent personal data were **provided by a third party**. Furthermore, it only covers personal data concerning the data subject. Thus, anonymous data and data that does not concern the data subject is not subject to the right to data portability. However, regarding the latter the Art. 29 Working Party takes a rather broad approach and also considers data to be covered that include details of third parties (see Art. 29 Working Party, Guidelines on the right to data portability, WP 242 rev. 01 (2017), at 9, available at http://ec.europa.eu/newsroom/just/item-detail.cfm?item_id=50083).

3   The limitation to personal data that the data subject "has provided" to the controller means that only such data are covered which the **data subject has transferred to the controller knowingly and willingly**. However, according to the Art. 29 Working Party's broad interpretation, this also includes "observed data provided by the data subject by virtue of the use of the service or the device" which may for example "include a person's search history, traffic data and location data" as well as "other raw data such as the heartbeat tracked by a wearable device". In any case, the Art. 29 Working Party does not consider data to be covered that "are created by the data controller (using the data observed or directly provided as input)" (see Art. 29 Working Party, Guidelines on the right to data portability, WP 242 rev. 01 (2017), at 10, available at http://ec.europa.eu/newsroom/just/item-detail.cfm?item_id=50083).

4   The right to data portability **only applies vis-à-vis a controller**, not vis-à-vis a processor. If a cloud provider processes the data of the user not for its own purposes but only upon instruction of the user – as is common with almost all cloud services offered in exchange for a fee – the user does not have a right to data portability because the cloud provider is not a controller. The right to data portability neither applies between a controller and a processor.

5   Pursuant to Recital 68 sentence 1, the data format also has to be interoperable. However, pursuant to Recital 68 sentence 7, the controller is not obligated "to adopt or maintain processing systems which are technically compatible". The Art. 29 Working Party also emphasises that "portability aims to produce interoperable systems, not compatible systems" but on the other hand

"strongly encourages cooperation between industry stakeholders and trade associations to work together on a common set of interoperable standards and formats to deliver the requirements of the right to data portability" (see Art. 29 Working Party, Guidelines on the right to data portability, WP 242 rev. 01 (2017), at 17 et seq., available at http://ec.europa.eu/newsroom/just/item-detail.cfm?item_id=50083).

6   According to the Art. 29 Working Party, such hindrance "can be characterised as any legal, technical or financial obstacles placed by data controller in order to refrain or slow down access, transmission or reuse by the data subject or by another data controller" (see Art. 29 Working Party, Guidelines on the right to data portability, WP 242 rev. 01 (2017), at 15, available at http://ec.europa.eu/newsroom/just/item-detail.cfm?item_id=50083).

7   Recital 68 sentence 4 clarifies that the right to data portability does not apply where processing is based on a legal ground other than consent or contract (listed in para. 1). Cf. also para. 3 sentence 2. By way of example, in the HR context, the Art. 29 Working Party outlines that some employee data "are based on the legal ground of legitimate interest, or are necessary for compliance with specific legal obligations in the field of employment". Thus, according to the Art. 29 Working Party "the right to data portability in an HR context will undoubtedly concern some processing operations (such as pay and compensation services, internal recruitment) but in many other situations a case by case approach will be needed to verify whether all conditions applying to the right to data portability are met" (see Art. 29 Working Party, Guidelines on the right to data portability, WP 242 rev. 01 (2017), at 9, available at http://ec.europa.eu/newsroom/just/item-detail.cfm?item_id=50083).

8   The provision of para. 2 is designed to enable a direct data transfer from one cloud provider to another cloud provider. However, as mentioned in cmt. 4, cloud providers are often not subject to a data portability obligation. Potential cases of applicability might be the transfer of account data and usage data of social networks. In this regard, the Art. 29 Working Party points out that Recital 68 further clarifies the limits of what is "technically feasible", indicating that it "should not create an obligation for the controllers to adopt or maintain processing systems which are technically compatible" (Recital 68 sentence 7). However, the Art. 29 Working Party further states that "on a technical level, data controllers should explore and assess two different and complimentary paths for making portable data available to the data subjects or to other data controllers: (i) a direct transmission of the overall dataset of portable data (or several extracts of parts of the global dataset); (ii) an automated tool that allows extraction of relevant data" (see Art. 29 Working Party, Guidelines on the right to data portability, WP 242 rev. 01 (2017), at 16, available at http://ec.europa.eu/newsroom/just/item-detail.cfm?item_id=50083).

With regard to the direct transmission, the Art. 29 Working Party further mentions that "the data controller is not responsible for compliance of the receiving data controller with data protection law, considering that it is not the sending data controller that chooses the recipient"; however, "the controller should set safeguards that they genuinely act on the data subject's behalf" (see *id.*, at 6). The Art. 29 Working Party also states that controllers "have no specific obligation to check and verify the quality of the data before transmitting it" and that "data portability does not impose an obligation on the data controller to retain personal data for longer than is necessary or beyond any specified retention period" (see *id.*, at 6). However, the "receiving data controller is responsible for ensuring that the portable data provided are relevant and not excessive with regard to the new data processing" (see *id.*).

With regard to "technically feasible", the Art. 29 Working Party further outlines that "if the size of data requested by the data subject makes transmission via the internet problematic, rather than potentially allowing for an extended time period of a maximum of three months to comply with the request, the data controller may also need to consider alternative means of providing the data such as using streaming or saving to a CD, DVD or other physical media or allowing for the personal data to be transmitted directly to another data controller" (see *id.*, at 14).

9   Para. 4 primarily refers to the rights and freedoms of other persons, in particular the freedom of speech and the freedom of information (cf. Recital 68 sentence 8). According to Art. 29 Working Party, it must be ensured that "where personal data of third parties are included in the data set[,] another legal basis for the processing must be identified" (Art. 29 Working Party, Guidelines on the right to data portability, WP 242 rev. 01 (2017), at 11, available at http://ec.europa.eu/newsroom/just/item-detail.cfm?item_id=50083). Moreover, the Art. 29 Working Party states that rights and freedoms of others "can be understood as including trade secrets or intellectual property and in particular the copyright protecting the software" (*id.*, at 12). However, according to the Art. 29 Working Party "a potential business risk cannot [...] in and of itself serve as the basis for a refusal to answer the portability request and data controllers can transmit the personal data provided by data subjects in a form that does not release information covered by trade secrets or intellectual property rights" (see *id.*, at 12). In addition, it can also be concluded that another controller is, in principle, not obligated to support the data format of the original controller.

Section 4 – Right to object and automated individual decision-making

Article 21

Right to object[1]

1. The data subject shall have the right to object, on grounds relating to his or her particular situation, at any time to processing of personal data concerning him or her which is based on point (e) or (f) of Article 6(1), including profiling based on those provisions.[2,3] The controller shall no longer process the personal data unless the controller demonstrates compelling legitimate grounds for the processing[4] which override the interests, rights and freedoms of the data subject or for the establishment, exercise or defence of legal claims.

2. Where personal data are processed for direct marketing purposes, the data subject shall have the right to object at any time to processing of personal data concerning him or her for such marketing, which includes profiling[5] to the extent that it is related to such direct marketing.

3. Where the data subject objects to processing for direct marketing purposes, the personal data shall no longer be processed for such purposes.[6]

4. At the latest at the time of the first communication with the data subject, the right referred to in paragraphs 1 and 2 shall be explicitly brought to the attention of the data subject[7] and shall be presented clearly and separately from any other information.[8]

5. In the context of the use of information society services, and notwithstanding Directive 2002/58/EC, the data subject may exercise his or her right to object by automated means using technical specifications.[9]

6. Where personal data are processed for scientific or historical research purposes or statistical purposes pursuant to Article 89(1), the data subject, on grounds relating to his or her particular situation, shall have the right to object to processing of personal data[10] concerning him or her, unless the processing is necessary for the performance of a task carried out for reasons of public interest.[11]

Recitals:
Regarding para. 1:

(69) *Where personal data might lawfully be processed because processing is necessary for the performance of a task carried out in the public interest or in the exercise of official authority vested in the controller, or on grounds of the legitimate interests of a controller or a third party, a data subject should, nevertheless, be entitled to object to the processing of any personal data relating to his or her particular situation. It should be for the controller to demonstrate that its compelling legitimate interest overrides the interests or the fundamental rights and freedoms of the data subject.*

Regarding para. 2 and 3:

(70) *Where personal data are processed for the purposes of direct marketing, the data subject should have the right to object to such processing, including profiling to the*

extent that it is related to such direct marketing, whether with regard to initial or further processing, at any time and free of charge. That right should be explicitly brought to the attention of the data subject and presented clearly and separately from any other information.

Commentary:

1   Regarding the regulatory concept of Art. 21: Art. 21 para. 1 provides for a right to object to the processing based on a particular legal basis, whereas para. 2 and para. 6 provide a right to object to the processing for particular purposes. The **legal consequence of a legitimate objection** pursuant to para. 1 is that any further processing of the data becomes impermissible (para. 1 sentence 2), whereas an objection pursuant to paras. 2 or 6 only makes it impermissible to process the data for the respective purposes (cf. para. 3 and cmt. 10 below).

Furthermore, it must be noted that a legitimate objection pursuant to para. 1 requires a balancing of interests in favour of the data subject (taking into account the shifting of the burden of proof), whereas an objection pursuant to paras. 2 or 6 does not require such a balancing of interests.

2   See Art. 4 No. 4 regarding the definition of the term "profiling"; see Art. 22 regarding the right of the data subject not to be subject to a decision based solely on automated processing.

3   As a result, the **right to object to profiling** exists only if the profiling neither has legal consequences concerning the data subject nor similarly affects him or her. In these serious cases of profiling, the legal bases Art. 6 para. 1 subpara. 1 lit. e or f do not apply to begin with (see Art. 22 para. 2).

4   Therefore, the controller bears the **burden of proof** pursuant to para. 1 sentence 2 that its interests prevail over the interests of the data subject (cf. also Recital 69 last sentence).

5   See cmts. 2 and 3 above. Since **profiling for purposes of direct marketing** neither has legal consequences concerning the data subject nor similarly affects the data subject, it is not covered by Art. 22. However, in such a case, para. 2 provides for a right to object to the profiling performed for direct marketing purposes.

6   An objection to the processing of personal data for **direct marketing** purposes does **not require a balancing of interests** pursuant to para. 3.

7   Given that the first communication can take place before the collection of personal data, the deadline to comply with the **information obligation** pursuant to para. 4 may end before the deadline to comply with the information obligation pursuant to Art. 13. Therefore, the timing of the provision of information pursuant to Art. 13 et seq. and the provision of information pursuant to para. 4 could differ.

8   "Other information" within the meaning of para. 4 is to be interpreted in a manner that it does not cover information pursuant to Art. 13 et seq. It is permissible to insert the information on the right to object pursuant to paras. 1 and 2 into the privacy statement.

9   The controller's obligation to take into account **objections by automated**

means in the context of the use of information society services should only apply if the "technical specifications" within the meaning of para. 5 are a technical standard of an internationally recognised standardisation organisation (eg, of the IETF). The "Do Not Track" specification would not yet fulfill these requirements (currently there is only a draft of an IETF standard; cf. https://tools.ietf.org/html/draft-mayer-do-not-track-00).

10   Although para. 6 does not contain an explicit provision regarding the consequences of an objection to the data processing **for scientific or historical research purposes or statistical purposes**, it can be assumed that after such an objection, personal data may not be processed for these purposes, unless the processing is necessary for the performance of a task carried out for reasons of public interest.

11   National law may provide for further exceptions from the right codified in para. 6 to object to the processing of personal data for scientific or historical research purposes or statistical purposes (see Art. 89 para. 2).

Article 22

Automated individual decision-making, including profiling

1. The data subject shall have the right not to be subject to a decision based solely on automated processing,[1] including profiling,[2] which produces legal effects concerning him or her[3] or similarly significantly affects him or her.[4]

2. Paragraph 1 shall not apply[5] if the decision:

   (a) is necessary for entering into, or performance of, a contract between the data subject and a data controller;

   (b) is authorised by Union or Member State law[6] to which the controller is subject and which also lays down suitable measures[7] to safeguard the data subject's rights and freedoms and legitimate interests; or

   (c) is based on the data subject's explicit consent.[8]

3. In the cases referred to in points (a) and (c) of paragraph 2, the data controller shall implement suitable measures to safeguard the data subject's rights and freedoms and legitimate interests, at least[9] the right to obtain human intervention on the part of the controller, to express his or her point of view and to contest the decision.

4. Decisions referred to in paragraph 2 shall not be based on special categories of personal data referred to in Article 9(1), unless point (a) or (g) of Article 9(2) applies[10] and suitable measures to safeguard the data subject's rights and freedoms and legitimate interests are in place.

Recitals:

(71) The data subject should have the right not to be subject to a decision, which may include a measure, evaluating personal aspects relating to him or her which is based solely on automated processing and which produces legal effects concerning him or her or similarly significantly affects him or her, such as automatic refusal of an online credit application or e-recruiting practices without any human intervention. Such processing includes 'profiling' that consists of any form of automated processing of personal data evaluating the personal aspects relating to a natural person, in particular to analyse or predict aspects concerning the data subject's performance at work, economic situation, health, personal preferences or interests, reliability or behaviour, location or movements, where it produces legal effects concerning him or her or similarly significantly affects him or her. However, decision-making based on such processing, including profiling, should be allowed where expressly authorised by Union or Member State law to which the controller is subject, including for fraud and tax-evasion monitoring and prevention purposes conducted in accordance with the regulations, standards and recommendations of Union institutions or national oversight bodies and to ensure the security and reliability of a service provided by the controller, or necessary for the entering or performance of a contract between the data subject and a controller, or when the data subject has given his or her explicit consent. In any case, such processing should be subject to suitable safeguards, which should include specific information to the data subject and the right to obtain human intervention, to express his or her point of view, to obtain an explanation of the

decision reached after such assessment and to challenge the decision. Such measure should not concern a child.

In order to ensure fair and transparent processing in respect of the data subject, taking into account the specific circumstances and context in which the personal data are processed, the controller should use appropriate mathematical or statistical procedures for the profiling, implement technical and organisational measures appropriate to ensure, in particular, that factors which result in inaccuracies in personal data are corrected and the risk of errors is minimised, secure personal data in a manner that takes account of the potential risks involved for the interests and rights of the data subject and that prevents, inter alia, discriminatory effects on natural persons on the basis of racial or ethnic origin, political opinion, religion or beliefs, trade union membership, genetic or health status or sexual orientation, or that result in measures having such an effect. Automated decision-making and profiling based on special categories of personal data should be allowed only under specific conditions.

(72) Profiling is subject to the rules of this Regulation governing the processing of personal data, such as the legal grounds for processing or data protection principles. The European Data Protection Board established by this Regulation (the 'Board') should be able to issue guidance in that context.

Commentary:

1   The term "decision" must, in principle, be understood broadly and covers in particular a measure (cf. Recital 71 sentence 1). Whether it must be an **individual decision** is not clear from the plain language (in contrast to Art. 15 Data Protection Directive). However, the heading of Art. 22 and the heading of Section 4 mention an "individual" decision-making. Therefore, it can be assumed that the scope of Art. 22 is limited to profiling and individual decisions.

Moreover, the wording of para. 1 does not clarify whether it is required that **a decision is based on an evaluation of certain personal aspects relating to the data subject** (Art. 15 Data Protection Directive was explicit in this regard). Recital 71 sentence 1 explicitly states that data subjects "should have the right not to be subject to a decision [...] evaluating personal aspects relating to him or her". This could lead to the conclusion that the prohibition in para. 1 only covers decisions which are based on the evaluation of aspects relating to the data subject. However, pursuant to the regulatory concept of para. 1, profiling only constitutes a subset of the term "decision" and if the term "decision" was interpreted so narrowly, there would be no scope of applicability beyond profiling (cf. Art. 4 No. 4). Until clarified by the courts, it should be assumed that the prohibition in para. 1 also covers decisions that are not based on evaluations of personal aspects relating to the data subject.

2   See Art. 4 No. 4 regarding the definition of the term "profiling".

3   A decision which produces **"legal effect"** is, for example, the termination of a contract.

4   Examples of **similarly significant effects** as a decision with legal effect are in particular: (i) an automatic refusal of an online credit application; or (ii) e-

recruiting practices without any human intervention (cf. Recital 71 sentence 1). However, the automated decision concerning the display of personal advertisement to the data subject is not a decision that significantly affects the data subject.

5   In addition to the requirements of para. 2, an automated decision or profiling must also comply with the other requirements of the GDPR such as the principles in Art. 5 (cf. Recital 72 sentence 2) as well as the **information obligations** in Art. 13 and Art. 14 (cf. cmt. 9 below). If para. 2 applies, a data subject's **right to object does not exist** (see Art. 21 cmts. 3 and 5).

Pursuant to Art. 70 para. 1 lit. f, the Board may issue guidelines, recommendations and best practices to provide more details on the criteria and conditions for the decisions based on profiling pursuant to para. 2.

6   Regarding the prohibition of automated decisions and profiling, para. 2 lit. b provides for an **opening clause** which enables the national legislature to enact new statutory authorisations for automated decisions and profiling. Pursuant to Recital 71 sentence 3 these statutory permissions may in particular serve the purpose of monitoring and preventing fraud and tax fraud as well as to ensure security and reliability of the service offered by the controller.

7   The **suitable measures** mentioned in para. 2 lit. b **which the national legislature must set out when making use of the opening clause** must at least include: (i) the right to obtain human intervention on the part of the controller; (ii) the right for the data subject to express his or her point of view; and (iii) the right to contest the decision (cf. para. 3 regarding the measures to be implemented by the controller if the profiling or the automated decision is not based on para. 2 lit. b).

8   See Art. 4 No. 11 regarding the definition of the term "consent", Art. 7 et seq. regarding the further requirements of consent, and Art. 9 cmt. 7 regarding the requirements for "explicit" consent. However, pursuant to Recital 71 sentence 5 **"such measure should not concern a child"** (see Art. 6 cmt. 9 regarding the definition of the term "child") which leads to the conclusion that profiling of a child is in principle impermissible even if the child validly consented or consent is given by the holder of parental responsibility (cf. Art. 8).

9   The **"suitable measures" that must at least be implemented** by the controller within the meaning of para. 3, include – in addition to the rights of human intervention, expression of the data subject's own point of view and contesting the decision mentioned in para. 3 – "specific information to the data subject" and "an explanation of the decision reached after such assessment" (see Recital 71 sentence 4). The requirement to provide specific information to the data subject will be deemed complied with when providing the information pursuant to Art. 13 para. 2 lit. f, respectively Art. 14 para. 2 lit. g. However, it remains unclear whether a decision is sufficiently explained if "meaningful information about the logic involved, as well as the significance and the envisaged consequences of such processing for the data subject" are provided to the data subject (cf. Art. 13 para. 2 lit. f; Art. 14 para. 2 lit. g). Since it can be assumed that the legislature of the Union would have included additional

information obligations in Art. 13 para. 2 lit. f and Art. 14 para. 2 lit. g, if it had intended to impose broader information obligations, it can be assumed that the implementation of the measures mentioned in para. 3 in combination with compliance with the information obligations in Art. 13 para. 2 lit. f respectively Art. 14 para. 2 lit. g exhaustively describe the "suitable measures" that must "at least" be implemented.

Recital 71 para. 2 mentions additional **measures that must be implemented depending on the specific circumstances**: (i) the use of appropriate mathematical or statistical procedures for the profiling; (ii) technical and organisational measures appropriate to ensure, in particular that factors which result in inaccuracies in personal data are corrected and the risk of errors is minimised; and (iii) measures that prevent, inter alia, discriminatory effects on natural persons on the basis of racial or ethnic origin, political opinion, religion or beliefs, trade union membership, genetic or health status or sexual orientation, or that result in measures having such an effect.

10 The references to Art. 9 para. 2 lit. a (explicit consent) and lit. g (statutory basis) contained in para. 4 mean that a profiling or automated decision by **using sensitive data** is permissible only if based on para. 2 lit. b or lit. c. The use of sensitive data for profiling or automated decisions on the basis of the necessity to enter into or to perform a contract (para. 2 lit. a) is, on the other hand, in principle unlawful.

Section 5 – Restrictions

Article 23

Restrictions[1]

1. Union or Member State law to which the data controller or processor is subject[2] may restrict by way of a legislative measure the scope of the obligations and rights provided for in Articles 12 to 22 and Article 34, as well as Article 5 in so far as its provisions correspond to the rights and obligations provided for in Articles 12 to 22, when such a restriction respects the essence of the fundamental rights and freedoms and is a necessary and proportionate measure[3] in a democratic society to safeguard:

(a) national security;[4]

(b) defence;

(c) public security;[5]

(d) the prevention, investigation, detection or prosecution of criminal offences or the execution of criminal penalties, including the safeguarding against and the prevention of threats to public security;[6]

(e) other important objectives of general public interest of the Union or of a Member State, in particular an important economic or financial interest of the Union or of a Member State, including monetary, budgetary and taxation a matters, public health and social security;[7]

(f) the protection of judicial independence and judicial proceedings;

(g) the prevention, investigation, detection and prosecution of breaches of ethics for regulated professions;

(h) a monitoring, inspection or regulatory function connected, even occasionally, to the exercise of official authority in the cases referred to in points (a) to (e) and (g);

(i) the protection of the data subject or the rights and freedoms of others;[8]

(j) the enforcement of civil law claims.[9]

2. In particular, any legislative measure referred to in paragraph 1 shall contain specific provisions at least, where relevant,[10] as to:

(a) the purposes of the processing or categories of processing;

(b) the categories of personal data;

(c) the scope of the restrictions introduced;

(d) the safeguards to prevent abuse or unlawful access or transfer;

(e) the specification of the controller or categories of controllers;

(f) the storage periods and the applicable safeguards taking into account the nature, scope and purposes of the processing or categories of processing;

(g) the risks to the rights and freedoms of data subjects; and

(h) the right of data subjects to be informed about the restriction, unless that may be prejudicial to the purpose of the restriction.

Recital:

(73) Restrictions concerning specific principles and the rights of information, access to and rectification or erasure of personal data, the right to data portability, the right to object, decisions based on profiling, as well as the communication of a personal data breach to a data subject and certain related obligations of the controllers may be imposed by Union or Member State law, as far as necessary and proportionate in a democratic society to safeguard public security, including the protection of human life especially in response to natural or manmade disasters, the prevention, investigation and prosecution of criminal offences or the execution of criminal penalties, including the safeguarding against and the prevention of threats to public security, or of breaches of ethics for regulated professions, other important objectives of general public interest of the Union or of a Member State, in particular an important economic or financial interest of the Union or of a Member State, the keeping of public registers kept for reasons of general public interest, further processing of archived personal data to provide specific information related to the political behaviour under former totalitarian state regimes or the protection of the data subject or the rights and freedoms of others, including social protection, public health and humanitarian purposes. Those restrictions should be in accordance with the requirements set out in the Charter and in the European Convention for the Protection of Human Rights and Fundamental Freedoms.

Commentary:

1   This clause is the most **far-reaching opening clause** in the GDPR. It allows Member States to restrict to a large extent **all rights of the data subjects and the corresponding obligations of the controller**, including information obligations, the right of access, the right to rectification, the right to erasure, the right to object, the right to restriction of processing, data portability, profiling and data breach notifications. To the extent Arts. 12 to 22 already contain opening clauses which set out precise requirements regarding the content of the national law, these are leges specialis which precede the general opening clause in Art. 23.

In Germany, the new Federal Data Protection Act (Federal Law Gazette, No. 44, at 2097 et seqq., 5 July 2017) which will come into effect on the same date as the GDPR, that is, on 25 May 2018, contains restrictions of the data subject rights.

2   The GDPR does not stipulate which Member State's law applies. Regarding the **conflict of laws** in general, see Art. 92 cmt. 5.

3   The proportionality and necessity in a democratic society refers to the limitations of Art. 8 para. 2 ECHR (cf. also Recital 73 last sentence).

4   Mentioning "national security" in para. 1 lit. a is not necessary because national security is not subject to Union law to begin with (see Art. 2 cmt. 5). To the extent national security is concerned, the obligations in para. 2 do not apply.

5   Public security pursuant to para. 1 lit. c covers the protection of human life especially in response to natural or man-made disasters, the prevention,

      investigation and prosecution of criminal offences or the execution of criminal penalties (Recital 73 sentence 1).

6   To the extent data is processed by the competent national authority to prevent, investigate, detect or prosecute criminal **offences** or the execution of criminal penalties, the GDPR does not apply to begin with (Art. 2 para. 2 lit. d). Therefore, the scope of applicability of para. 1 lit. d is limited to the processing for these purposes by other persons than the competent authorities.

7   Based on para. 1 lit. e, a Member State may, for example, provide for restrictions of the data subject rights in connection with: (i) the keeping of public registers for reasons of general public interest; or (ii) important economic or financial interests of the Member State (Recital 73 sentence 1).

8   Regarding the conflict between the right to data protection on the one hand and the freedom of speech and the freedom of information on the other hand, the Member States have an even broader legislative competence pursuant to Art. 85. The balancing of fundamental rights is therefore largely left to the Member States.

9   Due to the provisions of Art. 9 para. 2 lit. f, Art. 17 para. 3 lit. e, Art. 18 para. 2, Art. 21 para. 1 and Art. 49 para. 1 lit. e, the opening clause in para. 1 lit. j would not have been necessary.

10   The content mentioned in para. 2 must "at least, where relevant" be included into national legislation. A **mandatory minimum content for national laws** cannot be derived therefrom.

Chapter IV – Controller and processor

Section 1 – General obligations

Article 24

Responsibility of the controller[1]

1. Taking into account the nature, scope, context and purposes of processing as well as the risks of varying likelihood and severity[2] for the rights and freedoms of natural persons, the controller[3] shall implement appropriate technical and organisational measures[4] to ensure and to be able to demonstrate[5] that processing is performed in accordance with this Regulation. Those measures shall be reviewed and updated where necessary.[6]

2. Where proportionate in relation to processing activities, the measures referred to in paragraph 1 shall include the implementation of appropriate data protection policies[7] by the controller.

3. Adherence to approved codes of conduct as referred to in Article 40 or approved certification mechanisms as referred to in Article 42 may be used as an element by which to demonstrate compliance with the obligations of the controller.

Recitals:

(74) *The responsibility and liability of the controller for any processing of personal data carried out by the controller or on the controller's behalf should be established. In particular, the controller should be obliged to implement appropriate and effective measures and be able to demonstrate the compliance of processing activities with this Regulation, including the effectiveness of the measures. Those measures should take into account the nature, scope, context and purposes of the processing and the risk to the rights and freedoms of natural persons.*

(75) *The risk to the rights and freedoms of natural persons , of varying likelihood and severity, may result from personal data processing which could lead to physical, material or non-material damage, in particular: where the processing may give rise to discrimination, identity theft or fraud, financial loss, damage to the reputation, loss of confidentiality of personal data protected by professional secrecy, unauthorised reversal of pseudonymisation, or any other significant economic or social disadvantage; where data subjects might be deprived of their rights and freedoms or prevented from exercising control over their personal data; where personal data are*

processed which reveal racial or ethnic origin, political opinions, religion or philosophical beliefs, trade union membership, and the processing of genetic data, data concerning health or data concerning sex life or criminal convictions and offences or related security measures; where personal aspects are evaluated, in particular analysing or predicting aspects concerning performance at work, economic situation, health, personal preferences or interests, reliability or behaviour, location or movements, in order to create or use personal profiles; where personal data of vulnerable natural persons, in particular of children, are processed; or where processing involves a large amount of personal data and affects a large number of data subjects.

(76) The likelihood and severity of the risk to the rights and freedoms of the data subject should be determined by reference to the nature, scope, context and purposes of the processing. Risk should be evaluated on the basis of an objective assessment, by which it is established whether data processing operations involve a risk or a high risk.

(77) Guidance on the implementation of appropriate measures and on the demonstration of compliance by the controller or the processor, especially as regards the identification of the risk related to the processing, their assessment in terms of origin, nature, likelihood and severity, and the identification of best practices to mitigate the risk, could be provided in particular by means of approved codes of conduct, approved certifications, guidelines provided by the Board or indications provided by a data protection officer. The Board may also issue guidelines on processing operations that are considered to be unlikely to result in a high risk to the rights and freedoms of natural persons and indicate what measures may be sufficient in such cases to address such risk.

Commentary:

1   Art. 24 substantiates the principle of **accountability** codified in Art. 5 para. 2 which contains two elements: On the one hand the obligation to implement risk-appropriate **technical and organisational measures** to comply with the GDPR (cmt. 4 below) and on the other hand a **material obligation to demonstrate compliance** (see cmt. 5 below; cf. also Art. 5 cmt. 13).

Despite the fact that Art. 83 does not provide for administrative fines in case of violations of Art. 24, technical and organisational measures are necessary in particular to comply with the obligations pursuant to Art. 25, a violation of which is subject to administrative fines pursuant to Art. 83 para. 4 lit. a. Furthermore, the obligation to demonstrate compliance may be subject to the powers of the supervisory authority and non-compliance in this regard may be taken into consideration for sentencing (see cmt. 5 below).

2   Pursuant to Recital 76 sentence 1, the likelihood and severity of the risk should be determined by reference to the: (i) nature; (ii) scope; (iii) context; and (iv) purposes of the processing. In principle, a qualitative risk assessment (ie, a ranking using risk classes) as well as a quantitative risk assessment (ie, a mathematical calculation) can be considered. However, Recital 76 sentence 2 provides that the risk "should be evaluated on the basis of an objective assessment, by which it is established whether data processing operations involve a risk or a high risk". Therefore, a **qualitative risk assessment** using the risk categories "medium" and "high" is generally sufficient.

3   Since Art. 24 **only refers to controllers and not to processors**, this provision only applies to controllers (regarding the personal scope of application of the principle of accountability in general cf. also Art. 5 cmt. 12).

4   Whereas the term "technical and organisational measures" pursuant to the Data Protection Directive was limited to data security (cf. Art. 17 para. 1 Data Protection Directive), the term **"technical and organisational measures"** (in practice also referred to as "TOMs") in the GDPR is more comprehensive and includes all measures to provide and demonstrate data protection compliance.

The measures taken, including the implemented internal strategies pursuant to para. 2 must in particular comply with the principles of **data protection by design** (Art. 25 para. 1) and **data protection by default** (Art. 25 para. 2) (see Recital 78 sentence 2).

Examples for possible technical and organisational measures within the meaning of para. 1 are the following: (i) voluntary appointment of a data protection officer (Art. 37) and other individuals with responsibility for data protection; (ii) offering adequate data protection training and education to staff members; (iii) setting up of procedures to manage access, correction and deletion requests which should be transparent to data subjects; (iv) establishment of an internal complaints handling mechanism; and (v) implementation and supervision of verification procedures to ensure that all the measures not only exist on paper but that they are implemented and work in practice (cf. Art. 29 Working Party, Opinion 3/2010 on the principle of accountability, WP 173 (2010), at 11 et seq.; Art. 22 Madrid Resolution dated 5 November 2009, available at https://icdppc.org/wp-content/uploads/2015/02/The-Madrid-Resolution.pdf).

5   Since the implementation of technical and organisational measures pursuant to para. 1 is necessary "to demonstrate compliance with the obligations of the controller", it could be concluded that the controller bears the burden of proof for compliance with the GDPR (see also Recital 74 sentence 2 which states that the controller should "be able to demonstrate the compliance of processing activities with this Regulation"). However, in the context of a proceeding regarding the imposing of administrative fines pursuant to Art. 83, this would be incompatible with the presumption of innocence pursuant to Art. 48 para. 1 of the Charter. Therefore, the obligation to demonstrate compliance as set out in para. 1 (cf. also Art. 5 para. 2) does **not address the burden of proof** but is rather a **material obligation to demonstrate compliance** (see also Art. 5 cmt. 13).

In contrast to the proposal of the EU Commission (cf. Art. 79 para. 6 lit. e in conjunction with Art. 22 of the proposal of the Commission, COM(2012) 11 final), the GDPR does not contain a provision imposing administrative fines for a violation of the obligation to demonstrate compliance. This obligation is also not covered by a right of the data subject (cf. the catalogue of the rights of the data subject in Art. 12 et seqq.) which excludes the possibility of an enforcement of the obligation by private individuals. However, the obligation to demonstrate compliance is subject to enforcement by the supervisory authorities when making use of their powers pursuant to Art. 58 para. 1 (cf. Art. 5 cmt. 13). In addition, the obligation to demonstrate compliance could be considered in sentencing pursuant to Art. 83 para. 2 lit. f. Moreover, it is possible that the controller has an obligation to demonstrate compliance vis-à-vis the data subject in connection with damage claim proceedings (see Art. 82 cmt. 5) which could lead to disadvantages in case of non-compliance.

6   A regular **data protection audit** pursuant to para. 1 last sentence is not always required (Art. 24 para. 1 says "where necessary") but in most cases.

7   Based on para. 2 (cf. also Recital 78 sentence 2), it can be concluded that there is a general obligation to issue **data protection policies**. Otherwise the demonstration of compliance with the GDPR could be difficult, unless the controller complies with approved codes of conducts pursuant to Art. 40 or with approved certification mechanisms pursuant to Art. 42 (cf. para. 3).

Article 25

Data protection by design and by default[1]

1.[2] Taking into account the state of the art, the cost of implementation and the nature, scope, context and purposes of processing as well as the risks of varying likelihood and severity for rights and freedoms of natural persons posed by the processing, the controller shall, both at the time of the determination of the means for processing and at the time of the processing itself, implement appropriate technical and organisational measures,[3] such as pseudonymisation,[4] which are designed to implement data-protection principles, such as data minimisation,[5] in an effective manner and to integrate the necessary safeguards into the processing in order to meet the requirements of this Regulation and protect the rights of data subjects.

2.[6] The controller shall implement appropriate technical and organisational measures for ensuring that, by default, only personal data which are necessary for each specific purpose of the processing are processed.[7] That obligation applies to the amount of personal data collected, the extent of their processing, the period of their storage and their accessibility. In particular, such measures shall ensure that by default personal data are not made accessible without the individual's intervention to an indefinite number of natural persons.[8]

3. An approved certification mechanism pursuant to Article 42 may be used as an element to demonstrate compliance with the requirements set out in paragraphs 1 and 2 of this Article.

Recital:

(78) The protection of the rights and freedoms of natural persons with regard to the processing of personal data require that appropriate technical and organisational measures be taken to ensure that the requirements of this Regulation are met. In order to be able to demonstrate compliance with this Regulation, the controller should adopt internal policies and implement measures which meet in particular the principles of data protection by design and data protection by default. Such measures could consist, inter alia, of minimising the processing of personal data, pseudonymising personal data as soon as possible, transparency with regard to the functions and processing of personal data, enabling the data subject to monitor the data processing, enabling the controller to create and improve security features. When developing, designing, selecting and using applications, services and products that are based on the processing of personal data or process personal data to fulfil their task, producers of the products, services and applications should be encouraged to take into account the right to data protection when developing and designing such products, services and applications and, with due regard to the state of the art, to make sure that controllers and processors are able to fulfil their data protection obligations. The principles of data protection by design and by default should also be taken into consideration in the context of public tenders.

Commentary:

1   In contrast to the general obligation under Art. 24 to implement risk-appropriate technical and organisational measures, violations of Art. 25 may be subject to administrative fines pursuant to Art. 83 para. 4 lit. a. However, the obligations specifically resulting from Art. 25 are limited (cf. cmts. 3, 7 and 8 below).

    The most substantial practical relevance of Art. 25 could be seen in the provision that the principles of privacy by design (para. 1) and privacy by default (para. 2) **"should also be taken into consideration in the context of public tenders"** (Recital 78 last sentence). Additionally, Recital 78 sentence 4 provides that producers of the products, services and applications should be encouraged to take into account the right to data protection when developing and designing such products, services and applications. That means that data protection requirements become mandatory for public IT tenders.

    Pursuant to the unambiguous wording of paras. 1 and 2, the principles of data protection by design and by default are **not directly applicable to processors**.

2   Para. 1 describes the principle of data protection by design.

3   The **data protection by design measures** that must be implemented have to be determined pursuant to: (i) the technical feasibility ("state of the art"); (ii) the costs of implementation; and (iii) the data protection risks for the data subjects ("the risks of the varying likelihood and severity"). This requires a **risk assessment** (cf. Art. 24 cmt. 2) and a **cost/benefit analysis**.

    Pursuant to Recital 78 sentence 3, such measures could consist, *inter alia*, of: (i) minimising the processing of personal data (cf. Art. 5 para. 1 lit. c); (ii) pseudonymising personal data as soon as possible (cf. Art. 5 para. 1 lit. e); (iii) transparency with regard to the functions and processing of personal data (Art. 12 et seqq.); (iv) enabling the data subject to monitor the data processing; and (v) enabling the controller to create and improve security features (Art. 32). It is noteworthy that the measures contained in that list are measures that are mandatory anyway pursuant to other provisions of the GDPR (cf. the provisions mentioned above in brackets). Therefore, para. 1 will in practice barely set out new obligations for controllers.

4   See Art. 4 No. 5 regarding the definition of the term "pseudonymisation".

5   See Art. 5 para. 1 lit. c.

6   Para. 2 describes the principle of **data protection by default**.

7   The obligation of para. 2 sentence 1 already results from the principles of data minimisation (Art. 5 para. 1 lit. c) and purpose limitation (Art. 5 para. 1 lit. b).

8   The obligation set out in para. 2 last sentence, **to not make accessible personal data to an indefinite number of natural persons by default**, is an obligation that results specifically from para. 2 and is not contained in any other provisions of the GDPR. From a practical perspective, para. 2 last sentence will in particular be of relevance for information society services (cf. Art. 4 No. 24).

Article 26

Joint controllers

1. Where two or more controllers jointly determine the purposes and means of processing, they shall be joint controllers. They shall in a transparent manner determine their respective responsibilities for compliance with the obligations under this Regulation, in particular as regards the exercising of the rights of the data subject and their respective duties to provide the information referred to in Articles 13 and 14, by means of an arrangement between them unless, and in so far as, the respective responsibilities of the controllers are determined by Union or Member State law to which the controllers are subject. The arrangement may designate a contact point for data subjects.

2. The arrangement referred to in paragraph 1 shall duly reflect the respective roles and relationships of the joint controllers vis-à-vis the data subjects.[1] The essence of the arrangement shall be made available to the data subject.[2]

3. Irrespective of the terms of the arrangement referred to in paragraph 1, the data subject may exercise his or her rights under this Regulation in respect of and against each of the controllers.[3]

Recital:

(79) The protection of the rights and freedoms of data subjects as well as the responsibility and liability of controllers and processors, also in relation to the monitoring by and measures of supervisory authorities, requires a clear allocation of the responsibilities under this Regulation, including where a controller determines the purposes and means of the processing jointly with other controllers or where a processing operation is carried out on behalf of a controller.

Commentary:

1   Para. 3 clarifies that both joint controllers are **jointly liable** for the fulfillment of the controller obligations vis-à-vis the data subjects. However, it does not set out the distribution of the liability for administrative fines. On the basis of para. 3, an *argumentum a contrario* can be developed that a particular joint controller is only liable for administrative fines if an obligation was violated that was assigned to that joint controller in the arrangement concluded pursuant to para. 1.

2   The GDPR does not contain any indication concerning the required timing or format of the **information on the "essence of the arrangement"** pursuant to para. 2. From a practical perspective, joint controllers should use the requirements of Art. 12 for guidance and include the information in the privacy statement pursuant to Art. 13 and/or Art. 14.

3   The rights of the data subjects in para. 3 include in particular the right to claim damages pursuant to Art. 82.

Article 27

Representatives of controllers or processors not established in the Union[1]
1. Where Article 3(2) applies, the controller or the processor shall designate in writing a representative[2] in the Union.[3]
2. The obligation laid down in paragraph 1 of this Article shall not apply to:
  (a) processing which is occasional, does not include, on a large scale, processing of special categories of data as referred to in Article 9(1) or processing of personal data relating to criminal convictions and offences referred to in Article 10, and is unlikely to result in a risk to the rights and freedoms of natural persons, taking into account the nature, context, scope and purposes of the processing;[4] or
  (b) a public authority or body.[5]
3. The representative shall be established in one of the Member States where the data subjects, whose personal data are processed in relation to the offering of goods or services to them, or whose behaviour is monitored, are.
4. The representative shall be mandated by the controller or processor to be addressed in addition to or instead of the controller or the processor by, in particular, supervisory authorities and data subjects, on all issues related to processing, for the purposes of ensuring compliance with this Regulation.
5. The designation of a representative by the controller or processor shall be without prejudice to legal actions which could be initiated 'against the controller or the processor themselves.[6]

Recital:
(80) Where a controller or a processor not established in the Union is processing personal data of data subjects who are in the Union whose processing activities are related to the offering of goods or services, irrespective of whether a payment of the data subject is required, to such data subjects in the Union, or to the monitoring of their behaviour as far as their behaviour takes place within the Union, the controller or the processor should designate a representative, unless the processing is occasional, does not include processing, on a large scale, of special categories of personal data or the processing of personal data relating to criminal convictions and offences, and is unlikely to result in a risk to the rights and freedoms of natural persons, taking into account the nature, context, scope and purposes of the processing or if the controller is a public authority or body. The representative should act on behalf of the controller or the processor and may be addressed by any supervisory authority. The representative should be explicitly designated by a written mandate of the controller or of the processor to act on its behalf with regard to its obligations under this Regulation. The designation of such representative does not affect the responsibility or liability of the controller or the processor under this Regulation. Such a representative should perform its tasks according to the mandate received from the controller or processor, including cooperating with the competent supervisory authorities with regard to any action taken to ensure compliance with this Regulation. The designated representative should be subject to enforcement proceedings in the event of non-compliance by the controller or processor.

Commentary:

1   The purpose of a **representative** is to ensure that the competent supervisory authority can execute law enforcement measures against a controller or processor that is not established in the EEA, without being limited to their territorial scope of competence (cf. *Dammann/Simitis*, Data Protection Directive (1997) Art. 4 cmt. 10 regarding Art. 4 para. 2 Data Protection Directive). The last sentence of Recital 80 provides that "the designated representative should be subject to enforcement proceedings in the event of non-compliance by the controller or processor". However, it cannot be concluded that the representative is subject to damage claims (see Art. 82 para. 1 which states that in case of a violation of the GDPR, the data subject has the right to receive compensation "from the controller or processor" only).

2   See Art. 4 No. 17 regarding the definition of the term "representative".

3   Pursuant to Recital 80 sentence 3, the representative should explicitly be designated by a written mandate. The designation must contain the scope of para. 4.

4   The requirements contained in para. 2 lit. a must be fulfilled cumulatively. In particular the requirement of "occasional" processing will rarely be met.

5   See Art. 37 cmt. 2 regarding the definition of the term "public authority or body".

6   The controller's or processor's liability will not be reduced by designating a representative.

Article 28

Processor

1. Where processing is to be carried out on behalf of a controller, the controller shall use only processors providing sufficient guarantees[1] to implement appropriate technical and organisational measures in such a manner that processing will meet the requirements of this Regulation and ensure the protection of the rights of the data subject.

2. The processor shall not engage another processor[2] without prior specific or general written[3] authorisation of the controller. In the case of general written authorisation, the processor shall inform the controller of any intended changes concerning the addition or replacement of other processors, thereby giving the controller the opportunity to object to such changes.[4]

3. Processing by a processor shall be governed by a contract or other legal act under Union or Member State law, that is binding on the processor with regard to the controller and that sets out the subject-matter and duration of the processing, the nature and purpose of the processing, the type of personal data and categories of data subjects and the obligations and rights of the controller.[5] That contract or other legal act shall stipulate, in particular, that the processor:[6]

(a) processes the personal data only on documented instructions from the controller, including with regard to transfers of personal data to a third country or an international organisation,[7] unless required to do so by Union or Member State law to which the processor is subject; in such a case, the processor shall inform the controller of that legal requirement before processing, unless that law prohibits such information on important grounds of public interest;

(b) ensures that persons authorised to process the personal data have committed themselves to confidentiality or are under an appropriate statutory obligation of confidentiality;

(c) takes all measures required pursuant to Article 32;

(d) respects the conditions referred to in paragraphs 2 and 4 for engaging another processor;

(e) taking into account the nature of the processing, assists the controller by appropriate technical and organisational measures, insofar as this is possible, for the fulfilment of the controller's obligation to respond to requests for exercising the data subject's rights laid down in Chapter III;

(f) assists the controller in ensuring compliance with the obligations pursuant to Articles 32 to 36 taking into account the nature of processing and the information available to the processor;[8,9]

(g) at the choice of the controller, deletes or returns all the personal data to the controller after the end of the provision of services relating to processing, and deletes existing copies unless Union or Member State law requires storage of the personal data;

(h) makes available to the controller all information necessary to demonstrate compliance with the obligations laid down in this Article and allow for and contribute to audits, including inspections, conducted by the controller or another auditor mandated by the controller.[10]

With regard to point (h) of the first subparagraph, the processor shall immediately inform the controller if, in its opinion, an instruction infringes this Regulation or other Union or Member State data protection provisions.

4. Where a processor engages another processor[11] for carrying out specific processing activities on behalf of the controller, the same data protection obligations as set out in the contract or other legal act between the controller and the processor as referred to in paragraph 3 shall be imposed on that other processor by way of a contract or other legal act under Union or Member State law, in particular providing sufficient guarantees[12] to implement appropriate technical and organisational measures in such a manner that the processing will meet the requirements of this Regulation. Where that other processor fails to fulfil its data protection obligations, the initial processor shall remain fully liable to the controller for the performance of that other processor's obligations.[13]

5. Adherence of a processor to an approved code of conduct as referred to in Article 40 or an approved certification mechanism as referred to in Article 42 may be used as an element by which to demonstrate sufficient guarantees as referred to in paragraphs 1 and 4 of this Article.

6. Without prejudice to an individual contract between the controller and the processor, the contract or the other legal act referred to in paragraphs 3 and 4 of this Article may be based, in whole or in part, on standard contractual clauses referred to in paragraphs 7 and 8 of this Article,[14] including when they are part of a certification granted to the controller or processor pursuant to Articles 42 and 43.

7. The Commission may lay down standard contractual clauses[15] for the matters referred to in paragraph 3 and 4 of this Article and in accordance with the examination procedure referred to in Article 93(2).

8. A supervisory authority may adopt standard contractual clauses for the matters referred to in paragraph 3 and 4 of this Article and in accordance with the consistency mechanism referred to in Article 63.[16]

9. The contract or the other legal act referred to in paragraphs 3 and 4 shall be in writing, including in electronic form.

10. Without prejudice to Articles 82, 83 and 84, if a processor infringes this Regulation by determining the purposes and means of processing, the processor shall be considered to be a controller in respect of that processing.[17]

Recital:

(81) *To ensure compliance with the requirements of this Regulation in respect of the processing to be carried out by the processor on behalf of the controller, when entrusting a processor with processing activities, the controller should use only processors providing sufficient guarantees, in particular in terms of expert knowledge, reliability and resources, to implement technical and organisational measures which will meet the requirements of this Regulation, including for the security of processing.*

The adherence of the processor to an approved code of conduct or an approved certification mechanism may be used as an element to demonstrate compliance with the obligations of the controller. The carrying-out of processing by a processor should be governed by a contract or other legal act under Union or Member State law, binding the processor to the controller, setting out the subject-matter and duration of the processing, the nature and purposes of the processing, the type of personal data and categories of data subjects, taking into account the specific tasks and responsibilities of the processor in the context of the processing to be carried out and the risk to the rights and freedoms of the data subject. The controller and processor may choose to use an individual contract or standard contractual clauses which are adopted either directly by the Commission or by a supervisory authority in accordance with the consistency mechanism and then adopted by the Commission. After the completion of the processing on behalf of the controller, the processor should, at the choice of the controller, return or delete the personal data, unless there is a requirement to store the personal data under Union or Member State law to which the processor is subject.

Commentary:

1 Pursuant to para. 5 the guarantees mentioned in para. 1 can be demonstrated by the processor by complying with approved codes of conduct pursuant to Art. 40 or with approved certification mechanisms pursuant to Art. 42 (cf. also Recital 81 sentence 2). For the area of data security, certifications pursuant to technical standards are also common, in particular certifications pursuant to ISO/IEC 27001:2013, "Information technology – Security techniques – Information security management systems – Requirements".

2 The term "another processor" does not clarify whether para. 2 only covers **subprocessors** (ie, processors which were engaged by the processor in its own name) or also setups where the processor receives a power of attorney from the controller to engage additional processors by concluding data processing agreements in the name of the controller. From a practical perspective, it is recommended to assume that both setups are covered by the term "another processor" until clarified by the CJEU.

3 To approve a subprocessor, a stricter formal requirement than that of the original data processing agreement should not apply. Therefore, electronic form is sufficient (cf. para. 9).

4 Para. 2 does not clarify to what extent the controller's decision autonomy may be limited. For example, if the processor has a right to terminate the agreement with the controller for cause in case the controller objects to the subprocessor, the controller's autonomy would be limited. This applies in particular if the change from one processor to another processor would require substantial time and financial resources on the controller's part.

5 Regarding the level of detail of the subject matter and duration of the processing, the nature and purpose of the processing, the type of personal data and categories of data subjects and the obligations and rights of the controller, **appendix 1 of the standard contractual clauses (Commission decision 2010/87/EC) may provide guidance** from a practical perspective.

6   **Present data processing agreements** that, for example, in Austria include the minimum requirements pursuant to Sec. 11 of the Austrian Data Protection Act 2000, or in Germany include the minimum requirements pursuant to Sec. 11 of the currently applicable German Data Protection Act, do not comply with these requirements – see in particular cmt. 8 regarding para. 3 lit. f and cmt. 10 regarding para. 3 lit. h.

7   See Art. 4 No. 26 regarding the definition of the term "international organisation".

8   Para. 3 lit. f goes beyond what is required, for example, pursuant to Sec. 11 Austrian Data Protection Act 2000 and Sec. 11 German Data Protection Act. In particular, para. 3 lit. f requires that the processor is contractually obligated to inform the controller about personal data breaches, so that the controller can comply with its information obligation pursuant to Art. 33 et seq. (cf. also Art. 33 para. 2).

9   Since the right to data portability does not apply between controllers and processors (see Art. 20 cmt. 4), there is a high risk for the controller that para. 3 lit. g does not contain a right to receive the data in a particular (reusable) format. Controllers should expressly include such a right in the agreement.

10 The processor's obligation to not only provide information but also to **allow for and contribute to audits** pursuant to para. 3 lit. h goes beyond what was necessary under the Austrian Data Protection Act 2000, but corresponds, for example, with the opinion of the German data protection authorities regarding the current German Data Protection Act. It is noteworthy that the processor must have the right to conduct the audit by itself or to engage an auditor. An audit conducted by an auditor engaged by the processor would not be sufficient pursuant to the plain language of para. 3 lit. g.

11 See cmt. 2 above regarding the term "another processor".

12 See cmt. 1 above.

13 Para. 4 last sentence provides for a liability as a vicarious agent.

14 Para. 6 clarifies that the use of standard contractual clauses pursuant to paras. 7 and 8 is not mandatory.

15 In contrast to the Data Protection Directive and the past legal practice, the GDPR uses the term "**standard contractual clauses**" not only to designate contract terms that should compensate the lack of an adequate level of data protection in a third country, but also to designate contract terms which apply to a processor located in the EU, respectively the EEA. The latter clauses could also be designated as "intra-EU standard contractual clauses".

    Furthermore, the GDPR also uses the term "standard data protection clauses" as a synonym for "standard contractual clauses" (cf. Art. 58 para. 3 lit. g).

16 Before adopting standard contractual clauses pursuant to para. 8, they must be presented to the Board for it to issue an opinion (Art. 64 para. 1 lit. d).

17 Cf. also Art. 29.

Article 29

Processing under the authority of the controller or processor

The processor and any person acting under the authority of the controller or of the processor, who has access to personal data, shall not process those data except on instructions from the controller, unless required to do so by Union or Member State law.[1]

Commentary:

1   A violation of Art. 29 has the consequence that the processor, respectively the person acting under its authority, will be qualified as a controller (see Art. 28 para. 10).

Article 30

Records of processing activities

1. Each controller and, where applicable, the controller's representative,[1] shall maintain a record of processing activities[2] under its responsibility. That record shall contain all of the following information:[3]

    (a) the name and contact details[4] of the controller and, where applicable, the joint controller, the controller's representative and the data protection officer;

    (b) the purposes of the processing;

    (c) a description of the categories of data subjects and of the categories of personal data;

    (d) the categories of recipients[5] to whom the personal data have been or will be disclosed including recipients in third countries or international organisations;

    (e) where applicable, transfers of personal data to a third country or an international organisation,[6] including the identification of that third country or international organisation and, in the case of transfers referred to in the second subparagraph of Article 49(1), the documentation of suitable safeguards;[7]

    (f) where possible, the envisaged time limits for erasure of the different categories of data;

    (g) where possible, a general description of the technical and organisational security measures referred to in Article 32(1).

2. Each processor and, where applicable, the processor's representative shall maintain a record of all categories of processing activities carried out on behalf of a controller, containing:[8]

    (a) the name and contact details of the processor or processors and of each controller on behalf of which the processor is acting, and, where applicable, of the controller's or the processor's representative, and the data protection officer;

    (b) the categories of processing carried out on behalf of each controller;

    (c) where applicable, transfers of personal data to a third country or an international organisation, including the identification of that third country or international organisation and, in the case of transfers referred to in the second subparagraph of Article 49(1), the documentation of suitable safeguards;[9]

    (d) where possible, a general description of the technical and organisational security measures referred to in Article 32(1).

3. The records referred to in paragraphs 1 and 2 shall be in writing, including in electronic form.

4. The controller or the processor and, where applicable, the controller's or the processor's representative, shall make the record available to the supervisory authority[10] on request.[11]

5. The obligations referred to in paragraphs 1 and 2 shall not apply to an

enterprise[12] or an organisation employing fewer than 250 persons[13] unless the processing it carries out is likely to result in a risk to the rights and freedoms of data subjects, the processing is not occasional, or the processing includes special categories of data as referred to in Article 9(1) or personal data relating to criminal convictions and offences referred to in Article 10.

Recital:

(82) In order to demonstrate compliance with this Regulation, the controller or processor should maintain records of processing activities under its responsibility. Each controller and processor should be obliged to cooperate with the supervisory authority and make those records, on request, available to it, so that it might serve for monitoring those processing operations.

Commentary:

1   See Art. 4 No. 17 regarding the definition of the term "representative". Despite the fact that para. 1 also requires the representative to maintain records of processing activities, Art. 83 para. 4 lit. a only provides for fines in case of violations of "obligations of the controller or the processor".

2   The term **processing activity** which is not defined in the GDPR generally corresponds with the term "data application" in the Austrian Data Protection Act 2000 and the term "processing activity" in the German Data Protection Act. The term "processing activity" can be understood as the sum of all data processing for a particular purpose or for several related purposes. This applies irrespective of which and how many software products are used to carry out the processing.

3   The information that must be included in the record pursuant to para. 1 must to a large extent also be included in the notice to the data subjects pursuant to Art. 13 et seq. This does not apply to: (i) the name of the data protection officer pursuant to para. 1 lit. a; and (ii) the general description of the technical and organisational security measures pursuant to para. 1 lit. g.

4   See Art. 13 cmt. 7 regarding the definition of the term "contact details".

5   See Art. 4 No. 9 regarding the definition of the term "recipient" which does not include public authorities which may receive personal data in the framework of a particular inquiry in accordance with Union or Member State law. Pursuant to the wording of para. 1 lit. d in conjunction with Art. 4 No. 9, a lawful transfer to law enforcement agencies of a Member State does not have to be documented. However, a controller would be well advised to document such a transfer in order to comply with its burden of proof (Art. 24 cmt. 5).

6   See Art. 4 No. 26 regarding the definition of the term "international organisation".

7   Together with data transfers pursuant to Art. 49 para. 1 subpara. 2 that are mentioned in para. 1 lit. e, the conducted assessment also has to be documented (Art. 49 para. 6).

8   Para. 2 provides an **obligation for processors to maintain a record** which is independent from the record of the controller. The record to be maintained by

a processor does not have to contain all "processing activities" (cf. para. 1), but only "all categories of processing activities carried out on behalf of a controller", that is, the record can be more general.

9 Together with the data transfers pursuant to Art. 49 para. 1 subpara. 2 that are mentioned in para. 2 lit. c, the conducted assessment also has to be documented (Art. 49 para. 6).

10 By implication of para. 4, there is **no obligation to provide the records of processing activities to the data subject.**

11 Regarding the obligation to cooperate with the supervisory authority in general, see Art. 31.

12 See Art. 4 No. 18 regarding the definition of the term "enterprise".

13 Cf. Recital 13 which states that the exception in para. 5 was introduced to "take account of the specific situation of micro, small and medium-sized enterprises".

Article 31

Cooperation with the supervisory authority

The controller and the processor and, where applicable, their representatives,[1] shall cooperate, on request, with the supervisory authority in the performance of its tasks.[2]

Commentary:

1   See Art. 4 No. 17 regarding the definition of the term "representative". Despite the fact that para. 1 also requires the representative to cooperate with the supervisory authority, Art. 83 para. 4 lit. a only provides for fines in case of violations of "obligations of the controller or the processor".

2   A violation of the obligation to cooperate can be **sanctioned with administrative fines** pursuant to Art. 83 para. 4 lit. a. This is very problematic in light of the privilege against [...] self-incrimination (**nemo tenetur principle**) deriving from the right to a fair trial (Art. 47 para. 2 Charter), in particular since the degree of cooperation must be taken into account anyway when deciding whether to impose a fine and when deciding on the amount of the fine. To interpret the provision in line with fundamental rights, it must be assumed that the obligation to cooperate applies only to the extent that it does not result in a risk of self-incrimination.

Section 2 – Security of personal data

Article 32

Security of processing[1]
1. Taking into account the state of the art, the costs of implementation and the nature, scope, context and purposes of processing as well as the risk of varying likelihood[2] and severity for the rights and freedoms of natural persons, the controller and the processor[3] shall implement appropriate technical and organisational measures[4] to ensure a level of security[5,6] appropriate to the risk, including[7] inter alia as appropriate:[8]
    (a) the pseudonymisation[9] and encryption of personal data;
    (b) the ability to ensure the ongoing confidentiality, integrity, availability and resilience of processing systems and services;[10]
    (c) the ability to restore the availability and access to personal data in a timely manner in the event of a physical or technical incident;[11]
    (d) a process for regularly testing, assessing and evaluating the effectiveness of technical and organisational measures for ensuring the security of the processing.
2. In assessing the appropriate level of security account shall be taken in particular of the risks that are presented by processing, in particular from accidental or unlawful destruction, loss, alteration, unauthorised disclosure of, or access to personal data transmitted, stored or otherwise processed.[12]
3. Adherence to an approved code of conduct as referred to in Article 40 or an approved certification mechanism as referred to in Article 42 may be used as an element by which to demonstrate compliance with the requirements set out in paragraph 1 of this Article.
4. The controller and processor shall take steps to ensure that any natural person acting under the authority of the controller or the processor who has access to personal data does not process them except on instructions from the controller, unless he or she is required to do so by Union or Member State law.

Recitals:
(83) In order to maintain security and to prevent processing in infringement of this Regulation, the controller or processor should evaluate the risks inherent in the processing and implement measures to mitigate those risks, such as encryption. Those measures should ensure an appropriate level of security, including confidentiality, taking into account the state of the art and the costs of implementation in relation to the risks and the nature of the personal data to be protected. In assessing data security risk, consideration should be given to the risks that are presented by personal data processing, such as accidental or unlawful destruction, loss, alteration, unauthorised disclosure of, or access to, personal data transmitted, stored or otherwise processed which may in particular lead to physical, material or non-material damage.
[Recital 84 can be found with Art. 35.]

Commentary:

1   The subject matter of Art. 32 are the technical and organisational measures to protect the **confidentiality, integrity, and availability** of personal data (see cmt. 6 below). Technical and organisational measures to protection the lawfulness of the processing are the subject matter of Art. 24.

Not every violation of the security to be provided pursuant to Art. 33 constitutes a "personal data breach" within the meaning of Art. 4 No. 12 and therefore does not trigger a notification obligation pursuant to Art. 33 et seq. For example, temporary violations of the availability of personal data must be prevented pursuant to Art. 32 but do not trigger a notification obligation pursuant to Art. 33 et seq. (see cmt. 6 below).

2   Pursuant to the last sentence of Recital 83, "in assessing data security risk, consideration should be given to the risks that are presented by personal data processing, such as accidental or unlawful destruction, loss, alteration, unauthorised disclosure of, or access to, personal data". In particular it should be taken into consideration, whether it "may lead to physical, material or non-material damage".

Art. 32 – in contrast to Art. 24 – does not indicate which type of risk assessment should be performed. In general, a **qualitative risk assessment** (ie, a ranking of risks in risk classes) and a **quantitative risk assessment** (ie, a mathematical calculation) as well as a mixture of both could be considered. When conducting a quantitative risk assessment, risks are usually represented in monetary figures which, in practice, often is the expected annual damage – the Annualised Loss Expectancy (ALE). ALE is defined as the mathematical product of the potential damage and the likelihood of occurrence as follows (cf., eg, Landoll, *The Security Risk Assessment Handbook* (2006) 416; Endorf, "Measuring ROI on Security" in Tipton/Krause (editors), *Information Security Management Handbook*6 (2007) 133 (135)):

ALE = Annual Rate of Occurrence (ARO) × Single Loss Expectancy (SLE)

The amount of damage in case of a one-time occurrence of the event (SLE) could be determined on the basis of the "physical, material or non-material damage" mentioned in the last sentence of Recital 83. The quantification of damage is a significant challenge but a necessity in any case for the purposes of Art. 82. Calculation models will therefore have to be developed.

In contrast, the Annual Rate of Occurrence (ARO) can be determined to a large extent on the basis of past experience. Therefore, a quantification of individual data security risks is possible and the "costs of implementation" of a security measure mentioned in para. 1 could be contrasted directly with the calculated ALE to determine whether the respective security measure is appropriate.

3   The obligations pursuant to Art. 32 do **not only apply to the controller but also to the processor** – in contrast with the obligations in Art. 24 and in Art. 17 Data Protection Directive.

4   The term "technical and organisational measures" or "TOMs" is used for the measures required pursuant to Art. 24 and for the necessary data security

measures pursuant to Art. 32 (see also Art. 24 cmt. 4). The following table shows the connection between the TOMs to be implemented by a controller and a processor and the notification obligation in case of security breaches (cf. also Art. 33 cmt. 2):

	Controller		Processor	
	TOM	Breach Notification	TOM	Breach Notification
Confidentiality	Art. 32	Art. 33 et seq.	Art. 32	Art. 33 para. 2
Integrity	Art. 32	Art. 33 et seq.	Art. 32	Art. 33 para. 2
General availability	Art. 32	Art. 33 et seq.	Art. 32	Art. 33 para. 2
uninterrupted availability	Art. 32		Art. 32	
Lawfulness	Art. 24			

5   The German version of the GDPR incorrectly uses the term "protection" ("Schutz") as a synonym for "security". The heading of Art. 32 says "security of processing" ("Sicherheit der Verarbeitung"), whereas para. 1 sentence 1 uses the term "level of protection" ("Schutzniveau"). The English version of the GDPR constantly uses "security" – in the heading "Security of processing" and in para. 1 sentence 1 "level of security".

6   The GDPR does not explicitly define the term "**security**". However, from para. 2 it can be derived that personal data pursuant to para. 1 must be protected against violations of: (i) availability ("destruction, loss"); (ii) integrity ("alteration"); and (iii) confidentiality ("unauthorized disclosure" and "unauthorized access"). The protection against "accidental or unlawful" processing used in Art. 17 para. 1 Data Protection Directive and mentioned in Art. 5 para. 1 lit. f is not the subject matter of Art. 32 but of Art. 24 (cf. also Art. 5 cmt. 11).

    From the security measures mentioned in para. 1 lit. b and c, it can be derived that personal data must be protected against a temporary loss of availability which is more than Art. 17 Data Protection Directive required (cf. Feiler, "Risikoadäquate Datensicherheitsmaßnahmen gemäß § 14 DSG 2000 – Eine kritische Betrachtung" in Jahnel (Hrsg), *Jahrbuch Datenschutzrecht* (2015) 97 (99)). However, such a **temporary loss of availability** does not constitute a personal data breach pursuant to Art. 4 No. 12 and therefore does not result in a notification obligation pursuant to Art. 33 et seq. (cf. Art. 4 cmt. 30).

7   Although it is not strictly mandatory to implement the measures mentioned in para. 1 lit. a to d, they will in most cases be regarded as part of the measures required under para. 1.

8   In the area of information security it is common practice to classify security measures based on their nature and effect: Based on their effect, they can be **deterrent** (eg, a disciplinary policy), **preventive** (eg, encryption measures, cf. para. 1 lit. a), **detective** (eg, a network-based intrusion detection system), or

reactive (eg, a data recovery system, cf. para. 1 lit. c). Based on their nature, security measures can be **technical** (eg, anti-virus software), **organisational** (eg, employee training), or **physical** (eg, a lock) (cf. Feiler, *Information Security Law in the EU and the U.S.* (2011) 61).

9   See Art. 4 No. 5 regarding the definition of the term "pseudonymisation".

10   To the extent personal data is processed in IT systems, the security of these systems constitutes a logic pre-condition for the security of the personal data. Therefore, it is appropriate that para. 1 lit. b requires measures of IT security.

11   Para. 1 lit. c requires **reactive measures** which enable a recovery after an incident. These include in particular data **backup and restore processes.**

12   The list of protection objectives does not – in contrast to Art. 17 para. 1 Data Protection Directive and Art. 5 para. 1 lit. f – include the protection against the risk of "accidental and unlawful" processing. This protection objective and any related measures are not the subject matter of Art. 32 but of Art. 24 (cf. cmt. 6 above and Art. 5 cmt. 11).

Article 33

Notification of a personal data breach to the supervisory authority[1]

1. In the case of a personal data breach,[2] the controller shall without undue delay[3] and, where feasible, not later than 72 hours after having become aware of it, notify the personal data breach to the supervisory authority competent in accordance with Article 55,[4] unless the personal data breach is unlikely to result in a risk to the rights and freedoms of natural persons[5] Where the notification to the supervisory authority is not made within 72 hours, it shall be accompanied by reasons for the delay.

2. The processor shall notify the controller without undue delay after becoming aware of a personal data breach.[6]

3. The notification referred to in paragraph 1 shall at least:[7]
    (a) describe the nature of the personal data breach including where possible, the categories and approximate number of data subjects concerned and the categories and approximate number of personal data records concerned;
    (b) communicate the name and contact details of the data protection officer or other contact point where more information can be obtained;
    (c) describe the likely consequences of the personal data breach;
    (d) describe the measures taken or proposed to be taken by the controller to address the personal data breach, including, where appropriate, measures to mitigate its possible adverse effects.

4. Where, and in so far as, it is not possible to provide the information at the same time, the information may be provided in phases without undue further delay.

5. The controller shall document any personal data breaches,[8] comprising the facts relating to the personal data breach, its effects and the remedial action taken. That documentation shall enable the supervisory authority to verify compliance with this Article.

Recital:

(85) A personal data breach may, if not addressed in an appropriate and timely manner, result in physical, material or non-material damage to natural persons such as loss of control over their personal data or limitation of their rights, discrimination, identity theft or fraud, financial loss, unauthorised reversal of pseudonymisation, damage to reputation, loss of confidentiality of personal data protected by professional secrecy or any other significant economic or social disadvantage to the natural person concerned. Therefore, as soon as the controller becomes aware that a personal data breach has occurred, the controller should notify the personal data breach to the supervisory authority without undue delay and, where feasible, not later than 72 hours after having become aware of it, unless the controller is able to demonstrate, in accordance with the accountability principle, that the personal data breach is unlikely to result in a risk to the rights and freedoms of natural persons. Where such notification cannot be achieved within 72 hours, the reasons for the delay should accompany the notification and information may be provided in phases without undue further delay.

Commentary:

1   The obligation to notify personal data breaches is in practice often called "**data breach notification**". The obligation to **notify the supervisory authority** applies pursuant to Art. 33 if there is a risk for the rights and freedoms of natural persons which generally applies save for exceptional cases ("unless..."). The **obligation to notify the data subject** pursuant to Art. 34 only applies if the risk is high. Irrespective of the degree of the risk, every data breach must be **documented** by the controller (Art. 33 para. 5).

    The details of the information obligation vis-à-vis the supervisory authority (Art. 70 para. 1 lit. g) and vis-à-vis the data subject (Art. 70 para. 1 lit. h) can be stipulated by the Board in guidelines, recommendations and best practices.

2   See Art. 4 No. 12 regarding the definition of the term "**personal data breach**" which includes a permanent violation of the availability, a violation of the integrity and a violation of the confidentiality of personal data. Therefore, a temporary violation of availability (eg, a server outage) does not qualify as a "personal data breach". Notwithstanding the foregoing, measures pursuant to Art. 32 have to be implemented to prevent such temporary loss of availability (Art. 32 cmt. 4 and 6).

    Pursuant to Art. 70 para. 1 lit. g, the Board may issue guidelines, recommendations and best practices for establishing what constitutes a personal data breach and for the particular circumstances in which a controller or a processor is required to notify the personal data breach.

3   Pursuant to Art. 70 para. 1 lit. g, the Board may issue guidelines, recommendations and best practices for determining the undue delay.

4   Since para. 1 only refers to the general competence pursuant to Art. 55, it could be assumed that a notification to the competent supervisory authority is also required if there is a lead competence pursuant to Art. 56. However, Art. 56 para. 6 stipulates that "the **lead supervisory authority shall be the sole interlocutor** of the controller or processor for the cross-border processing carried out by that controller or processor". Therefore, if there is a lead competence pursuant to Art. 56, it can be assumed that a notification of a personal data breach must only be made to the lead authority.

    However, if there is no lead competence, the notification must be made to the authority competent in general. Therefore, in many cases it might be required to notify the supervisory authorities of multiple Member States (see Art. 55 cmt. 5).

5   Therefore, the notification obligation does not apply if there is no risk for the rights and freedoms of natural persons. This would, for example, be the case if the data was **encrypted** using a secure cryptographic method and the required cryptographic key was neither compromised nor could it be guessed or calculated, in particular due to insufficient complexity of the key.

6   Regarding the requirement of a **contractual arrangement** concerning the notification obligation of the processor vis-à-vis the controller, see Art. 28 para. 3 lit. f.

7   The minimum content for the notification listed in para. 3 must also apply to the **notification obligation of the processor** pursuant to para. 2.

8   The **documentation obligation** pursuant to para. 5 applies to every personal data breach, irrespective of whether the breach leads to a risk for the rights and freedoms of natural persons and, thus, a notification obligation pursuant to para. 1.

Article 34

Communication of a personal data breach to the data subject[1]

1. When the personal data breach[2] is likely to result in a high risk[3] to the rights and freedoms of natural persons, the controller shall communicate[4] the personal data breach to the data subject without undue delay.[5]

2. The communication to the data subject referred to in paragraph 1 of this Article shall describe in clear and plain language the nature of the personal data breach and contain at least the information and measures referred to in points (b), (c) and (d) of Article 33(3).[6]

3. The communication to the data subject referred to in paragraph 1 shall not be required if any of the following conditions are met:

   (a) the controller has implemented appropriate technical and organisational protection measures, and those measures were applied to the personal data affected by the personal data breach, in particular those that render the personal data unintelligible to any person who is not authorised to access it, such as encryption;

   (b) the controller has taken subsequent measures which ensure that the high risk to the rights and freedoms of data subjects referred to in paragraph 1 is no longer likely to materialise;

   (c) it would involve disproportionate effort. In such a case, there shall instead be a public communication or similar measure whereby the data subjects are informed in an equally effective manner.

4. If the controller has not already communicated the personal data breach to the data subject, the supervisory authority, having considered the likelihood of the personal data breach resulting in a high risk, may require it to do so or may decide that any of the conditions referred to in paragraph 3 are met.

Recitals:

(86) The controller should communicate to the data subject a personal data breach, without undue delay, where that personal data breach is likely to result in a high risk to the rights and freedoms of the natural person in order to allow him or her to take the necessary precautions. The communication should describe the nature of the personal data breach as well as recommendations for the natural person concerned to mitigate potential adverse effects. Such communications to data subjects should be made as soon as reasonably feasible and in close cooperation with the supervisory authority, respecting guidance provided by it or by other relevant authorities such as law-enforcement authorities. For example, the need to mitigate an immediate risk of damage would call for prompt communication with data subjects whereas the need to implement appropriate measures against continuing or similar personal data breaches may justify more time for communication.

(87) It should be ascertained whether all appropriate technological protection and organisational measures have been implemented to establish immediately whether a personal data breach has taken place and to inform promptly the supervisory authority and the data subject. The fact that the notification was made without undue delay

should be established taking into account in particular the nature and gravity of the personal data breach and its consequences and adverse effects for the data subject. Such notification may result in an intervention of the supervisory authority in accordance with its tasks and powers laid down in this Regulation.

(88) In setting detailed rules concerning the format and procedures applicable to the notification of personal data breaches, due consideration should be given to the circumstances of that breach, including whether or not personal data had been protected by appropriate technical protection measures, effectively limiting the likelihood of identity fraud or other forms of misuse. Moreover, such rules and procedures should take into account the legitimate interests of law-enforcement authorities where early disclosure could unnecessarily hamper the investigation of the circumstances of a personal data breach.

Commentary:

1   The **purpose of the information obligation** to the data subject is "to allow him or her to take the necessary precautions" (Recital 86 sentence 1) in order to mitigate the consequences of the breach as much as possible.

The details of the information obligation may be stipulated by the Board in guidelines, recommendations and best practices (Art. 70 para. 1 lit. h).

2   See Art. 4 No. 12 regarding the definition of the term "**personal data breach**" which includes a permanent violation of the availability, a violation of the integrity and a violation of the confidentiality of personal data. Therefore, a temporary violation of availability (eg, a server outage) does not qualify as a "personal data breach". Notwithstanding the foregoing, measures pursuant to Art. 32 have to be implemented to prevent such temporary losses of availability (Art. 32 cmt. 6).

3   There is a **high risk** within the meaning of para. 1 in particular if there is a violation of the security of a data processing activity that required a data protection impact assessment pursuant to Art. 35.

The Board may issue guidelines, recommendations and best practices as to the circumstances in which a personal data breach is likely to result in a high risk to the rights and freedoms of natural persons (Art. 70 para. 1 lit. h).

4   See Art. 12 regarding the **form and method of the notification**; in particular, the notification may also be provided electronically (eg, via email; Art. 12 para. 1 sentence 2).

5   Pursuant to the last sentence of Recital 86 "**prompt communication** with data subjects" is required if there is a "**need to mitigate an immediate risk of damage**", "whereas the need to implement appropriate measures against continuing or similar personal data breaches may justify more time for communication".

Regarding the question whether the notification was made without undue delay, Recital 87 outlines that "it should be ascertained whether all appropriate technological protection and organisational measures have been implemented to establish immediately whether a personal data breach has taken place and to inform promptly the supervisory authority and the data subject". Therefore, it can be assumed that appropriate detective security measures must be implemented (eg, intrusion detection systems) to comply with the obligation of providing the notification without undue delay.

6   The data subjects do not have to be notified about: (i) the categories and approximate number of data subjects concerned; and (ii) the categories and the approximate number of personal data records concerned. This reduces transparency but lowers the controller's barrier for a notification to the data subjects.

In addition to the information mentioned in para. 2, the notification to the data subject must also include "**recommendations (…) to mitigate potential adverse effects**" (Recital 86 sentence 2).

Section 3 – Data protection impact assessment and prior consultation

Article 35

Data protection impact assessment[1]

1. Where a type of processing in particular using new technologies, and taking into account the nature, scope, context and purposes of the processing, is likely to result in a high risk to the rights and freedoms of natural persons,[2] the controller[3] shall, prior[4] to the processing, carry out an assessment of the impact of the envisaged processing operations on the protection of personal data. A single assessment may address a set of similar processing operations that present similar high risks.[5]

2. The controller shall seek the advice of the data protection officer, where designated, when carrying out a data protection impact assessment.

3. A data protection impact assessment referred to in paragraph 1 shall in particular be required in the case of:[6]

(a) a systematic and extensive evaluation of personal aspects relating to natural persons which is based on automated processing, including profiling,[7] and on which decisions are based that produce legal effects concerning the natural person or similarly significantly affect the natural person;

(b) processing on a large scale[8] of special categories of data referred to in Article 9(1), or of personal data relating to criminal convictions and offences referred to in Article 10; or

(c) a systematic monitoring of a publicly accessible area on a large scale.[9]

4. The supervisory authority[10] shall establish and make public[11] a list of the kind of processing operations which are subject to the requirement for a data protection impact assessment pursuant to paragraph 1. The supervisory authority shall communicate those lists to the Board referred to in Article 68.[12]

5. The supervisory authority[13] may also establish and make public a list of the kind of processing operations for which no data protection impact assessment is required.[14] The supervisory authority shall communicate those lists to the Board.

6. Prior to the adoption of the lists referred to in paragraphs 4 and 5, the competent supervisory authority shall apply the consistency mechanism referred to in Article 63 where such lists involve processing activities which are related to the offering of goods or services to data subjects or to the monitoring of their behaviour in several Member States, or may substantially affect the free movement of personal data within the Union.[15]

7. The assessment shall contain at least:[16]

(a) a systematic description of the envisaged processing operations and the purposes of the processing, including, where applicable, the legitimate interest pursued by the controller;

(b) an assessment of the necessity and proportionality of the processing operations in relation to the purposes;

(c) an assessment of the risks to the rights and freedoms of data subjects referred to in paragraph 1;[17] and

(d) the measures envisaged to address the risks, including safeguards, security measures and mechanisms to ensure the protection of personal data and to demonstrate compliance with this Regulation taking into account the rights and legitimate interests of data subjects and other persons concerned.

8. Compliance with approved codes of conduct referred to in Article 40 by the relevant controllers or processors shall be taken into due account in assessing the impact of the processing operations performed by such controllers or processors, in particular for the purposes of a data protection impact assessment.[18]

9. Where appropriate, the controller shall seek the views of data subjects or their representatives[19] on the intended processing, without prejudice to the protection of commercial or public interests or the security of processing operations.

10. Where processing pursuant to point (c) or (e) of Article 6(1) has a legal basis in Union law or in the law of the Member State to which the controller is subject, that law regulates the specific processing operation or set of operations in question, and a data protection impact assessment has already been carried out as part of a general impact assessment in the context of the adoption of that legal basis, paragraphs 1 to 7 shall not apply unless Member States deem it to be necessary to carry out such an assessment prior to processing activities.[20]

11. Where necessary, the controller shall carry out a review to assess if processing is performed in accordance with the data protection impact assessment at least when there is a change of the risk represented by processing operations.[21]

Recitals:

(84) *In order to enhance compliance with this Regulation where processing operations are likely to result in a high risk to the rights and freedoms of natural persons, the controller should be responsible for the carrying-out of a data protection impact assessment to evaluate, in particular, the origin, nature, particularity and severity of that risk. The outcome of the assessment should be taken into account when determining the appropriate measures to be taken in order to demonstrate that the processing of personal data complies with this Regulation. Where a data-protection impact assessment indicates that processing operations involve a high risk which the controller cannot mitigate by appropriate measures in terms of available technology and costs of implementation, a consultation of the supervisory authority should take place prior to the processing.*

(89) *Directive 95/46/EC provided for a general obligation to notify the processing of personal data to the supervisory authorities. While that obligation produces administrative and financial burdens, it did not in all cases contribute to improving the protection of personal data. Such indiscriminate general notification obligations should therefore be abolished, and replaced by effective procedures and mechanisms which focus instead on those types of processing operations which are likely to result in a high risk to the rights and freedoms of natural persons by virtue of their nature, scope, context and purposes. Such types of processing operations may be those which*

in, particular, involve using new technologies, or are of a new kind and where no data protection impact assessment has been carried out before by the controller, or where they become necessary in the light of the time that has elapsed since the initial processing.

(90) In such cases, a data protection impact assessment should be carried out by the controller prior to the processing in order to assess the particular likelihood and severity of the high risk, taking into account the nature, scope, context and purposes of the processing and the sources of the risk. That impact assessment should include, in particular, the measures, safeguards and mechanisms envisaged for mitigating that risk, ensuring the protection of personal data and demonstrating compliance with this Regulation.

(91) This should in particular apply to large-scale processing operations which aim to process a considerable amount of personal data at regional, national or supranational level and which could affect a large number of data subjects and which are likely to result in a high risk, for example, on account of their sensitivity, where in accordance with the achieved state of technological knowledge a new technology is used on a large scale as well as to other processing operations which result in a high risk to the rights and freedoms of data subjects, in particular where those operations render it more difficult for data subjects to exercise their rights. A data protection impact assessment should also be made where personal data are processed for taking decisions regarding specific natural persons following any systematic and extensive evaluation of personal aspects relating to natural persons based on profiling those data or following the processing of special categories of personal data, biometric data, or data on criminal convictions and offences or related security measures. A data protection impact assessment is equally required for monitoring publicly accessible areas on a large scale, especially when using optic-electronic devices or for any other operations where the competent supervisory authority considers that the processing is likely to result in a high risk to the rights and freedoms of data subjects, in particular because they prevent data subjects from exercising a right or using a service or a contract, or because they are carried out systematically on a large scale. The processing of personal data should not be considered to be on a large scale if the processing concerns personal data from patients or clients by an individual physician, other health care professional or lawyer. In such cases, a data protection impact assessment should not be mandatory.

(92) There are circumstances under which it may be reasonable and economical for the subject of a data protection impact assessment to be broader than a single project, for example where public authorities or bodies intend to establish a common application or processing platform or where several controllers plan to introduce a common application or processing environment across an industry sector or segment or for a widely used horizontal activity.

(93) In the context of the adoption of the Member State law on which the performance of the tasks of the public authority or public body is based and which regulates the specific processing operation or set of operations in question, Member States may deem it necessary to carry out such assessment prior to the processing activities.

Commentary:

1   In practice, the term "Privacy Impact Assessment" and the abbreviation "PIA" are also common.

2   A processing operation "**is likely to result in a high risk**" and therefore requires a data processing impact assessment if: (i) one of the cases of para. 3 applies; (ii) the kind of processing operation is included on a "black list" of the competent data protection authority pursuant to para. 4; or (iii) a high risk is identified on the basis of a preliminary assessment taking into account the nature, scope, context and purposes of the processing (cf. Recital 90 sentence 1), in particular because it includes the use of "new technologies" (Recital 89 sentence 4).

   Conversely, a processing operation will not result in a high risk if it is mentioned on the "white list" of the competent supervisory authority. According to the Art. 29 Working Party "a 'risk' is a scenario describing an event and its consequences, estimated in terms of severity and likelihood". Furthermore, the Art. 29 Working Party states that "the reference to 'the rights and freedoms' of the data subjects primarily concerns the right to privacy but may also involve other fundamental rights such as freedom of speech, freedom of thought, freedom of movement, prohibition of discrimination, right to liberty, conscience and religion" (see Art. 29 Working Party, Guidelines on Data Protection Impact Assessment (DPIA) and determining whether processing is "likely to result in a high risk" for the purposes of Regulation 2016/679, WP 248 (2017), at 15, available at http://ec.europa.eu/newsroom/just/item-detail.cfm? item_id=50083).

3   Carrying out a data protection impact assessment is generally **not the data protection officer's task**. The data protection officer only has to provide advice as regards the data protection impact assessment where requested (Art. 39 para. 1 lit. c). That advice, according to the Art. 29 Working Party, should be documented within the data protection impact assessment. Also, a controller may decide to have the data protection impact assessment carried out by someone else, inside or outside of the organisation; in any case, "the controller remains ultimately accountable for that task" (see Art. 29 Working Party, Guidelines on Data Protection Impact Assessment (DPIA) and determining whether processing is "likely to result in a high risk" for the purposes of Regulation 2016/679, WP 248 (2017), at 13, available at http://ec.europa.eu/ newsroom/just/item-detail.cfm?item_id=50083).

4   That the data protection impact assessment must be carried out "**prior**" to the processing means that the processing may not begin before the data protection impact assessment has been completed (and, if required, before the initiation of the consultation with the supervisory authority pursuant to Art. 36). According to the Art. 29 Working Party, carrying out a data protection impact assessment "is a continual process, not a one-time exercise" and should be "started as early as possible in the design of the processing operation" (see Art. 29 Working Party, Guidelines on Data Protection Impact Assessment (DPIA) and determining whether processing is "likely to result in a high risk" for the

purposes of Regulation 2016/679", WP 248 (2017), at 13, available at http://ec.europa.eu/newsroom/just/item-detail.cfm?item_id=50083).

However, it is questionable whether a data protection impact assessment will also be required for processing operations that began before the applicability of the GDPR on 25 May 2018. Since, in such cases, it is not possible to carry out a data protection impact assessment "prior" to the processing (the processing has already started) and the obligation in para. 1 cannot be complied with, there are, in our opinion, good arguments that a **data protection impact assessment** does not have to be carried out **for "old" processing operations** that started before 25 May 2018 (see Art. 36 cmt. 3 regarding the same issue concerning the consultation obligation and Art. 13 cmt. 3 regarding compliance with the information obligations).

The Art. 29 Working Party, however, strongly recommends to carry out data protection impact assessments for processing operations already underway prior to May 2018. Also, a data protection impact assessment might become necessary according to the Art. 29 Working Party "where a significant change to the processing operations has taken place after May 2018, for example because a new technology has come into force or because personal data is being processed for a different purpose" because in cases like this "the processing in effect becomes a new data processing operation" (see Art. 29 Working Party, Guidelines on Data Protection Impact Assessment (DPIA) and determining whether processing is "likely to result in a high risk" for the purposes of Regulation 2016/679, WP 248 (2017), at 12, available at http://ec.europa.eu/newsroom/just/item-detail.cfm?item_id=50083).

5   It could also be reasonable "for the subject of a data protection impact assessment to be broader than a single project" and to also cover, for example, a common application processing platform that was introduced by several controllers (cf. Recital 92). According to the Art. 29 Working Party "the data controller deploying the product remains obliged to carry out its own DPIA with regard to the specific implementation, but this can be informed by a DPIA prepared by the product provider, if appropriate" (see Art. 29 Working Party, Guidelines on Data Protection Impact Assessment (DPIA) and determining whether processing is "likely to result in a high risk" for the purposes of Regulation 2016/679, WP 248 (2017), at 6, available at http://ec.europa.eu/newsroom/just/item-detail.cfm?item_id=50083).

6   The enumeration in para. 3 is not comprehensive ("in particular") which means that in addition to the cases mentioned in para. 3 and the black list of the competent supervisory authority pursuant to para. 4, further cases that require a data protection impact assessment are easily conceivable. According to the Art. 29 Working Party, the following criteria should be considered when deciding on whether a data protection impact assessment is required: "(i) evaluation or scoring; (ii) automated decision making with legal or similar significant effect; (iii) systematic monitoring; (iv) sensitive data; (v) data processed on a large scale; (vi) datasets that have been matched or combined; (vii) data concerning vulnerable data subjects, e.g. kids and employees; (viii) innovative use or applying

technological or oganisational solutions; (ix) if the processing itself prevents data subjects from exercising a right or using a service or a contract". The Art. 29 Working Party states that "as a rule of thumb a processing operation meeting less than two criteria may not require a DPIA due to the lower level of risk, and processing operations which meet at least two of these criteria will require a DPIA" (see Art. 29 Working Party, Guidelines on Data Protection Impact Assessment (DPIA) and determining whether processing is "likely to result in a high risk" for the purposes of Regulation 2016/679, WP 248 (2017), at 10, available at http://ec.europa.eu/newsroom/just/item-detail.cfm?item_id=50083).

The Art. 29 Working Party lists the following examples of processing that require a data protection impact assessment: (i) a hospital processing its patients' genetic and health data; (ii) the use of a camera system to monitor driving behaviour on highways (the controller envisages to use an intelligent video analysis system to single out cars and automatically recognise license plates); (iii) a company monitoring its employees' activities, including the monitoring of the employees' work station, internet activity, etc.; (iv) the gathering of public social media profiles data to be used by private companies generating profiles for contact directories.

The following are examples of processing operations that do not require a data protection impact assessment: (i) an online magazine using a mailing list to send a generic daily digest to its subscribers; (ii) an e-commerce website displaying adverts for vintage car parts involving limited profiling based on past purchases behaviour on certain parts of its website (see Art. 29 Working Party, Guidelines on Data Protection Impact Assessment (DPIA) and determining whether processing is "likely to result in a high risk" for the purposes of Regulation 2016/679, WP 248 (2017), at 10, available at http://ec.europa.eu/newsroom/just/item-detail.cfm?item_id=50083).

7   See Art. 4 No. 4 regarding the definition of the term "profiling". See Art. 22 regarding the right of a data subject not to be subject to a decision based solely on automated processing, including profiling.

8   The processing will not be considered to be **"on a large scale" within the meaning of para. 3 lit. b**, "if the processing concerns personal data from patients or clients by an individual physician, other health care professional or lawyer" (Recital 91 sentence 4). In such cases, a data protection impact assessment is generally not required. According to the Art. 29 Working Party in particular the following factors should be considered when determining whether the processing is carried out on a large scale: "(i) the number of data subjects concerned, either as a specific number or as a proportion of the relevant population; (ii) the volume of data and/or the range of different data items being processed; (iii) the duration, or permanence, of the data processing activity; and (iv) the geographical extent of the processing activity" (see Art. 29 Working Party, Guidelines on Data Protection Impact Assessment (DPIA) and determining whether processing is "likely to result in a high risk" for the purposes of Regulation 2016/679, WP 248 (2017), at 9, available at http://ec.europa.eu/newsroom/just/item-detail.cfm?item_id=50083).

9   As an example of **"monitoring of a publicly accessible area"** that requires a
        data protection impact assessment pursuant to para. 3 lit. c, Recital 91
        sentence 3 mentions the use of "optic-electronic devices", that is, electronic
        video surveillance. At least the use of a larger amount of electronic video
        cameras might constitute a "systematic monitoring (…) on a large scale" which
        requires a data protection impact assessment pursuant to para. 3 lit. c.

10   The "supervisory authority" mentioned in para. 4 (and para. 5) means, in our
        opinion, the competent supervisory authority(ies) pursuant to Art. 55. If there
        is a lead competence pursuant to Art. 56, only the lead authority should be
        relevant (cf. Art. 56 para. 6).

11   The list with processing operations pursuant to para. 4 is a **"black list"**.

12   Art. 64 para. 1 lit. a clarifies that the list with processing operations in para. 4
        that requires a data protection impact assessment pursuant to para. 1 must be
        communicated to the Board for it to issue an opinion on it prior to its adoption
        by the supervisory authority.

13   See cmt. 10 above.

14   The list with processing operations pursuant to para. 5 is a **"white list"**.
        Additionally, a data protection impact assessment will not be required
        according to the Art. 29 Working Party "when the nature, scope, context and
        purposes of the processing are very similar to the processing for which DPIA
        have been carried out". In such cases, "results of DPIA for similar processing can
        be used" (see Art. 29 Working Party, Guidelines on Data Protection Impact
        Assessment (DPIA) and determining whether processing is "likely to result in a
        high risk" for the purposes of Regulation 2016/679, WP 248 (2017), at 11,
        available at http://ec.europa.eu/newsroom/just/item-detail.cfm?item_id=
        50083).

15   The limitation of the obligation to apply the consistency mechanism in the
        second half-sentence of para. 6 before adopting a black list pursuant to para. 4
        or a white list pursuant to para. 5 is unfortunate. As a result, there will be
        different black lists and different white lists in the various Member States.

16   According to the Art. 29 Working Party, the generic iterative process for
        carrying out a data protection impact assessment includes the following steps:
        "(i) description of the envisaged processing, (ii) assessment of the necessity and
        proportionality, (iii) measures envisaged to demonstrate compliance,
        (iv) assessment of the risks to the rights and freedoms, (iv) measures envisaged
        to address the risk, (v) documentation, and (vi) monitoring and review".
        However, the Art. 29 Working Party states that "the GDPR provides data
        controllers with flexibility to determine the precise structure and form of the
        DPIA in order to allow for this to fit with existing working practices". Annex 1
        of the Guidelines of the Art. 29 Working Party contains examples of existing EU
        data protection impact assessments (methodology) and Annex 2 contains
        criteria that controllers can use to assess whether a data protection impact
        assessment is sufficiently comprehensive to comply with the GDPR (see Art. 29
        Working Party, Guidelines on Data Protection Impact Assessment (DPIA) and
        determining whether processing is "likely to result in a high risk" for the

purposes of Regulation 2016/679, WP 248 (2017), Annex 1 and 2, available at http://ec.europa.eu/just/item-detail.cfm?item_id=50083).

According to the Art. 29 Working Party, controllers should also "consider publishing their DPIA, or perhaps parts of it". However, the Art. 29 Working Party also states that this is not a legal requirement (see Art. 29 Working Party, Guidelines on Data Protection Impact Assessment (DPIA) and determining whether processing is "likely to result in a high risk" for the purposes of Regulation 2016/679, WP 248 (2017), at 17, available at http://ec.europa.eu/newsroom/just/item-detail.cfm?item_id=50083).

17   An **assessment of the risks pursuant to para. 7 lit.** c must be carried out taking into consideration the envisaged measures to address the risks pursuant to para. 7 lit. d. For the question whether a consultation with the supervisory authority pursuant to Art. 36 para. 1 is necessary, a final risk assessment is required which also considers the measures to address the risks pursuant to para. 7 lit. d (Art. 36 cmt. 5).

It follows from Art. 36 para. 1 that para. 7 lit. c requires a **qualitative risk assessment that clearly answers the question whether there is a "high risk"**. Such a qualitative assessment is required for the purposes of Art. 36 to determine whether a consultation with the supervisory authority has to be performed.

A high risk will be indicated (cf. cmt. 2 above): (i) in the cases of para. 3; or (ii) if the kind of processing operation is included on a "black list" of the competent supervisory authority pursuant to para. 4. However, there are conceivable measures pursuant to para. 7 lit. d that mitigate the risk in such a manner that the threshold to a "high risk" is not reached. This is likely to apply, for example, in case of pseudonymisation within the meaning of Art. 4 No. 5.

18   Compliance with approved codes of conducts pursuant to Art. 40 is likely to only have to be taken into consideration, to the extent they provide for measures to address the risks within the meaning of para. 7 lit. d.

19   The term "representative" as used here is different from the one defined in Art. 4 No. 17. This term may include, for example, the works councils.

20   Unless provided otherwise by the legislature, the obligation to carry out a data protection impact assessment does not apply in the cases of Art. 6 para. 1 subpara. 1 lit. c and e.

21   A **re-evaluation of the data protection impact assessment** will therefore generally be required after each personal data breach within the meaning of Art. 4 No. 12 and after each violation of the provisions of the GDPR. According to the Art. 29 Working Party, a data protection impact assessment "should be re-assessed after 3 years, perhaps sooner, depending on the nature of the processing and the rate of change in the processing operation and general circumstances" (see Art. 29 Working Party, Guidelines on Data Protection Impact Assessment (DPIA) and determining whether processing is "likely to result in a high risk" for the purposes of Regulation 2016/679, WP 248 (2017), at 12, available at http://ec.europa.eu/newsroom/just/item-detail.cfm?item_id= 50083).

Article 36

Prior consultation[1]
1. The controller shall consult the supervisory authority[2] prior[3] to processing where a data protection impact assessment under Article 35 indicates that the processing would result in a high risk[4] in the absence of measures taken by the controller to mitigate the risk.[5]
2. Where the supervisory authority is of the opinion that the intended processing referred to in paragraph 1 would infringe this Regulation, in particular where the controller has insufficiently identified or mitigated the risk, the supervisory authority shall, within period of up to eight weeks of receipt of the request for consultation, provide written advice to the controller and, where applicable to the processor,[6] and may use any of its powers referred to in Article 58.[7] That period may be extended by six weeks, taking into account the complexity of the intended processing. The supervisory authority shall inform the controller and, where applicable, the processor, of any such extension within one month of receipt of the request for consultation together with the reasons for the delay. Those periods may be suspended until the supervisory authority has obtained information it has requested for the purposes of the consultation.[8]
3. When consulting the supervisory authority pursuant to paragraph 1, the controller shall provide the supervisory authority with:
   (a) where applicable, the respective responsibilities of the controller, joint controllers and processors involved in the processing, in particular for processing within a group of undertakings;
   (b) the purposes and means of the intended processing;
   (c) the measures and safeguards provided to protect the rights and freedoms of data subjects pursuant to this Regulation;
   (d) where applicable, the contact details[9] of the data protection officer;
   (e) the data protection impact assessment provided for in Article 35; and
   (f) any other information requested by the supervisory authority.
4. Member States shall consult the supervisory authority during the preparation of a proposal for a legislative measure to be adopted by a national parliament, or of a regulatory measure based on such a legislative measure, which relates to processing.[10]
5. Notwithstanding paragraph 1, Member State law may require controllers to consult with, and obtain prior authorisation from, the supervisory authority in relation to processing by a controller for the performance of a task carried out by the controller in the public interest,[11] including processing in relation to social protection and public health.

Recitals:
(94) Where a data protection impact assessment indicates that the processing would, in the absence of safeguards, security measures and mechanisms to mitigate the risk, result in a high risk to the rights and freedoms of natural persons and the controller is of the

opinion that the risk cannot be mitigated by reasonable means in terms of available technologies and costs of implementation, the supervisory authority should be consulted prior to the start of processing activities. Such high risk is likely to result from certain types of processing and the extent and frequency of processing, which may result also in a realisation of damage or interference with the rights and freedoms of the natural person. The supervisory authority should respond to the request for consultation within a specified period. However, the absence of a reaction of the supervisory authority within that period should be without prejudice to any intervention of the supervisory authority in accordance with its tasks and powers laid down in this Regulation, including the power to prohibit processing operations. As part of that consultation process, the outcome of a data protection impact assessment carried out with regard to the processing at issue may be submitted to the supervisory authority, in particular the measures envisaged to mitigate the risk to the rights and freedoms of natural persons.

(95) *The processor should assist the controller, where necessary and upon request, in ensuring compliance with the obligations deriving from the carrying out of data protection impact assessments and from prior consultation of the supervisory authority.*

(96) *A consultation of the supervisory authority should also take place in the course of the preparation of a legislative or regulatory measure which provides for the processing of personal data, in order to ensure compliance of the intended processing with this Regulation and in particular to mitigate the risk involved for the data subject.*

Commentary:

1   The purpose of the prior consultation mechanism in connection with the instrument of a data protection impact assessment is to abolish the general notification obligation pursuant to Art. 18 para. 1 Data Protection Directive (cf. Recital 89). Despite the foregoing, the consultation by nature constitutes a notification, in particular since the consultation procedure concludes, if at all, with a recommendation of the supervisory authority but **not an approval**. After having initiated the consultation procedure, the controller does not have to wait for a reaction of the supervisory authority before beginning with the processing of the personal data. An approval procedure may be introduced by the national legislature in limited cases pursuant to para. 5 only.

2   If there is a **lead competence** for a particular supervisory authority pursuant to Art. 56, only that supervisory authority has to be consulted (cf. Art. 56 para. 6). If there is no lead authority, the generally competent supervisory authority pursuant to Art. 55 para. 1 must be consulted. Due to the different factors determining the competence pursuant to Art. 55 para. 1, it will likely be necessary to consult with the supervisory authorities of various Member States (see Art. 55 cmt. 5) if a lead competence does not exist.

3   Para. 1 clarifies that the consultation with the supervisory authority **must be initiated (but not completed) prior to processing**.

      In cases where the processing began before the application of the GDPR on 25 May 2018, it is not possible to consult with the supervisory authority "prior" to the processing (the processing has already begun). Therefore, there are good arguments in our opinion that the **consultation with the supervisory authority regarding old processing operations which began before 25 May 2018 is not required** (cf. Art. 35 cmt 4 regarding the same issue concerning data protection impact assessments and Art. 13 cmt 3 regarding compliance with information obligations).

4   Whether the processing results in a **"high risk"** must be determined in the context of a risk assessment pursuant to Art. 35 para. 7 lit. c (see in particular Art. 35 cmt. 17).

5   Pursuant to para. 1, a consultation with the supervisory authority is required if the data protection impact assessment indicates that the processing operation would result in a high risk. When assessing the level of risk, the measures to address risks must already be considered. Recital 84 last sentence clarifies that the supervisory authority should be consulted "where a data-protection impact assessment indicates that processing operations involve a high risk which the controller cannot mitigate by appropriate measures". Recital 94 sentence 1, too, outlines that a consultation is required "where a data protection impact assessment indicates that the processing would, in the absence of safeguards, security measures and mechanisms to mitigate the risk, result in a high risk to the rights and freedoms of natural persons and the controller is of the opinion that the risk cannot be mitigated by reasonable means in terms of available technologies and costs of implementation".

Subject to para. 5, a consultation with the supervisory authority is required only if the risk continues to be high despite the measures taken to address the risk.

6   Pursuant to para. 2, the **processor, too, can be the addressee of an advice** of the supervisory authority. In this regard, Recital 95 states that "the processor should assist the controller, where necessary and upon request, in ensuring compliance with the obligations deriving from the carrying out of data protection impact assessments and from prior consultation of the supervisory authority". This does not constitute a legal obligation for the data processor.

7   Despite the supervisory authority's obligation in para. 2 to provide advice within a **period of up to eight weeks (which can be extended to up to 14 weeks)**, the supervisory authority may use its powers laid down in the GDPR, including the power to prohibit processing operations, even if the supervisory authority did not react within that period.

8   In case of a request by the supervisory authority for additional information, the periods may be suspended.

9   See Art. 13 cmt. 7 regarding the definition of the term "contact details".

10 Para. 4 outlines the Member States' obligation to consult their respective supervisory authority during the preparation "of a legislative or regulatory measure which provides for the processing of personal data" (cf. Recital 96).

11 Para. 5 mentions the "processing for the performance of a task carried out in the public interest" based on Art. 6 para. 1 subpara. 1 lit. e or Art. 9 para. 2 lit. i and allows Member States to enact national laws that require controllers to

consult with, and obtain prior authorisation from, the supervisory authority in certain circumstances.

Section 4 – Data protection officer

Article 37

Designation of the data protection officer

1. The controller and the processor shall designate[1] a data protection officer in any case where:

    (a) the processing is carried out by a public authority or body,[2] except for courts acting in their judicial capacity;

    (b) the core activities[3] of the controller or the processor consist of processing operations which, by virtue of their nature, their scope and/or their purposes, require regular and systematic monitoring of data subjects on a large scale;[4] or

    (c) the core activities[5] of the controller or the processor consist of processing on a large scale of special categories of data pursuant to Article 9 and personal data relating to criminal convictions and offences referred to in Article 10.[6]

2. A group of undertakings[7] may appoint a single data protection officer provided that a data protection officer is easily accessible from each establishment[8,9]

3. Where the controller or the processor is a public authority or body, a single data protection officer may be designated for several such authorities or bodies, taking account of their organisational structure[10] and size.

4. In cases other than those referred to in paragraph 1, the controller or processor or associations and other bodies representing categories of controllers or processors may[11] or, where required by Union or Member State law shall,[12] designate a data protection officer. The data protection officer may act for such associations and other bodies representing controllers or processors.

5. The data protection officer shall be designated on the basis of professional qualities and, in particular, expert knowledge of data protection law and practices and the ability to fulfil the tasks referred to in Article 39.[13]

6. The data protection officer may be a staff member of the controller or processor, or fulfil the tasks on the basis of a service contract.[14]

7. The controller or the processor shall publish the contact details[15] of the data protection officer and communicate them to the supervisory authority.

Recital:

(97) Where the processing is carried out by a public authority, except for courts or independent judicial authorities when acting in their judicial capacity, where, in the private sector, processing is carried out by a controller whose core activities consist of processing operations that require regular and systematic monitoring of the data subjects on a large scale, or where the core activities of the controller or the processor consist of processing on a large scale of special categories of personal data and data relating to criminal convictions and offences, a person with expert knowledge of data protection law and practices should assist the controller or processor to monitor internal compliance with this Regulation. In the private sector, the core activities of a controller

relate to its primary activities and do not relate to the processing of personal data as
ancillary activities. The necessary level of expert knowledge should be determined in
particular according to the data processing operations carried out and the protection
required for the personal data processed by the controller or the processor. Such data
protection officers, whether or not they are an employee of the controller, should be in
a position to perform their duties and tasks in an independent manner.

Commentary:

1   Pursuant to para. 1, a processor, too, is obligated (subject to the requirements in para. 1 lit. a to c) to appoint a data protection officer. According to the Art. 29 Working Party, "depending on who fulfils the criteria on mandatory designation, in some cases only the controller or only the processor, in other cases both the controller and its processor are required to appoint a DPO" (see Art. 29 Working Party, Guidelines on Data Protection Officers, WP 243 rev. 01 (2017), at 9, available at http://ec.europa.eu/newsroom/just/item-detail.cfm?item_id=50083).

2   The term **"public authority or body"** is not defined in the GDPR. Based on the purpose of the GDPR it seems to be reasonable to define the term "public authority or body" (which does not cover public companies) analogously to the term "contracting authorities" in Art. 2 para. 1 No. 1 Directive 2014/24/EU: "State, regional or local authorities, bodies governed by public law or associations formed by one or more such authorities or one or more such bodies governed by public law". Public companies are not subject to the obligation to appoint a data protection officer pursuant to para. 1 lit. a (and cannot be exempted from the national legislature pursuant to Art. 83 para. 7 from administrative fines; see Art. 83 cmt. 19). The Art. 29 Working Party, however, is of the opinion that whether an entity qualifies as a "public authority or body" is to be determined under national law (see Art. 29 Working Party, Guidelines on Data Protection Officers, WP 243 rev. 01 (2017), at 6, available at http://ec.europa.eu/newsroom/just/item-detail.cfm?item_id=50083).

3   Regarding the term **"core activities"** as used in para. 1 lit. b, Recital 97 sentence 2 states "in the private sector, the core activities of a controller relate to its primary activities and do not relate to the processing of personal data as ancillary activities". According to the Art. 29 Working Party "'core activities' can be considered as the key operations necessary to achieve the controller's or processor's goals", however, "should not be interpreted as excluding activities where the processing of data forms an inextricable part of the controller's or processor's activity". Thus, the Art. 29 Working Party is of the opinion that, for example, the processing of patients' health records "should be considered to be one of any hospital's core activities and hospitals must therefore designate data protection officers". The same applies to a private security company that carries out the surveillance of a number of private shopping centers and public spaces (see Art. 29 Working Party, Guidelines on Data Protection Officers, WP 243 rev. 01 (2017), at 7, available at http://ec.europa.eu/newsroom/just/item-detail.cfm?item_id=50083).

4   That the core activity pursuant to para. 1 lit. b consists of processing activities that **"require regular and systematic monitoring of data subjects on a large scale"** will basically only apply to data driven business models that collect personal data by monitoring the data subjects (eg, via logging of their Internet activities). The operation of video surveillance cameras in a retail store would likely not be subject to para. 1 lit. b because the monitoring is just an "ancillary service" of the retail store (cf. cmt. 3 above). The Art. 29 Working Party recommends that in particular the following factors should be taken into consideration when determining whether the processing is carried out on a large scale: "(i) the number of data subjects concerned – either as a specific number or as a proportion of the relevant population, (ii) the volume of data and/or the range of different data items being processed, (iii) the duration, or permanence, of the data processing activity, and (iv) the geographical extent of the processing activity". As examples of large-scale processing, the Art. 29 Working Party lists: "(i) processing of patient data in the regular course of business by a hospital, (ii) processing of travel data of individuals using a city's public transport system (e.g. tracking via travel cards), (iii) processing of real time geo-location data of customers of an international fast food chain for statistical purposes by a processor specialised in providing these services, (iv) processing of customer data in the regular course of business by an insurance company or a bank, (v) processing of personal data for behavioural advertising by a search engine, and (vi) processing of data (content, traffic, location) by telephone or internet service providers" (see Art. 29 Working Party, Guidelines on Data Protection Officers, WP 243 rev. 01 (2017), at 8, available at http://ec.europa.eu/newsroom/just/item-detail.cfm?item_id=50083).

The Art. 29 Working Party interprets "regular" as meaning one or more of the following: "(i) ongoing or occurring at particular intervals for a particular period, (ii) recurring or repeated at fixed times, (iii) constantly or periodically taking place". The Art. 29 Working Party interprets "systematic" as meaning one or more of the following: "(i) occurring according to a system, (ii) pre-arranged, organised or methodical, (ii) taking place as part of a general plan for data collection, (iv) carried out as part of a strategy" (see Art. 29 Working Party, Guidelines on Data Protection Officers, WP 243 rev. 01 (2017), at 21, available at http://ec.europa.eu/newsroom/just/item-detail.cfm?item_id=50083).

5   See cmt. 3 regarding the term "core activity".

6   That the core activity pursuant to para. 1 lit. c consists of the **processing on a large scale of special categories of data and personal data relating to criminal convictions and offences** will primarily apply to data driven business models. This would, for example, be the case, if a company specialised in DNA analyses. However, where the data processing is just an ancillary service, it is – in the light of Recital 97 sentence 2 – doubtful whether para. 1 lit. c applies. According to the Art. 29 Working Party examples that do not constitute large-scale processing, include the following; "(i) processing of patient data by an individual physician, and (ii) processing of personal data relating to criminal convictions and offences by an individual lawyer" (see Art. 29 Working Party,

Guidelines on Data Protection Officers, WP 243 rev. 01 (2017), at 21, available at http://ec.europa.eu/newsroom/just/item-detail.cfm?item_id=50083). Para. 1 lit. c will not apply if an employer only processes the social security number and the number of sick days of its employees.

7   See Art. 4 No. 19 regarding the definition of the term "group of undertakings".

8   See Art. 3 cmt. 3 regarding the definition of the term "establishment".

9   The requirement that the **data protection officer must be easily accessible** pursuant to para. 2 will likely be complied with if contact is possible via telephone and direct electronic communication (eg, via email). According to the Art. 29 Working Party "the availability of a DPO (whether physically on the same premises as employees, via a hotline or other secure means of communication) is essential to ensure that data subjects will be able to contact the DPO". The Art. 29 Working Party states that the data protection officer "with the help of a team if necessary, must be in a position to efficiently communicate with data subjects and cooperate with the supervisory authorities concerned". According to the Art. 29 Working Party this "also means that this communication must take place in the language or languages used by the supervisory authorities and the data subjects concerned" (see Art. 29 Working Party, Guidelines on Data Protection Officers, WP 243 rev. 01 (2017), at 10, available at http://ec.europa.eu/newsroom/just/item-detail.cfm?item_id= 50083).

The Art. 29 Working Party recommends "that the DPO be located within the European Union, whether or not the controller or the processor is established in the European Union", however, it also states that "it cannot be excluded that, in some situations where the controller or the processor has no establishment within the European Union, a DPO may be able to carry out his or her activities more effectively if located outside the EU" (see Art. 29 Working Party, Guidelines on Data Protection Officers, WP 243 rev. 01 (2017), at 11, available at http://ec.europa.eu/newsroom/just/item-detail.cfm?item_id=50083).

10   The wording used in para. 3, "taking account of their organisational structure and size", does not mean that the public authorities or bodies for which a single data protection officer has been appointed, have to necessarily be subordinate. It would in our opinion, for example, be permissible – and in order to avoid redundancies and to concentrate competences even preferable – to appoint a single data protection officer for several federal ministries.

11   Para. 4 sentence 1 half-sentence 1 clarifies that a controller, respectively a processor, **may appoint a data protection officer anytime voluntarily** without any obligation to do so. If an organisation designates a DPO on a voluntary basis "the requirements under Articles 37 to 39 will apply to his or her designation, position and tasks as if the designation had been mandatory" (see Art. 29 Working Party, Guidelines on Data Protection Officers, WP 243 rev. 01 (2017), at 5, available at http://ec.europa.eu/newsroom/just/item-detail.cfm?item_id=50083).

12   The **opening clause** in para. 4 sentence 1 half-sentence 2 authorises the national legislature to enact additional laws that require the appointment of a

data protection officer. The German legislature made use of this opening clause in the new German Data Protection Act supplementing the GDPR (Federal Law Gazette, No. 44, at 2097 et seqq., 5 July 2017) and stipulates that in addition to Art. 37 para. 1 GDPR, a data protection officer must be appointed if: (i) a company generally deploys at least 10 persons with the continuous automatic processing of personal data; (ii) the data processing activities require a data protection impact assessment; or (iii) companies process personal data for the purpose of transfer, the purpose of anonymous transfer or for purposes of market or opinion research.

13 With regard to para. 5, Recital 97 sentence 3 provides that "**the necessary level of expert knowledge** should be determined in particular according to the data processing operations carried out and the protection required for the personal data processed by the controller or the processor". In general, the expert knowledge under para. 5 will likely require: (i) a completed pertinent college degree; (ii) technical knowhow; and (iii) special knowledge in the field of data protection law. According to the Art. 29 Working Party, "the required level of expertise is not strictly defined but it must be commensurate with the sensitivity, complexity and amount of data an organisation processes" (see Art. 29 Working Party, Guidelines on Data Protection Officers, WP 243 rev. 01 (2017), at 11, available at http://ec.europa.eu/newsroom/just/item-detail.cfm?item_id=50083). Regarding the professional qualities, the Art. 29 Working Party states that "it is a relevant element that DPOs must have expertise in national and European data protection laws and practices and an in-depth understanding of the GDPR". They further state that "knowledge of the business sector and of the organisation of the controller is useful" and that "the DPO should also have a good understanding of the processing operations carried out, as well as on the systems, and data security and data protection needs of the controller" (see Art. 29 Working Party, Guidelines on Data Protection Officers, WP 243 rev. 01 (2017), at 11, available at http://ec.europa.eu/newsroom/just/item-detail.cfm?item_id=50083). According to the Art. 29 Working Party, the "ability to fulfil its tasks" refers to personal qualities and knowledge but also to their position within the organisation: "Personal qualities should include for instance integrity and high professional ethics; the DPO's primary concern should be enabling compliance with the GDPR" (see Art. 29 Working Party, Guidelines on Data Protection Officers, WP 243 rev. 01 (2017), at 12, available at http://ec.europa.eu/newsroom/just/item-detail.cfm?item_id=50083).

14 Pursuant to para. 6, the **data protection officer may also be a person external to the organisation**. Irrespective of whether the data protection officer is an employee of the controller or a contractor, data protection officers "should be in a position to perform their duties and tasks in an independent manner" (Recital 97 sentence 4; cf. also Art. 38 para. 3). There are good arguments that an external data protection officer may also be a legal entity and does not have to be a natural person. According to the Art. 29 Working Party, the function of a data protection officer can also be exercised by an organisation. In such a case

the Art. 29 Working Party deems it essential "that each member of the organisation exercising the functions of a DPO fulfils all applicable requirements of Section 4 of the GDPR" and that "each such member be protected by the provisions of the GDPR". However, according to the Art. 29 Working Party, individual skills and strengths can be combined so that several individuals, working in a team, may more efficiently serve their clients" (see Art. 29 Working Party, Guidelines on Data Protection Officers, WP 243 rev. 01 (2017), at 12, available at http://ec.europa.eu/newsroom/just/item-detail.cfm?item_id=50083).

15 See Art. 13 cmt. 7 regarding the definition of the term "contact details". According to the Art. 29 Working Party, the contact details of the data protection officer "should include information allowing data subjects and the supervisory authority to reach the DPO in an easy way (a postal address, a dedicated telephone number, and/or a dedicated e-mail address)"; however it does not require the name of the data protection officer (see Art. 29 Working Party, Guidelines on Data Protection Officers, WP 243 rev. 01 (2017), at 13, available at http://ec.europa.eu/newsroom/just/item-detail.cfm?item_id=50083).

Article 38

Position of the data protection officer

1. The controller and the processor shall ensure that the data protection officer is involved, properly and in a timely manner, in all issues which relate to the protection of personal data.[1]

2. The controller and processor shall support[2] the data protection officer in performing the tasks referred to in Article 39 by providing resources necessary to carry out those tasks and access to personal data and processing operations, and to maintain[3] his or her expert knowledge.

3. The controller and processor shall ensure that the data protection officer does not receive any instructions regarding the exercise of those tasks.[4] He or she shall not be dismissed or penalised by the controller or the processor for performing his tasks.[5] The data protection officer shall directly report to the highest management level of the controller or the processor.[6]

4. Data subjects may contact the data protection officer with regard to all issues related to processing of their personal data and to the exercise of their rights under this Regulation.[7]

5. The data protection officer shall be bound by secrecy or confidentiality concerning the performance of his or her tasks, in accordance with[8] Union or Member State law.

6. The data protection officer may fulfil other tasks and duties.[9] The controller or processor shall ensure that any such tasks and duties do not result in a conflict of interests.

Commentary:

1   According to the Art. 29 Working Party, "it is crucial that the DPO, or his/her team, is involved from the earliest stage possible in all issues relating to data protection" and companies "should ensure, for example, that (i) the DPO is invited to participate regularly in meetings of senior and middle management, (ii) his or her presence is recommended where decisions with data protection implications are taken" and that all relevant information must be passed on to the DPO in a timely manner in order to allow him or her to provide adequate advice. The Art. 29 Working Party further states that (iii) "the opinion of the DPO must always be given due weight" and that "in case of disagreement, the WP29 recommends, as good practice, to document the reasons for not following the DPO's advice". Moreover the Art. 29 Working Party outlines that (iv) "the DPO must be promptly consulted once a data breach or another incident has occurred" (see Art. 29 Working Party, Guidelines on Data Protection Officers, WP 243 rev. 01 (2017), at 13 seq., available at http://ec.europa.eu/newsroom/just/item-detail.cfm?item_id=50083).

2   In larger organisations the resources to be provided pursuant to para. 2 could also include staff resources (see Art. 29 Working Party, Guidelines on Data Protection Officers, WP 243 rev. 01, at 14, available at http://ec.europa.eu/newsroom/just/item-detail.cfm?item_id=50083). Additionally, the Art. 29

Working Party states that in particular the following types of resources are also to be considered: (i) active support by senior management; (ii) sufficient time for data protection officers to fulfill their duties; (iii) adequate support in terms of financial resources and infrastructure (premises, facilities, equipment); (iv) official communication of the designation of the data protection officer to all staff; (v) necessary access to other services, such as Human Resources, legal, IT, security, etc.; and (vi) continuous training. Pursuant to the Art. 29 Working Party, the resources also depend on the company: "In general, the more complex and/or sensitive the processing operations, the more resources must be given to the DPO" (Art. 29 Working Party, Guidelines on Data Protection Officers, WP 243 rev. 01 (2017), at 14, available at http://ec.europa.eu/ newsroom/just/item-detail.cfm?item_id=50083).

3   To maintain the required expert knowledge pursuant to para. 2, the required resources will primarily include expert literature and trainings. For internal data protection officers it will also include time resources.

4   Para. 3 sentence 1 stipulates the principle that the data protection officer **may not receive any instructions**. This applies to internal and external data protection officers. However, this independence is limited to the tasks pursuant to Art. 39 GDPR (see also Art. 29 Working Party, Guidelines on Data Protection Officers, WP 243 rev. 01 (2017), at 15, available at http://ec.europa.eu/ newsroom/just/item-detail.cfm?item_id=50083). According to the Art. 29 Working Party, independence means that "in fulfilling their tasks under Article 39, DPOs must not be instructed how to deal with a matter, for example, what result should be achieved, how to investigate a complaint or whether to consult the supervisory authority". Additionally, according to the Art. 29 Working Party, data protection officers "must not be instructed to take a certain view of an issue related to data protection law, for example, a particular interpretation of the law" (see Art. 29 Working Party, Guidelines on Data Protection Officers, WP 243 rev. 01 (2017), at 15, available at http://ec.europa.eu/ newsroom/just/item-detail.cfm?item_id=50083).

5   A termination of a data protection officer in violation of para. 3 sentence 2 could be challenged. Thus the data protection officer has comprehensive special **protection against termination**. Cf. also Recital 97 sentence 4 which requires that the data protection officer "should be in a position to perform their duties and tasks in an independent manner". According to the Art. 29 Working Party, "penalties may take a variety of forms and may be direct or indirect". They state that they "could consist, for example, of absence or delay of promotion; prevention from career advancement; denial from benefits that other employees receive". According to the Art. 29 Working Party, "it is not necessary that these penalties be actually carried out, a mere threat is sufficient as long as they are used to penalise the DPO on grounds related to his/her DPO activities" (see Art. 29 Working Party, Guidelines on Data Protection Officers, WP 243 rev. 01 (2017), at 15, available at http://ec.europa.eu/newsroom/ just/item-detail.cfm?item_id=50083). However, "penalties are only prohibited under the GDPR if they are imposed as a result of the DPO carrying out his or

her duties as a DPO" and "a DPO could still be dismissed legitimately for reasons other than for performing his or her tasks as a DPO" (see Art. 29 Working Party, Guidelines on Data Protection Officers, WP 243 rev. 01 (2017), at 16, available at http://ec.europa.eu/newsroom/just/item-detail.cfm?item_id=50083).

6   Para. 3 sentence 3 contains the principle of **direct reporting to the highest management level**. According to the Art. 29 Working Party, such direct reporting "ensures that senior management (e.g. board of directors) is aware of the DPO's advice and recommendations as part of the DPO's mission to inform and advise the controller or the processor", in particular if the data protection officer has a dissenting opinion (see Art. 29 Working Party, Guidelines on Data Protection Officers, WP 243 rev. 01 (2017), at 15, available at http://ec.europa.eu/newsroom/just/item-detail.cfm?item_id=50083).

7   The German language version of para. 4 contains a translation error because it says that data subjects may seek advice from the data protection officer ("mit Fragen zu Rate ziehen"). However, the English language version uses the wording **"may contact"**, the French version "peuvent prendre contact" and the Spanish version "podrán ponerse en contacto". Therefore, the data protection officer is **not obligated to advise the data subjects** (cf. Art. 39 cmt. 3) but only the controller and the processor pursuant to Art. 39 para. 1 lit. a. If the data protection officer had to also advise the data subjects, the prohibition to represent both parties stipulated in codes of professional conduct would make it impossible for attorneys to act as a data protection officer (cf., eg, in Austria Sec. 10 para. 1 Attorneys Code).

8   The German translation of para. 5 contains a translation error. The English version says "shall be bound by secrecy or confidentiality concerning the performance of his or her tasks, in accordance with Union or Member State law", that means, the **confidentiality obligation** derives directly from para. 5.
        Due to the wording that the confidentiality obligation must be "in accordance with" Union or Member State law, exceptions are possible, for example, the obligation to testify as a witness.

9   Para. 6 sentence 1 clarifies that a **part-time data protection officer**, too, may be permissible. According to the Art. 29 Working Party, "as a rule of thumb, conflicting positions within the organisation may include senior management positions (such as chief executive, chief operating, chief financial, chief medical officer, head of marketing department, head of Human Resources or head of IT departments) but also other roles lower down in the organisational structure if such positions or roles lead to the determination of purposes and means of processing" (see Art. 29 Working Party, Guidelines on Data Protection Officers, WP 243 rev. 01 (2017), at 16, available at http://ec.europa.eu/newsroom/just/item-detail.cfm?item_id=50083).

Article 39

Tasks of the data protection officer[1]

1. The data protection officer shall have at least the following tasks:[2]

(a) to inform and advise the controller or the processor and the employees who carry out processing of their obligations pursuant to this Regulation and to other Union or Member State data protection provisions;[3]

(b) to monitor compliance with this Regulation, with other Union or Member State data protection provisions and with the policies of the controller or processor in relation to the protection of personal data, including the assignment of responsibilities, awareness-raising and training of staff involved in processing operations, and the related audits;[4]

(c) to provide advice where requested as regards the data protection impact assessment and monitor its performance pursuant to Article 35;[5]

(d) to cooperate with the supervisory authority;

(e) to act as the contact point for the supervisory authority on issues relating to processing, including the prior consultation referred to in Article 36, and to consult, where appropriate, with regard to any other matter.[6]

2. The data protection officer shall in the performance of his or her tasks have due regard to the risk associated with processing operations, taking into account the nature, scope, context and purposes of processing.

Commentary:

1   A violation of Art. 39 is subject to fines pursuant to Art. 83 para. 4 lit. a. However, this applies only to "obligations of the controller and the processor". Thus, the GDPR itself **does not provide for sanctions for the data protection officer** in case he or she does not comply with his or her tasks under Art. 39. The Art. 29 Working Party also emphasises that "it is not the DPO who is personally responsible where there is an instance of non-compliance" and that "data protection compliance is a corporate responsibility of the data controller, not of the DPO" (see Art. 29 Working Party, Guidelines on Data Protection Officers, WP 243 rev. 01 (2017), at 17, available at http://ec.europa.eu/ newsroom/just/item-detail.cfm?item_id=50083). However, if a controller or processor suffers a damage due to a data protection officer's culpable violation of obligations, the data protection officer might be subject to general liability under civil law.

2   In addition to the tasks mentioned in para. 1 lit. a to e, the data protection officer is also the contact person for requests of data subjects (see Art. 38 para. 4). Maintaining the records of processing activities pursuant to Art. 30 is not one of the data protection officer's mandatory tasks but could be assigned to the data protection officer (see Art. 29 Working Party, Guidelines on Data Protection Officers, WP 243 rev. 01 (2017), at 25, available at http://ec.europa.eu/ newsroom/just/item-detail.cfm?item_id=50083).

3   Pursuant to para. 1 lit. b, the controller's or the processor's staff must only be advised on their obligations pursuant to the GDPR, that means, not in their role as data subjects (cf. also Art. 38 cmt. 7).

4 According to the Art. 29 Working Party, data protection officers may, as part of these duties to monitor compliance, in particular: "(i) collect information to identify processing activities; (ii) analyse and check the compliance of processing activities, (iii) inform, advise and issue recommendations to the controller or the processor" (see Art. 29 Working Party, Guidelines on Data Protection Officers", WP 243 rev. 01 (2017), at 17, available at http://ec.europa.eu/newsroom/just/item-detail.cfm?item_id=50083).

5 The Art. 29 Working Party recommends "that the controller should seek the advice of the DPO, on the following issues, amongst others: (i) whether or not to carry out a DPIA, (ii) what methodology to follow when carrying out a DPIA, (iii) whether to carry out the DPIA in-house or whether to outsource it, (iv) what safeguards (including technical and organisational measures) to apply to mitigate any risks to the rights and interests of the data subjects, (v) whether or not the data protection impact assessment has been correctly carried out and whether its conclusions (whether or not to go ahead with the processing and what safeguards to apply) are in compliance with the GDPR" (see Art. 29 Working Party, Guidelines on Data Protection Officers, WP 243 rev. 01 (2017), at 17, available at http://ec.europa.eu/newsroom/just/item-detail.cfm?item _id=50083).

6 According to the Art. 29 Working Party, lit. d and lit. e refer to the data protection officer's role as a "facilitator", that is., "to facilitate access by the supervisory authority to the documents and information for the performance of the tasks mentioned in Art. 57, as well as for the exercise of its investigative, corrective, authorisation, and advisory powers mentioned in Art. 58" (see Art. 29 Working Party, Guidelines on Data Protection Officers, WP 243 rev. 01 (2017), at 18, available at http://ec.europa.eu/newsroom/just/item-detail. cfm?item_id=50083).

Section 5 – Codes of conduct and certification

Article 40

Codes of conduct[1]
1. The Member States, the supervisory authorities, the Board and the Commission shall encourage the drawing up of codes of conduct intended to contribute to the proper application of this Regulation, taking account of the specific features of the various processing sectors and the specific needs of micro, small and medium-sized enterprises.[2,3]
2. Associations and other bodies representing categories of controllers or processors may prepare codes of conduct, or amend or extend such codes, for the purpose of specifying the application of this Regulation, such as with regard to:
  (a) fair and transparent processing;[4]
  (b) the legitimate interests pursued by controllers in specific contexts;[5]
  (c) the collection of personal data;
  (d) the pseudonymisation of personal data;[6]
  (e) the information provided to the public and to data subjects;[7]
  (f) the exercise of the rights of data subjects;[8]
  (g) the information provided to, and the protection of, children,[9] and the manner in which the consent of the holders of parental responsibility over children is to be obtained;[10]
  (h) the measures and procedures referred to in Articles 24 and 25 and the measures to ensure security of processing referred to in Article 32;
  (i) the notification of personal data breaches to supervisory authorities and the communication of such personal data breaches to data subjects;[11]
  (j) the transfer of personal data to third countries or international organisations;[12] or
  (k) out-of-court proceedings and other dispute resolution procedures for resolving disputes between controllers and data subjects with regard to processing, without prejudice to the rights of data subjects pursuant to Articles 77 and 79.
3. In addition to adherence by controllers or processors subject to this Regulation, codes of conduct approved pursuant to paragraph 5 of this Article and having general validity pursuant to paragraph 9 of this Article may also be adhered to by controllers or processors that are not subject to this Regulation pursuant to Article 3 in order to provide appropriate safeguards within the framework of personal data transfers to third countries or international organisations under the terms referred to in point (e) of Article 46(2). Such controllers or processors shall make binding and enforceable commitments, via contractual or other legally binding instruments, to apply those appropriate safeguards including with regard to the rights of data subjects.
4. A code of conduct referred to in paragraph 2 of this Article shall contain mechanisms which enable the body referred to in Article 41(1) to carry out the

mandatory monitoring of compliance with its provisions by the controllers or processors which undertake to apply it, without prejudice to the tasks and powers of supervisory authorities competent pursuant to Article 55 or 56.

5. Associations and other bodies referred to in paragraph 2 of this Article which intend to prepare a code of conduct or to amend or extend an existing code shall submit the draft code, amendment or extension to the supervisory authority which is competent pursuant to Article 55. The supervisory authority shall provide an opinion on whether the draft code, amendment or extension complies with this Regulation and shall approve that draft code, amendment or extension if it finds that it provides sufficient appropriate safeguards.

6. Where the draft code, or amendment or extension is approved in accordance with paragraph 5, and where the code of conduct concerned does not relate to processing activities in several Member States, the supervisory authority shall register and publish the code.

7. Where a draft code of conduct relates to processing activities in several Member States, the supervisory authority which is competent pursuant to Article 55 shall, before approving the draft code, amendment or extension, submit it in the procedure referred to in Article 63 to the Board[13] which shall provide an opinion on whether the draft code, amendment or extension complies with this Regulation or, in the situation referred to in paragraph 3 of this Article, provides appropriate safeguards.

8. Where the opinion referred to in paragraph 7 confirms that the draft code, amendment or extension complies with this Regulation, or, in the situation referred to in paragraph 3, provides appropriate safeguards, the Board shall submit its opinion to the Commission.

9. The Commission may, by way of implementing acts, decide that the approved code of conduct, amendment or extension submitted to it pursuant to paragraph 8 of this Article have general validity within the Union. Those implementing acts shall be adopted in accordance with the examination procedure set out in Article 93(2).

10. The Commission shall ensure appropriate publicity for the approved codes which have been decided as having general validity in accordance with paragraph 9.

11. The Board shall collate all approved codes of conduct, amendments and extensions in a register and shall make them publicly available by way of appropriate means.

Recitals:

(98) *Associations or other bodies representing categories of controllers or processors should be encouraged to draw up codes of conduct, within the limits of this Regulation, so as to facilitate the effective application of this Regulation, taking account of the specific characteristics of the processing carried out in certain sectors and the specific needs of micro, small and medium enterprises. In particular, such codes of conduct could calibrate the obligations of controllers and processors, taking into account the risk likely to result from the processing for the rights and freedoms of natural persons.*

(99) When drawing up a code of conduct, or when amending or extending such a code, associations and other bodies representing categories of controllers or processors should consult relevant stakeholders, including data subjects where feasible, and have regard to submissions received and views expressed in response to such consultations.

Commentary:

1   Whether codes of conducts will be relevant in practice remains to be seen. At least the **legal advantages of codes of conducts are limited**, since compliance with codes of conducts is **only an "element" by which to demonstrate compliance with the GDPR** (cf. Art. 24 para. 3; Art. 28 para. 5; Art. 32 para. 3) but does not result in an assumption of compliance with the GDPR. Furthermore, compliance with approved codes of conducts only "shall be taken into due account" for the purposes of a data protection impact assessment (cf. Art. 35 para. 8). Therefore, the development of and compliance with a code of conduct is not connected with a direct advantage regarding the legal certainty of complying with the requirements of the GDPR.

2   See Art. 4 No. 18 regarding the definition of the term "enterprise". Pursuant to Recital 13 last sentence "the notion of **micro, small and medium-sized enterprises** should draw from Article 2 of the Annex to Commission Recommendation 2003/361/EC" which provides:

Article 2 – Staff headcount and financial ceilings determining enterprise categories

(1) The category of micro, small and medium-sized enterprises (SMEs) is made up of enterprises which employ fewer than 250 persons and which have an annual turnover not exceeding EUR 50 million, and/or an annual balance sheet total not exceeding EUR 43 million.

(2) Within the SME category, a small enterprise is defined as an enterprise which employs fewer than 50 persons and whose annual turnover and/or annual balance sheet total does not exceed EUR 10 million.

(3) Within the SME category, a microenterprise is defined as an enterprise which employs fewer than 10 persons and whose annual turnover and/or annual balance sheet total does not exceed EUR 2 million.

3   Cf. Recital 98 which states that the "specific needs of micro, small and medium enterprises" must be taken into account. Cf. also Recital 13 which states that "Member States and their supervisory authorities, are encouraged to take account of the specific needs of micro, small and medium-sized enterprises in the application of this Regulation".

4   Cf. Art. 5 para. 1 lit. a; Arts. 12 to 14.

5   Cf. Art. 6 para. 1 subpara. 1 lit. f.

6   Cf. Art. 4 No. 5 regarding the definition of the term "pseudonymisation". Regarding potential regulatory areas see Art. 6 para. 4 lit. e, Art. 25 para. 1 and Art. 32 para. 1 lit. d.

7   Cf. in particular Art. 12 et seqq. and Art. 34.

8   See Arts. 12 to 22.

9   See Art. 6 cmt. 9 regarding the definition of the term "child".

10   See Art. 8.
11   See Arts. 33 et seq.
12   See Arts. 44 to 50.
13   See Art. 64 para. 1 lit. b.

Article 41

Monitoring of approved codes of conduct

1. Without prejudice to the tasks and powers of the competent supervisory authority under Articles 57 and 58, the monitoring of compliance with a code of conduct pursuant to Article 40 may be carried out by a body which has an appropriate level of expertise in relation to the subject-matter of the code and is accredited for that purpose by the competent supervisory authority.[1]

2. A body as referred to in paragraph 1 may be accredited to monitor compliance with a code of conduct where that body has:

   (a) demonstrated its independence and expertise in relation to the subject-matter of the code to the satisfaction of the competent supervisory authority;

   (b) established procedures which allow it to assess the eligibility of controllers and processors concerned to apply the code, to monitor their compliance with its provisions and to periodically review its operation;

   (c) established procedures and structures to handle complaints about infringements of the code or the manner in which the code has been, or is being, implemented by a controller or processor, and to make those procedures and structures transparent to data subjects and the public; and

   (d) demonstrated to the satisfaction of the competent supervisory authority that its tasks and duties do not result in a conflict of interests.[2]

3. The competent supervisory authority shall submit the draft criteria for accreditation of a body as referred to in paragraph 1 of this Article to the Board pursuant to the consistency mechanism referred to in Article 63.[3]

4. Without prejudice to the tasks and powers of the competent supervisory authority and the provisions of Chapter VIII, a body as referred to in paragraph 1 of this Article shall, subject to appropriate safeguards, take appropriate action in cases of infringement of the code by a controller or processor, including suspension or exclusion of the controller or processor concerned from the code. It shall inform the competent supervisory authority of such actions and the reasons for taking them.[4]

5. The competent supervisory authority shall revoke the accreditation of a body as referred to in paragraph 1 if the conditions for accreditation are not, or are no longer, met or where actions taken by the body infringe this Regulation.

6. This Article shall not apply to processing carried out by public authorities and bodies.[5]

Commentary:

1   The purpose of the accreditation requirement is that whether the monitoring body is able to comply with its tasks from a **professional and organisational** perspective is checked and verified by the supervisory authority **in advance**. Contrary to the wording, not only the professional knowledge is therefore examined. However, it remains unclear whether the supervisory authority is obligated at all to offer the possibility of such accreditation and how to shape the accreditation procedure.

2   A **conflict of interests** mentioned in para. 2 lit. d would in our opinion have
    to be assumed (but would not necessarily exist) if the monitoring body was
    mainly financed by payments of the controller or the processor to be
    monitored.

3   See Art. 64 para. 1 lit. c.

4   The monitoring body must inform the supervisory authority about the
    measures that are taken against a controller or a processor in case of a violation
    of the code of conduct pursuant to para. 4. The violation itself is not subject to
    an explicit notification obligation.

5   See Art. 37 cmt. 2 regarding the definition of the term "public authority or
    body".

Article 42

Certification[1]

1. The Member States, the supervisory authorities, the Board and the Commission shall encourage, in particular at Union level, the establishment of data protection certification mechanisms and of data protection seals and marks, for the purpose of demonstrating compliance with this Regulation of processing operations by controllers and processors. The specific needs of micro, small and medium-sized enterprises[2,3] shall be taken into account.

2. In addition to adherence by controllers or processors subject to this Regulation, data protection certification mechanisms, seals or marks approved pursuant to paragraph 5 of this Article may be established for the purpose of demonstrating the existence of appropriate safeguards provided by controllers or processors that are not subject to this Regulation pursuant to Article 3 within the framework of personal data transfers to third countries or international organisations under the terms referred to in point (f) of Article 46(2). Such controllers or processors shall make binding and enforceable commitments, via contractual or other legally binding instruments, to apply those appropriate safeguards, including with regard to the rights of data subjects.

3. The certification shall be voluntary and available via a process that is transparent.

4. A certification pursuant to this Article does not reduce the responsibility of the controller or the processor for compliance with this Regulation and is without prejudice to the tasks and powers of the supervisory authorities which are competent pursuant to Article 55 or 56.

5. A certification pursuant to this Article shall be issued by the certification bodies referred to in Article 43 or by the competent supervisory authority, on the basis of criteria approved by that competent supervisory authority pursuant to Article 58(3) or by the Board pursuant to Article 63. Where the criteria are approved by the Board, this may result in a common certification, the European Data Protection Seal.[4]

6. The controller or processor which submits its processing to the certification mechanism shall provide the certification body referred to in Article 43, or where applicable, the competent supervisory authority, with all information and access to its processing activities which are necessary to conduct the certification procedure.

7. Certification shall be issued to a controller or processor for a maximum period of three years and may be renewed, under the same conditions, provided that the relevant requirements continue to be met. Certification shall be withdrawn, as applicable, by the certification bodies referred to in Article 43 or by the competent supervisory authority where the requirements for the certification are not or are no longer met.

8. The Board shall collate all certification mechanisms and data protection seals and marks in a register and shall make them publicly available by any appropriate means.

Recital:

(100)In order to enhance transparency and compliance with this Regulation, the establishment of certification mechanisms and data protection seals and marks should be encouraged, allowing data subjects to quickly assess the level of data protection of relevant products and services.

Commentary:

1   It remains to be seen whether certifications become relevant in practice. The **legal advantages of certifications are limited**, since compliance with approved certification mechanisms may **only be regarded as a "factor"** to demonstrate compliance with the GDPR (cf. Art. 24 para. 3; Art. 25 para. 3; Art. 28 para. 5; Art. 32 para. 3) but does not result in an assumption of compliance with the GDPR.

2   See Art. 40 cmt. 2 regarding the definition of the term "micro, small and medium-sized enterprise".

3   Cf. Recital 13 sentence 4 which states that "Union institutions and bodies, and Member States and their supervisory authorities, are encouraged to take account of the specific needs of micro, small and medium-sized enterprises in the application of this Regulation".

4   A certification pursuant to criteria approved by the Board is called the "European Data Protection Seal". This refers neither to the existing European Privacy Seal (www.european-privacy-seal.eu/) nor to the data protection seal of one of the German data protection authorities ("Unabhängiges Landeszentrum für Datenschutz Schleswig-Holstein"; www.datenschutzzentrum.de/guetesiegel/).

Article 43

Certification bodies

1. Without prejudice to the tasks and powers of the competent supervisory authority under Articles 57 and 58, certification bodies which have an appropriate level of expertise in relation to data protection shall, after informing the supervisory authority[1] in order to allow it to exercise its powers pursuant to point (h) of Article 58(2) where necessary,[2] issue and renew certification. Member States shall ensure that those certification bodies are accredited by one or both of the following:

   (a) the supervisory authority which is competent pursuant to Article 55 or 56;[3]

   (b) the national accreditation body named in accordance with Regulation (EC) No 765/2008 of the European Parliament[4] and of the Council in accordance with EN-ISO/IEC 17065/2012[4] and with the additional requirements[5] established by the supervisory authority which is competent pursuant to Article 55 or 56.

2. Certification bodies referred to in paragraph 1 shall be accredited in accordance with that paragraph only where they have:

   (a) demonstrated their independence and expertise in relation to the subject-matter of the certification to the satisfaction of the competent supervisory authority;

   (b) undertaken to respect the criteria referred to in Article 42(5) and approved by the supervisory authority which is competent pursuant to Article 55 or 56 or by the Board pursuant to Article 63;

   (c) established procedures for the issuing, periodic review and withdrawal of data protection certification, seals and marks;

   (d) established procedures and structures to handle complaints about infringements of the certification or the manner in which the certification has been, or is being, implemented by the controller or processor, and to make those procedures and structures transparent to data subjects and the public; and

   (e) demonstrated, to the satisfaction of the competent supervisory authority, that their tasks and duties do not result in a conflict of interests.

3. The accreditation of certification bodies as referred to in paragraphs 1 and 2 of this Article shall take place on the basis of criteria approved by the supervisory authority which is competent pursuant to Article 55 or 56 or by the Board pursuant to Article 63.[6] In the case of accreditation pursuant to point (b) of paragraph 1 of this Article, those requirements shall complement those envisaged in Regulation (EC) No 765/2008 and the technical rules that describe the methods and procedures of the certification bodies.

4. The certification bodies referred to in paragraph 1 shall be responsible for the proper assessment leading to the certification or the withdrawal of such

---

4   Regulation (EC) Nr. 765/2008 of the European Parliament and of the Council of 9 July 2008 setting out the requirements for accreditation and market surveillance relating to the marketing of products and repealing Regulation (EEC) No 339/93.

certification without prejudice to the responsibility of the controller or processor for compliance with this Regulation. The accreditation shall be issued for a maximum period of five years and may be renewed on the same conditions provided that the certification body meets the requirements set out in this Article.

5. The certification bodies referred to in paragraph 1 shall provide the competent supervisory authorities with the reasons for granting or withdrawing the requested certification.

6. The requirements referred to in paragraph 3 of this Article and the criteria referred to in Article 42(5) shall be made public by the supervisory authority in an easily accessible form. The supervisory authorities shall also transmit those requirements and criteria to the Board. The Board shall collate all certification mechanisms and data protection seals in a register and shall make them publicly available by any appropriate means.[7]

7. Without prejudice to Chapter VIII, the competent supervisory authority or the national accreditation body shall revoke an accreditation of a certification body pursuant to paragraph 1 of this Article where the conditions for the accreditation are not, or are no longer, met or where actions taken by a certification body infringe this Regulation.

8. The Commission shall be empowered to adopt delegated acts in accordance with Article 92 for the purpose of specifying the requirements to be taken into account for the data protection certification mechanisms referred to in Article 42(1).

9. The Commission may adopt implementing acts laying down technical standards for certification mechanisms and data protection seals and marks, and mechanisms to promote and recognise those certification mechanisms, seals and marks. Those implementing acts shall be adopted in accordance with the examination procedure referred to in Article 93(2).

Commentary:

1   Pursuant to para. 1, the **supervisory authority competent** for certifying the controller or processor must be informed. If there is no lead competence pursuant to Art. 56 para. 1, each generally competent supervisory authority pursuant to Art. 55 para. 1 must be informed. Thus, in many cases, the supervisory authorities of several Member States will have to be informed (see Art. 55 cmt. 5).

2   Therefore, the competent supervisory authority effectively has a **right to object** to each certification pursuant to para. 1 in connection with Art 58 para. 2 lit. h.

3   The reference in para. 1 lit. a to the "supervisory authority which is competent pursuant to Article 55 or 56" must, in our opinion, be understood in a manner that – subject to para. 1 lit. b – a certification body must have an accreditation of a supervisory authority which is competent for the certification body (and not necessarily for the controller or processor to be certified).

4   The standard ISO/IEC 17065:2012 mentioned in para. 1 lit. b is titled "Conformity assessment – Requirements for bodies certifying products,

processes and services" and contains legal and financial requirements as well as requirements regarding the structure, resources, processes and the management system of the accreditation body.

5   The reference in para. 1 lit. b to the "**additional requirements established by the supervisory authority which is competent pursuant to Art. 55 or 56**" must in our opinion be understood in a manner that the competent supervisory authority for a particular controller or processor may determine substantive requirements regarding the designation of an accreditation body.

6   See Art. 64 para. 1 lit. c.

7   Regarding the maintenance of a public register with the accredited bodies by the Board pursuant to para. 6, see Art. 70 para. 1 lit. o.

Chapter V – Transfers of personal data to third countries or international organisations

Article 44

General principle for transfers

Any transfer[1] of personal data which are undergoing processing or are intended for processing after transfer to a third country[2,3] or to an international organisation[4] shall take place only if, subject to the other provisions of this Regulation, the conditions laid down in this Chapter are complied with by the controller and processor,[5] including for onward transfers of personal data from the third country or an international organisation to another third country or to another international organisation.[6] All provisions in this Chapter shall be applied in order to ensure that the level of protection of natural persons guaranteed by this Regulation is not undermined.

Recitals:

(101) *Flows of personal data to and from countries outside the Union and international organisations are necessary for the expansion of international trade and international cooperation. The increase in such flows has raised new challenges and concerns with regard to the protection of personal data. However, when personal data are transferred from the Union to controllers, processors or other recipients in third countries or to international organisations, the level of protection of natural persons ensured in the Union by this Regulation should not be undermined, including in cases of onward transfers of personal data from the third country or international organisation to controllers, processors in the same or another third country or international organisation. In any event, transfers to third countries and international organisations may only be carried out in full compliance with this Regulation. A transfer could take place only if, subject to the other provisions of this Regulation, the conditions laid down in the provisions of this Regulation relating to the transfer of personal data to third countries or international organisations are complied with by the controller or processor.*

(102) *This Regulation is without prejudice to international agreements concluded between the Union and third countries regulating the transfer of personal data including appropriate safeguards for the data subjects. Member States may conclude international agreements which involve the transfer of personal data to third countries or international organisations, as far as such agreements do not affect this Regulation or any other provisions of Union law and include an appropriate level of protection for the fundamental rights of the data subjects.*

Commentary:

1 The term **"transfer"** is not defined in the GDPR but generally covers a disclosure vis-à-vis another controller or processor, respectively a subprocessor.

Taking into consideration the purpose of Art. 44 et seqq., the following do not qualify as a transfer: (i) a controller established in a third country collects personal data in the Union; (ii) a controller established in a third country engages a processor established in the Union for the purpose of collecting data and in doing so the processor discloses personal data to the controller; or (iii) a controller discloses personal data vis-à-vis the data subject (eg, when answering a data access request pursuant to Art. 15).

2 The term **"third country"** which is not defined in the GDPR covers all states except: (1) the Member States of the Union; and (2) the Member States of the EEA, that is, in addition to the EU Member States also Island, Liechtenstein and Norway (see Art. 3 cmt. 5).

3 The GDPR does not define **"transfer to a third country"** and in particular does not expressly set out whether the establishment of the recipient or the place of the processing is relevant. It is likely that one of the two criteria will be sufficient to result in a "transfer to a third country". This will, in our opinion, apply irrespective of whether the recipient in the third country is subject to the GDPR pursuant to Art. 3 para. 2 (cf. Art. 3 cmt. 7).

A transfer to a company established in the Union which is controlled by a company established in a third country, does not qualify as a "transfer to a third country". This also applies if the controlling entity established in the third country can be forced pursuant to the laws of the third country to use its control over the company in the Union to force the disclosure of personal data to authorities in the third country (cf., eg, *Microsoft Corp. vs. U.S.*, U.S. Court of Appeals for the Second Circuit, Docket-No. 142985, 14. 7. 2016). Only the disclosure itself would have to be qualified as a "transfer to a third country".

4 See Art. 4 No. 26 regarding the definition of the term "international organisation".

5 In addition to the specific requirements regarding international data transfers set out in this chapter, the other requirements pursuant to Art. 5 et seq. must be complied with. In particular, the transfer must be based on a legal basis pursuant to Arts. 6, 9, or 10, and, in case of a transfer to a processor, a data processing agreement pursuant to Art. 28 must be concluded.

6 **Onward transfers** from the first recipient to a third party are generally subject to the same requirements as the original transfer to the first recipient. This also applies if the first recipient and the third party are established in the same third country (cf. Recital 101 sentence 3 which states that "the level of protection of natural persons ensured in the Union by this Regulation should not be undermined, including in cases of onward transfers of personal data from the third country or international organisation to controllers, processors in the same or another third country or international organisation").

Article 45

Transfers on the basis of an adequacy decision[1]

1. A transfer[2] of personal data to a third country[3,4] or an international organisation[5] may take place where the Commission has decided[6] that the third country, a territory or one or more specified sectors within that third country, or the international organisation in question ensures an adequate level of protection. Such a transfer shall not require any specific authorisation.[7]

2. When assessing the adequacy of the level of protection, the Commission shall, in particular, take account of the following elements:[8]

(a) the rule of law, respect for human rights and fundamental freedoms, relevant legislation, both general and sectoral, including concerning public security, defence, national security and criminal law and the access of public authorities to personal data, as well as the implementation of such legislation, data protection rules, professional rules and security measures, including rules for the onward transfer of personal data to another third country or international organisation which are complied with in that country or international organisation, case-law, as well as effective and enforceable data subject rights and effective administrative and judicial redress for the data subjects whose personal data are being transferred;

(b) the existence and effective functioning of one or more independent supervisory authorities in the third country or to which an international organisation is subject, with responsibility for ensuring and enforcing compliance with the data protection rules, including adequate enforcement powers, for assisting and advising the data subjects in exercising their rights and for cooperation with the supervisory authorities of the Member States; and

(c) the international commitments the third country or international organisation concerned has entered into, or other obligations arising from legally binding conventions or instruments as well as from its participation in multilateral or regional systems, in particular in relation to the protection of personal data.

3. The Commission, after assessing the adequacy of the level of protection, may decide, by means of implementing act, that a third country, a territory or one or more specified sectors within a third country, or an international organisation ensures an adequate level of protection within the meaning of paragraph 2 of this Article. The implementing act shall provide for a mechanism for a periodic review, at least every four years, which shall take into account all relevant developments in the third country or international organisation. The implementing act shall specify its territorial and sectoral application and, where applicable, identify the supervisory authority or authorities referred to in point (b) of paragraph 2 of this Article. The implementing act shall be adopted in accordance with the examination procedure referred to in Article 93(2).

4. The Commission shall, on an ongoing basis, monitor developments in third

countries and international organisations that could affect the functioning of decisions adopted pursuant to paragraph 3 of this Article and decisions adopted on the basis of Article 25(6) of Directive 95/46/EC.[9]

5. The Commission shall, where available information reveals, in particular following the review referred to in paragraph 3 of this Article, that a third country, a territory or one or more specified sectors within a third country, or an international organisation no longer ensures an adequate level of protection within the meaning of paragraph 2 of this Article, to the extent necessary, repeal, amend or suspend the decision referred to in paragraph 3 of this Article by means of implementing acts without retro-active effect. Those implementing acts shall be adopted in accordance with the examination procedure referred to in Article 93(2).

On duly justified imperative grounds of urgency, the Commission shall adopt immediately applicable implementing acts in accordance with the procedure referred to in Article 93(3).[10]

6. The Commission shall enter into consultations with the third country or international organisation with a view to remedying the situation giving rise to the decision made pursuant to paragraph 5.

7. A decision pursuant to paragraph 5 of this Article is without prejudice to transfers of personal data to the third country, a territory or one or more specified sectors within that third country, or the international organisation in question pursuant to Articles 46 to 49.[11]

8. The Commission shall publish in the Official Journal of the European Union and on its website[12] a list of the third countries, territories and specified sectors within a third country and international organisations for which it has decided that an adequate level of protection is or is no longer ensured.

9. Decisions adopted by the Commission on the basis of Article 25(6) of Directive 95/46/EC shall remain in force until amended, replaced or repealed by a Commission Decision adopted in accordance with paragraph 3 or 5 of this Article.[13]

Recitals:

Regarding para. 1:

(103) *The Commission may decide with effect for the entire Union that a third country, a territory or specified sector within a third country, or an international organisation, offers an adequate level of data protection, thus providing legal certainty and uniformity throughout the Union as regards the third country or international organisation which is considered to provide such level of protection. In such cases, transfers of personal data to that third country or international organisation may take place without the need to obtain any further authorisation. The Commission may also decide, having given notice and a full statement setting out the reasons to the third country or international organisation, to revoke such a decision.*

Regarding para. 2:

(104)In line with the fundamental values on which the Union is founded, in particular the protection of human rights, the Commission should, in its assessment of the third country, or of a territory or specified sector within a third country, take into account how a particular third country respects the rule of law, access to justice as well as international human rights norms and standards and its general and sectoral law, including legislation concerning public security, defence and national security as well as public order and criminal law. The adoption of an adequacy decision with regard to a territory or a specified sector in a third country should take into account clear and objective criteria, such as specific processing activities and the scope of applicable legal standards and legislation in force in the third country. The third country should offer guarantees ensuring an adequate level of protection essentially equivalent to that ensured within the Union, in particular where personal data are processed in one or several specific sectors. In particular, the third country should ensure effective independent data protection supervision and should provide for cooperation mechanisms with the Member States' data protection authorities, and the data subjects should be provided with effective and enforceable rights and effective administrative and judicial redress.

(105)Apart from the international commitments the third country or international organisation has entered into, the Commission should take account of obligations arising from the third country's or international organisation's participation in multilateral or regional systems in particular in relation to the protection of personal data, as well as the implementation of such obligations. In particular, the third country's accession to the Council of Europe Convention of 28 January 1981 for the Protection of Individuals with regard to the Automatic Processing of Personal Data and its Additional Protocol should be taken into account. The Commission should consult the Board when assessing the level of protection in third countries or international organisations.

Regarding para. 4:

(106)The Commission should monitor the functioning of decisions on the level of protection in a third country, a territory or specified sector within a third country, or an international organisation, and monitor the functioning of decisions adopted on the basis of Article 25(6) or Article 26(4) of Directive 95/46/EC. In its adequacy decisions, the Commission should provide for a periodic review mechanism of their functioning. That periodic review should be conducted in consultation with the third country or international organisation in question and take into account all relevant developments in the third country or international organisation. For the purposes of monitoring and of carrying out the periodic reviews, the Commission should take into consideration the views and findings of the European Parliament and of the Council as well as of other relevant bodies and sources. The Commission should evaluate, within a reasonable time, the functioning of the latter decisions and report any relevant findings to the Committee within the meaning of Regulation (EU) No 182/2011 of the European Parliament and of the Council as established under this Regulation, to the European Parliament and to the Council.

Regarding para. 5 to 7:

(107)*The Commission may recognise that a third country, a territory or a specified sector within a third country, or an international organisation no longer ensures an adequate level of data protection. Consequently the transfer of personal data to that third country or international organisation should be prohibited, unless the requirements in this Regulation relating to transfers subject to appropriate safeguards, including binding corporate rules, and derogations for specific situations are fulfilled. In that case, provision should be made for consultations between the Commission and such third countries or international organisations. The Commission should, in a timely manner, inform the third country or international organisation of the reasons and enter into consultations with it in order to remedy the situation.*

Commentary:

1   As in Art. 25 para. 6 Data Protection Directive, the European Commission has the possibility to adopt adequacy decisions with the consequence that the transfer of personal data does not require any specific authorisation (see para. 1). The adequacy decisions that were adopted on the basis of Art. 25 para. 6 Data Protection Directive remain in force (para. 9).

2   See Art. 44 cmt. 1 regarding the definition of the term "transfer".

3   See Art. 44 cmt. 2 regarding the definition of the term "third country".

4   See Art. 44 cmt. 3 regarding the definition of the term "transfer to a third country".

5   See Art. 4 No 26 regarding the definition of the term "international organisation".

6   An adequacy decision is adopted based on para. 3.

7   If there is an adequacy decision, the transfer to the third country does **not** require an **authorisation** pursuant to para. 1. Despite the foregoing, a transfer to a processor requires the conclusion of a data processing agreement pursuant to Art. 28.

8   Cf. Recitals 104 and 105.

9   Cf. Recital 106.

10   Regarding the **suspension of an adequacy decision due to imperative grounds of urgency** pursuant to para. 5 subpara. 2, Recital 169 states: "The Commission should adopt immediately applicable implementing acts where available evidence reveals that a third country, a territory or a specified sector within that third country, or an international organisation does not ensure an adequate level of protection, and imperative grounds of urgency so require."

11   Pursuant to para. 7 the **repeal of an adequacy decision** pursuant to para. 5 does not impact the transfer which is based on appropriate safeguards pursuant to Art. 46. Cf. Recital 107 sentence 2 which states that "the transfer of personal data to that third country or international organisation should be prohibited, unless the requirements in this Regulation relating to transfers subject to appropriate safeguards, including binding corporate rules, and derogations for specific situations are fulfilled".

12   The European Commission's website mentioned in para. 8 which publishes all

adequacy decisions can be found at: http://ec.europa.eu/justice/data-protection/international-transfers/adequacy/index_en.htm (last access on August 2017).

13 So far (as of August 2017) the European Commission **has recognised the following third countries as providing an adequate level of data protection** based on Art. 25 para. 6: Andorra, Argentina, Canada (to the extent the recipient is subject to the Canadian Personal Information Protection and Electronic Documents Act), Faeroe Islands, Guernsey, Isle of Man, Jersey, Israel, New Zealand, Switzerland, the United States of America (to the extent the recipient is self-certified under the Privacy Shield) and Eastern Republic of Uruguay.

Article 46

Transfers subject to appropriate safeguards[1]

1. In the absence of a decision pursuant to Article 45(3), a controller or processor may transfer[2] personal data to a third country[3,4] or an international organisation[5] only if the controller or processor has provided appropriate safeguards, and on condition that enforceable data subject rights and effective legal remedies for data subjects are available.

2. The appropriate safeguards referred to in paragraph 1 may be provided for, without requiring any specific authorisation from a supervisory authority,[6] by:[7]

(a) a legally binding and enforceable instrument between public authorities or bodies;[8]

(b) binding corporate rules in accordance with Article 47;[9]

(c) standard data protection clauses[10] adopted by the Commission in accordance with the examination procedure referred to in Article 93(2);[11,12]

(d) standard data protection clauses adopted by a supervisory authority[13] and approved by the Commission pursuant to the examination procedure referred to in Article 93(2);[14]

(e) an approved code of conduct pursuant to Article 40 together with binding and enforceable commitments of the controller or processor in the third country to apply the appropriate safeguards, including as regards data subjects' rights; or

(f) an approved certification mechanism pursuant to Article 42 together with binding and enforceable commitments of the controller or processor in the third country to apply the appropriate safeguards, including as regards data subjects' rights.

3. Subject to the authorisation from the competent supervisory authority, the appropriate safeguards referred to in paragraph 1 may also be provided for, in particular,[15] by:

(a) contractual clauses between the controller or processor and the controller, processor or the recipient[16] of the personal data in the third country or international organisation;[17] or

(b) provisions to be inserted into administrative arrangements between public authorities or bodies which include enforceable and effective data subject rights.[18]

4. The supervisory authority shall apply the consistency mechanism referred to in Article 63 in the cases referred to in paragraph 3 of this Article.

5. Authorisations by a Member State or supervisory authority on the basis of Article 26(2) of Directive 95/46/EC shall remain valid until amended, replaced or repealed, if necessary, by that supervisory authority. Decisions adopted by the Commission on the basis of Article 26(4) of Directive 95/46/EC shall remain in force until amended, replaced or repealed, if necessary, by a Commission Decision adopted in accordance with paragraph 2 of this Article.

Recitals:

(108)In the absence of an adequacy decision, the controller or processor should take measures to compensate for the lack of data protection in a third country by way of appropriate safeguards for the data subject. Such appropriate safeguards may consist of making use of binding corporate rules, standard data protection clauses adopted by the Commission, standard data protection clauses adopted by a supervisory authority or contractual clauses authorised by a supervisory authority. Those safeguards should ensure compliance with data protection requirements and the rights of the data subjects appropriate to processing within the Union, including the availability of enforceable data subject rights and of effective legal remedies, including to obtain effective administrative or judicial redress and to claim compensation, in the Union or in a third country. They should relate in particular to compliance with the general principles relating to personal data processing, the principles of data protection by design and by default. Transfers may also be carried out by public authorities or bodies with public authorities or bodies in third countries or with international organisations with corresponding duties or functions, including on the basis of provisions to be inserted into administrative arrangements, such as a memorandum of understanding, providing for enforceable and effective rights for data subjects. Authorisation by the competent supervisory authority should be obtained when the safeguards are provided for in administrative arrangements that are not legally binding.

(109)The possibility for the controller or processor to use standard data-protection clauses adopted by the Commission or by a supervisory authority should prevent controllers or processors neither from including the standard data-protection clauses in a wider contract, such as a contract between the processor and another processor, nor from adding other clauses or additional safeguards provided that they do not contradict, directly or indirectly, the standard contractual clauses adopted by the Commission or by a supervisory authority or prejudice the fundamental rights or freedoms of the data subjects. Controllers and processors should be encouraged to provide additional safeguards via contractual commitments that supplement standard protection clauses.

Commentary:

1   The permissibility of a transfer based on appropriate safeguards pursuant to Art. 46 is subject to the limitation of Art. 49 para. 5 which **allows limitations pursuant to national law** "in the absence of an adequacy decision".

2   See Art. 44 cmt. 1 regarding the definition of the term "transfer".

3   See Art. 44 cmt. 2 regarding the definition of the term "third country".

4   See Art. 44 cmt. 3 regarding the definition of the term "transfer to a third country".

5   See Art. 4 No 26 regarding the definition of the term "international organisation".

6   **If appropriate safeguards pursuant to para. 2 are provided** – such as the Standard Contractual Clauses (para. 2 lit. c) – the international data transfer does **not require an authorisation**.

7   The list with appropriate safeguards in para. 2 lit. a to f that do not require an authorisation is exhaustive. All other appropriate safeguards are subject to authorisation pursuant to para. 3.

8   Recital 108 last sentence clarifies that the transfer is not subject to an authorisation only if there is a legally binding administrative arrangement. If it is not legally binding the transfer is subject to authorisation pursuant to para. 3 lit. b.

9   Transfers based on **Binding Corporate Rules** do not have to be authorised, irrespective of which supervisory authority approved the binding corporate rules. This unlimited recognition among all Member States is justified because the approval pursuant to Art. 47 para. 1 is provided in accordance with the consistency mechanism under Art. 63.

10   The GDPR uses the terms "**standard data protection clauses**" and "**standard contractual clauses**" as synonyms for: (i) the contract templates published by the European Commission or a supervisory authority which compensate the lack of an adequate level of data protection in a third country (para. 2 lit. c and d); and (ii) templates for regular data processing agreements published by the European Commission or a supervisory authority (Art. 28 para. 7 and 8).

11   Pursuant to the law and administrative practice of some Member States, a transfer on the basis of standard contractual clauses was subject to an authorisation requirement if the standard contractual clauses were modified in any way. Recital 109 sentence 1 now states that controllers and processors should not be prevented "from adding other clauses or additional safeguards provided that they do not contradict, directly or indirectly, the standard contractual clauses adopted by the Commission or by a supervisory authority or prejudice the fundamental rights or freedoms of the data subjects". In addition, Recital 109 last sentence determines that "controllers and processors should be encouraged to provide additional safeguards via contractual commitments that supplement standard protection clauses". Based on this, it can be assumed that **modifications of the standard contractual clauses** which increase the level of protection or at least do not lower it do not give reason for an authorisation requirement; rather, para. 2 lit. c applies.

12   The Standard Contractual Clauses already adopted pursuant to Art. 26 para. 4 Data Protection Directive remain in force (cf. para. 5 sentence 2). These include the Standard Contractual Clauses for the transfer of personal data to third countries – controller to controller transfers (Commission Decision 2001/497/EC, Commission Decision 2004/915/EC) as well as the Standard Contractual Clauses for the transfer of personal data to processors established in third countries (Commission Decision 2010/87/EU).

13   Before their adoption, the standard data protection clauses mentioned in para. 2 lit. d must be provided to the Board for it to issue an opinion (Art. 64 para. 1 lit. d).

14   National supervisory authorities, too, are authorised to adopt standard data protection clauses pursuant to para. 2 lit. d. The obligation to provide them to the Board (Art. 64 para. 1 lit. d) as well as the examination procedure pursuant to Art. 93 para. 2 ensure a certain level of consistency.

15   The enumerations in para. 3 lit. a and b are exemplary in nature so that other appropriate safeguards are conceivable. A transfer based on para. 3 always requires an authorisation from the supervisory authority.

16 See Art. 4 No. 9 regarding the definition of the term "recipient".

17 Before standard contractual clauses pursuant to para. 3 lit. a are authorised they must be provided to the Board for it to issue an opinion (Art. 64 para. 1 lit. e).

18 Cf. Recital 108 sentence 5 which states that "transfers may also be carried out by public authorities or bodies with public authorities or bodies in third countries or with international organisations with corresponding duties or functions, including on the basis of provisions to be inserted into administrative arrangements, such as a memorandum of understanding, providing for enforceable and effective rights for data subjects".

Article 47

Binding corporate rules[1]

1. The competent supervisory authority shall approve binding corporate rules[2] in accordance with the consistency mechanism set out in Article 63,[3] provided that they:
  (a) are legally binding and apply to and are enforced by every member concerned of the group of undertakings,[4] or group of enterprises engaged in a joint economic activity,[5] including their employees;
  (b) expressly confer enforceable rights on data subjects with regard to the processing of their personal data; and
  (c) fulfil the requirements laid down in paragraph 2.
2. The binding corporate rules referred to in paragraph 1 shall specify at least:
  (a) the structure and contact details[6] of the group of undertakings, or group of enterprises engaged in a joint economic activity and of each of its members;[7]
  (b) the data transfers or set of transfers, including the categories of personal data, the type of processing and its purposes, the type of data subjects affected and the identification of the third country or countries in question;
  (c) their legally binding nature, both internally and externally;
  (d) the application of the general data protection principles, in particular purpose limitation, data minimisation, limited storage periods, data quality, data protection by design and by default, legal basis for processing, processing of special categories of personal data, measures to ensure data security, and the requirements in respect of onward transfers to bodies not bound by the binding corporate rules;
  (e) the rights of data subjects in regard to processing and the means to exercise those rights, including the right not to be subject to decisions based solely on automated processing, including profiling in accordance with Article 22, the right to lodge a complaint with the competent supervisory authority and before the competent courts of the Member States in accordance with Article 79, and to obtain redress and, where appropriate, compensation for a breach of the binding corporate rules;
  (f) the acceptance by the controller or processor established on the territory of a Member State of liability for any breaches of the binding corporate rules by any member concerned not established in the Union; the controller or the processor shall be exempt from that liability, in whole or in part, only if it proves that that member is not responsible for the event giving rise to the damage;
  (g) how the information on the binding corporate rules, in particular on the provisions referred to in points (d), (e) and (f) of this paragraph is provided to the data subjects in addition to Articles 13 and 14;
  (h) the tasks of any data protection officer designated in accordance with Article 37 or any other person or entity in charge of the monitoring compliance with the binding corporate rules within the group of

undertakings, or group of enterprises engaged in a joint economic activity, as well as monitoring training and complaint-handling;

(i) the complaint procedures;

(j) the mechanisms within the group of undertakings, or group of enterprises engaged in a joint economic activity for ensuring the verification of compliance with the binding corporate rules. Such mechanisms shall include data protection audits and methods for ensuring corrective actions to protect the rights of the data subject. Results of such verification should be communicated to the person or entity referred to in point (h) and to the board of the controlling undertaking of a group of undertakings, or of the group of enterprises engaged in a joint economic activity, and should be available upon request to the competent supervisory authority;

(k) the mechanisms for reporting and recording changes to the rules and reporting those changes to the supervisory authority;

(l) the cooperation mechanism with the supervisory authority to ensure compliance by any member of the group of undertakings, or group of enterprises engaged in a joint economic activity, in particular by making available to the supervisory authority the results of verifications of the measures referred to in point (j);

(m) the mechanisms for reporting to the competent supervisory authority any legal requirements to which a member of the group of undertakings, or group of enterprises engaged in a joint economic activity is subject in a third country which are likely to have a substantial adverse effect on the guarantees provided by the binding corporate rules; and

(n) the appropriate data protection training to personnel having permanent or regular access to personal data.

3. The Commission may specify the format and procedures for the exchange of information between controllers, processors and supervisory authorities for binding corporate rules within the meaning of this Article. Those implementing acts shall be adopted in accordance with the examination procedure set out in Article 93(2).

Recitals:

(110)A group of undertakings, or a group of enterprises engaged in a joint economic activity, should be able to make use of approved binding corporate rules for its international transfers from the Union to organisations within the same group of undertakings, or group of enterprises engaged in a joint economic activity, provided that such corporate rules include all essential principles and enforceable rights to ensure appropriate safeguards for transfers or categories of transfers of personal data.

Commentary:

1   **Binding corporate rules** are also known as "BCR". Pursuant to Art. 46 para. 2 lit. b, they constitute appropriate safeguards for all intra-group data transfers, however not with regard to transfers to external third parties. They therefore constitute a kind of privilege for groups of companies.

Pursuant to Art. 70 para. 1 lit. i, the Board may issue guidelines, recommendations and best practices to further specify the criteria and requirements for personal data transfers based on binding corporate rules mentioned in para. 2.

2   See Art. 4 No. 20 regarding the definition of the term "binding corporate rules".

3   The applicability of the **consistency mechanism** in Art. 63 in conjunction with Art. 64 para. 1 lit. f justifies an unlimited recognition of the BCR among all Member States (see Art. 46 cmt. 9).

4   See Art. 4 No. 19 regarding the definition of the term "group of undertakings".

5   See Art. 4 cmt. 49 regarding the interpretation of the term "group of undertakings engaged in a joint economic activity" and its differentiation from the "group of undertakings" within the meaning of Art. 4 No. 19.

6   See Art. 13 cmt. 7 regarding the definition of the term "contact details".

7   Despite para. 2 lit. a which provides that the BCR has to list the contact details of all group members, the acquisition of new group companies should in our opinion not necessarily require a new approval. In practice, the advice of the competent supervisory authority should be sought.

Article 48

Transfers or disclosures not authorised by Union law

Any judgment of a court or tribunal and any decision of an administrative authority of a third country[1] requiring a controller or processor to transfer or disclose personal data may only be recognised or enforceable in any manner if based on an international agreement, such as a mutual legal assistance treaty, in force between the requesting third country and the Union or a Member State, without prejudice to other grounds for transfer pursuant to this Chapter.[2]

Recital:

(115) Some third countries adopt laws, regulations and other legal acts which purport to directly regulate the processing activities of natural and legal persons under the jurisdiction of the Member States. This may include judgments of courts or tribunals or decisions of administrative authorities in third countries requiring a controller or processor to transfer or disclose personal data, and which are not based on an international agreement, such as a mutual legal assistance treaty, in force between the requesting third country and the Union or a Member State. The extraterritorial application of those laws, regulations and other legal acts may be in breach of international law and may impede the attainment of the protection of natural persons ensured in the Union by this Regulation. Transfers should only be allowed where the conditions of this Regulation for a transfer to third countries are met. This may be the case, inter alia, where disclosure is necessary for an important ground of public interest recognised in Union or Member State law to which the controller is subject.

Commentary:

1   See Art. 44 cmt. 2 regarding the definition of the term "third country".
2   Due to the lack of recognition of these decisions of a third country, the lawfulness of disclosures must be assessed pursuant to the GDPR only. In particular, there has to be a **legal basis pursuant to Arts. 6, 9, or 10** (eg, a prevailing legitimate interest pursuant to Art. 6 para. 1 subpara. 1 lit. f or a necessity for the establishment, exercise, or defense of legal claims pursuant to Art. 9 para. 2 lit. f).

Article 49

Derogations for specific situations[1]

1. In the absence of an adequacy decision pursuant to Article 45(3), or of appropriate safeguards pursuant to Article 46, including binding corporate rules,[2] a transfer[3] or a set of transfers of personal data to a third country[4] or an international organisation shall take place only on one of the following conditions:[5]

(a) the data subject has explicitly consented[6,7] to the proposed transfer, after having been informed of the possible risks of such transfers for the data subject due to the absence of an adequacy decision and appropriate safeguards;[8]

(b) the transfer is necessary for the performance of a contract between the data subject and the controller or the implementation of pre-contractual measures taken at the data subject's request;[9]

(c) the transfer is necessary for the conclusion or performance of a contract concluded in the interest of the data subject between the controller and another natural or legal person;[10,11]

(d) the transfer is necessary for important reasons of public interest;[12]

(e) the transfer is necessary for the establishment, exercise or defence of legal claims;[13]

(f) the transfer is necessary in order to protect the vital interests of the data subject or of other persons, where the data subject is physically or legally incapable of giving consent;[14]

(g) the transfer is made from a register which according to Union or Member State law is intended to provide information to the public and which is open to consultation either by the public in general or by any person who can demonstrate a legitimate interest,[15] but only to the extent that the conditions laid down by Union or Member State law for consultation are fulfilled in the particular case.[16]

Where a transfer could not be based on a provision in Article 45 or 46, including the provisions on binding corporate rules, and none of the derogations for a specific situation referred to in the first subparagraph of this paragraph is applicable, a transfer to a third country or an international organisation may take place only if the transfer is not repetitive, concerns only a limited number of data subjects, is necessary for the purposes of compelling legitimate interests pursued by the controller which are not overridden by the interests or rights and freedoms of the data subject, and the controller has assessed all the circumstances surrounding the data transfer and has on the basis of that assessment provided suitable safeguards with regard to the protection of personal data. The controller shall inform the supervisory authority of the transfer. The controller shall, in addition to providing the information referred to in Articles 13 and 14, inform the data subject of the transfer and on the compelling legitimate interests pursued.[17]

2. A transfer pursuant to point (g) of the first subparagraph of paragraph 1 shall

not involve the entirety of the personal data or entire categories of the personal data contained in the register. Where the register is intended for consultation by persons having a legitimate interest, the transfer shall be made only at the request of those persons or if they are to be the recipients.

3. Points (a), (b) and (c) of the first subparagraph of paragraph 1 and the second subparagraph thereof shall not apply to activities carried out by public authorities in the exercise of their public powers.

4. The public interest referred to in point (d) of the first subparagraph of paragraph 1 shall be recognised in Union law or in the law of the Member State to which the controller is subject.

5. In the absence of an adequacy decision, Union or Member State law may, for important reasons of public interest, expressly set limits to the transfer of specific categories of personal data to a third country or an international organisation. Member States shall notify such provisions to the Commission.

6. The controller or processor shall document the assessment as well as the suitable safeguards referred to in the second subparagraph of paragraph 1 of this Article in the records referred to in Article 30.

Recitals:

(111)Provisions should be made for the possibility for transfers in certain circumstances where the data subject has given his or her explicit consent, where the transfer is occasional and necessary in relation to a contract or a legal claim, regardless of whether in a judicial procedure or whether in an administrative or any out-of-court procedure, including procedures before regulatory bodies. Provision should also be made for the possibility for transfers where important grounds of public interest laid down by Union or Member State law so require or where the transfer is made from a register established by law and intended for consultation by the public or persons having a legitimate interest. In the latter case, such a transfer should not involve the entirety of the personal data or entire categories of the data contained in the register and, when the register is intended for consultation by persons having a legitimate interest, the transfer should be made only at the request of those persons or, if they are to be the recipients, taking into full account the interests and fundamental rights of the data subject.

(112)Those derogations should in particular apply to data transfers required and necessary for important reasons of public interest, for example in cases of international data exchange between competition authorities, tax or customs administrations, between financial supervisory authorities, between services competent for social security matters, or for public health, for example in the case of contact tracing for contagious diseases or in order to reduce and/or eliminate doping in sport. A transfer of personal data should also be regarded as lawful where it is necessary to protect an interest which is essential for the data subject's or another person's vital interests, including physical integrity or life, if the data subject is incapable of giving consent. In the absence of an adequacy decision, Union or Member State law may, for important reasons of public interest, expressly set limits to the transfer of specific categories of data to a third country or an international organisation. Member States should notify

such provisions to the Commission. Any transfer to an international humanitarian organisation of personal data of a data subject who is physically or legally incapable of giving consent, with a view to accomplishing a task incumbent under the Geneva Conventions or to complying with international humanitarian law applicable in armed conflicts, could be considered to be necessary for an important reason of public interest or because it is in the vital interest of the data subject.

(113) Transfers which can be qualified as not repetitive and that only concern a limited number of data subjects, could also be possible for the purposes of the compelling legitimate interests pursued by the controller, when those interests are not overridden by the interests or rights and freedoms of the data subject and when the controller has assessed all the circumstances surrounding the data transfer. The controller should give particular consideration to the nature of the personal data, the purpose and duration of the proposed processing operation or operations, as well as the situation in the country of origin, the third country and the country of final destination, and should provide suitable safeguards to protect fundamental rights and freedoms of natural persons with regard to the processing of their personal data. Such transfers should be possible only in residual cases where none of the other grounds for transfer are applicable. For scientific or historical research purposes or statistical purposes, the legitimate expectations of society for an increase of knowledge should be taken into consideration. The controller should inform the supervisory authority and the data subject about the transfer.

(114) In any case, where the Commission has taken no decision on the adequate level of data protection in a third country, the controller or processor should make use of solutions that provide data subjects with enforceable and effective rights as regards the processing of their data in the Union once those data have been transferred so that that they will continue to benefit from fundamental rights and safeguards.

[Recital 115 can be found with Art. 48.]

Commentary:

1   The permissibility of a transfer based on one of the derogations in Art. 47 is subject to para. 5 which allows for limitations under national law "in the absence of an adequacy decision".

2   See Art. 47.

3   See Art. 44 cmt. 1 regarding the definition of the term "transfer".

4   See Art. 44 cmt. 2 regarding the definition of the term "third country".

5   The Board may issue guidelines, recommendations and best practices to further specify the criteria and requirements for personal data transfers pursuant to para. 1 (Art. 70 para. 1 lit. j).

6   See Art. 4 No. 11 regarding the definition of the term "**consent**" and Art. 7 et seq. regarding the further requirements for consent. In addition to the requirements mentioned there, consent concerning international data transfers must be **explicit**. In particular clicking on a checkbox with a respective wording in the course of an online registration process is to be regarded as explicit consent.

7   The exception of the requirement of explicit consent in para. 1 subpara. 1 lit. a does not apply to activities carried out by public authorities in the exercise of their public powers (see para. 3).

8   The requirement that explicit consent can only be given after having been informed of the possible risks of such transfers due to the absence of an adequacy decision and appropriate safeguards corresponds to the requirement of informed consent (cf. Art. 4 cmt. 25). This makes it necessary to inform the data subject about the third country to which the data is transferred. Whether or not it must be informed about the identity of the recipient remains questionable, in particular because the recipients usually do not have any influence on the risk existing in the third country.

9   The derogation concerning the **necessity of contract performance respectively concerning the implementation of pre-contractual measures** pursuant to para. 1 subpara. 1 lit. b does not apply to activities carried out by public authorities in the exercise of their public powers (see para. 3).

10   Para. 1 subpara. 1 lit. c applies, in contrast to lit. b, if the respective contract was not concluded with the data subject but at least in the interests of the data subject.

11   The derogation concerning the **necessity for the conclusion or performance of a contract concluded in the interest of the data subject** pursuant to para. 1 subpara. 1 lit. c does not apply to activities carried out by public authorities in the exercise of their public powers (see para. 3).

12   The public interest within the meaning of para. 1 subpara. 1 lit. d must be an interest pursuant to para. 4 which is recognised in Union law or in the law of the Member State to which the controller is subject. As examples for "important reasons of public interest", Recital 112 mentions "international data exchange between competition authorities, tax or customs administrations, between financial supervisory authorities, between services competent for social security matters, or for public health, for example in the case of contact tracing for contagious diseases or in order to reduce and/or eliminate doping in sport". As a further example Recital 112 last sentence mentions the transfer "to an international humanitarian organisation [...], with a view to accomplishing a task incumbent under the Geneva Conventions or to complying with international humanitarian law applicable in armed conflicts".

13   Recital 111 sentence 1 clarifies that the transfer **necessary for the establishment, exercise or defense of legal claims** is not limited to court proceedings but applies more generally, "regardless of whether in a judicial procedure or whether in an administrative or any out-of-court procedure, including procedures before regulatory bodies". Regarding the general legal basis for the processing of sensitive data cf. Art. 9 para. 2 lit. f.

14   See Art. 4 No 11 regarding the definition of the term "consent".

15   A register within the meaning of para. 1 subpara. 1 lit. g is for example the commercial register or the land register.

16   See para. 2.

17   Based on para. 1 subpara. 2 and subpara. 3, the **following requirements** can be

derived to **exceptionally allow a data transfer** despite the absence of an adequacy decision, suitable safeguards or one of the derogations in para. 1 subpara. 1: (i) the transfer is not repetitive; (ii) the transfer concerns only a limited number of data subjects; (iii) there are prevailing legitimate interests of the controller; (iv) the controller provided suitable safeguards with regard to the protection of personal data; (v) the controller informs the supervisory authority of the transfer; and (vi) the controller informs the data subject *ad hoc* (and not prior pursuant to Art. 13 et seq.) about the transfer and the compelling legitimate interests (cf. also Recital 113).

Article 50

International cooperation for the protection of personal data
In relation to third countries[1] and international organisations,[2] the Commission and supervisory authorities shall take appropriate steps to:
- (a) develop international cooperation mechanisms to facilitate the effective enforcement of legislation for the protection of personal data;
- (b) provide international mutual assistance in the enforcement of legislation for the protection of personal data, including through notification, complaint referral, investigative assistance and information exchange, subject to appropriate safeguards for the protection of personal data and other fundamental rights and freedoms;
- (c) engage relevant stakeholders in discussion and activities aimed at furthering international cooperation in the enforcement of legislation for the protection of personal data;
- (d) promote the exchange and documentation of personal data protection legislation and practice, including on jurisdictional conflicts with third countries.

Recital:

(116) When personal data moves across borders outside the Union it may put at increased risk the ability of natural persons to exercise data protection rights in particular to protect themselves from the unlawful use or disclosure of that information. At the same time, supervisory authorities may find that they are unable to pursue complaints or conduct investigations relating to the activities outside their borders. Their efforts to work together in the cross-border context may also be hampered by insufficient preventative or remedial powers, inconsistent legal regimes, and practical obstacles like resource constraints. Therefore, there is a need to promote closer cooperation among data protection supervisory authorities to help them exchange information and carry out investigations with their international counterparts. For the purposes of developing international cooperation mechanisms to facilitate and provide international mutual assistance for the enforcement of legislation for the protection of personal data, the Commission and the supervisory authorities should exchange information and cooperate in activities related to the exercise of their powers with competent authorities in third countries, based on reciprocity and in accordance with this Regulation.

Commentary:
1 See Art. 44 cmt. 2 regarding the definition of the term "third country".
2 See Art. 4 No. 26 regarding the definition of the term "international organisation".

Chapter VI – Independent supervisory authorities

Section 1 – Independent status

Article 51

Supervisory authority

1. Each Member State shall provide for one or more[1] independent public authorities[2] to be responsible for monitoring the application of this Regulation, in order to protect the fundamental rights and freedoms of natural persons in relation to processing and to facilitate the free flow of personal data within the Union ('supervisory authority').[3,4]

2. Each supervisory authority shall contribute to the consistent application of this Regulation throughout the Union. For that purpose, the supervisory authorities shall cooperate with each other and the Commission in accordance with Chapter VII.

3. Where more than one supervisory authority is established in a Member State, that Member State shall designate the supervisory authority which is to represent those authorities in the Board and shall set out the mechanism to ensure compliance by the other authorities with the rules relating to the consistency mechanism referred to in Article 63.

4. Each Member State shall notify to the Commission the provisions of its law which it adopts pursuant to this Chapter, by 25 May 2018 and, without delay, any subsequent amendment affecting them.

Recital:

(117)The establishment of supervisory authorities in Member States, empowered to perform their tasks and exercise their powers with complete independence, is an essential component of the protection of natural persons with regard to the processing of their personal data. Member States should be able to establish more than one supervisory authority, to reflect their constitutional, organisational and administrative structure.

Commentary:

1   Therefore, it can be expected that in federally structured Member States, such as the Federal Republic of Germany, there will still be (at least) one supervisory authority per state and one on the federal level. A (certain) synchronisation will in particular be ensured by para. 3 (cf. Recital 119).

2   The term "authority" is not further specified in the GDPR. Since the wording did not change, content-related changes to the present legal situation cannot be assumed.

3   This provision implements Art. 16 para. 2 last sentence TFEU which provides for the monitoring of data protection law compliance by independent authorities in primary EU law. See also Art. 8 para. 3 Charter.

4   For this purpose, cross-border cooperation between the supervisory authorities is necessary "without the need for any agreement between Member States on the provision of mutual assistance or on such cooperation" (Recital 123).

Article 52

Independence

1. Each supervisory authority shall act with complete independence in performing its tasks and exercising its powers in accordance with this Regulation.[1,2]

2. The member or members[3] of each supervisory authority shall, in the performance of their tasks and exercise of their powers in accordance with this Regulation, remain free from external influence, whether direct or indirect, and shall neither seek nor take instructions from anybody.

3. Member or members of each supervisory authority shall refrain from any action incompatible with their duties and shall not, during their term of office, engage in any incompatible occupation, whether gainful or not.

4. Each Member State shall ensure that each supervisory authority is provided with the human, technical and financial resources, premises and infrastructure necessary for the effective performance of its tasks and exercise of its powers, including those to be carried out in the context of mutual assistance, cooperation and participation in the Board.[4]

5. Each Member State shall ensure that each supervisory authority chooses and has its own staff which shall be subject to the exclusive direction of the member or members of the supervisory authority concerned.

6. Each Member State shall ensure that each supervisory authority is subject to financial control which does not affect its independence and that it has separate, public annual budgets, which may be part of the overall state or national budget.

Recitals:

(118)The independence of supervisory authorities should not mean that the supervisory authorities cannot be subject to control or monitoring mechanisms regarding their financial expenditure or to judicial review.

(119)Where a Member State establishes several supervisory authorities, it should establish by law mechanisms for ensuring the effective participation of those supervisory authorities in the consistency mechanism. That Member State should in particular designate the supervisory authority which functions as a single contact point for the effective participation of those authorities in the mechanism, to ensure swift and smooth cooperation with other supervisory authorities, the Board and the Commission.

(120)Each supervisory authority should be provided with the financial and human resources, premises and infrastructure necessary for the effective performance of their tasks, including those related to mutual assistance and cooperation with other supervisory authorities throughout the Union. Each supervisory authority should have a separate, public annual budget, which may be part of the overall state or national budget.

Commentary:

1   Regarding the independency of the Austrian Data Protection Authority cf. CJEU October 16, 2012, C-614/10 – *Commission/Austria*; cf. also CJEU 9 March 2010, C-518/07 – *Commission/Germany*.

2   The fact that the supervisory authorities are subject to control or monitoring mechanisms regarding their financial expenditure or to judicial review does not impact their independence (Recital 118).

3   In the case of a monocratic authority such as the Austrian Data Protection Authority, there is only one "member", that is, the head of the supervisory authority.

4   The new tasks of the Austrian Data Protection Authority, including carrying out administrative procedures due to violations of the GDPR, will require an increase of the financial and personal resources of the Austrian Data Protection Authority. The budget of the Austrian Data Protection Authority in 2016 was EUR 1,403,000 pursuant to information provided by the deputy director of the Austrian Data Protection Authority.

Article 53

General conditions for the members of the supervisory authority

1. Member States shall provide for each member[1] of their supervisory authorities to be appointed by means of a transparent procedure by:
- their parliament;
- their government;
- their head of State;[2] or
- an independent body entrusted with the appointment under Member State law.

2. Each member shall have the qualifications, experience and skills, in particular in the area of the protection of personal data, required to perform its duties and exercise its powers.[3]

3. The duties of a member shall end in the event of the expiry of the term of office, resignation or compulsory retirement, in accordance with the law of the Member State concerned.

4. A member shall be dismissed only in cases of serious misconduct or if the member no longer fulfils the conditions required for the performance of the duties.

Recital:

(121)The general conditions for the member or members of the supervisory authority should be laid down by law in each Member State and should in particular provide that those members are to be appointed, by means of a transparent procedure, either by the parliament, government or the head of State of the Member State on the basis of a proposal from the government, a member of the government, the parliament or a chamber of the parliament, or by an independent body entrusted under Member State law. In order to ensure the independence of the supervisory authority, the member or members should act with integrity, refrain from any action that is incompatible with their duties and should not, during their term of office, engage in any incompatible occupation, whether gainful or not. The supervisory authority should have its own staff, chosen by the supervisory authority or an independent body established by Member State law, which should be subject to the exclusive direction of the member or members of the supervisory authority.

Commentary:

1   In the case of a monocratic authority like the Austrian Data Protection Authority, there is only one "member", that is, the head of the supervisory authority.

2   In Austria, the principles on the appointment of the director of the Austrian Data Protection Authority may remain.

3   The appointment of a person that does not have sufficient qualifications, experience and skills in the area of data protection will not be permitted under the GDPR. The requirements are (likely) higher than those that a data protection officer must fulfil (see in this regard Art. 37 para. 5) and therefore

include at least: (i) a pertinent college degree; (ii) technical knowhow; (iii) special knowledge in the field of data protection law; and (iv) experience in data protection law and data protection supervision.

Article 54

Rules on the establishment of the supervisory authority
1. Each Member State shall provide by law for all of the following:
   (a) the establishment of each supervisory authority;
   (b) the qualifications and eligibility conditions required to be appointed as member of each supervisory authority;
   (c) the rules and procedures for the appointment of the member or members of each supervisory authority;
   (d) the duration of the term of the member or members of each supervisory authority of no less than four years, except for the first appointment after 24 May 2016, part of which may take place for a shorter period where that is necessary to protect the independence of the supervisory authority by means of a staggered appointment procedure;
   (e) whether and, if so, for how many terms[1] the member or members of each supervisory authority is eligible for reappointment;
   (f) the conditions governing the obligations of the member or members and staff of each supervisory authority, prohibitions on actions, occupations and benefits incompatible therewith during and after the term of office and rules governing the cessation of employment.
2. The member or members and the staff of each supervisory authority shall, in accordance with Union or Member State law, be subject to a duty of professional secrecy both during and after their term of office, with regard to any confidential information which has come to their knowledge in the course of the performance of their tasks or exercise of their powers.[2] During their term of office, that duty of professional secrecy shall in particular apply to reporting by natural persons of infringements of this Regulation.[3]

Commentary:
1   A re-appointment therefore remains permissible.
2   Cf., for example, Sec. 310 para. 1 Austrian Criminal Code.
3   The Board may issue guidelines, recommendations and best practices for establishing common procedures regarding para. 2 (Art. 70 para. 1 lit. m).

Section 2 – Competence, tasks and powers

Article 55

Competence[1]
1. Each supervisory authority[2] shall be competent for the performance of the tasks[3] assigned to and the exercise of the powers[4] conferred on it in accordance with this Regulation on the territory of its own Member State.[5,6]
2. Where processing is carried out by public authorities or private bodies acting on the basis of point (c) or (e) of Article 6(1), the supervisory authority of the Member State concerned shall be competent.[7] In such cases Article 56 does not apply.[8]
3. Supervisory authorities shall not be competent to supervise processing operations of courts acting in their judicial capacity.[9]

Recitals:

(122)Each supervisory authority should be competent on the territory of its own Member State to exercise the powers and to perform the tasks conferred on it in accordance with this Regulation. This should cover in particular the processing in the context of the activities of an establishment of the controller or processor on the territory of its own Member State, the processing of personal data carried out by public authorities or private bodies acting in the public interest, processing affecting data subjects on its territory or processing carried out by a controller or processor not established in the Union when targeting data subjects residing on its territory. This should include handling complaints lodged by a data subject, conducting investigations on the application of this Regulation and promoting public awareness of the risks, rules, safeguards and rights in relation to the processing of personal data.

(123)The supervisory authorities should monitor the application of the provisions pursuant to this Regulation and contribute to its consistent application throughout the Union, in order to protect natural persons in relation to the processing of their personal data and to facilitate the free flow of personal data within the internal market. For that purpose, the supervisory authorities should cooperate with each other and with the Commission, without the need for any agreement between Member States on the provision of mutual assistance or on such cooperation.

Commentary:

1   Although the rules on competence of the Data Protection Directive in particular as interpreted by the CJEU often result in parallel competences, they are phrased clearly. In contrast, the **rules on competences** in the GDPR are very **complex**. Whereas Art. 55 para. 1 provides for a general competence of a supervisory authority in its own territory, Art. 56 provides for specific competences for cross-border situations.

2   See Art. 4 No. 21 in conjunction with Art. 51 regarding the definition of the term "supervisory authority".

3   See Art. 57 regarding the tasks of the supervisory authorities.

4   See Art. 58 regarding the powers of the supervisory authorities.

5   This **general competence pursuant to para. 1** should, pursuant to Recital 122, "cover in particular" the following: (1) "the **processing in the context of the activities of an establishment** of the controller or processor on the territory of its own Member State" (this corresponds with Art. 4 No. 1 lit. a Data Protection Directive), (2) "the processing of personal data carried out by public authorities or private bodies acting in the public interest" (cf. Art. 55 para. 2), (3) "processing **affecting data subjects on its territory**", or (4) "processing carried out by a controller or processor not established in the Union **when targeting data subjects residing on its territory**". In particular the alternative triggers of the processing in the context of the activities of an establishment on the one hand and the effect on data subjects in the territory of the supervisory authority on the other hand, will in practice often mean that a general competence pursuant to Art. 55 will exist for several supervisory authorities of different Member States (cf., eg, Art. 33 cmt. 4).

6   A supervisory authority competent pursuant to para. 1 **is not necessarily the supervisory authority concerned** within the meaning of Art. 4 No. 22. If the processing activities do not have a substantial effect on the data subjects in the territory of the supervisory authority, it is generally competent pursuant to para. 1 without Art. 4 No. 22 having to be fulfilled, in particular because Art. 4 No. 22 lit. b requires 'substantial effects' ("substantially affected").

7   **In the cases of para. 2, the exclusive competence rests with the supervisory authority of the Member State where the public authority or private body is established** (cf. Recital 128 sentence 2 which states that in cases of para. 2 "the only supervisory authority competent to exercise the powers conferred to it in accordance with this Regulation should be the supervisory authority of the Member State where the public authority or private body is established").

8   Regarding para. 2, cf. also Recital 128 sentence 1 which states that "the rules on the lead supervisory authority and the one-stop-shop mechanism should not apply where the processing is carried out by public authorities or private bodies in the public interest".

9   Cf. Recital 20 which states that "the competence of the supervisory authorities should not cover the processing of personal data when **courts are acting in their judicial capacity**, in order to safeguard the independence of the judiciary in the performance of its judicial tasks, including decision-making". Recital 20 further states that it "should be possible to entrust supervision of such data processing operations to specific bodies within the judicial system of the Member State, which should, in particular ensure compliance with the rules of this Regulation, enhance awareness among members of the judiciary of their obligations under this Regulation and handle complaints in relation to such data processing operations".

Article 56

Competence of the lead supervisory authority[1]

1. Without prejudice to Article 55, the supervisory authority of the main establishment[2] or of the single establishment[3,4] of the controller or processor[5] shall be competent to act as lead supervisory authority for the cross-border processing carried out by that controller or processor in accordance with the procedure provided in Article 60.[6,7,8]

2. By derogation from paragraph 1,[9] each supervisory authority shall be competent to handle a complaint lodged with it or a possible infringement of this Regulation, if the subject matter[10] relates only to an establishment in its Member State or substantially affects data subjects only in its Member State.[11]

3. In the cases referred to in paragraph 2 of this Article, the supervisory authority shall inform the lead supervisory authority without delay on that matter. Within a period of three weeks after being informed the lead supervisory authority shall decide whether or not it will handle the case in accordance with the procedure provided in Article 60, taking into account whether or not there is an establishment of the controller or processor in the Member State of which the supervisory authority informed it.

4. Where the lead supervisory authority decides to handle the case, the procedure provided in Article 60 shall apply. The supervisory authority which informed the lead supervisory authority may submit to the lead supervisory authority a draft for a decision.[12] The lead supervisory authority shall take utmost account of that draft when preparing the draft decision referred to in Article 60(3).

5. Where the lead supervisory authority decides not to handle the case, the supervisory authority which informed the lead supervisory authority shall handle it according to Articles 61 and 62.[13]

6. The lead supervisory authority shall be the sole interlocutor[14] of the controller or processor for the cross-border[15] processing carried out by that controller or processor.

Recitals:

(124) *Where the processing of personal data takes place in the context of the activities of an establishment of a controller or a processor in the Union and the controller or processor is established in more than one Member State, or where processing taking place in the context of the activities of a single establishment of a controller or processor in the Union substantially affects or is likely to substantially affect data subjects in more than one Member State, the supervisory authority for the main establishment of the controller or processor or for the single establishment of the controller or processor should act as lead authority. It should cooperate with the other authorities concerned, because the controller or processor has an establishment on the territory of their Member State, because data subjects residing on their territory are substantially affected, or because a complaint has been lodged with them. Also where a data subject not residing in that Member State has lodged a complaint, the supervisory authority*

with which such complaint has been lodged should also be a supervisory authority concerned. Within its tasks to issue guidelines on any question covering the application of this Regulation, the Board should be able to issue guidelines in particular on the criteria to be taken into account in order to ascertain whether the processing in question substantially affects data subjects in more than one Member State and on what constitutes a relevant and reasoned objection.

(125) The lead authority should be competent to adopt binding decisions regarding measures applying the powers conferred on it in accordance with this Regulation. In its capacity as lead authority, the supervisory authority should closely involve and coordinate the supervisory authorities concerned in the decision-making process. Where the decision is to reject the complaint by the data subject in whole or in part, that decision should be adopted by the supervisory authority with which the complaint has been lodged.

(126) The decision should be agreed jointly by the lead supervisory authority and the supervisory authorities concerned and should be directed towards the main or single establishment of the controller or processor and be binding on the controller and processor. The controller or processor should take the necessary measures to ensure compliance with this Regulation and the implementation of the decision notified by the lead supervisory authority to the main establishment of the controller or processor as regards the processing activities in the Union.

(127) Each supervisory authority not acting as the lead supervisory authority should be competent to handle local cases where the controller or processor is established in more than one Member State, but the subject matter of the specific processing concerns only processing carried out in a single Member State and involves only data subjects in that single Member State, for example, where the subject matter concerns the processing of employees' personal data in the specific employment context of a Member State. In such cases, the supervisory authority should inform the lead supervisory authority without delay about the matter. After being informed, the lead supervisory authority should decide, whether it will handle the case pursuant to the provision on cooperation between the lead supervisory authority and other supervisory authorities concerned ('one-stop-shop mechanism'), or whether the supervisory authority which informed it should handle the case at local level. When deciding whether it will handle the case, the lead supervisory authority should take into account whether there is an establishment of the controller or processor in the Member State of the supervisory authority which informed it in order to ensure effective enforcement of a decision vis-à-vis the controller or processor. Where the lead supervisory authority decides to handle the case, the supervisory authority which informed it should have the possibility to submit a draft for a decision, of which the lead supervisory authority should take utmost account when preparing its draft decision in that one-stop-shop mechanism.

(128) The rules on the lead supervisory authority and the one-stop-shop mechanism should not apply where the processing is carried out by public authorities or private bodies in the public interest. In such cases the only supervisory authority competent to exercise the powers conferred to it in accordance with this Regulation should be the supervisory authority of the Member State where the public authority or private body is established.

[Recital 129 can be found with Art. 58.]

(130) Where the supervisory authority with which the complaint has been lodged is not the lead supervisory authority, the lead supervisory authority should closely cooperate with the supervisory authority with which the complaint has been lodged in accordance with the provisions on cooperation and consistency laid down in this Regulation. In such cases, the lead supervisory authority should, when taking measures intended to produce legal effects, including the imposition of administrative fines, take utmost account of the view of the supervisory authority with which the complaint has been lodged and which should remain competent to carry out any investigation on the territory of its own Member State in liaison with the competent supervisory authority.

(131) Where another supervisory authority should act as a lead supervisory authority for the processing activities of the controller or processor but the concrete subject matter of a complaint or the possible infringement concerns only processing activities of the controller or processor in the Member State where the complaint has been lodged or the possible infringement detected and the matter does not substantially affect or is not likely to substantially affect data subjects in other Member States, the supervisory authority receiving a complaint or detecting or being informed otherwise of situations that entail possible infringements of this Regulation should seek an amicable settlement with the controller and, if this proves unsuccessful, exercise its full range of powers. This should include: specific processing carried out in the territory of the Member State of the supervisory authority or with regard to data subjects on the territory of that Member State; processing that is carried out in the context of an offer of goods or services specifically aimed at data subjects in the territory of the Member State of the supervisory authority; or processing that has to be assessed taking into account relevant legal obligations under Member State law.

Commentary:

1   **Regarding the differentiation** between the general competence pursuant to Art. 55 para. 1, the lead competence pursuant to Art. 56 para. 1 and the subsidiary competence pursuant to Art. 56 para. 2: A **lead competence** pursuant to para. 1 requires that: (1) the main establishment or the only establishment of the controller respectively the processor is located in the territory of the supervisory authority; and (2) the controller or processor conducts a cross-border processing (cf. Art. 4 cmt. 55).

A **subsidiary competence** of a supervisory authority pursuant to para. 2 applies if para. 1 is fulfilled (cf. cmt. 9 below) and the subject of the complaint or the infringement: (1) is connected with only one establishment in a Member State; or (2) the data subjects of only one Member State are substantially affected (cf. cmt. 10 below). However, if para. 1 is not fulfilled, there is no lead competence pursuant to para. 1, no subsidiary competence pursuant to para. 2, and also the limitation of para. 2 does not apply. In such a case, the competence of the supervisory authorities results from the general competence of Art. 55 para. 1.

This may result in substantial legal uncertainty as outlined in the following cases: a controller with a single establishment in Germany: (1) has its entire data processed by a processor in Austria; or (2) processes, *inter alia*, personal data of Austrian data subjects without "substantially affecting" them; or (3) processes exclusively personal data of Austrian data subjects so that the processing substantially affects exclusively them or is likely to substantially affect exclusively them.

None of these cases constitutes a "cross-border processing" within the meaning of Art. 4 No. 23 (there are neither establishments nor substantial impacts in more than one Member State). Therefore, the competence does not derive from Art. 56 but exclusively from Art. 55 para. 1. In all three cases, the German supervisory authority will be competent because "the processing [takes place] in the context of the activities of an establishment of the controller or processor on the territory of its own Member State" (Recital 122 sentence 2). In the first case, the Austrian supervisory authority could also be generally competent pursuant to Art. 55 para. 1 because the enumeration of elements causing competence in Recital 122 is only exemplary ("in particular") and therefore, due to the broad wording of Art. 55 para. 1, also the place of the data processing could be reason enough to assume a competence. For the second and third case, the competence of the Austrian supervisory authority can be derived directly from Recital 122 because it lists "processing affecting data subjects on its territory", without requiring "substantial effects". This would result in the competence of the Austrian supervisory authority (due to the place of the data processing, respectively the place of residence of the data subjects) and the competence of the German supervisory authority (due to the place of the establishment of the controller), without one of the supervisory authorities having a lead competence or the cooperation procedure pursuant to Art. 60 being applicable.

A plurality of supervisory authorities with general competence pursuant to Art. 55 para. 1 also exists if the processing activity affects data subjects in several Member States (cf. Art. 55 para. 1 in connection with Recital 122) but: (i) the controller does not have an establishment in the Union (in such case Art. 56 para. 1 would not apply; see cmt. 2 below); or (ii) the controller has several establishments, but not a main establishment in the Union (also in such a case Art. 56 para. 1 does not apply; see cmt. 4 below).

The purpose of the GDPR to ensure a consistent enforcement of data protection law (cf. Recital 10) will be achieved only to a limited extent by the rules on competence in the GDPR. Conflicts on competences that will have to be clarified by the CJEU are to be expected.

2 See Art. 4 No. 16 regarding the definition of the term "**main establishment**". In effect: (i) a controller, respectively a processor, can only have a "main establishment" if at least one establishment is located in the Union (cf. Art. 4 cmt. 38 and 45); (ii) the term "main establishment" is relative regarding the respective processing activity, that means, a controller, respectively processor, could not only have one main establishment but multiple main establishments depending on the data processing activity focused on (see Art. 4 cmt. 42 and 45); (iii) controllers generally do not have a group-wide main establishment (see Art. 4 cmt. 42), whereas processors could have a group-wide main

establishment (see Art. 4 cmt. 44); and (iv) a controller that makes its decisions on purposes and means in an establishment in a third country and also has its central administration in a third country does not have a "main establishment" within the meaning of Art. 4 No. 16 lit. a (Art. 4 cmt. 40 and 41).

3   See Art. 3 cmt. 3 regarding the definition of the term "establishment".

4   It follows from the wording "supervisory authority of the main establishment or of the single establishment" that there will be **no lead competence** for a controller or processor **without an establishment in the Union** because such controller or processor will neither have an establishment (in the Union) nor a "main establishment" (see Art. 4 cmt. 38). The same derives from the element "cross-border processing" which will only apply if the controller, respectively the processor, has an establishment in the Union (see Art. 4 cmt. 58).

Furthermore, it follows from the wording "supervisory authority of the main establishment or of the single establishment" that para. 1 will not apply – and therefore the general competence pursuant to Art. 55 para. 1 will apply – if the controller has **several establishments but not its main establishment in the Union**. This fact pattern applies to many globally operating IT companies (eg, cloud service providers) since typically only the parent company decides on the purposes and means of the processing, has its central administration in the US, and its subsidiaries in several Member States are only tasked with the distribution and, possibly, the technical development.

The fact that this practically very relevant fact pattern – the controller has many establishments but not its main establishment in the Union – does not result in a lead competence pursuant to Art. 56 para. 1 (but, in most cases, in multiple general competences pursuant to Art. 55 para. 1) constitutes a disadvantage for these controllers. Additionally, this could lead to disadvantages for the data subjects because a general competence of all supervisory authorities could easily result in a situation where none of the supervisory authorities feel compelled to act or where multiple supervisory authorities pursue inconsistent enforcement strategies against the same controllers.

5   Due to the dual reference to: (i) the main establishment of the controller; and (ii) the main establishment of the processor, the wording of Art. 56 para. 1 could lead to different lead competences in the same matter for the controller on the one hand and for the processor on the other hand. To avoid that, Recital 36 sentence 5 provides that **"the competent lead supervisory authority [of the controller] should remain the supervisory authority"** for the entire case; the supervisory authority of the Member State where the processor has its main establishment "should be considered to be a supervisory authority concerned and that supervisory authority should participate in the cooperation procedure" pursuant to Art. 60. As a consequence, if a processor provides services to multiple controllers located in different Member States, the processor may have to deal with multiple supervisory authorities (see Art. 29 Working Party, Guidelines for identifying a controller or processor's lead supervisory authority, WP 244 rev. 1 (2017), at 9, available at http://ec.europa.eu/newsroom/just/item-detail.cfm?item_id=50083).

6   See Art. 4 No. 23 regarding the definition of the term **"cross-border processing"**. A cross-border processing pursuant to Art. 4 No. 23 only exists if the processing of personal data: (1) takes place in the context of the activities of establishments in more than one Member State of a controller or processor in the Union (lit. a); or (2) takes place in the context of the activities of a single establishment of a controller or processor in the Union but substantially affects or is likely to substantially affect data subjects in more than one Member State (lit. b). Due to a lack of a "cross-border processing", Art. 56 para. 1 (and, thus, para. 2) do not apply in particular to: (1) controllers respectively processors without an establishment in the EU; or (2) controllers, respectively processors, with only one establishment in the EU, whose processing does not substantially affect data subjects in several Member States. In these cases the competence of the supervisory authority follows exclusively from Art. 55 para. 1.

7   **Art. 56 does not apply if** the processing takes place by authorities or private bodies based on **Art. 6 para. 1 lit. c or e** (see Art. 55 para. 2).

8   If there are conflicting views regarding the lead competence, a **binding decision of the Board** can be adopted. In our opinion, also the controller respectively the processor has a right to apply (cf. Art. 65 cmt. 2).

9   Para. 2 is a *lex specialis* in relation to para. 1, that means, **in order to apply para. 2, all elements of para. 1 need to be fulfilled.** This is supported by para. 3 sentence 1 which requires that a competent supervisory authority pursuant to para. 2 must inform the competent lead authority pursuant to para. 1. In addition to that, this can be derived from the systematic location of the rules on the subsidiary competence in Art. 56 with the heading "Competence of the lead supervisory authority".

10   The wording of Art. 56 para. 2 is unfortunate because it does not unambiguously state whether the two alternative requirements "relates only to an establishment in its Member State" and "substantially affects data subjects only in its Member State" only apply to infringements or also to complaints. However, the wording in Recital 131 clearly states that "the concrete subject matter of a complaint or the possible infringement concerns only processing activities of the controller or processor in the Member State where the complaint has been lodged or the possible infringement detected". Therefore, the requirements apply to infringements and complaints.

11   Pursuant to Recital 127 sentence 1, para. 2 applies if "the subject matter concerns the **processing of employees' personal data in the specific employment context** of a Member State".

12   It remains to be seen which national law must be applied to prepare the draft of a decision. Regarding the issues resulting from the missing **conflict of laws rules** in general, see in detail Art. 92 cmt. 5.

13   According to the Art. 29 Working Party, an example for this might be "where a marketing company with its main establishment in Paris launches a product that only affects data subjects residing in Portugal". According to the Art. 29 Working Party, "in such case the French and Portuguese supervisory authority might agree that it is appropriate for the Portuguese supervisory authority to

take the lead in dealing with the matter" (see Art. 29 Working Party, Guidelines for identifying a controller or processor's lead supervisory authority, WP 244 rev. 1 (2017), at 9 seq., available at http://ec.europa.eu/newsroom/just/item-detail.cfm?item_id=50083).

14   The provision in para. 6 that **"the lead supervisory authority shall be the sole interlocutor"** of the controller, or the processor, applies only if the lead authority decides to handle the case pursuant to para. 3. Otherwise, the lead authority would be the sole interlocutor of the controller, or the processor, but pursuant to the wording of para. 4, the cooperation procedure under Art. 60 would not apply and, thus, the interaction between the lead authority and the authority that has subsidiary competence would be unregulated. In particular, it would not be clear which supervisory authority would be competent to adopt the decision (Art. 60 paras. 7, 8 and 9 would not apply).

15   See cmt. 6 regarding the definition of the term "cross-border processing".

Article 57

Tasks

1. Without prejudice to other tasks[1] set out under this Regulation, each supervisory authority shall on its territory:[2]

(a) monitor and enforce the application of this Regulation;

(b) promote public awareness and understanding of the risks, rules, safeguards and rights in relation to processing.[3] Activities addressed specifically to children[4] shall receive specific attention;

(c) advise, in accordance with Member State law, the national parliament, the government, and other institutions and bodies on legislative and administrative measures relating to the protection of natural persons' rights and freedoms with regard to processing;

(d) promote the awareness of controllers and processors of their obligations under this Regulation;

(e) upon request, provide information to any data subject concerning the exercise of their rights under this Regulation and, if appropriate, cooperate with the supervisory authorities in other Member States to that end;

(f) handle complaints lodged by a data subject, or by a body, organisation or association in accordance with Article 80, and investigate, to the extent appropriate, the subject matter of the complaint and inform the complainant of the progress and the outcome of the investigation within a reasonable period, in particular if further investigation or coordination with another supervisory authority is necessary;

(g) cooperate with, including sharing information and provide mutual assistance to, other supervisory authorities with a view to ensuring the consistency of application and enforcement of this Regulation;

(h) conduct investigations on the application of this Regulation, including on the basis of information received from another supervisory authority or other public authority;

(i) monitor relevant developments, insofar as they have an impact on the protection of personal data, in particular the development of information and communication technologies and commercial practices;

(j) adopt standard contractual clauses referred to in Article 28(8) and in point (d) of Article 46(2);

(k) establish and maintain a list in relation to the requirement for data protection impact assessment pursuant to Article 35(4);

(l) give advice on the processing operations referred to in Article 36(2);

(m) encourage the drawing up of codes of conduct pursuant to Article 40(1) and provide an opinion and approve such codes of conduct which provide sufficient safeguards, pursuant to Article 40(5);

(n) encourage the establishment of data protection certification mechanisms and of data protection seals and marks pursuant to Article 42(1), and approve the criteria of certification pursuant to Article 42(5);

(o) where applicable, carry out a periodic review of certifications issued in accordance with Article 42(7);

(p) draft and publish the criteria for accreditation of a body for monitoring codes of conduct pursuant to Article 41 and of a certification body pursuant to Article 43;

(q) conduct the accreditation of a body for monitoring codes of conduct pursuant to Article 41 and of a certification body pursuant to Article 43;

(r) authorise contractual clauses and provisions referred to in Article 46(3);

(s) approve binding corporate rules pursuant to Article 47;

(t) contribute to the activities of the Board;

(u) keep internal records of infringements of this Regulation and of measures taken in accordance with Article 58(2); and

(v) fulfil any other tasks related to the protection of personal data.

2. Each supervisory authority shall facilitate the submission of complaints referred to in point (f) of paragraph 1 by measures such as a complaint submission form which can also be completed electronically, without excluding other means of communication.

3. The performance of the tasks of each supervisory authority shall be free of charge for the data subject and, where applicable, for the data protection officer.

4. Where requests are manifestly unfounded or excessive, in particular because of their repetitive character, the supervisory authority may charge a reasonable fee based on administrative costs, or refuse to act on the request. The supervisory authority shall bear the burden of demonstrating the manifestly unfounded or excessive character of the request.

Recitals:

(132) Awareness-raising activities by supervisory authorities addressed to the public should include specific measures directed at controllers and processors, including micro, small and medium-sized enterprises, as well as natural persons in particular in the educational context.

(133) The supervisory authorities should assist each other in performing their tasks and provide mutual assistance, so as to ensure the consistent application and enforcement of this Regulation in the internal market. A supervisory authority requesting mutual assistance may adopt a provisional measure if it receives no response to a request for mutual assistance within one month of the receipt of that request by the other supervisory authority.

(134) Each supervisory authority should, where appropriate, participate in joint operations with other supervisory authorities. The requested supervisory authority should be obliged to respond to the request within a specified time period.

Commentary:

1   Other tasks could result from a notification of the data subject due to a personal data breach (see Recital 86) which may also "result in an intervention of the supervisory authority in accordance with its tasks and powers laid down in this Regulation" (Recital 87 sentence 3).

2   Regarding the other tasks mentioned in para. 1, it must be referred to Recital 129 sentence 3 which states that "Member States may specify other tasks related to the protection of personal data under this Regulation".

3   This clarifies that a supervisory authority may not act only reactively to (asserted) infringements but also has to perform awareness-raising proactively. In our opinion, this includes the necessity to respond to questions regarding the application and interpretation of data protection law provisions.

4   See Art. 6 cmt. 9 regarding the definition of the term "child".

Article 58

Powers[1]

1. Each supervisory authority shall have all of the following investigative powers:
    (a) to order the controller and the processor, and, where applicable, the controller's or the processor's representative[2] to provide any information it requires for the performance of its tasks;
    (b) to carry out investigations in the form of data protection audits;
    (c) to carry out a review on certifications issued pursuant to Article 42(7);
    (d) to notify the controller or the processor of an alleged infringement of this Regulation;
    (e) to obtain, from the controller and the processor, access to all personal data and to all information necessary for the performance of its tasks;[3]
    (f) to obtain access to any premises of the controller and the processor, including to any data processing equipment and means, in accordance with Union or Member State procedural law.[4,5]
2. Each supervisory authority shall have all of the following corrective powers:
    (a) to issue warnings to a controller or processor that intended processing operations are likely to infringe provisions of this Regulation;
    (b) to issue reprimands to a controller or a processor where processing operations have infringed provisions of this Regulation;[6]
    (c) to order the controller or the processor to comply with the data subject's requests to exercise his or her rights pursuant to this Regulation;
    (d) to order the controller or processor to bring processing operations into compliance with the provisions of this Regulation, where appropriate, in a specified manner and within a specified period;
    (e) to order the controller to communicate[7] a personal data breach to the data subject;[8]
    (f) to impose a temporary or definitive limitation including a ban on processing;
    (g) to order the rectification or erasure of personal data or restriction of processing pursuant to Articles 16, 17 and 18 and the notification of such actions to recipients[9] to whom the personal data have been disclosed pursuant to Article 17(2) and Article 19;
    (h) to withdraw a certification or to order the certification body to withdraw a certification issued pursuant to Articles 42 and 43, or to order the certification body not to issue certification if the requirements for the certification are not or are no longer met;
    (i) to impose an administrative fine pursuant to Article 83, in addition to, or instead of measures referred to in this paragraph, depending on the circumstances of each individual case;
    (j) to order the suspension of data flows to a recipient in a third country or to an international organisation.[10]
3. Each supervisory authority shall have all of the following authorisation and advisory powers:

(a) to advise the controller in accordance with the prior consultation procedure referred to in Article 36;

(b) to issue, on its own initiative or on request, opinions to the national parliament, the Member State government or, in accordance with Member State law, to other institutions and bodies as well as to the public on any issue related to the protection of personal data;

(c) to authorise processing referred to in Article 36(5), if the law of the Member State requires such prior authorisation;

(d) to issue an opinion and approve draft codes of conduct pursuant to Article 40(5);

(e) to accredit certification bodies pursuant to Article 43;

(f) to issue certifications and approve criteria of certification in accordance with Article 42(5);

(g) to adopt standard data protection clauses referred to in Article 28(8) and in point (d) of Article 46(2);

(h) to authorise contractual clauses referred to in point (a) of Article 46(3);

(i) to authorise administrative arrangements referred to in point (b) of Article 46(3);

(j) to approve binding corporate rules pursuant to Article 47.

4. The exercise of the powers conferred on the supervisory authority pursuant to this Article shall be subject to appropriate safeguards, including effective judicial remedy and due process, set out in Union and Member State law in accordance with the Charter.

5. Each Member State shall provide by law that its supervisory authority shall have the power to bring infringements of this Regulation to the attention of the judicial authorities and where appropriate, to commence or engage otherwise in legal proceedings, in order to enforce the provisions of this Regulation.

6. Each Member State may provide by law that its supervisory authority shall have additional powers to those referred to in paragraphs 1, 2 and 3. The exercise of those powers shall not impair the effective operation of Chapter VII.

Recital:

(129)In order to ensure consistent monitoring and enforcement of this Regulation throughout the Union, the supervisory authorities should have in each Member State the same tasks and effective powers, including powers of investigation, corrective powers and sanctions, and authorisation and advisory powers, in particular in cases of complaints from natural persons, and without prejudice to the powers of prosecutorial authorities under Member State law, to bring infringements of this Regulation to the attention of the judicial authorities and engage in legal proceedings. Such powers should also include the power to impose a temporary or definitive limitation, including a ban, on processing. Member States may specify other tasks related to the protection of personal data under this Regulation. The powers of supervisory authorities should be exercised in accordance with appropriate procedural safeguards set out in Union and Member State law, impartially, fairly and within a reasonable time. In particular each measure should be appropriate, necessary and

proportionate in view of ensuring compliance with this Regulation, taking into account the circumstances of each individual case, respect the right of every person to be heard before any individual measure which would affect him or her adversely is taken and avoid superfluous costs and excessive inconveniences for the persons concerned. Investigatory powers as regards access to premises should be exercised in accordance with specific requirements in Member State procedural law, such as the requirement to obtain a prior judicial authorisation. Each legally binding measure of the supervisory authority should be in writing, be clear and unambiguous, indicate the supervisory authority which has issued the measure, the date of issue of the measure, bear the signature of the head, or a member of the supervisory authority authorised by him or her, give the reasons for the measure, and refer to the right of an effective remedy. This should not preclude additional requirements pursuant to Member State procedural law. The adoption of a legally binding decision implies that it may give rise to judicial review in the Member State of the supervisory authority that adopted the decision.

Commentary:

1. The Board may draw up guidance concerning the application of the measures referred to in paras. 1 to 3 (Art. 70 para. 1 lit. k).

2. See Art. 4 No. 17 regarding the definition of the term "representative".

3. The power pursuant to **para. 1 lit. e** mirrors a respective **obligation of the controller or the processor** (see Art. 83 para. 5 lit. e).

4. Pursuant to Recital 129 sentence 6, "investigatory powers as regards access to premises should be exercised in accordance with specific requirements in Member State procedural law, such as the requirement to obtain a prior judicial authorisation".

5. The power pursuant to **para. 1 lit. f** mirrors a respective **obligation of the controller or the processor** (see Art. 83 para. 5 lit. e).

6. See Art. 83 cmt. 2 regarding the requirements for a warning instead of an administrative fine.

7. See Art. 34 para. 4.

8. See Art. 4 No. 12 regarding the definition of the term "personal data breach".

9. See Art. 4 No. 9 regarding the definition of the term "recipient".

10. See Art. 4 No. 26 regarding the definition of the term "international organisation".

Article 59

Activity reports

Each supervisory authority[1] shall draw up an annual report[2] on its activities, which may include a list of types of infringement notified and types of measures taken in accordance with Article 58(2). Those reports shall be transmitted to the national parliament, the government and other authorities as designated by Member State law. They shall be made available to the public, to the Commission and to the Board.[3,4]

Commentary:

1   The European Data Protection Supervisor, too, publishes an annual report, cf. https://edps.europa.eu/annual-reports_en.

2   In addition to this formal report, there are numerous informal public statements by the respective heads of supervisory authorities, for example, of the European Data Protection Officer, https://edps.europa.eu/press-publications/press-news/blog_en.

3   The reports of the Austrian Data Protection Authority are currently published at www.dsb.gv.at/dokumente – since 2014 on an annual basis.

4   The reports of the German federal and state data protection authorities are available at www.thm.de/zaftda/.

Chapter VII – Cooperation and consistency

Section 1 – Cooperation[1]

Article 60

Cooperation between the lead supervisory authority and the other supervisory authorities concerned

1. The lead supervisory authority shall cooperate with the other supervisory authorities concerned[2] in accordance with this Article in an endeavour to reach consensus. The lead supervisory authority and the supervisory authorities concerned shall exchange all relevant information with each other.

2. The lead supervisory authority may request at any time other supervisory authorities concerned to provide mutual assistance pursuant to Article 61 and may conduct joint operations pursuant to Article 62, in particular for carrying out investigations or for monitoring the implementation of a measure concerning a controller or processor established in another Member State.

3. The lead supervisory authority shall, without delay, communicate the relevant information on the matter to the other supervisory authorities concerned. It shall without delay submit a draft decision[3] to the other supervisory authorities concerned for their opinion and take due account of their views.

4. Where any of the other supervisory authorities concerned within a period of four weeks after having been consulted in accordance with paragraph 3 of this Article, expresses a relevant and reasoned objection[4] to the draft decision, the lead supervisory authority shall, if it does not follow the relevant and reasoned objection or is of the opinion that the objection is not relevant or reasoned, submit the matter to the consistency mechanism referred to in Article 63.

5. Where the lead supervisory authority intends to follow the relevant and reasoned objection made, it shall submit to the other supervisory authorities concerned a revised draft decision for their opinion. That revised draft decision shall be subject to the procedure referred to in paragraph 4 within a period of two weeks.

6. Where none of the other supervisory authorities concerned has objected to the draft decision submitted by the lead supervisory authority within the period referred to in paragraphs 4 and 5, the lead supervisory authority and the supervisory authorities concerned shall be deemed to be in agreement with that draft decision and shall be bound by it.

7. The lead supervisory authority shall adopt and notify the decision to the main establishment[5] or single establishment[6] of the controller or processor, as the case may be and inform the other supervisory authorities concerned and the Board of the decision in question, including a summary of the relevant facts and grounds. The supervisory authority with which a complaint has been lodged shall inform the complainant on the decision.

8. By derogation from paragraph 7, where a complaint is dismissed or rejected, the supervisory authority with which the complaint was lodged shall adopt the decision and notify it to the complainant and shall inform the controller thereof.[7]

9. Where the lead supervisory authority and the supervisory authorities concerned agree[8] to dismiss or reject parts of a complaint and to act on other parts of that complaint, a separate decision shall be adopted for each of those parts of the matter. The lead supervisory authority shall adopt the decision for the part concerning actions in relation to the controller, shall notify it to the main establishment or single establishment of the controller or processor on the territory of its Member State and shall inform the complainant thereof, while the supervisory authority of the complainant shall adopt the decision for the part concerning dismissal or rejection of that complaint,[9] and shall notify it to that complainant and shall inform the controller or processor thereof.

10. After being notified of the decision of the lead supervisory authority pursuant to paragraphs 7 and 9, the controller or processor shall take the necessary measures to ensure compliance with the decision as regards processing activities in the context of all its establishments in the Union. The controller or processor shall notify the measures taken for complying with the decision to the lead supervisory authority, which shall inform the other supervisory authorities concerned.

11. Where, in exceptional circumstances, a supervisory authority concerned has reasons to consider that there is an urgent need to act in order to protect the interests of data subjects, the urgency procedure referred to in Article 66 shall apply.

12. The lead supervisory authority and the other supervisory authorities concerned shall supply the information required under this Article to each other by electronic means, using a standardised format.

Commentary:

1 Given that para. 1 refers to the term lead authority, Art. 60 will, pursuant to its unambiguous language, **only apply if a lead competence exists pursuant to Art. 56 para. 1.**

 In summary, the procedure of cooperation provides the following: (1) The lead supervisory authority must **submit the draft decision to the other supervisory authorities concerned for their opinion without undue delay** and take due account of their views (para. 3); (2) the supervisory authorities concerned may, within a period of four weeks, express a **relevant and reasoned objection** (para. 4); and (3) the lead supervisory authority must submit the matter to the **consistency mechanism** pursuant to Art. 63 in conjunction with

Art. 65 para. 1 lit. a if it does not follow the objection or is of the opinion that the objection is not relevant or reasoned (para. 4). Where the lead supervisory authority intends to follow the objection, it must submit a revised draft decision to the other supervisory authorities concerned for their opinion pursuant to para. 5 sentence 1. The other supervisory authorities concerned may object within a shorter period of two weeks (para. 5 sentence 2).

2   See Art. 4 No. 22 regarding the definition of the term "supervisory authority concerned".

3   The GDPR does not stipulate in which **language** the supervisory authorities have to communicate with each other. In particular, it is not clear in which language the draft decision in para. 3 needs to be submitted to the supervisory authorities concerned. In order to minimise the translation costs of the Member States, it would be preferable if the supervisory authorities could develop a practice according to which the lead authority prepares an English translation of the draft decision and submits that to all other supervisory authorities concerned. However, this practice could bear the risk that problems are analysed less intensively or that results are distorted due to language problems. As an alternative, all translation activities could be centralised at the secretariat that is provided by the European Data Protection Supervisor (cf. Art. 75 para. 1 lit. e)

4   See Art. 4 No. 24 regarding the definition of the term "relevant and reasoned objection".

5   See Art. 4 No. 16 regarding the definition of the term "main establishment".

6   See Art. 3 cmt. 3 regarding the definition of the term "establishment".

7   Due to the remarkable provision of para. 8, **the international competence of the authority for the adoption of the decision derives from the substantive assessment** of the case and, thus, results in a "Catch-22" regarding the conflict of laws and competence to issue the decision. However, the GDPR does not answer the question which national law applies to a particular case (regarding the question of the conflict of laws rules in general, see Art. 92 cmt. 5).

8   To the extent the resolution of the case also depends on national law, the lead authority and the supervisory authority concerned must, first of all, **agree on the applicable national law**. Thus, this provision implicitly requires that the question on the applicable national law is resolved by every supervisory authority pursuant to the same criteria, that means, autonomously in the Union. If the question on the applicable national law was determined by national conflict of laws rules, the supervisory authorities of different Member States could – based on different conflict of laws rules – regularly disagree on whether to dismiss or reject parts of a complaint and to act on other parts of the complaint. See Art. 92 cmt. 5 regarding the question on the conflict of laws in general.

9   In case of a **mixed decision** (partly acting on and partly rejecting the complaint), the **competence will be split**. As a result, two decisions could be adopted concerning the same facts where the two decisions are then challenged before courts of different Member States. Given that the same preliminary issues may have to be resolved in both administrative procedures, contradicting decisions regarding the same set of facts are conceivable.

Article 61

Mutual assistance

1. Supervisory authorities shall provide each other with relevant information and mutual assistance in order to implement and apply this Regulation in a consistent manner, and shall put in place measures for effective cooperation with one another. Mutual assistance shall cover, in particular, information requests and supervisory measures, such as requests to carry out prior authorisations and consultations, inspections and investigations.

2. Each supervisory authority shall take all appropriate measures required to reply to a request[1] of another supervisory authority without undue delay and no later than one month after receiving the request. Such measures may include, in particular, the transmission of relevant information on the conduct of an investigation.

3. Requests for assistance shall contain all the necessary information, including the purpose of and reasons for the request. Information exchanged shall be used only for the purpose for which it was requested.

4. The requested supervisory authority shall not refuse to comply with the request unless:

   (a) it is not competent for the subject-matter of the request or for the measures it is requested to execute;[2] or
   (b) compliance with the request would infringe this Regulation or Union or Member State law to which the supervisory authority receiving the request is subject.

5. The requested supervisory authority shall inform the requesting supervisory authority of the results or, as the case may be, of the progress of the measures taken in order to respond to the request. The requested supervisory authority shall provide reasons for any refusal to comply with a request pursuant to paragraph 4.

6. Requested supervisory authorities shall, as a rule, supply the information requested by other supervisory authorities by electronic means, using a standardised format.

7. Requested supervisory authorities shall not charge a fee for any action taken by them pursuant to a request for mutual assistance. Supervisory authorities may agree on rules to indemnify each other for specific expenditure arising from the provision of mutual assistance in exceptional circumstances.

8. Where a supervisory authority does not provide the information referred to in paragraph 5 of this Article within one month of receiving the request of another supervisory authority, the requesting supervisory authority may adopt a provisional measure on the territory of its Member State in accordance with Article 55(1). In that case, the urgent need to act under Article 66(1) shall be presumed to be met and require an urgent binding decision from the Board pursuant to Article 66(2).

9. The Commission may, by means of implementing acts, specify the format and procedures for mutual assistance referred to in this Article and the arrangements

for the exchange of information by electronic means between supervisory authorities, and between supervisory authorities and the Board, in particular the standardised format referred to in paragraph 6 of this Article. Those implementing acts shall be adopted in accordance with the examination procedure referred to in Article 93(2).

Commentary:

1   In contrast to the supply of information by the requested supervisory authority (cf. para. 6), it is not specified in which language and form the requesting supervisory authority must submit its request. There are good arguments to apply paras. 6 and 9 by analogy so that a request can be done by electronic means.

2   Regarding the competence of a supervisory authority mentioned in para. 4, it can be assumed that Art. 55 will be primarily relevant.

Article 62

Joint operations of supervisory authorities

1. The supervisory authorities shall, where appropriate, conduct joint operations including joint investigations and joint enforcement measures in which members or staff of the supervisory authorities of other Member States are involved.

2. Where the controller or processor has establishments[1] in several Member States or where a significant number of data subjects in more than one Member State are likely to be substantially affected by processing operations, a supervisory authority of each of those Member States shall have the right to participate in joint operations. The supervisory authority which is competent pursuant to Article 56(1) or (4) shall invite the supervisory authority of each of those Member States to take part in the joint operations and shall respond without delay to the request of a supervisory authority to participate.

3. A supervisory authority may, in accordance with Member State law, and with the seconding supervisory authority's authorisation, confer powers, including investigative powers on the seconding supervisory authority's members or staff involved in joint operations or, in so far as the law of the Member State of the host supervisory authority permits, allow the seconding supervisory authority's members or staff to exercise their investigative powers in accordance with the law of the Member State of the seconding supervisory authority. Such investigative powers may be exercised only under the guidance and in the presence of members or staff of the host supervisory authority. The seconding supervisory authority's members or staff shall be subject to the Member State law of the host supervisory authority.

4. Where, in accordance with paragraph 1, staff of a seconding supervisory authority operate in another Member State, the Member State of the host supervisory authority shall assume responsibility for their actions, including liability, for any damage caused by them during their operations, in accordance with the law of the Member State in whose territory they are operating.[2]

5. The Member State in whose territory the damage was caused shall make good such damage under the conditions applicable to damage caused by its own staff. The Member State of the seconding supervisory authority whose staff has caused damage to any person in the territory of another Member State shall reimburse that other Member State in full any sums it has paid to the persons entitled on their behalf.

6. Without prejudice to the exercise of its rights vis-à-vis third parties[3] and with the exception of paragraph 5, each Member State shall refrain, in the case provided for in paragraph 1, from requesting reimbursement from another Member State in relation to damage referred to in paragraph 4.

7. Where a joint operation is intended and a supervisory authority does not, within one month, comply with the obligation laid down in the second sentence of paragraph 2 of this Article, the other supervisory authorities may adopt a provisional measure on the territory of its Member State in accordance

with Article 55. In that case, the urgent need to act under Article 66(1) shall be presumed to be met and require an opinion or an urgent binding decision from the Board pursuant to Article 66(2).

Commentary:
1   See Art. 3 cmt. 3 regarding the definition of the term "establishment".
2   Pursuant to para. 4 in conjunction with national public liability laws, a Member State may be liable for foreign supervisory authorities. It would be preferable if there was a clarification which legal entity will be liable.
3   See Art. 4 No. 10 regarding the definition of the term "third party".

Section 2 – Consistency

Article 63

Consistency mechanism

In order to contribute to the consistent application of this Regulation throughout the Union, the supervisory authorities shall cooperate with each other and, where relevant, with the Commission, through the consistency mechanism as set out in this Section.

Recital:

(135) *In order to ensure the consistent application of this Regulation throughout the Union, a consistency mechanism for cooperation between the supervisory authorities should be established. That mechanism should in particular apply where a supervisory authority intends to adopt a measure intended to produce legal effects as regards processing operations which substantially affect a significant number of data subjects in several Member States. It should also apply where any supervisory authority concerned or the Commission requests that such matter should be handled in the consistency mechanism. That mechanism should be without prejudice to any measures that the Commission may take in the exercise of its powers under the Treaties.*

Article 64

Opinion of the Board[1]

1. The Board shall issue an opinion where a competent supervisory authority[2] intends to adopt any of the measures below.[3] To that end, the competent supervisory authority shall communicate the draft decision to the Board, when it:

(a) aims to adopt a list of the processing operations subject to the requirement for a data protection impact assessment pursuant to Article 35(4);[4]

(b) concerns a matter pursuant to Article 40(7) whether a draft code of conduct or an amendment or extension to a code of conduct complies with this Regulation;

(c) aims to approve the criteria for accreditation of a body pursuant to Article 41(3) or a certification body pursuant to Article 43(3);

(d) aims to determine standard data protection clauses referred to in point (d) of Article 46(2) and in Article 28(8);

(e) aims to authorise contractual clauses referred to in point (a) of Article 46(3); or

(f) aims to approve binding corporate rules within the meaning of Article 47.

2. Any supervisory authority, the Chair[5] of the Board or the Commission may request that any matter of general application or producing effects in more than one Member State be examined by the Board with a view to obtaining an opinion,[6] in particular where a competent supervisory authority does not comply with the obligations for mutual assistance in accordance with Article 61 or for joint operations in accordance with Article 62.[7]

3. In the cases referred to in paragraphs 1 and 2, the Board shall issue an opinion on the matter submitted to it provided that it has not already issued an opinion on the same matter. That opinion shall be adopted within eight weeks by simple majority of the members of the Board. That period may be extended by a further six weeks, taking into account the complexity of the subject matter.[8] Regarding the draft decision referred to in paragraph 1 circulated to the members of the Board in accordance with paragraph 5, a member which has not objected within a reasonable period indicated by the Chair, shall be deemed to be in agreement with the draft decision.

4. Supervisory authorities and the Commission shall, without undue delay, communicate by electronic means to the Board, using a standardised format any relevant information, including as the case may be a summary of the facts, the draft decision, the grounds which make the enactment of such measure necessary, and the views of other supervisory authorities concerned.

5. The Chair of the Board shall, without undue, delay inform by electronic means:

(a) the members of the Board and the Commission of any relevant information which has been communicated to it using a standardised format. The secretariat[9] of the Board shall, where necessary, provide translations of relevant information; and

(b) the supervisory authority referred to, as the case may be, in paragraphs 1 and 2, and the Commission of the opinion and make it public.

6. The competent supervisory authority shall not adopt its draft decision referred to in paragraph 1 within the period referred to in paragraph 3.

7. The supervisory authority referred to in paragraph 1 shall take utmost account of the opinion of the Board and shall, within two weeks after receiving the opinion, communicate to the Chair of the Board by electronic means whether it will maintain or amend its draft decision and, if any, the amended draft decision, using a standardised format.

8. Where the supervisory authority concerned[10] informs the Chair of the Board within the period referred to in paragraph 7 of this Article that it does not intend to follow the opinion of the Board, in whole or in part, providing the relevant grounds, Article 65(1) shall apply.

Commentary:

1   The **procedure for the Board to issue an opinion can be summarised as follows:** If a competent authority intends to adopt a decision in any of the cases listed in para. 1 lit. a to f, it must communicate the draft decision to the Board (by electronic means using a standardised format, para. 4) and wait for its opinion (para. 6). The Board must adopt the opinion by a simple majority of its members (para. 3 sentence 2 and 3) within eight weeks (which can be extended to 14 weeks). If a member of the Board does not object in time, the member shall be deemed to be in agreement with the draft decision (para. 3 sentence 4). Within two weeks after the adoption of the opinion, the competent authority will communicate to the Board: (i) whether it will maintain or amend its draft decision (para. 7); and (ii) whether it intends not to follow the opinion of the Board in whole or in part in which case a dispute resolution procedure pursuant to Art. 65 must be conducted (para. 8). From the communication of the draft decision pursuant to para. 1 until the initiation of a dispute resolution procedure pursuant to para. 8, it can therefore take up to 16 weeks.

A matter of general application (what is meant is likely "relevance") or producing effects in more than one Member State may be submitted to the Board by any supervisory authority, the Chair of the Board, or the Commission (para. 2). In such case, an abstention from voting cannot be deemed as an affirmative vote (para. 3 sentence 4 *a contrario*) and a dispute resolution process cannot be initiated (cmt. 7 below).

2   Since Art. 64 does not refer to a lead competence, it also applies if the requirements of Art. 56 para. 1 are not fulfilled and there is only a general competence pursuant to Art. 55.

3   Pursuant to Art. 70 para. 1 lit. a, the Board must generally act *ex officio* ("on its own initiative").

4   Regarding the list of processing operations that require a data protection impact assessment, see also Art. 35 cmt. 12.

5   See Art. 73 et seq.

6   Regarding the general task of the Board to issue guidelines, recommendations

and best practices in order to encourage the consistent application of the GDPR, cf. Art. 70 para. 1 lit. e.

7   Due to the following provisions it is, in our opinion, **doubtful whether opinions pursuant to para. 2 can be subject to a binding decision pursuant to Art. 65**: (1) para. 6 prohibits the adoption of the draft decision by the competent supervisory authority within the period for the opinion only in cases of para. 1; (2) para. 7 only stipulates an obligation to inform the Board of the intention not to follow an opinion with reference to para. 1; and (3) para. 8 only refers to Art. 65 para. 1 with respect to para. 7 in conjunction with para. 1.

8   In case of an urgency procedure pursuant to Art. 66, the opinion must be adopted within a time period of two weeks which cannot be extended (Art. 66 para. 4).

9   See Art. 75.

10 See Art. 4 No. 22 regarding the definition of the term "supervisory authority concerned".

Article 65

Dartis resolution by the Board[1]

Dispute resolution by the Board[1]

1. In order to ensure the correct and consistent application of this Regulation in individual cases, the Board shall adopt a binding decision in the following cases:[2]

- (a) where, in a case referred to in Article 60(4), a supervisory authority concerned[3] has raised a relevant and reasoned objection[4] to a draft decision of the lead authority or the lead authority has rejected such an objection as being not relevant or reasoned. The binding decision shall concern all the matters which are the subject of the relevant and reasoned objection, in particular whether there is an infringement of this Regulation;[5]
- (b) where there are conflicting views on which of the supervisory authorities concerned is competent for the main establishment[6,7]
- (c) where a competent supervisory authority does not request the opinion of the Board in the cases referred to in Article 64(1), or does not follow the opinion of the Board issued under Article 64.[8] In that case, any supervisory authority concerned or the Commission may communicate the matter to the Board.

2. The decision referred to in paragraph 1 shall be adopted within one month from the referral of the subject-matter by a two-thirds majority of the members of the Board. That period may be extended by a further month on account of the complexity of the subject-matter. The decision referred to in paragraph 1 shall be reasoned and addressed to the lead supervisory authority and all the supervisory authorities concerned and binding on them.

3. Where the Board has been unable to adopt a decision within the periods referred to in paragraph 2, it shall adopt its decision within two weeks following the expiration of the second month referred to in paragraph 2 by a simple majority of the members of the Board. Where the members of the Board are split, the decision shall by adopted by the vote of its Chair.

4. The supervisory authorities concerned shall not adopt a decision on the subject matter submitted to the Board under paragraph 1 during the periods referred to in paragraphs 2 and 3.

5. The Chair of the Board shall notify, without undue delay, the decision referred to in paragraph 1 to the supervisory authorities concerned. It shall inform the Commission thereof. The decision shall be published on the website of the Board without delay after the supervisory authority has notified the final decision referred to in paragraph 6.

6. The lead supervisory authority or, as the case may be, the supervisory authority with which the complaint has been lodged[9] shall adopt its final decision on the basis of the decision referred to in paragraph 1 of this Article, without undue delay and at the latest by one month after the Board has notified its decision.[10] The lead supervisory authority or, as the case may be, the supervisory authority with which the complaint has been lodged, shall inform the Board of the date when its final decision is notified respectively to the

controller or the processor and to the data subject. The final decision of the supervisory authorities concerned shall be adopted under the terms of Article 60(7), (8) and (9). The final decision shall refer to the decision referred to in paragraph 1 of this Article and shall specify that the decision referred to in that paragraph will be published on the website of the Board in accordance with paragraph 5 of this Article. The final decision shall attach the decision referred to in paragraph 1 of this Article.[11]

Recital:

(136)In applying the consistency mechanism, the Board should, within a determined period of time, issue an opinion, if a majority of its members so decides or if so requested by any supervisory authority concerned or the Commission. The Board should also be empowered to adopt legally binding decisions where there are disputes between supervisory authorities. For that purpose, it should issue, in principle with a two thirds majority of its members, legally binding decisions in clearly specified cases where there are conflicting views among supervisory authorities, in particular in the cooperation mechanism between the lead supervisory authority and supervisory authorities concerned on the merits of the case, in particular whether there is an infringement of this Regulation.

Commentary:

1   **In short, the dispute resolution process can be described as follows:** The Board must adopt a decision within a time period of one month (which can be extended in complex cases by one further month) by a two-thirds majority (para. 2); where the Board is unable to do so, it must adopt its decision within two further weeks by a simple majority (para. 3). This decision is binding for all supervisory authorities concerned as well as the lead supervisory authority and must be addressed to them (para. 2 sentence 3). The decision of the Board must be sent to the controller, the processor and the data subject together with the decision from the competent authority (para. 6 last sentence) and must be published on the website of the Board (para. 6).

2   Para. 1 does not clarify whether the Board may only adopt a binding decision upon request. Neither does it clarify who is entitled to submit such a request. Only para. 1 lit. c contains an indication that **at least a supervisory authority concerned and the European Commission may submit a request.** In contrast, Art. 70 para. 1 lit. a outlines that the Board monitors and ensures the correct application of the GDPR "in the cases provided for in Articles 64 and 65 without prejudice to the tasks of national supervisory authorities [...] on its own initiative".

Because adopting a binding decision is not only in the interest of the supervisory authorities, but may also be in the interest of the controller, the processor and the data subject, respectively, they also should have a right to submit a request. In particular, a decision regarding the main establishment of a controller, respectively a processor, pursuant to para. 1 lit. b **should also be adopted upon request of such a controller or processor.**

3   See Art. 4 No. 22 regarding the definition of the term "supervisory authority concerned".

4   See Art. 4 No. 24 regarding the definition of the term "relevant and reasoned objection".

5   From para. 1 lit. a last sentence, it follows that the Board will also have to interpret and apply national data protection law which has been adopted by a Member State based on one of the numerous opening clauses (see Art. 92 cmt. 4). This requires that the Board decides as a preliminary question which national data protection law applies. Since the GDPR does – apart from one exception (see Art. 80 cmt. 4) – **not contain conflict of laws provisions**, the GDPR contains an **omission which must be remedied by analogy**; see in this regard 92 cmt. 5.

6   See Art. 4 No. 16 regarding the definition of the term **"main establishment"**. From the definition of this term, it follows that: (i) a controller, respectively processor, can only have a "main establishment" if it has at least one establishment in the Union (cf. Art. 4 cmt. 38 and 45); (ii) the term "main establishment" is relative regarding the respective processing activity, that is, a controller respectively processor might not have only one main establishment but, depending on which processing operation it is focused on, might have different main establishments (see Art. 4 cmt. 42 and 45); (iii) for a group of companies, there is basically no group-wide main establishment (see Art. 4 cmt. 42), whereas a group-wide main establishment for processors is possible (see Art. 4 cmt. 44); and (iv) a controller that makes its decisions regarding the purposes and means of the processing in an establishment in a third country and also has its central administration in a third country does not have a "main establishment" within the meaning of Art. 4 No. 16 lit. a (Art. 4 cmt. 40 and 41).

7   It is questionable whether a **competence decision** pursuant to para. 1 lit. b may only be adopted if Art. 56 para. 1 applies and therefore a lead competence can be determined. There are good arguments for this view because the decision of the Board pursuant to para. 2 sentence 3 is binding only for the lead authority and the supervisory authorities concerned. In any case, a main establishment within the meaning of Art. 4 No. 16 is required (see cmt. 6).

       A competence decision may – in case of conflicting views of different supervisory authorities – in our opinion, **also be requested by the controller or the processor** (see cmt. 2 above).

8   Para. 1 lit. c does not clearly state whether, in addition to an **opinion pursuant to Art. 64 para. 1**, an opinion pursuant to Art. 64 para. 2 may also be subject to a **binding decision of the Board**. This is doubtful in our opinion (see Art. 64 cmt. 7).

9   Regarding the competence to adopt a decision mentioned in para. 6 sentence 1, see Art. 60 para. 7 until 9.

10   From the initiation of the process pursuant to Art. 65, it can take two months (para. 2) plus two weeks (para. 3) until the adoption of the decision of the Board as well as one further month until the adoption of the final decision of the

competent supervisory authority, that is, a total of three months and two weeks. In the course of an urgency procedure, the decision would have to be adopted within two weeks by simple majority (Art. 66 para. 4).

If the dispute resolution (without applying the urgency procedure pursuant to Art. 66) is carried out due to a non-compliance with an opinion (para. 1 lit. c), the entire decision-making process may take more than seven months (to be exact: three months and 18 weeks) from the submission of the draft opinion (cf. Art. 64 cmt. 1).

If the dispute resolution (without applying the urgency procedure pursuant to Art. 66) is performed to resolve an objection of a supervisory authority concerned against the draft opinion of the lead authority (para. 1 lit. a), the entire decision-making process may take about four and a half months (to be exact three months and six weeks; cf. Art. 60 para. 4) from the communication of the draft opinion to the competent supervisory authority pursuant to Art. 60 para. 3 sentence 2.

11   If the decision of the Board is of **direct and individual concern** to a controller, processor, or the complainant, these persons may bring an **action for annulment** pursuant to Art. 263 TFEU within two months after the publication of the decision on the website of the Board (see Recital 143 sentence 1 and sentence 3). If these persons do not bring an action for annulment within the period laid down by Article 263 TFEU, a national court may not – when dealing with a legal remedy against the decision of the supervisory authority (see Art. 78) – refer a question on the validity of the decision of the Board to the CJEU upon request of these persons (see Recital 143 last sentence). Thus, if the data protection authority adopts a decision based on a decision of the Board, the person or legal entity receiving the decision should take action against the decision of the national supervisory authority before the national court and take action against the decision of the Board before the CJEU (cf. also Art. 78 cmt. 5).

Article 66

Urgency procedure[1]

1. In exceptional circumstances, where a supervisory authority concerned[2] considers that there is an urgent need to act in order to protect the rights and freedoms of data subjects, it may, by way of derogation from the consistency mechanism referred to in Articles 63, 64 and 65 or the procedure referred to in Article 60, immediately adopt provisional measures intended to produce legal effects on its own territory with a specified period of validity which shall not exceed three months.[3] The supervisory authority shall, without delay, communicate those measures and the reasons for adopting them to the other supervisory authorities concerned, to the Board and to the Commission.

2. Where a supervisory authority has taken a measure pursuant to paragraph 1 and considers that final measures need urgently be adopted, it may request an urgent opinion or an urgent binding decision from the Board, giving reasons for requesting such opinion or decision.

3. Any supervisory authority may request an urgent opinion or an urgent binding decision, as the case may be, from the Board where a competent supervisory authority has not taken an appropriate measure in a situation where there is an urgent need to act, in order to protect the rights and freedoms of data subjects, giving reasons for requesting such opinion or decision, including for the urgent need to act.

4. By derogation from Article 64(3) and Article 65(2), an urgent opinion or an urgent binding decision referred to in paragraphs 2 and 3 of this Article shall be adopted within two weeks by simple majority of the members of the Board.

Recitals:

(137) There may be an urgent need to act in order to protect the rights and freedoms of data subjects, in particular when the danger exists that the enforcement of a right of a data subject could be considerably impeded. A supervisory authority should therefore be able to adopt duly justified provisional measures on its territory with a specified period of validity which should not exceed three months.

(138) The application of such mechanism should be a condition for the lawfulness of a measure intended to produce legal effects by a supervisory authority in those cases where its application is mandatory. In other cases of cross-border relevance, the cooperation mechanism between the lead supervisory authority and supervisory authorities concerned should be applied and mutual assistance and joint operations might be carried out between the supervisory authorities concerned on a bilateral or multilateral basis without triggering the consistency mechanism.

Commentary:

1   If there is an urgent need to act in order to protect the rights and freedoms of data subjects, a supervisory authority concerned may adopt provisional measures with a validity not exceeding three months **without applying the**

consistency mechanism, that is, without obtaining an opinion of the Board pursuant to Art. 64 or a dispute resolution pursuant to Art. 65 (see para. 1).

If the supervisory authority: (i) has adopted such a provisional measure; and (ii) considers that final measures urgently need to be adopted, it may request an urgent opinion or an urgent binding decision from the Board (para. 2) within two weeks (cf. para. 4).

If the competent supervisory authority does not adopt provisional measures pursuant to para. 1 despite the urgency, every other supervisory authority may request an opinion or a binding decision from the Board by applying the shortened time period of two weeks (para. 3 and 4).

2 See Art. 4 No. 22 regarding the definition of the term "supervisory authority concerned".

3 There may be an **urgent need to act** within the meaning of para. 1 in particular when the danger exists that the enforcement of a right of a data subject could be considerably impeded (Recital 137 sentence 1).

Article 67

Exchange of information

The Commission may adopt implementing acts of general scope in order to specify the arrangements for the exchange of information by electronic means between supervisory authorities, and between supervisory authorities and the Board, in particular the standardised format referred to in Article 64.[1]

Those implementing acts shall be adopted in accordance with the examination procedure referred to in Article 93(2).

Commentary:

1   Since the **language issue** (cf. Art. 60 cmt. 3) is of "general scope" for the (electronic) exchange of information, it could, in our opinion, potentially be subject to an implementing act.

Section 3 – European data protection board

Article 68

European Data Protection Board

1. The European Data Protection Board (the 'Board') is hereby established as a body of the Union and shall have legal personality.
2. The Board shall be represented by its Chair.[1]
3. The Board shall be composed of the head of one supervisory authority of each Member State and of the European Data Protection Supervisor,[2] or their respective representatives.
4. Where in a Member State more than one supervisory authority is responsible for monitoring the application of the provisions pursuant to this Regulation, a joint representative shall be appointed in accordance with that Member State's law.
5. The Commission shall have the right to participate in the activities and meetings of the Board without voting right. The Commission shall designate a representative. The Chair of the Board shall communicate to the Commission the activities of the Board.
6. In the cases referred to in Article 65, the European Data Protection Supervisor shall have voting rights only on decisions which concern principles and rules applicable to the Union institutions, bodies, offices and agencies which correspond in substance to those of this Regulation.

Recital:

(139)In order to promote the consistent application of this Regulation, the Board should be set up as an independent body of the Union. To fulfil its objectives, the Board should have legal personality. The Board should be represented by its Chair. It should replace the Working Party on the Protection of Individuals with Regard to the Processing of Personal Data established by Directive 95/46/EC. It should consist of the head of a supervisory authority of each Member State and the European Data Protection Supervisor or their respective representatives. The Commission should participate in the Board's activities without voting rights and the European Data Protection Supervisor should have specific voting rights. The Board should contribute to the consistent application of this Regulation throughout the Union, including by advising the Commission, in particular on the level of protection in third countries or international organisations, and promoting cooperation of the supervisory authorities throughout the Union. The Board should act independently when performing its tasks.

Commentary:

1   See Art. 73 et seq. regarding the Chair of the Board.
2   Regarding the European Data Protection Supervisor's limited voting rights see para. 6.

Article 69

Independence

1. The Board shall act independently when performing its tasks or exercising its powers pursuant to Articles 70 and 71.[1]

2. Without prejudice to requests by the Commission referred to in point (b) of Article 70(1) and in Article 70(2), the Board shall, in the performance of its tasks or the exercise of its powers, neither seek nor take instructions from anybody.

Commentary:

1   See Art. 52 regarding the independence of the individual supervisory authorities as well as Art. 44 Regulation (EG) No 45/2001 regarding the independence of the European Data Protection Supervisor.

Article 70

Tasks of the Board

1. The Board shall ensure the consistent application of this Regulation. To that end, the Board shall, on its own[1] initiative or, where relevant, at the request of the Commission, in particular:

(a) monitor and ensure the correct application of this Regulation in the cases provided for in Articles 64 and 65 without prejudice to the tasks of national supervisory authorities;

(b) advise the Commission on any issue related to the protection of personal data in the Union, including on any proposed amendment of this Regulation;

(c) advise the Commission on the format and procedures for the exchange of information between controllers, processors and supervisory authorities for binding corporate rules;[2]

(d) issue guidelines, recommendations, and best practices on procedures for erasing links, copies or replications of personal data from publicly available communication services as referred to in Article 17(2);

(e) examine, on its own initiative, on request of one of its members or on request of the Commission, any question covering the application of this Regulation and issue guidelines, recommendations and best practices in order to encourage consistent application of this Regulation;[3]

(f) issue guidelines, recommendations and best practices in accordance with point (e) of this paragraph for further specifying the criteria and conditions for decisions based on profiling pursuant to Article 22(2);[4]

(g) issue guidelines, recommendations and best practices in accordance with point (e) of this paragraph for establishing the personal data breaches and determining the undue delay referred to in Article 33(1) and (2) and for the particular circumstances in which a controller or a processor is required to notify the personal data breach[5;6]

(h) issue guidelines, recommendations and best practices in accordance with point (e) of this paragraph as to the circumstances in which a personal data breach is likely to result in a high risk to the rights and freedoms of the natural persons referred to in Article 34(1);[7]

(i) issue guidelines, recommendations and best practices in accordance with point (e) of this paragraph for the purpose of further specifying the criteria and requirements for personal data transfers based on binding corporate rules[8] adhered to by controllers and binding corporate rules adhered to by processors and on further necessary requirements to ensure the protection of personal data of the data subjects concerned referred to in Article 47;

(j) issue guidelines, recommendations and best practices in accordance with point (e) of this paragraph for the purpose of further specifying the criteria and requirements for the personal data transfers on the basis of Article 49(1);

(k) draw up guidelines for supervisory authorities concerning the application of measures referred to in Article 58(1), (2) and (3) and the setting of administrative fines pursuant to Article 83;

(l) review the practical application of the guidelines, recommendations and best practices referred to in points (e) and (f);[9]

(m) issue guidelines, recommendations and best practices in accordance with point (e) of this paragraph for establishing common procedures for reporting by natural persons of infringements of this Regulation pursuant to Article 54(2);

(n) encourage the drawing-up of codes of conduct and the establishment of data protection certification mechanisms and data protection seals and marks pursuant to Articles 40 and 42;

(o) carry out the accreditation of certification bodies and its periodic review pursuant to Article 43 and maintain a public register of accredited bodies pursuant to Article 43(6) and of the accredited controllers or processors established in third countries pursuant to Article 42(7);

(p) specify the requirements referred to in Article 43(3) with a view to the accreditation of certification bodies under Article 42;[10]

(q) provide the Commission with an opinion on the certification requirements referred to in Article 43(8);

(r) provide the Commission with an opinion on the icons referred to in Article 12(7);

(s) provide the Commission with an opinion for the assessment of the adequacy of the level of protection in a third country or international organisation,[11] including for the assessment whether a third country, a territory or one or more specified sectors within that third country, or an international organisation no longer ensures an adequate level of protection. To that end, the Commission shall provide the Board with all necessary documentation, including correspondence with the government of the third country, with regard to that third country, territory or specified sector, or with the international organisation.

(t) issue opinions on draft decisions of supervisory authorities pursuant to the consistency mechanism referred to in Article 64(1), on matters submitted pursuant to Article 64(2) and to issue binding decisions pursuant to Article 65, including in cases referred to in Article 66;

(u) promote the cooperation and the effective bilateral and multilateral exchange of information and best practices between the supervisory authorities;

(v) promote common training programmes and facilitate personnel exchanges between the supervisory authorities and, where appropriate, with the supervisory authorities of third countries or with international organisations;

(w) promote the exchange of knowledge and documentation on data protection legislation and practice with data protection supervisory authorities worldwide;

(x) issue opinions on codes of conduct drawn up at Union level pursuant to Article 40(9); and

(y) maintain a publicly accessible electronic register of decisions taken by supervisory authorities and courts on issues handled in the consistency mechanism.

2. Where the Commission requests advice from the Board, it may indicate a time limit, taking into account the urgency of the matter.

3. The Board shall forward its opinions, guidelines, recommendations, and best practices to the Commission and to the committee referred to in Article 93 and make them public.

4. The Board shall, where appropriate, consult interested parties and give them the opportunity to comment within a reasonable period. The Board shall, without prejudice to Article 76, make the results of the consultation procedure publicly available.

Commentary:

1   In principle, the Board is required to act *ex officio* pursuant to para. 1.

2   See Art. 47.

3   Para. 1 lit. e is the central provision for the Board to issue guidelines, recommendations and best practices regarding all questions concerning the GDPR and, thus, to encourage a further **harmonisation by soft law** (cf. also para. 1 lit. f to j and m, which each refer to para. 1 lit. e). The Board is free to decide to which extent to make use of this option.

4   Cf. Recital 72.

5   See Art. 4 No. 12 regarding the definition of the term "personal data breach".

6   Cf. Recital 88 sentence 1, according to which "in setting detailed rules concerning the format and procedures applicable to the notification of personal data breaches, due consideration should be given to the circumstances of that breach, including whether or not personal data had been protected by appropriate technical protection measures, effectively limiting the likelihood of identity fraud or other forms of misuse".

7   Cf. Recital 88 sentence 2, according to which the rules and procedures pursuant to para. 1 lit. h "should take into account the legitimate interests of law-enforcement authorities where early disclosure could unnecessarily hamper the investigation of the circumstances of a personal data breach".

8   See Art. 47.

9   The reference was kept unchanged in the political agreement during the trilogue negotiations although in addition to lit. e and f, additional litera were added. This obviously seems to be an oversight. Thus, it can be assumed that the Board must review the practical application of all guidelines, recommendations and best practices issued by the Board.

10   See Art. 64 para. 1 lit. c.

11   See Art. 4 No. 26 regarding the definition of the term "international organisation".

Article 71

Reports

1. The Board shall draw up an annual report regarding the protection of natural persons with regard to processing in the Union and, where relevant, in third countries[1] and international organisations. The report shall be made public and be transmitted to the European Parliament, to the Council and to the Commission.[2]

2. The annual report shall include a review of the practical application of the guidelines, recommendations and best practices referred to in point (l)[3] of Article 70(1) as well as of the binding decisions referred to in Article 65.

Commentary:

1.   This will in particular concern third countries where an adequate level of data protection has been confirmed. However, the Commission, too, should monitor the functioning of decisions on the level of protection in a third country and the functioning of adequacy decisions (cf. Recital 106).

2.   Due to the lack of provisions on competence, the responsibility for this is (probably) with the chair.

3.   It must be assumed that a limitation to lit. l is not intended and that the practical application of all guidelines, recommendations and best practices pursuant to Art. 70 para. 1 should be reviewed and reported about.

Article 72

Procedure

1. The Board shall take decisions by a simple majority of its[1] members, unless otherwise provided for in this Regulation.[2]

2. The Board shall adopt its own rules of procedure[3] by a two-thirds majority of its members and organise its own operational arrangements.[4]

Commentary:

1 Para. 1 requires a simple majority of all of the Board's members, not only the members present at a particular meeting.

2 See para. 2 as well as Art. 65 para. 2.

3 The rules of procedure must include rules regarding confidentiality (cf. Recital 140 sentence 2, according to which the staff engaged in the secretariat of the Board "should perform its tasks exclusively under the instructions of, and report to, the Chair of the Board").

4 This quorum also applies regarding changes of the rules of procedure and operational arrangements.

Article 73

Chair

1. The Board shall elect a chair and two deputy chairs from amongst its members by simple majority.[1,2]

2. The term of office of the Chair and of the deputy chairs shall be five years and be renewable once.

Commentary:

1   The members of the Board are defined in Art. 68 para. 3 as the head of one supervisory authority of each Member State and of the European Data Protection Supervisor. Thus, **the European Data Protection Supervisor, too, could be the chair.** Since the chair provides for the secretariat of the Board (see Art. 75 para. 1), this would on the one hand be practical. On the other hand, the chair could be a natural counterbalance to the European Data Protection Supervisor who anyway has a very prominent role that significantly exceeds his monitoring tasks.

2   In addition to the rights and obligations mentioned in Art. 74, an additional task is the representation of the Board (Art. 68 para. 2).

Article 74

Tasks of the Chair

1. The Chair shall have the following tasks:
   - (a) to convene the meetings of the Board and prepare its agenda;
   - (b) to notify decisions adopted by the Board pursuant to Article 65 to the lead supervisory authority and the supervisory authorities concerned;
   - (c) to ensure the timely performance of the tasks of the Board, in particular in relation to the consistency mechanism referred to in Article 63.

2. The Board shall lay down the allocation of tasks between the Chair and the deputy chairs in its rules of procedure.[1]

Commentary:

1   See Art. 72 para. 2 regarding the rules of procedure of the Board.

Article 75

Secretariat

1. The Board shall have a secretariat, which shall be provided by the European Data Protection Supervisor.

2. The secretariat shall perform its tasks exclusively under the instructions of the Chair of the Board.

3. The staff of the European Data Protection Supervisor involved in carrying out the tasks conferred on the Board by this Regulation shall be subject to separate reporting lines from the staff involved in carrying out tasks conferred on the European Data Protection Supervisor.[1]

4. Where appropriate,[2] the Board and the European Data Protection Supervisor shall establish and publish a Memorandum of Understanding implementing this Article, determining the terms of their cooperation, and applicable to the staff of the European Data Protection Supervisor involved in carrying out the tasks conferred on the Board by this Regulation.

5. The secretariat shall provide analytical,[3] administrative and logistical support to the Board.

6. The secretariat shall be responsible in particular for:

    (a) the day-to-day business of the Board;[4]

    (b) communication between the members of the Board, its Chair and the Commission;

    (c) communication with other institutions and the public;

    (d) the use of electronic means for the internal and external communication;

    (e) the translation of relevant information;

    (f) the preparation and follow-up of the meetings of the Board;

    (g) the preparation, drafting and publication of opinions, decisions on the settlement of disputes between supervisory authorities and other texts adopted by the Board.

Recital:

(140) The Board should be assisted by a secretariat provided by the European Data Protection Supervisor. The staff of the European Data Protection Supervisor involved in carrying out the tasks conferred on the Board by this Regulation should perform its tasks exclusively under the instructions of, and report to, the Chair of the Board.

Commentary:

1   The staff engaged in the secretariat of the European Data Protection Supervisor "should perform its tasks exclusively under the instructions of, and report to, the Chair of the Board" (Recital 140 sentence 2).

2   It is uncertain (cf. Art. 73 cmt. 1) whether the European Data Protection Supervisor will at the same time serve as the Chair of the Board.

3   This (likely) means in particular legal assistance by researching the factual and legal situation.

4   This is a "catch-all" clause because the tasks mentioned in lit. b to lit. g also constitute day-to-day business.

Article 76

Confidentiality

1. The discussions of the Board shall be confidential where the Board deems it necessary, as provided for in its rules of procedure.[1]

2. Access to documents submitted to members of the Board, experts and representatives of third parties[2] shall be governed by Regulation (EC) No 1049/2001 of the European Parliament and of the Council.

Commentary:

1   See Art. 72 para. 2 regarding the rules of procedure of the Board.

2   See Art. 4 No. 10 regarding the definition of the term "third party".

Chapter VIII – Remedies, liability and penalties

Article 77

Right to lodge a complaint with a supervisory authority

1. Without prejudice to any other administrative or judicial remedy,[1] every data subject shall have the right to lodge a complaint with a[2] supervisory authority, in particular in the Member State of his or her habitual residence, place of work or place of the alleged infringement if the data subject considers that the processing of personal data relating to him or her infringes this Regulation.

2. The supervisory authority with which the complaint has been lodged shall inform the complainant on the progress and the outcome of the complaint including the possibility of a judicial remedy pursuant to Article 78.

Recital:

(141)Every data subject should have the right to lodge a complaint with a single supervisory authority, in particular in the Member State of his or her habitual residence, and the right to an effective judicial remedy in accordance with Article 47 of the Charter if the data subject considers that his or her rights under this Regulation are infringed or where the supervisory authority does not act on a complaint, partially or wholly rejects or dismisses a complaint or does not act where such action is necessary to protect the rights of the data subject. The investigation following a complaint should be carried out, subject to judicial review, to the extent that is appropriate in the specific case. The supervisory authority should inform the data subject of the progress and the outcome of the complaint within a reasonable period. If the case requires further investigation or coordination with another supervisory authority, intermediate information should be given to the data subject. In order to facilitate the submission of complaints, each supervisory authority should take measures such as providing a complaint submission form which can also be completed electronically, without excluding other means of communication.

Commentary:

1   **The right to lodge a complaint** with a supervisory authority applies, according to the unambiguous wording of para. 1, irrespective of the right to a judicial remedy against the controller or the processor (Art. 79). This results in **dual legal protection**.

2   Recital 141 sentence 1 clarifies that a data subject only has the right "to lodge

a complaint with a single supervisory authority". Thus, the same subject matter may not be submitted by the data subject with multiple supervisory authorities.

Article 78

Right to an effective judicial remedy against a supervisory authority[1]

1. Without prejudice to any other administrative or non-judicial remedy, each natural or legal person[2] shall have the right to an effective judicial remedy against a legally binding decision of a supervisory authority concerning them.[3]

2. Without prejudice to any other administrative or non-judicial remedy, each data subject shall have the right to an effective judicial remedy where the supervisory authority which is competent pursuant to Articles 55 and 56 does not handle a complaint or does not inform the data subject within three months on the progress or outcome of the complaint lodged pursuant to Article 77.[4]

3. Proceedings against a supervisory authority shall be brought before the courts of the Member State where the supervisory authority is established.

4. Where proceedings are brought against a decision of a supervisory authority which was preceded by an opinion or a decision of the Board in the consistency mechanism,[5] the supervisory authority shall forward that opinion or decision to the court.

Recitals:

(143)Any natural or legal person has the right to bring an action for annulment of decisions of the Board before the Court of Justice under the conditions provided for in Article 263 TFEU. As addressees of such decisions, the supervisory authorities concerned which wish to challenge them have to bring action within two months of being notified of them, in accordance with Article 263 TFEU. Where decisions of the Board are of direct and individual concern to a controller, processor or complainant, the latter may bring an action for annulment against those decisions within two months of their publication on the website of the Board, in accordance with Article 263 TFEU. Without prejudice to this right under Article 263 TFEU, each natural or legal person should have an effective judicial remedy before the competent national court against a decision of a supervisory authority which produces legal effects concerning that person. Such a decision concerns in particular the exercise of investigative, corrective and authorisation powers by the supervisory authority or the dismissal or rejection of complaints. However, the right to an effective judicial remedy does not encompass measures taken by supervisory authorities which are not legally binding, such as opinions issued by or advice provided by the supervisory authority. Proceedings against a supervisory authority should be brought before the courts of the Member State where the supervisory authority is established and should be conducted in accordance with that Member State's procedural law. Those courts should exercise full jurisdiction, which should include jurisdiction to examine all questions of fact and law relevant to the dispute before them.

Where a complaint has been rejected or dismissed by a supervisory authority, the complainant may bring proceedings before the courts in the same Member State. In the context of judicial remedies relating to the application of this Regulation, national courts which consider a decision on the question necessary to enable them to give judgment, may, or in the case provided for in Article 267 TFEU, must, request the Court of Justice to give a preliminary ruling on the interpretation of Union law, including this Regulation. Furthermore, where a decision of a supervisory authority implementing a decision of the Board is challenged before a national court and the validity of the decision of the Board is at issue, that national court does not have the power to declare the Board's decision invalid but must refer the question of validity to the Court of Justice in accordance with Article 267 TFEU as interpreted by the Court of Justice, where it considers the decision invalid. However, a national court may not refer a question on the validity of the decision of the Board at the request of a natural or legal person which had the opportunity to bring an action for annulment of that decision, in particular if it was directly and individually concerned by that decision, but had not done so within the period laid down in Article 263 TFEU.

Commentary:

1   Art. 78 grants an effective judicial remedy not only against a legally binding decision of a supervisory authority (para. 1) but also against the inactivity of a supervisory authority (lasting longer than three months) (para. 2).

2   Pursuant to para. 1, the **right to an effective judicial remedy against a supervisory authority** is granted to every natural or legal person, that is, data subjects, controllers and processors.

3   The judicial remedy can **only be directed against a decision of the supervisory authority that has legal effect on the person making use of the judicial remedy.** Such a decision concerns in particular "the exercise of investigative, corrective and authorisation powers by the supervisory authority or the dismissal or rejection of complaints" (Recital 143 sentence 5). The judicial remedy does not encompass "measures taken by supervisory authorities which are not legally binding, such as opinions issued by or advice provided by the supervisory authority" (Recital 143 sentence 6).

4   See Recital 141 sentence 1 according to which the data subject should have the right to an effective judicial remedy against a supervisory authority if the **"supervisory authority does not act on a complaint" (complaint for failure to act).**

5   Recital 143 clarifies that the courts competent to review a decision of a supervisory authority are **bound to the decisions of the Board**: "Where a decision of a supervisory authority implementing a decision of the Board is challenged before a national court and the validity of the decision of the Board is at issue, that national court does not have the power to declare the Board's decision invalid but **must refer the question of validity to the Court of Justice in accordance with Article 267 TFEU as interpreted by the Court of Justice**, where it considers the decision invalid" (**Preliminary Ruling Procedure**; Recital 143 sentence 11).

However, a referral of the decision of the Board to the CJEU **may not be made, if the person "had the opportunity to bring an action for annulment of that decision**, in particular if it was directly and individually concerned by that decision, but had not done so within the period laid down by Article 263 TFEU" (Recital 143 last sentence, see also Art. 65 cmt. 11).

Article 79

Right to an effective judicial remedy against a controller or processor

1. Without prejudice to any available administrative or non-judicial remedy, including the right to lodge a complaint with a supervisory authority pursuant to Article 77, each data subject shall have the right to an effective judicial remedy where he or she considers that his or her rights[1] under this Regulation have been infringed as a result of the processing of his or her personal data in non-compliance with this Regulation.[2]

2. Proceedings against a controller or a processor shall be brought before the courts of the Member State where the controller or processor has an establishment[3,4] Alternatively, such proceedings may be brought before the courts of the Member State where the data subject[5] has his or her habitual residence,[6] unless the controller or processor is a public authority of a Member State acting in the exercise of its public powers.[7]

Recital:

(145)*For proceedings against a controller or processor, the plaintiff should have the choice to bring the action before the courts of the Member States where the controller or processor has an establishment or where the data subject resides, unless the controller is a public authority of a Member State acting in the exercise of its public powers.*

Commentary:

1   The exclusive reference to "the right to an effective judicial remedy where [the data subject] considers that his or her rights under this Regulation have been infringed" in para. 1 results in the conclusion (which could be questioned under primary law) that the data subject **only has legal standing to sue regarding the provisions of Chapter III of the GDPR ("Rights of the data subject", Arts. 12 to 23)**. The data subject would not have legal standing to claim in court other infringements under the GDPR.

2   The **question whether civil courts are bound by a decision of the supervisory authority** is not addressed in the GDPR and must therefore be assessed from a national law perspective.

In any case, civil courts of a particular Member State will not be bound by decisions of foreign lead authorities to which the Member State's supervisory authority did not object to (Art. 60 para. 6 *argumentum a contrario*).

Moreover, civil courts will generally not be bound by decisions of the Board (Art. 65 para. 2 last sentence in conjunction with Art. 288 para. 4 sentence 2 TFEU).

3   See Art. 3 cmt. 3 regarding the definition of the term "establishment".

4   This **general jurisdiction** of para. 2 substantially exceeds the general jurisdiction of Art. 4 No. 1 of the Brussels Ia-Regulation because pursuant to Art. 4 No. 1 in conjunction with Art. 63 para. 1 Brussels Ia-Regulation, legal persons may only be sued in the Member State where they have: (a) their registered seat; (b) their central administration; or (c) their main establishment.

In contrast, Art. 79 para. 2 stipulates a general jurisdiction in every Member State where the defendant has an establishment which covers legally dependent and legally independent establishments pursuant to Recital 22 (see Art. 3 cmt. 3). That means in particular that internationally operating companies may be sued in every Member State where they have a subsidiary. Thus, the claimant has the possibility to engage in **forum shopping**.

5   The plain language of para. 2 does not require that the claimant is identical to the data subject. Thus, there are good arguments that the general jurisdiction pursuant to para. 2 sentence 1 as well as the selected jurisdiction pursuant to para. 2 sentence 2 **also apply to actions of a data protection not-for-profit body, organisation or association within the meaning of Art. 80 para. 1.** The unconditional reference to Art. 79 (see Art. 80 cmt. 1) leads to the conclusion that the jurisdictions of Art. 79 para. 2 also apply to actions brought by a data protection not-for-profit body, organisation or association. Moreover, Recital 145 only mentions "claimant" and therefore does not indicate any limitation to data subjects.

6   In contrast to the general jurisdiction of para. 2 sentence 1 (see cmt. 4 above), para. 2 sentence 2 provides a **selected jurisdiction.**

7   The GDPR does not expressly stipulate the relationship between the jurisdictions of the GDPR and those of the Brussels Ia-Regulation. Recital 147 states that "general jurisdiction rules such as those of Regulation (EU) No 1215/2012 of the European Parliament and of the Council should not prejudice the application of such specific rules". It could be derived from this Recital that also a prorogation of jurisdiction pursuant to Art. 25 Brussels Ia-Regulation should not "prejudice" the application of the jurisdictions pursuant to the GDPR, that is, that the jurisdictions of Art. 79 para. 2 **cannot be excluded by a jurisdiction clause in a contract.** Otherwise, it would be very likely that, in practice, the jurisdictions of the GDPR will be excluded to a large extent and an advantageous international competence for the controller will be agreed in general terms and conditions. Since this is not in line with the purpose of the rules of competence of the GDPR, these rules are *leges speciales* and **supersede Art. 25 Brussels Ia-Regulation.**

Article 80

Representation of data subjects

1. The data subject shall have the right to mandate a not-for-profit body, organisation or association which has been properly constituted in accordance with the law of a Member State, has statutory objectives which are in the public interest, and is active in the field of the protection of data subjects' rights and freedoms with regard to the protection of their personal data to lodge the complaint on his or her behalf, to exercise the rights referred to in Articles 77, 78 and 79[1] on his or her behalf, and to exercise[2] the right to receive compensation referred to in Article 82 on his or her behalf where provided for by Member State law.[3]

2. Member States may provide that any body, organisation or association referred to in paragraph 1 of this Article, independently of a data subject's mandate, has the right to lodge, in that Member State,[4] a complaint with the supervisory authority which is competent pursuant to Article 77 and to exercise the rights referred to in Articles 78 and 79[5] if it considers that the rights of a data subject under this Regulation have been infringed as a result of the processing.

Recital:

(142)Where a data subject considers that his or her rights under this Regulation are infringed, he or she should have the right to mandate a not-for-profit body, organisation or association which is constituted in accordance with the law of a Member State, has statutory objectives which are in the public interest and is active in the field of the protection of personal data to lodge a complaint on his or her behalf with a supervisory authority, exercise the right to a judicial remedy on behalf of data subjects or, if provided for in Member State law, exercise the right to receive compensation on behalf of data subjects. A Member State may provide for such a body, organisation or association to have the right to lodge a complaint in that Member State, independently of a data subject's mandate, and the right to an effective judicial remedy where it has reasons to consider that the rights of a data subject have been infringed as a result of the processing of personal data which infringes this Regulation. That body, organisation or association may not be allowed to claim compensation on a data subject's behalf independently of the data subject's mandate.

[Recital 143 can be found with Art. 78.]

Commentary:

1   The unconditional references to Art. 79 lead to the conclusion that the **jurisdictions** of Art. 79 para. 2 also apply for actions brought by not-for-profit data protection bodies, organisations or associations (cf. Art. 79 cmt. 5).

2   Given that the rights mentioned in para. 1 including the right to lodge a complaint pursuant to Art. 77 and the right to a judicial remedy against controllers or processors pursuant to Art. 79 can be exercised on "his or her behalf" (ie, on behalf of the data subject), para. 1 does, in our opinion, **not**

provide for a selected litigation in one's own name on another's behalf, but a judicial right to representation through not-for-profit data protection bodies, organisations or associations within the meaning of para. 1.

3   Whether a not-for-profit data protection body, organisation or association within the meaning of para. 1 also has the right to claim damages in the name of the data subject must be answered under national law. However, the GDPR does not clarify which Member State law is relevant in this regard – this could potentially be either: (i) the law of the country of establishment of the not-for-profit data protection body, organisation or association; (ii) the law of the country of residence of the data subject; or (iii) the *lex fori*. Regarding the question of the conflict of laws, see in detail Art. 92 cmt. 5.

4   Para. 2 contains the **only provision in the GDPR regarding conflict of laws**. Whether a not-for-profit data protection body, organisation or association is entitled to act without a mandate of the data subject, in particular to lodge a complaint with the competent supervisory authority (Art. 77), to take a judicial remedy against a supervisory authority (Art. 78) or to take a judicial action against a controller or processor (Art. 79) without a mandate of the data subject, must be determined pursuant to the *lex fori*.

5   The right to **representative action pursuant to para. 2** excludes the right to claim compensation. Recital 142 last sentence stipulates that the data protection bodies, organisations or associations "may not be allowed to claim compensation on a data subject's behalf independently of the data subject's mandate".

Article 81

Suspension of proceedings[1]

1. Where a competent court of a Member State has information on proceedings, concerning the same subject matter[2] as regards processing by the same controller or processor, that are pending in a court in another Member State, it shall contact that court in the other Member State to confirm the existence of such proceedings.

2. Where proceedings concerning the same subject matter as regards processing of the same controller or processor are pending in a court in another Member State, any competent court other than the court first seized may[3] suspend its proceedings.

3. Where those proceedings are pending at first instance, any court other than the court first seized may also, on the application of one of the parties, decline jurisdiction if the court first seized has jurisdiction over the actions in question and its law permits the consolidation thereof.[4]

Recitals:

(144)Where a court seized of proceedings against a decision by a supervisory authority has reason to believe that proceedings concerning the same processing, such as the same subject matter as regards processing by the same controller or processor, or the same cause of action, are brought before a competent court in another Member State, it should contact that court in order to confirm the existence of such related proceedings. If related proceedings are pending before a court in another Member State, any court other than the court first seized may stay its proceedings or may, on request of one of the parties, decline jurisdiction in favour of the court first seized if that court has jurisdiction over the proceedings in question and its law permits the consolidation of such related proceedings. Proceedings are deemed to be related where they are so closely connected that it is expedient to hear and determine them together in order to avoid the risk of irreconcilable judgments resulting from separate proceedings.

[Recital 145 can be found with Art. 79.]

Commentary:

1   A suspension of the proceeding pursuant to Art. 81 is, in our opinion, only possible in proceedings initiated pursuant to Art. 78. It can be derived from Recital 144 sentence 1 that exclusively "a court seized of proceedings against a decision by a supervisory authority" may decide on the suspension of the proceeding. Thus, Art. 81 **does not apply in civil law proceedings**.

2   Regarding the question when two proceedings within the meaning of para. 1 concern "the same subject matter", Recital 144 last sentence states that "proceedings are deemed to be related where they are so closely connected that it is expedient to hear and determine them together in order to avoid the risk of irreconcilable judgments resulting from separate proceedings".

3   Pursuant to para. 2, any competent court seized later **can** suspend the pending

proceedings. However, if the same infringement is the subject matter of both proceedings, the proceeding **must** be suspended due to the principle *ne bis in idem* to avoid a double sanctioning.

4   Para. 3 concerns proceedings where the subject matter is a different infringement. This results from the fact that a connection of the proceedings is a prerequisite for the suspension of proceeding.

Article 82

Right to compensation and liability[1]

1. Any person who has suffered material[2] or non-material[3] damage as a result of an infringement of this Regulation shall have the right to receive compensation from the controller or processor for the damage suffered.

2. Any controller involved in processing shall be liable for the damage caused by processing which infringes this Regulation. A processor shall be liable for the damage caused by processing[4] only where it has not complied with obligations of this Regulation specifically directed to processors or where it has acted outside or contrary to lawful instructions of the controller.

3. A controller or processor shall be exempt from liability under paragraph 2 if it proves that it is not in any way responsible for the event giving rise to the damage.[5]

4. Where more than one controller or processor, or both a controller and a processor, are involved in the same processing and where they are, under paragraphs 2 and 3, responsible for any damage caused by processing, each controller or processor shall be held liable for the entire damage in order to ensure effective compensation of the data subject.[6]

5. Where a controller or processor has, in accordance with paragraph 4, paid full compensation for the damage suffered, that controller or processor shall be entitled to claim back from the other controllers or processors involved in the same processing that part of the compensation corresponding to their part of responsibility for the damage, in accordance with the conditions set out in paragraph 2.[7]

6. Court proceedings for exercising the right to receive compensation shall be brought before the courts competent under the law of the Member State referred to in Article 79(2).[8]

Recitals:

(146) *The controller or processor should compensate any damage which a person may suffer as a result of processing that infringes this Regulation. The controller or processor should be exempt from liability if it proves that it is not in any way responsible for the damage. The concept of damage should be broadly interpreted in the light of the case-law of the Court of Justice in a manner which fully reflects the objectives of this Regulation. This is without prejudice to any claims for damage deriving from the violation of other rules in Union or Member State law. Processing that infringes this Regulation also includes processing that infringes delegated and implementing acts adopted in accordance with this Regulation and Member State law specifying rules of this Regulation. Data subjects should receive full and effective compensation for the damage they have suffered. Where controllers or processors are involved in the same processing, each controller or processor should be held liable for the entire damage. However, where they are joined to the same judicial proceedings, in accordance with Member State law, compensation may be apportioned according to the responsibility of each controller or processor for the damage caused by the processing, provided that*

full and effective compensation of the data subject who suffered the damage is ensured. Any controller or processor which has paid full compensation may subsequently institute recourse proceedings against other controllers or processors involved in the same processing.

(147)*Where specific rules on jurisdiction are contained in this Regulation, in particular as regards proceedings seeking a judicial remedy including compensation, against a controller or processor, general jurisdiction rules such as those of Regulation (EU) No 1215/2012 of the European Parliament and of the Council1 should not prejudice the application of such specific rules.*

Commentary:

1   A compensation claim pursuant to Art. 82 requires: (i) a material or non-material **damage** (para. 1); (ii) **unlawfulness** ("processing which infringes this Regulation" pursuant to para. 2); (iii) **causality** (para. 2); and (iv) **culpability**, where the defendant has the burden of proof that it is not culpable (para. 3).

2   The term **material damage** will generally cover any impairment of the plaintiff's existing financial position as well as loss of profits.

3   The term **non-material damage** must be interpreted autonomously and is not limited to damages in connection with a humiliation or a similarly severe impairment.

Recital 146 sentence 3 clarifies that "the concept of damage should be broadly interpreted in the light of the case-law of the Court of Justice in a manner which fully reflects the objectives of this Regulation".

According to Recitals 75 and 85 in particular the following circumstances might result in a non-material (or material) damage: (i) discrimination; (ii) identity theft or fraud; (iii) damage to the reputation; (iv) loss of confidentiality of personal data protected by professional secrecy (eg, the professional secrecy obligation of physicians); (v) unauthorised reversal of pseudonymisation; (vi) significant social disadvantages for the concerned data subject; (vii) the unlawful processing of sensitive or data with criminal relevance; (viii) unlawful profiling; or (ix) if personal data of vulnerable natural persons, in particular data of children, is processed unlawfully.

4   The processing also infringes the GDPR and is therefore **unlawful** pursuant to para. 2 if the processing "infringes delegated and implementing acts adopted in accordance with this Regulation and Member State law specifying rules of this Regulation" (Recital 146 sentence 5).

5   Thus, para. 3 stipulates – as did Art. 23 para. 2 Data Protection Directive – **the possibility of the defendant to prove that it is not culpable** because, for example, the occurrence of the damage could not be avoided due to *force majeure*.

In our opinion, the controller will also not be culpable if it can demonstrate it has implemented all required technical and organisational measures pursuant to Art. 24 that are necessary to mitigate the risk that occurred in the specific case (eg, if personal data was entered incorrectly due to human error and, thus, the principle of accuracy pursuant to Art. 5 para. 1 lit. d was infringed in spite of appropriate training measures and appropriate technical measures to identify and prevent input errors).

6   Para. 4 stipulates a **joint liability** for all accomplices. This covers in particular joint controllers within the meaning of Art. 26 or a controller and a processor who are both responsible for not implementing appropriate security measures in violation of Art. 32.

    If one of the controllers or the processors pays full compensation, it is entitled to take recourse pursuant to para. 5.

7   Given that the GDPR does not contain any provision to the contrary, the **right to recourse** pursuant to para. 5 may, in our opinion, be subject to an agreement such as a data processing agreement or a joint controller agreement pursuant to Art. 26.

8   Para. 6 in conjunction with Art. 79 para. 2 provides the possibility of forum shopping for data subjects (cf. Art. 79 cmt. 4).

Article 83

General conditions for imposing administrative fines[1]

1. Each supervisory authority shall ensure that the imposition of administrative fines pursuant to this Article in respect of infringements of this Regulation referred to in paragraphs 4, 5 and 6 shall in each individual case be effective, proportionate and dissuasive.

2. Administrative fines shall, depending on the circumstances of each individual case, be imposed in addition to, or instead of, measures referred to in points (a) to (h) and (j) of Article 58(2).[2] When deciding whether to impose an administrative fine and deciding on the amount of the administrative fine in each individual case due regard shall be given to the following:[3]

   (a) the nature, gravity and duration of the infringement taking into account the nature scope or purpose of the processing concerned as well as the number of data subjects affected and the level of damage suffered by them;[4]

   (b) the intentional or negligent character of the infringement;

   (c) any action taken by the controller or processor to mitigate the damage suffered by data subjects;

   (d) the degree of responsibility of the controller or processor taking into account technical and organisational measures implemented by them pursuant to Articles 25 and 32;[5]

   (e) any relevant[6] previous infringements by the controller or processor;

   (f) the degree of cooperation with the supervisory authority, in order to remedy the infringement and mitigate the possible adverse effects of the infringement;

   (g) the categories of personal data affected by the infringement;[7]

   (h) the manner in which the infringement became known to the supervisory authority, in particular whether, and if so to what extent, the controller or processor notified the infringement;

   (i) where measures referred to in Article 58(2) have previously been ordered against the controller or processor concerned with regard to the same subject-matter, compliance with those measures;

   (j) adherence to approved codes of conduct pursuant to Article 40 or approved certification mechanisms pursuant to Article 42; and

   (k) any other aggravating or mitigating factor applicable to the circumstances of the case,[8] such as financial benefits gained, or losses avoided, directly or indirectly, from the infringement.

3. If a controller or processor intentionally or negligently,[9] for the same or linked processing operations, infringes several provisions of this Regulation, the total amount of the administrative fine shall not exceed the amount specified for the gravest infringement.[10]

4. Infringements of the following provisions shall, in accordance with paragraph 2, be subject to administrative fines up to 10 000 000 EUR, or in the case of an undertaking,[11] up to 2 % of the total worldwide annual turnover of the preceding financial year, whichever is higher:

(a) the obligations of the controller and the processor pursuant to Articles 8, 11, 25 to 39 and 42 and 43;

(b) the obligations of the certification body pursuant to Articles 42 and 43;

(c) the obligations of the monitoring body pursuant to Article 41(4).

5. Infringements of the following provisions shall, in accordance with paragraph 2, be subject to administrative fines up to 20 000 000 EUR, or in the case of an undertaking,[12] up to 4 % of the total worldwide annual turnover of the preceding financial year, whichever is higher:

(a) the basic principles for processing, including conditions for consent, pursuant to Articles 5, 6, 7 and 9;

(b) the data subjects' rights pursuant to Articles 12 to 22;

(c) the transfers of personal data to a recipient[13] in a third country or an international organisation[14] pursuant to Articles 44 to 49;

(d) any obligations pursuant to Member State law adopted under Chapter IX;[15]

(e) non-compliance with an order or a temporary or definitive limitation on processing or the suspension of data flows by the supervisory authority pursuant to Article 58(2) or failure to provide access in violation of Article 58(1).[16]

6. Non-compliance with an order by the supervisory authority as referred to in Article 58(2) shall, in accordance with paragraph 2 of this Article, be subject to administrative fines up to 20 000 000 EUR, or in the case of an undertaking,[17] up to 4 % of the total worldwide annual turnover of the preceding financial year, whichever is higher.[18]

7. Without prejudice to the corrective powers of supervisory authorities pursuant to Article 58(2), each Member State may lay down the rules on whether and to what extent administrative fines may be imposed on public authorities and bodies[19] established in that Member State.

8. The exercise by the supervisory authority of its powers under this Article shall be subject to appropriate procedural safeguards in accordance with Union and Member State law, including effective judicial remedy and due process.

9. Where the legal system of the Member State does not provide for administrative fines,[20] this Article may be applied in such a manner that the fine is initiated by the competent supervisory authority and imposed by competent national courts, while ensuring that those legal remedies are effective and have an equivalent effect to the administrative fines imposed by supervisory authorities. In any event, the fines imposed shall be effective, proportionate and dissuasive. Those Member States shall notify to the Commission the provisions of their laws which they adopt pursuant to this paragraph by 25 May 2018 and, without delay, any subsequent amendment law or amendment affecting them.

Recital:

(148)In order to strengthen the enforcement of the rules of this Regulation, penalties including administrative fines should be imposed for any infringement of this Regulation, in addition to, or instead of appropriate measures imposed by the supervisory authority pursuant to this Regulation. In a case of a minor infringement

or if the fine likely to be imposed would constitute a disproportionate burden to a natural person, a reprimand may be issued instead of a fine. Due regard should however be given to the nature, gravity and duration of the infringement, the intentional character of the infringement, actions taken to mitigate the damage suffered, degree of responsibility or any relevant previous infringements, the manner in which the infringement became known to the supervisory authority, compliance with measures ordered against the controller or processor, adherence to a code of conduct and any other aggravating or mitigating factor. The imposition of penalties including administrative fines should be subject to appropriate procedural safeguards in accordance with the general principles of Union law and the Charter, including effective judicial protection and due process.

[Recital 149 can be found with Art. 84]

(150)In order to strengthen and harmonise administrative penalties for infringements of this Regulation, each supervisory authority should have the power to impose administrative fines. This Regulation should indicate infringements and the upper limit and criteria for setting the related administrative fines, which should be determined by the competent supervisory authority in each individual case, taking into account all relevant circumstances of the specific situation, with due regard in particular to the nature, gravity and duration of the infringement and of its consequences and the measures taken to ensure compliance with the obligations under this Regulation and to prevent or mitigate the consequences of the infringement. Where administrative fines are imposed on an undertaking, an undertaking should be understood to be an undertaking in accordance with Articles 101 and 102 TFEU for those purposes. Where administrative fines are imposed on persons that are not an undertaking, the supervisory authority should take account of the general level of income in the Member State as well as the economic situation of the person in considering the appropriate amount of the fine. The consistency mechanism may also be used to promote a consistent application of administrative fines. It should be for the Member States to determine whether and to which extent public authorities should be subject to administrative fines. Imposing an administrative fine or giving a warning does not affect the application of other powers of the supervisory authorities or of other penalties under this Regulation.

(151)The legal systems of Denmark and Estonia do not allow for administrative fines as set out in this Regulation. The rules on administrative fines may be applied in such a manner that in Denmark the fine is imposed by competent national courts as a criminal penalty and in Estonia the fine is imposed by the supervisory authority in the framework of a misdemeanour procedure, provided that such an application of the rules in those Member States has an equivalent effect to administrative fines imposed by supervisory authorities. Therefore the competent national courts should take into account the recommendation by the supervisory authority initiating the fine. In any event, the fines imposed should be effective, proportionate and dissuasive.

Commentary:

1   Art. 83 para. 2 contains factors relevant for sentencing. Para. 3 contains a

provision regarding the absorption or cumulation of administrative fines (see cmt. 10). From para. 3, it can also be derived that the imposition of fines is subject to the principle of culpability (see cmt. 9). Paras. 4 to 6 contain offences for which the administrative fines will be calculated based on the total worldwide annual turnover of the group of companies (see cmt. 11 below). Para. 7 defers the decision whether administrative fines may also be imposed to public authorities to each Member State.

The Board may draw up guidelines concerning the setting of administrative fines (Art. 70 para 1 lit. k).

2   In case of a "minor infringement" or if the "fine likely to be imposed would constitute a disproportionate burden to a natural person" (Recital 148 sentence 2), **a reprimand** pursuant to Art. 58 para. 2 lit. b **may be issued instead of a fine**.

3   The list of **factors relevant for sentencing** in para. 2 is a non-exhaustive list (see para. 2 lit. k).

4   See Art. 82 cmt. 2 and 3 regarding the terms "material" and "non-material" damage.

5   The technical and organisational measures pursuant to Art. 24 implemented by the controller are not mentioned in para. 2 lit. d, however, they will likely have to be considered pursuant to para. 2 lit. k.

6   The element of any **relevant previous infringements** in para. 2 lit. e means that there must be a certain factual connection between the previous infringement of the GDPR and the infringement now at issue in order to provide for an aggravating factor. However, it remains unclear whether violations against national data protection law before 25 May 2018 must be considered too.

7   Corresponding to the assessment of the EU legislature (cf. Arts. 9 and 10), will likely have to be considered as an aggravating factor if the infringement of the GDPR affects sensitive data or crime-related data.

8   Para. 2 lit. k will likely make it necessary to take into consideration, for example, the **technical and organisational measures pursuant to Art. 24** implemented by the controller.

If administrative fines are imposed on persons that are not an undertaking, "the supervisory authority should take account of the general level of income in the Member State as well as the economic situation of the person in considering the appropriate amount of the fine" (Recital 150 sentence 4).

9   Pursuant to para. 3, the cases referred therein will be subject to the principle of absorption (see cmt. 10 below) if a controller or processor "intentionally or negligently" infringes the GDPR. From this wording it can be derived that the EU legislature requires **culpability** such as intent or negligence for any administrative fines to be imposed.

10   Pursuant to para. 3, the **principle of absorption** applies in case the same or linked processing operations infringe several provisions of the GDPR, that is, the total amount of the administrative fine may not exceed the amount specified for the gravest infringement. If the infringements concern multiple

processing operations that are not linked, the **principle of cumulation** applies, that means, the fines for each of the infringements must be added.

11 See Art. 4 No. 18 regarding the general definition of the term "undertaking". For the purposes of Art. 83, Recital 150 sentence 3 stipulates that the term "undertaking" should be understood "to be an undertaking in accordance with Articles 101 and 102 TFEU", that means, that the **antitrust term of "undertaking"** applies.

Thus, for the purposes of Art. 83, the term undertaking "encompasses any entity engaged in an economic activity, regardless of its legal status and the way in which it is financed" whereby the economic unit is of relevance "even if in law that economic unit consists of several persons, natural or legal" (CJEU 11 July 2013, C-440/11P – *Stichting Administratiekantoor Portielje*, para. 36). This definition of the term "undertaking" significantly affects the calculation of the maximum administrative fines as well as the attribution of data protection infringements.

The maximum administrative fine pursuant to paras. 4 to 6 is either the mentioned fixed amount or "in case of an undertaking" a certain percentage "of the total worldwide annual turnover of the preceding financial year". When calculating the maximum administrative fine, the turnover of the undertaking within the meaning of Art. 101 et seq. TFEU, that means, from a practical perspective, the **global group-wide turnover** will be the basis.

Pursuant to the antitrust case law of the CJEU, the term "undertaking" also significantly affects the attribution of infringements. Pursuant to the case law of the CJEU, the parent company is co-responsible for anti-competitive actions of the controlled entity if the entity violating antitrust law "does not decide independently upon its own conduct on the market, but carries out, in all material respects, the instructions given to it by the parent company" (CJEU 14 July 1972, C-48/69 – ICI, para. 133; CJEU 25 October 1983, C-107/82 – AEG, para. 49). In the case of a wholly-owned subsidiary there is a rebuttable presumption that the subsidiary does not decide independently upon its own conduct (CJEU 25 October 1983, C-107/82 – AEG, para. 50; CJEU 19 July 2010, C-628/10 P and C-14/11 P – *Alliance One International*, para. 46 et seq.).

Given that the GDPR does not contain an explicit provision regarding the attribution of an infringement but refers to the antitrust term of "undertaking" regarding the calculation of the maximum administrative fines, there is a high risk for controllers, respectively processors, that the antitrust term of "undertaking" will also be relevant for the attribution of data protection infringements. In such a case, the following would apply, taking into consideration the antitrust case law of the CJEU.

If the entity that infringes data protection law does not decide independently upon its own conduct in data protection matters but basically follows the instructions of the controlling entity due to commercial and legal dependencies – for which there is a rebuttable presumption in case of a wholly-owned subsidiary – the administrative fine may be imposed on the controlling entity instead of the controlled entity. That means that in many cases the **parent** company will be liable for the administrative fines and also the amount of administrative fines will be calculated on the basis of the total group-wide turnover.

12   See cmt. 11 above.

13   See Art. 4 No. 9 regarding the definition of the term "recipient".

14   See Art. 4 No. 26 regarding the definition of the term "international organisation".

15   The violation of national laws which were enacted within the scope of the GDPR but are not covered by Chapter IX ("Provisions relating to specific processing situations", Arts. 85 to 91; cf. Art. 92 cmt. 5) may, pursuant to para. 5 lit. d, not be sanctioned with administrative fines pursuant to Art. 83 but are subject to national sanction laws enacted by each Member State pursuant to Art. 84.

16   The failure to provide access mentioned in para. 5 lit. e refers to the obligation to grant the supervisory authority access to: (i) all personal data and all information necessary for the performance of its tasks (Art. 58 para. 1 lit. e); and (ii) any premises, including to any data processing equipment and means (Art. 58 para. 1 lit. f).

17   See cmt. 11 above.

18   Para. 6 which was inserted in the course of the political agreement during the trilogue negotiations is redundant in relation to para. 5 lit. e.

19   See Art. 37 cmt. 2 regarding the definition of the term "public authority or body" which, in our opinion, does not cover public companies. Thus, it is not the national legislature's decision whether administrative fines may also be imposed on public companies.

20   Para. 9 contains a special provision for Denmark and Estonia because their legal systems make it impossible for a supervisory authority to impose administrative fines provided for in Art. 83 (see Recital 151 first sentence).

Article 84

Penalties

1. Member States shall lay down the rules on other penalties applicable to infringements of this Regulation in particular for infringements which are not subject to administrative fines pursuant to Article 83,[1] and shall take all measures necessary to ensure that they are implemented. Such penalties shall be effective, proportionate and dissuasive.[2]

2. Each Member State shall notify to the Commission the provisions of its law which it adopts pursuant to paragraph 1, by 25 May 2018 and, without delay, any subsequent amendment affecting them.

Recitals:

(149)Member States should be able to lay down the rules on criminal penalties for infringements of this Regulation, including for infringements of national rules adopted pursuant to and within the limits of this Regulation. Those criminal penalties may also allow for the deprivation of the profits obtained through infringements of this Regulation. However, the imposition of criminal penalties for infringements of such national rules and of administrative penalties should not lead to a breach of the principle of ne bis in idem, as interpreted by the Court of Justice.
[Recitals 150 and 151 can be found with Art. 83.]

(152)Where this Regulation does not harmonise administrative penalties or where necessary in other cases, for example in cases of serious infringements of this Regulation, Member States should implement a system which provides for effective, proportionate and dissuasive penalties. The nature of such penalties, criminal or administrative, should be determined by Member State law.

Commentary:

1   The following infringements are not subject to administrative fines pursuant to Art. 83: (i) violations against national provisions which were enacted within the scope of the GDPR but are not covered by chapter IX ("Provisions relating to Specific Processing Situations"; Art. 85 to 91; cf. Art. 83 para. 5 lit. d); (ii) violations against Art. 10; and (iii) violations against the principle of accountability pursuant to Art. 5 para. 2 in conjunction with Art. 24. In particular for these violations **only national law may provide for penalties**.

2   Observing the principle *ne bis in idemi*, national legislatures may also lay down rules on criminal penalties, including the seizure of profits (disgorgement of profits) obtained through infringements (Recital 149).

Chapter IX – Provisions relating to specific processing situations

Article 85

Processing and freedom of expression and information[1]

1. Member States shall by law reconcile the right to the protection of personal data pursuant to this Regulation with the right to freedom of expression and information, including[2] processing for journalistic purposes and the purposes of academic, artistic or literary expression.

2. For processing carried out for journalistic purposes[3] or the purpose of academic artistic or literary expression, Member States shall provide for exemptions or derogations from Chapter II (principles), Chapter III (rights of the data subject), Chapter IV (controller and processor), Chapter V (transfer of personal data to third countries or international organisations), Chapter VI (independent supervisory authorities), Chapter VII (cooperation and consistency) and Chapter IX (specific data processing situations) if they are necessary to reconcile the right to the protection of personal data with the freedom of expression and information.

3. Each Member State shall notify to the Commission the provisions of its law which it has adopted pursuant to paragraph 2[4] and, without delay, any subsequent amendment law or amendment affecting them.

Recital:

(153)Member States law should reconcile the rules governing freedom of expression and information, including journalistic, academic, artistic and or literary expression with the right to the protection of personal data pursuant to this Regulation. The processing of personal data solely for journalistic purposes, or for the purposes of academic, artistic or literary expression should be subject to derogations or exemptions from certain provisions of this Regulation if necessary to reconcile the right to the protection of personal data with the right to freedom of expression and information, as enshrined in Article 11 of the Charter. This should apply in particular to the processing of personal data in the audiovisual field and in news archives and press libraries. Therefore, Member States should adopt legislative measures which lay down the exemptions and derogations necessary for the purpose of balancing those fundamental rights. Member States should adopt such exemptions and derogations on general principles, the rights of the data subject, the controller and the processor, the transfer of personal data to third countries or international organisations, the independent

supervisory authorities, cooperation and consistency, and specific data-processing situations. Where such exemptions or derogations differ from one Member State to another, the law of the Member State to which the controller is subject should apply. In order to take account of the importance of the right to freedom of expression in every democratic society, it is necessary to interpret notions relating to that freedom, such as journalism, broadly.

Commentary:

1   The provision of Art. 85 is remarkable because the EU legislature delegates the task to **reconcile the fundamental rights with the GDPR to the Member States**. Pursuant to Recital 153 sentence 2, the national legislature must provide for derogations "if necessary to reconcile the right to the protection of personal data with the right to freedom of expression and information, as enshrined in Article 11 of the Charter".

    The reasons why the legislature of the Union delegates to the Member States its original responsibility to not adopt law that violates the Charter are difficult to understand from a political perspective. If a Member State does not comply with this delegated responsibility, it is questionable whether the CJEU may repeal individual provisions of the GDPR due to a violation of Art. 11 Charter.

2   Thus – in contrast to para. 2 – **the scope of para. 1** does not only encompass the "processing for journalistic purposes and the purposes of academic, artistic or literary expression" but also the reconciliation of any other conflicts between the right to protection of personal data (Art. 8 Charter) and the right to freedom of expression and information (Art. 11 Charter).

    That the regulatory power of the Member States exceeds para. 2 is confirmed by Recital 153 sentence 1 which provides that "Member States law should reconcile the rules governing freedom of expression and information, including journalistic, academic, artistic and or literary expression with the right to the protection of personal data pursuant to this Regulation".

3   In particular the **term journalism** must be **interpreted broadly** (Recital 153 last sentence).

4   Pursuant to the plain language of para. 3, there is no **obligation to notify** national provisions that are based exclusively on para. 1.

Article 86

Processing and public access to official documents

Personal data in official documents held by a public authority or a public body or a private body for the performance of a task carried out in the public interest may be disclosed by the authority or body in accordance with Union or Member State law to which the public authority or body is subject in order to reconcile public access to official documents with the right to the protection of personal data pursuant to this Regulation.[1,2]

Recital:

(154)This Regulation allows the principle of public access to official documents to be taken into account when applying this Regulation. Public access to official documents may be considered to be in the public interest. Personal data in documents held by a public authority or a public body should be able to be publicly disclosed by that authority or body if the disclosure is provided for by Union or Member State law to which the public authority or public body is subject. Such laws should reconcile public access to official documents and the reuse of public sector information with the right to the protection of personal data and may therefore provide for the necessary reconciliation with the right to the protection of personal data pursuant to this Regulation. The reference to public authorities and bodies should in that context include all authorities or other bodies covered by Member State law on public access to documents. Directive 2003/98/EC of the European Parliament and of the Council leaves intact and in no way affects the level of protection of natural persons with regard to the processing of personal data under the provisions of Union and Member State law, and in particular does not alter the obligations and rights set out in this Regulation. In particular, that Directive should not apply to documents to which access is excluded or restricted by virtue of the access regimes on the grounds of protection of personal data, and parts of documents accessible by virtue of those regimes which contain personal data the re-use of which has been provided for by law as being incompatible with the law concerning the protection of natural persons with regard to the processing of personal data.

Commentary:

1   Pursuant to Art. 86, personal data "may be disclosed by the authority [...] in order to reconcile **the right to public access to official documents** with the right to the protection of personal data". This clarifies that the **GDPR does not preclude a granting of access**. It is the national legislatures' task to "reconcile public access to official documents and the reuse of public sector information with the right to the protection of personal data" (Recital 154 sentence 4).

2   In this context, it must be considered that against a Member State **a right to access documents might directly be based on Art. 11 Charter** if the Member State acts in the implementation of Union law (cf. Art. 51 para. 1 Charta). Pursuant to the case law of the ECtHR, the ECtHR recognises a right to access documents under Art. 10 ECHR if: (i) the party requesting access has a social "watchdog" function which does not only encompass the press but also NGOs;

(ii) the requested information relates to a subject matter that is of public interest; and (iii) the requesting party acts with the intention to disclose the received information to the public and, thus, to contribute to the public discourse (ECtHR 14 April 2009, *Társaság a Szabadságjogokért v Hungary*, No. 37374/05; 26 May 2009, *Kenedi v Hungary*, No. 31475/05; 25 September 2013, *Youth Initiative For Human Rights v Serbia*, No. 48135/06; 28 November 2013, *Austrian Association for the preservation, strengthening and establishment of an economically healthy agricultural and forestry property v Austria*, No. 39534/07). Pursuant to Art. 52 para. 3 Charter, this case law of the ECtHR must be considered when interpreting Art. 11 Charter (see in detail Feiler, "Informationsfreiheit vs. Datenschutz – Datenschutz als Hemmschuh und Wegbereiter für das Grundrecht auf Zugang zu amtlichen Informationen" in Jahnel (Hrsg), *Jahrbuch Datenschutzrecht* 2014 (2014), 55 (61 et seqq.)).

Article 87

Processing of the national identification number

Member States may further determine[1] the specific conditions for the processing of a national identification number or any other identifier of general application.[2] In that case the national identification number or any other identifier of general application shall be used only under appropriate safeguards for the rights and freedoms of the data subject pursuant to this Regulation.

Commentary:

1   From the wording "further determine", it can be derived that the Member States may provide for detailed provisions which supplement the provisions of the GDPR but may not contradict them. However, it is also clarified that providing national identification numbers generally complies with the GDPR.

2   Neither the term "**national identification number**" nor the term "**any other identifier of general application**" are defined in the GDPR. However, from the heading it can be derived that such identification numbers or identifiers must be identification numbers or identifiers that are valid only within one Member State and that are issued by the Member State itself or at least used for official purposes of identification.

Thus, Art. 87 does in particular not apply to IP addresses, VAT identification numbers (not a national but a Union-wide identification number pursuant to Art. 214 of the Directive on the Common System of Value Added Tax, 2006/112/EC) or license plates (recognition in the entire Union pursuant to Art. 3 of Regulation (EC) No 2411/98).

Numbers contained in identification cards or passports (eg, in Austria pursuant to the Passport Act of 1992 and in Germany pursuant to the Identity Card Act and the Passport Act) are covered by Art. 87 GDPR.

To the extent that social security numbers may already be covered by the term "health data" within the meaning of Art. 4 No. 15 (see Art. 4 cmt. 35), it would not be necessary to apply Art. 87 too.

Article 88

Processing in the context of employment

1. Member States may, by law or by collective agreements,[1] provide for more specific rules[2] to ensure the protection of the rights and freedoms in respect of the processing of employees' personal data in the employment context,[3] in particular for the purposes of the recruitment, the performance of the contract of employment, including discharge of obligations laid down by law or by collective agreements, management, planning and organisation of work, equality and diversity in the workplace, health and safety at work, protection of employer's or customer's property and for the purposes of the exercise and enjoyment, on an individual or collective basis, of rights and benefits related to employment, and for the purpose of the termination of the employment relationship.

2. Those rules shall include suitable and specific measures to safeguard the data subject's human dignity, legitimate interests and fundamental rights, with particular regard to the transparency of processing, the transfer of personal data within a group of undertakings,[4] or a group of enterprises engaged in a joint economic activity[5] and monitoring systems at the work place.

3. Each Member State shall notify to the Commission those provisions of its law which it adopts pursuant to paragraph 1, by 25 May 2018 and, without delay, any subsequent amendment affecting them.

Recital:

(155)*Member State law or collective agreements, including 'works agreements', may provide for specific rules on the processing of employees' personal data in the employment context, in particular for the conditions under which personal data in the employment context may be processed on the basis of the consent of the employee, the purposes of the recruitment, the performance of the contract of employment, including discharge of obligations laid down by law or by collective agreements, management, planning and organisation of work, equality and diversity in the workplace, health and safety at work, and for the purposes of the exercise and enjoyment, on an individual or collective basis, of rights and benefits related to employment, and for the purpose of the termination of the employment relationship.*

Commentary:

1   The term **"collective agreement"** encompasses collective bargaining agreements as well as works council agreements ("works agreements"; see Recital 155 sentence 1).

2   Art. 88 contains an **extremely broad** regulatory competence for the Member States because the Member States are not limited to "further determine" the conditions for the processing (as provided for in Art. 87) or "within the limits of this Regulation" (as provided for in the proposal of the Commission).

The only limitations derive from: (1) the wording that national laws must be limited to the "processing of employees' personal data in the employment context" (see cmt. 3 below); and that (2) the requirements of para. 2 must be met.

Recital 155 sets out that Member State law or collective agreements may in particular provide rules "for the conditions under which personal data in the employment context may be processed on the basis of the consent of the employee". Thus, the **validity of consent in the employment context** is also subject to national laws.

In Germany, the new Federal Data Protection Act (Federal Law Gazette, No. 44, at 2097 et seqq., 5 July 2017) which will come into effect on the same date as the GDPR, that is, on 25 May 2018, basically maintains the rules that already exist in Germany (see Sec. 26 new Federal Data Protection Act). Therefore, personal data of employees may be processed for the purposes of the employment relationship, for example, for the purposes of establishing, carrying out, or terminating an employment relationship. Also, personal data of employees may be processed to detect a crime if there is a documented reason to believe the data subject has committed a crime while employed, the processing of such employee data is necessary to investigate the crime, and the data subject does not have an overriding legitimate interest. The new German Federal Data Protection Act also stipulates that the processing of personal data of employees can be based on consent if the employee has given consent voluntarily. When determining whether a consent was voluntary, the dependency within the employment relationship and the circumstances of the consent must be considered. Consent can in particular be given freely if the employee gained a legal or financial benefit through the consent or if the employee and employer pursue similar interests.

3   The term "employees' personal data in the employment context" is the central wording for the regulatory competence of the Member States. Due to the lack of a definition of the term **employment** in the GDPR, it is likely that it covers all professional actions of, for example: (i) employees, apprentices and other persons that are subject to a mandatory national insurance; as well as (ii) officials. Regarding the processing of personal data at work, please see also Art. 29 Working Party, Opinion 2/2017 on data processing at work, WP 249 (2017), available at http://ec.europa.eu/newsroom/just/item-detail.cfm?item_id= 50083).

4   See Art. 4 No. 19 regarding the definition of the term "group of undertakings".

5   See Art. 4 cmt. 49 regarding the interpretation of the term "group of enterprises engaged in a joint economic activity" and – in contrast – the term "group of undertaking" within the meaning of Art. 4 No. 19.

Article 89

Safeguards and derogations relating to processing for archiving purposes in the public interest, scientific or historical research purposes or statistical purposes[1]

1. Processing for archiving purposes in the public interest,[2] scientific[3] or historical[4] research purposes or statistical[5] purposes, shall be subject to appropriate safeguards, in accordance with this Regulation, for the rights and freedoms of the data subject. Those safeguards shall ensure that technical and organisational measures are in place in particular in order to ensure respect for the principle of data minimisation.[6] Those measures may include pseudonymisation[7] provided that those purposes can be fulfilled in that manner. Where those purposes can be fulfilled by further processing which does not permit or no longer permits the identification of data subjects, those purposes shall be fulfilled in that manner.[8]

2. Where personal data are processed for scientific or historical research purposes or statistical purposes, Union or Member State law may provide for derogations from the rights referred to in Articles 15, 16, 18 and 21[9] subject to the conditions and safeguards referred to in paragraph 1 of this Article[10] in so far as such rights are likely to render impossible or seriously impair the achievement of the specific purposes, and such derogations are necessary for the fulfilment of those purposes.

3. Where personal data are processed for archiving purposes in the public interest, Union or Member State law may provide for derogations from the rights referred to in Articles 15, 16, 18, 19, 20 and 21 subject to the conditions and safeguards referred to in paragraph 1 of this Article[11] in so far as such rights are likely to render impossible or seriously impair the achievement of the specific purposes, and such derogations are necessary for the fulfilment of those purposes.

4. Where processing referred to in paragraphs 2 and 3 serves at the same time another purpose, the derogations shall apply only to processing for the purposes referred to in those paragraphs.

Recitals:

(156) The processing of personal data for archiving purposes in the public interest, scientific or historical research purposes or statistical purposes should be subject to appropriate safeguards for the rights and freedoms of the data subject pursuant to this Regulation. Those safeguards should ensure that technical and organisational measures are in place in order to ensure, in particular, the principle of data minimisation. The further processing of personal data for archiving purposes in the public interest, scientific or historical research purposes or statistical purposes is to be carried out when the controller has assessed the feasibility to fulfil those purposes by processing data which do not permit or no longer permit the identification of data subjects, provided that appropriate safeguards exist (such as, for instance, pseudonymisation of the data). Member States should provide for appropriate safeguards for the processing of personal

data for archiving purposes in the public interest, scientific or historical research purposes or statistical purposes. Member States should be authorised to provide, under specific conditions and subject to appropriate safeguards for data subjects, specifications and derogations with regard to the information requirements and rights to rectification, to erasure, to be forgotten, to restriction of processing, to data portability, and to object when processing personal data for archiving purposes in the public interest, scientific or historical research purposes or statistical purposes. The conditions and safeguards in question may entail specific procedures for data subjects to exercise those rights if this is appropriate in the light of the purposes sought by the specific processing along with technical and organisational measures aimed at minimising the processing of personal data in pursuance of the proportionality and necessity principles. The processing of personal data for scientific purposes should also comply with other relevant legislation such as on clinical trials.

(157) By coupling information from registries, researchers can obtain new knowledge of great value with regard to widespread medical conditions such as cardiovascular disease, cancer and depression. On the basis of registries, research results can be enhanced, as they draw on a larger population. Within social science, research on the basis of registries enables researchers to obtain essential knowledge about the long-term correlation of a number of social conditions such as unemployment and education with other life conditions. Research results obtained through registries provide solid, high-quality knowledge which can provide the basis for the formulation and implementation of knowledge-based policy, improve the quality of life for a number of people and improve the efficiency of social services. In order to facilitate scientific research, personal data can be processed for scientific research purposes, subject to appropriate conditions and safeguards set out in Union or Member State law.

(158) Where personal data are processed for archiving purposes, this Regulation should also apply to that processing, bearing in mind that this Regulation should not apply to deceased persons. Public authorities or public or private bodies that hold records of public interest should be services which, pursuant to Union or Member State law, have a legal obligation to acquire, preserve, appraise, arrange, describe, communicate, promote, disseminate and provide access to records of enduring value for general public interest. Member States should also be authorised to provide for the further processing of personal data for archiving purposes, for example with a view to providing specific information related to the political behaviour under former totalitarian state regimes, genocide, crimes against humanity, in particular the Holocaust, or war crimes.

(159) Where personal data are processed for scientific research purposes, this Regulation should also apply to that processing. For the purposes of this Regulation, the processing of personal data for scientific research purposes should be interpreted in a broad manner including for example technological development and demonstration, fundamental research, applied research and privately funded research. In addition, it should take into account the Union's objective under Article 179(1) TFEU of achieving a European Research Area. Scientific research purposes should also include studies conducted in the public interest in the area of public health. To meet the specificities of processing personal data for scientific research purposes, specific conditions should apply in particular as regards the publication or otherwise disclosure of personal data in the context of scientific

research purposes. If the result of scientific research in particular in the health context gives reason for further measures in the interest of the data subject, the general rules of this Regulation should apply in view of those measures.

(160) Where personal data are processed for historical research purposes, this Regulation should also apply to that processing. This should also include historical research and research for genealogical purposes, bearing in mind that this Regulation should not apply to deceased persons.

(161) For the purpose of consenting to the participation in scientific research activities in clinical trials, the relevant provisions of Regulation (EU) No 536/2014 of the European Parliament and of the Council should apply.

(162) Where personal data are processed for statistical purposes, this Regulation should apply to that processing. Union or Member State law should, within the limits of this Regulation, determine statistical content, control of access, specifications for the processing of personal data for statistical purposes and appropriate measures to safeguard the rights and freedoms of the data subject and for ensuring statistical confidentiality. Statistical purposes mean any operation of collection and the processing of personal data necessary for statistical surveys or for the production of statistical results. Those statistical results may further be used for different purposes, including a scientific research purpose. The statistical purpose implies that the result of processing for statistical purposes is not personal data, but aggregate data, and that this result or the personal data are not used in support of measures or decisions regarding any particular natural person.

(163) The confidential information which the Union and national statistical authorities collect for the production of official European and official national statistics should be protected. European statistics should be developed, produced and disseminated in accordance with the statistical principles as set out in Article 338(2) TFEU, while national statistics should also comply with Member State law. Regulation (EC) No 223/2009 of the European Parliament and of the Council provides further specifications on statistical confidentiality for European statistics.

Commentary:

1   Para. 1 basically repeats the **principles of data minimisation and storage limitation**. Para. 2 and para. 3 entitle the Member States to provide for derogations from certain rights of the data subjects.

The scope of application of para. 2 is limited to processing for: (i) scientific or historical research purposes; and (ii) statistical purposes and provides for derogations from the rights of information, erasure, access, rectification, restriction of processing and objection.

Para. 3 applies to archiving purposes in the public interest and, going beyond para. 2, provides for derogations from the notification obligation vis-à-vis third parties (Art. 19) and the right to data portability (Art. 20).

It must be noted that the lawfulness of processing of **sensitive data** for archiving purposes in the public interest or for scientific and historical research purposes or for statistical purposes may also be stipulated in national law (Art. 9 para. 2 lit. j). The **principle of purpose limitation** is not contrary to a further processing of personal data for archiving purposes in the public interest, for scientific and historical research purposes or for statistical purposes (Art. 5 para. 1 lit. b half-sentence 2), so that other purposes are possible. Against the background of the broad understanding of the term science (cf. cmt. 3) this constitutes a significant restriction of the principle of purpose limitation.

Consent to the participation in scientific research activities in clinical trials must, however, comply with the relevant provisions of Regulation (EU) No 536/2014 (cf. Recital 161). Outside the scope of application of such Regulation (in particular outside of clinical trials), a purpose-changing processing of personal data for purposes of researching a scientific medical question is permitted even without consent of the data subject.

2   The term "**archiving purposes**" includes in particular "providing specific information related to the political behaviour under former totalitarian state regimes, genocide, crimes against humanity, in particular the Holocaust, or war crimes" (Recital 158 sentence 3).

Regarding the processing of personal data for archiving purposes it must be taken into consideration that data referring to deceased persons do not constitute personal data (Art. 4 cmt. 2; cf. also Recital 158 sentence 1).

3   The term "**scientific research purposes**" "should be interpreted in a broad manner" (Recital 159 sentence 2) and includes in particular: (i) clinical trials (Recital 156 last sentence); (ii) research in the area of public health (Recital 157 sentence 1 and 2; Recital 159 sentence 4); (iii) social science research (cf. Recital 157 sentence 3 and 4); and (iv) "technological development and demonstration, fundamental research, applied research and privately funded research" (Recital 159 sentence 2). Thus, research may also be conducted by a private organisation.

4   The term "**historical research purposes**" includes in particular "research for genealogical purposes" (Recital 160 sentence 2).

5   The term "**statistical purposes**" means pursuant to Recital 162 sentence 3 "any operation of collection and the processing of personal data necessary for statistical surveys or for the production of statistical results". Pursuant to Recital 162 sentence 5 the following additional requirements must be met: (1) "the result of processing for statistical purposes is not personal data, but aggregate data"; and (2) "this result or the personal data are not used in support of measures or decisions regarding any particular natural person".

Recital 162 sentence 4 clarifies that statistical results may further be used for purposes other than scientific research purposes.

6   See Art 5 para. 1 lit. c regarding the principle of data minimisation mentioned in para. 1.

7   See Art. 4 No. 5 regarding the definition of the term "pseudonymisation".

8   Para. 1 last sentence repeats the **principle of storage limitation** stipulated in Art. 5 para. 1 lit. e. Pursuant to Recital 156 sentence 3, the controller must actively assess compliance with the principle of storage limitation before the further processing.

9   Regarding the **limitation of the right to object** to the processing of personal

data for scientific or historical research purposes or for statistical purposes pursuant to para. 2, see also Art. 21 para. 6.

10   Pursuant to Art. 14 para. 5 lit. b, the obligation to inform data subjects pursuant to Art. 14 ("Information to be provided where personal data have not been obtained from the data subject") may be limited under the conditions set out there (cf. Recital 156 sentence 5: "Member States should be authorised to provide, under specific conditions and subject to appropriate safeguards for data subjects, specifications and derogations with regard to the information requirements [...]").

Under the conditions set out in Art. 17 para. 3 lit. d, the right to erasure, too, may be limited.

11   Regarding the additionally existing **options to limit the information obligations pursuant to Art. 14 and the right to erasure pursuant to Art. 17**, see cmt. 10 above.

Article 90

Obligations of secrecy

1. Member States may adopt specific rules to set out the powers of the supervisory authorities laid down in points (e) and (f) of Article 58(1) in relation to controllers or processors that are subject, under Union or Member State law or rules established by national competent bodies, to an obligation of professional secrecy or other equivalent obligations of secrecy[1] where this is necessary and proportionate to reconcile the right of the protection of personal data with the obligation of secrecy. Those rules shall apply only with regard to personal data which the controller or processor has received as a result of or has obtained in an activity covered by that obligation of secrecy.

2. Each Member State shall notify to the Commission the rules adopted pursuant to paragraph 1, by 25 May 2018 and, without delay, any subsequent amendment affecting them.

Recital:

(164)As regards the powers of the supervisory authorities to obtain from the controller or processor access to personal data and access to their premises, Member States may adopt by law, within the limits of this Regulation, specific rules in order to safeguard the professional or other equivalent secrecy obligations, in so far as necessary to reconcile the right to the protection of personal data with an obligation of professional secrecy. This is without prejudice to existing Member State obligations to adopt rules on professional secrecy where required by Union law.

Commentary:

1   Secrecy obligations can, for example, be found in the respective national laws for attorneys, notaries, and physicians.

Article 91

Existing data protection rules of churches and religious associations

1. Where in a Member State, churches and religious associations or communities apply, at the time of entry into force of this Regulation, comprehensive rules relating to the protection of natural persons with regard to processing, such rules may continue to apply, provided that they are brought into line with this Regulation.[1]

2. Churches and religious associations which apply comprehensive rules in accordance with paragraph 1 of this Article shall be subject to the supervision of an independent supervisory authority, which may be specific, provided that it fulfils the conditions laid down in Chapter VI of this Regulation.

Recital:

(165) This Regulation respects and does not prejudice the status under existing constitutional law of churches and religious associations or communities in the Member States, as recognised in Article 17 TFEU.

Commentary:

1   In Austria, the **Decretum Generale on Data Protection within the Catholic Church in Austria** (official journal of the Austrian Bishops Conference, No. 52, 15 September 2010, II. 1., available at www.bischofskonferenz.at/ dl/LnuMJKJKKkNKMJqx4KoJK/Amtsblatt_52.pdf) and the **Protestant Data Protection Rules** (Church Law of the Protestant Church A.u.H.B., Official Journal No. 195/1994, 214/1994, 156/1995, 207/1998, 199/2002, 36/2006, 95/2008, 201/2008, 231/2011, 209/2012 and 7/2015) should, in our opinion, be regarded as "comprehensive rules relating to the protection of natural persons with regard to processing" within the meaning of para. 1.

In Germany, the Instruction on Data Protection in the Church ("Anordnung über den kirchlichen Datenschutz", available at www.erzbistumberlin.de/ fileadmin/user_mount/PDF-Dateien/Amtsblaetter/Amtsblatt_201403 Anlage_KDO.pdf), for the catholic church and the Church Law on Data Protection of the Protestant Church in Germany ("Kirchengesetz über den Datenschutz der Evangelischen Kirche in Deutschland", available at http://kirchenrecht-ekd.de/document/25764) are comprehensive rules relating to the protection of natural persons.

Chapter X – Delegated acts and implementing acts

Article 92

Exercise of the delegation[1]

1. The power to adopt delegated acts is conferred on the Commission subject to the conditions laid down in this Article.

2. The delegation of power referred to in Article 12(8) and Article 43(8)[2] shall be conferred on the Commission for an indeterminate period of time from 24 May 2016.[3,4,5]

3. The delegation of power referred to in Article 12(8) and Article 43(8) may be revoked at any time by the European Parliament or by the Council. A decision of revocation shall put an end to the delegation of power specified in that decision. It shall take effect the day following that of its publication in the Official Journal of the European Union or at a later date specified therein. It shall not affect the validity of any delegated acts already in force.

4. As soon as it adopts a delegated act, the Commission shall notify it simultaneously to the European Parliament and to the Council.

5. A delegated act adopted pursuant to Article 12(8) and Article 43(8) shall enter into force only if no objection has been expressed by either the European Parliament or the Council within a period of three months of notification of that act to the European Parliament and the Council or if, before the expiry of that period, the European Parliament and the Council have both informed the Commission that they will not object. That period shall be extended by three months at the initiative of the European Parliament or of the Council.

Recitals:

(166)In order to fulfil the objectives of this Regulation, namely to protect the fundamental rights and freedoms of natural persons and in particular their right to the protection of personal data and to ensure the free movement of personal data within the Union, the power to adopt acts in accordance with Article 290 TFEU should be delegated to the Commission. In particular, delegated acts should be adopted in respect of criteria and requirements for certification mechanisms, information to be presented by standardised icons and procedures for providing such icons. It is of particular importance that the Commission carry out appropriate consultations during its preparatory work, including at expert level. The Commission, when preparing and

drawing-up delegated acts, should ensure a simultaneous, timely and appropriate
transmission of relevant documents to the European Parliament and to the Council.

(167) In order to ensure uniform conditions for the implementation of this Regulation,
implementing powers should be conferred on the Commission when provided for by
this Regulation. Those powers should be exercised in accordance with Regulation (EU)
No 182/2011. In that context, the Commission should consider specific measures for
micro, small and medium-sized enterprises.

Commentary:

1   Pursuant to Art. 92, the European Commission has the power – which may be
     revoked at any time (see para. 3) – to adopt certain delegated acts (see para. 2).
     The **Council and the European Parliament have a right to object** to any
     particular delegated act (para. 4 and 5)

2   Thus, the European Commission has the power to adopt two delegated acts
     (which are relatively unimportant in the overall context): (i) determining the
     information to be presented by icons pursuant to Art. 12 para. 8; and
     (ii) specifying the requirements to be taken into account for certification
     mechanisms pursuant to Art. 43 para. 8.

3   The GDPR proposal of the European Commission provided for 26 different
     competences regarding the adoption of implementing regulations (cf. Feiler,
     Der Vorschlag der Europäischen Kommission für eine Datenschutz-Grundverordnung
     der EU, MRInt 2011, 127 (127)). This was partly criticised as a concentration of
     powers to the benefit of the Commission (see, eg, Engel/Gmain, *Die EU-*
     Datenschutz-Grundverordnung: Was sich ändert, was bleibt – Teil II, jusIT 2013, 178
     (180)). In the course of the legislative process, the amount of provisions
     granting legislative competences to the Commission was reduced by the
     European Parliament to ten and finally to only two mentioned in Art. 86
     para. 2. In contrast, the provisions granting legislative competences to the
     Member States were increased significantly from three in the proposal of the
     European Commission (see cmt. 4 below).

4   The two competence provisions for the European Commission to adopt
     implementing acts must be seen in contrast to the **competences of the**
     national legislatures (opening clauses) to stipulate questions of data
     protection law within the scope of the GDPR (regarding the lack of conflict of
     laws provisions, see cmt. 5 below), in particular the following:

     i.   Pursuant to Art. 8 para. 1 ("Conditions for a child's consent regarding
           information society services") the processing of personal data of a child
           that is below the age of 16 based on consent is basically lawful only if
           consent is given by the holder of parental responsibility (or by the child
           authorized by the holder of parental responsibility). In deviation of this,
           any Member State may lower the age to 15, 14 or 13 years (Art. 8
           para. 1 subpara. 2).

     ii.   Pursuant to Art. 9 para. 2 lit. a ("Processing of special categories of
           personal data"), the processing of sensitive data is generally lawful, if
           the data subject explicitly consented, except where Member State law

provides that the prohibition may not be lifted by the data subject. That means that the **validity of consent to the processing of sensitive data** must be assessed also under national law.

iii. Pursuant to Art. 9 para. 2 lit. b, the processing of sensitive data is additionally lawful, if "necessary for the purposes of carrying out the obligations and exercising specific rights of the controller [...] in the field of **employment and social security and social protection law** in so far as it is authorized by [...] Member State law providing for appropriate safeguards for the fundamental rights and the interests of the data subject".

iv. Pursuant to Art. 9 para. 2 lit. j, the processing of sensitive data for **archiving purposes in the public interest, scientific or historical research purposes or statistical purposes** is lawful only if based on national law (or Union law) – subject to other legal bases pursuant to Art. 9 para. 2.

v. Pursuant to Art. 9 para. 4, the Member States may "maintain or introduce further conditions, including limitations with regard to the processing of **genetic data, biometric data or data concerning health**".

vi. Pursuant to Art. 10, the processing of "**personal data relating to criminal convictions and offences** or related security measures [...] shall be carried out only under the control of official authority or when the processing is authorised by Union or Member State law providing for appropriate safeguards for the rights and freedoms of data subjects". Whether and to what extent crime-related data may be processed must in most cases be assessed on the basis of national law.

vii. Pursuant to Art 22 para. 1 ("Automated individual decision-making, including profiling"), every data subject has the right "not to be subject to a **decision based solely on automated processing, including profiling**, which produces legal effects concerning him or her or similarly significantly affects him or her". Pursuant to para. 2 lit. b, this does not apply if the decision is "authorised by [...] Member State law to which the controller is subject and which also lays down suitable measures to safeguard the data subject's rights and freedoms and legitimate interests".

viii. Pursuant to Art. 23 ("Restrictions"), Member States may restrict, by way of a legislative measure, "the scope of the obligations and rights provided for in Articles 12 to 22 and Article 34", that means, **all data subject rights** when such restriction is a necessary and proportionate measure in a democratic society to safeguard the objectives mentioned in Art. 23 para. 1. In particular the following objectives mentioned in para. 1 are far-reaching: (i) the protection of "**other important objectives of general public interest** of the Union or of a Member State, in particular an important economic or financial interest of the Union or of a Member State, including monetary, budgetary and taxation a matters, public health and social security" (Art. 23 para. 1 lit. e); (ii) "the **protection of the data subject or the rights and freedoms of others**" (Art. 23 para. 1 lit. i); and (iii) "the **enforcement of civil law claims**" (Art. 23 para. 1 lit. j). Therefore, Art. 23 authorises the Member States to reconcile conflicts between different fundamental rights by national law.

ix. Pursuant to Art. 36 para. 1, a controller must conduct a prior consultation with the supervisory authority in principle only if the data protection impact assessment pursuant to Art. 35 indicates that the processing would result in a high risk. In contrast, Art. 36 para. 5 provides that "Member State law may require controllers to consult with, and obtain **prior authorisation** from, the supervisory authority in relation to processing by a controller for the performance of a task carried out by the controller in the public interest, including processing in relation to social protection and public health".

x. Pursuant to Art. 37, the obligation to appoint a data protection officer applies to controllers or processors only in limited cases (see Art. 37 para. 1 lit. a to c). In spite of this, a **data protection officer must be appointed** where required by Member State law (Art. 37 para. 4).

xi. Pursuant to Art. 83 para. 7, every Member State "may lay down the rules on whether and to what extent **administrative fines may be imposed on public authorities and bodies** established in that Member State".

xii. Pursuant to Art. 88 para. 1, Member States "may, by law or by collective agreements, provide for more specific rules to ensure the protection of the rights and freedoms in respect of the **processing of employees' personal data in the employment context**."

xiii. Pursuant to Art. 80 para. 1, a data subject only has the right **to mandate a not-for-profit body, organisation or association to exercise damage claims on his or her behalf** where provided for by Member State law.

xiv. Art. 80 para. 2 stipulates that the Member States may provide that any **data protection organisation, "independently of a data subject's mandate"**, has the right to lodge a complaint with the supervisory authority (Art. 77), to take judicial action against a supervisory authority (Art. 78), and to take judicial action against the controller or processor (Art. 79).

5   It is a remarkable shortfall of the GDPR that it does **not contain conflict of laws provisions**, apart from one exception (see Art. 80 cmt. 4). Thus, it is not clear which national data protection law applies. This shortfall results from the fact that the proposal of the European Commission would have achieved an almost complete unification of the law (cf. Knyrim, *Die Datenschutz-Grundverordnung: Entwicklung und Anwendungsbereich* (Teil I), Dako 2015, 32 (33)) and, therefore, conflict of laws provisions regarding the applicable law were not regarded necessary (cf. Lachmayer, *Zur Reform des europäischen Datenschutzes – Eine erste Analyse des Entwurfs der Datenschutz-Grundverordnung*, ÖJZ 2012/92, 841 (842)). Thus, Art. 94 para. 1 stipulates that the Data

Protection Directive is repealed without maintaining the effectiveness of the conflict of laws provision in Art. 4 Data Protection Directive (cf. Art. 94 cmt. 1).

To the extent a lead competence pursuant to Art. 56 para. 1 applies, this constitutes an **omission** of the Union legislature:

First, Art. 60 para. 4 provides that the Board must issue a binding decision if the lead authority and the supervisory authority concerned cannot agree on the content of a decision and thus the supervisory authority concerned raises an objection that is not followed by the lead authority (cf. Art. 65 para. 1 lit. a). As a preliminary issue, the Board will have to decide which national data protection law applies (see Art. 65 cmt. 5).

Secondly, Art. 60 para. 8 provides that the international competence to adopt the decision depends on the substantive resolution of a case which also leads to a "Catch-22" regarding the conflict of laws and the competence (see Art. 60 cmt. 7).

In cases of a lead competence pursuant to Art. 56 para. 1, the question of the applicable national data protection law is therefore not left to national law but has to be answered on the basis of Union law. Given that the GDPR does not contain conflict of laws provisions – apart from one exception (see Art. 80 cmt. 4) – this constitutes an unintended omission that must be remedied by analogy.

Since there is an **unintended omission only in case of a lead competence** pursuant to Art. 56 para. 1, the question of applicable national data protection law must be answered by **analogy to the rules of competence of the GDPR**. Thus, the national data protection law of the Member State of the controller's or processor's lead supervisory authority applies. The data protection law of another Member State should only be relevant if the prerequisites of a subsidiary competence pursuant to Art. 56 para. 2 apply, that is, if the subject matter of a complaint, or of an infringement: (1) relates to only an establishment in one Member State; or (2) substantially affects data subjects only in one Member State. In deviation from the above, the applicability of national employment law provisions should be answered pursuant to the Rome I Regulation.

If there is **no lead competence** (in particular, if the controller does not have an establishment in the Union or there is no cross-border processing within the meaning of Art. 4 No. 23), there is **no unintended omission** and it is subject to national law to regulate when to apply the data protection law of which Member State. The Rome II Regulation is not applicable because it does not apply to administrative matters (Art. 1 para. 1 Rome II Regulation) and expressly excludes from its scope non-contractual obligations arising out of violations of privacy and rights relating to personality (Art. 1 para. 2 lit. g Rome II Regulation).

Article 93

Committee procedure

1. The Commission shall be assisted by a committee. That committee shall be a committee within the meaning of Regulation (EU) No 182/2011.
2. Where reference is made to this paragraph,[1] Article 5 of Regulation (EU) No 182/2011 shall apply.
3. Where reference is made to this paragraph,[2] Article 8 of Regulation (EU) No 182/2011, in conjunction with Article 5 thereof, shall apply.

Recitals:

(168) The examination procedure should be used for the adoption of implementing acts on standard contractual clauses between controllers and processors and between processors; codes of conduct; technical standards and mechanisms for certification; the adequate level of protection afforded by a third country, a territory or a specified sector within that third country, or an international organisation; standard protection clauses; formats and procedures for the exchange of information by electronic means between controllers, processors and supervisory authorities for binding corporate rules; mutual assistance; and arrangements for the exchange of information by electronic means between supervisory authorities, and between supervisory authorities and the Board.

(169) The Commission should adopt immediately applicable implementing acts where available evidence reveals that a third country, a territory or a specified sector within that third country, or an international organisation does not ensure an adequate level of protection, and imperative grounds of urgency so require.

Commentary:

1   A **reference to para. 2 is made by**: (i) Art. 28 para. 7 (adoption of standard contractual clauses for regular data processing agreements); (ii) Art. 40 para. 9 (decision on the general validity of codes of conduct within the Union); (iii) Art. 43 para. 9 (implementing acts laying down technical standards for certification mechanisms and data protection seals and marks and mechanism to promote and recognise those certification mechanisms, seals and marks); (iv) Art. 45 para. 3 (adequacy decision); (v) Art. 45 para. 5 subpara. 1 (suspension of an adequacy decision); (vi) Art. 46 para. 2 lit. c (adoption of standard contractual clauses for data transfers to third countries or international organisations); (vii) Art. 46 para. 2 lit. d (approval of standard contractual clauses for data transfers to third countries or international organisations); (viii) Art. 47 para. 3 (specification of the format and procedure for the exchange of information with supervisory authorities in case of BCR); (ix) Art. 61 para. 9 (format and procedure for mutual assistance and arrangements for the exchange of information between supervisory authorities); and (x) Art. 67 para. 2 (exchange of information by electronic means between the supervisory authorities).

2   A **reference to para. 3 is made by** Art. 45 para. 5 subpara. 2 (urgent suspension of an adequacy decision; cf. Recital 169).

Chapter XI – Final provisions

Repeal of Directive 95/46/EC

1. Directive 95/46/EC is repealed with effect from 25 May 2018.[1,2]

2. References to the repealed Directive shall be construed as references to this Regulation.[3] References to the Working Party on the Protection of Individuals with regard to the Processing of Personal Data established by Article 29 of Directive 95/46/EC shall be construed as references to the European Data Protection Board established by this Regulation.

Recitals:

(170) Since the objective of this Regulation, namely to ensure an equivalent level of protection of natural persons and the free flow of personal data throughout the Union, cannot be sufficiently achieved by the Member States and can rather, by reason of the scale or effects of the action, be better achieved at Union level, the Union may adopt measures, in accordance with the principle of subsidiarity as set out in Article 5 of the Treaty on European Union (TEU). In accordance with the principle of proportionality as set out in that Article, this Regulation does not go beyond what is necessary in order to achieve that objective.

(171) Directive 95/46/EC should be repealed by this Regulation. Processing already under way on the date of application of this Regulation should be brought into conformity with this Regulation within the period of two years after which this Regulation enters into force. Where processing is based on consent pursuant to Directive 95/46/EC, it is not necessary for the data subject to give his or her consent again if the manner in which the consent has been given is in line with the conditions of this Regulation, so as to allow the controller to continue such processing after the date of application of this Regulation. Commission decisions adopted and authorisations by supervisory authorities based on Directive 95/46/EC remain in force until amended, replaced or repealed.

(172) The European Data Protection Supervisor was consulted in accordance with Article 28(2) of Regulation (EC) No 45/2001 and delivered an opinion on 7 March 2012.

Commentary:

1   The **repeal of the Data Protection Directive** stipulated in para. 1 **applies unconditionally**. Therefore, the conflict of laws provision in Art. 4 Data Protection Directive will be ineffective from 25 May 2018.

2   See Art. 4 cmt. 29 regarding the question of whether a data subject consent
     obtained under the Data Protection Directive continues to apply.

3   For example, the reference in Art. 5 para. 3 ePrivacy Directive (2009/136/EC)
     must be seen as a reference to the GDPR.

Article 95

Relationship with Directive 2002/58/EC

This Regulation shall not impose additional obligations on natural or legal persons in relation to processing in connection with the provision of publicly available electronic communications services in public communication networks in the Union in relation to matters for which they are subject to specific obligations with the same objective set out in Directive 2002/58/EC.[1]

Recital:

(173)This Regulation should apply to all matters concerning the protection of fundamental rights and freedoms vis-à-vis the processing of personal data which are not subject to specific obligations with the same objective set out in Directive 2002/58/EC of the European Parliament and of the Council, including the obligations on the controller and the rights of natural persons. In order to clarify the relationship between this Regulation and Directive 2002/58/EC, that Directive should be amended accordingly. Once this Regulation is adopted, Directive 2002/58/EC should be reviewed in particular in order to ensure consistency with this Regulation.

Commentary:

1   The differentiating criterion "the same objective" would lead to a significant legal uncertainty when applying the GDPR. The following provisions of the GDPR very likely pursue the same objectives as the ePrivacy Directive and will therefore not apply to providers of publicly available electronic communication services: Art. 32 (cf. Art. 4 para. 1 and 1a ePrivacy Directive); Art. 33 (cf. Art. 4 para. 3 subpara. 1 ePrivacy Directive); and Art. 34 (cf. Art. 4 para. 3 subpara. 2 ePrivacy Directive).

It remains to be seen whether the ePrivacy Directive (2002/58/EC as amended by Directive 2009/136/EC) will be replaced in time. On 10 January 2017, the Commission published a proposal for a Regulation on Privacy and Electronic Communication (COM(2017) 10 final) which is supposed to repeal the ePrivacy Directive and to supplement the GDPR from the same time as the GDPR, that is, from 25 May 2018.

Article 96

Relationship with previously concluded Agreements
International agreements involving the transfer of personal data to third countries or international organisations[1] which were concluded by Member States prior to 24 May 2016, and which comply with Union law as applicable prior to that date, shall remain in force until amended, replaced or revoked.

Commentary:
1   Cf. Art. 4 No. 26 regarding the definition of the term "international organisation".

Article 97

Commission reports

1. By 25 May 2020 and every four years thereafter, the Commission shall submit a report on the evaluation and review of this Regulation to the European Parliament and to the Council. The reports shall be made public.

2. In the context of the evaluations and reviews referred to in paragraph 1, the Commission shall examine, in particular, the application and functioning of:

(a) Chapter V on the transfer of personal data to third countries or international organisations[1] with particular regard to decisions adopted pursuant to Article 45(3) of this Regulation and decisions adopted on the basis of Article 25(6) of Directive 95/46/EC;

(b) Chapter VII on cooperation and consistency.

3. For the purpose of paragraph 1, the Commission may request information from Member States and supervisory authorities.

4. In carrying out the evaluations and reviews referred to in paragraphs 1 and 2, the Commission shall take into account the positions and findings of the European Parliament, of the Council, and of other relevant bodies or sources.

5. The Commission shall, if necessary, submit appropriate proposals to amend this Regulation, in particular taking into account of developments in information technology and in the light of the state of progress in the information society.

Commentary:

1   Cf. Art. 4 No. 26 regarding the definition of the term "international organisation".

Article 98

Review of other Union legal acts on data protection

The Commission shall, if appropriate, submit legislative proposals with a view to amending other Union legal acts on the protection of personal data, in order to ensure uniform and consistent protection of natural persons with regard to processing. This shall in particular concern the rules relating to the protection of natural persons with regard to processing by Union institutions, bodies, offices and agencies and on the free movement of such data.[1]

Commentary:

1   This applies in particular to Regulation No. 45/2001 of the European Parliament and of the Council of 18 December 2000 on the protection of individuals with regard to the processing of personal data by the Community institutions and bodies and on the free movement of such data.

Article 99

Entry into force and application

1. This Regulation shall enter into force on the twentieth day following that of its publication in the Official Journal of the European Union.[1]

2. It shall apply from 25 May 2018. This Regulation shall be binding in its entirety and directly applicable in all Member States.

Commentary:

1   The GDPR was published in the Official Journal of the EU on 4 May 2016 and therefore **entered into force on 24 May 2016.** If transitional provisions are not enacted, **currently applicable data protection law will apply until 24 May 2018 and from 25 May 2018 the GDPR will apply.**

Keyword index

About the authors

Dr Lukas Feiler

Attorney, Baker McKenzie

Lukas.Feiler@bakermckenzie.com

Dr Feiler is an attorney in the IT practice group of Baker McKenzie's Vienna office and a Fellow of the Stanford-Vienna Transatlantic Technology Law Forum (TTLF). Dr Feiler holds a PhD in law from the University of Vienna, a certification as a Systems Security Certified Practitioner (SSCP), and a certification as a Certified Information Privacy Professional/Europe (CIPP/E). He holds a teaching position for 'European and International Privacy Law' at the University of Vienna School of Law and is the author of numerous articles on information technology and data protection law.

Dr Michaela Weigl

Attorney, Baker McKenzie

Michaela.Weigl@bakermckenzie.com

Dr Weigl is an attorney in the IT practice group of Baker McKenzie's Frankfurt office. She advises German and international companies on all aspects of IT law, with a strong focus on data protection law. Dr Weigl holds a PhD in law from the University of Passau and certifications as a Certified Information Privacy Professional/Europe (CIPP/E) and a Certified Information Privacy Professional/US (CIPP/US). She frequently gives presentations in San Francisco and Silicon Valley. She is the author of numerous articles on IT law and data protection law.

Prof. Dr Nikolaus Forgó

Professor, University of Vienna

nikolaus.forgo@univie.ac.at

Prof. Dr Nikolaus Forgó has studied law in Vienna and Paris. From 2000 to 2017 he was full professor for legal informatics and IT law at Leibniz Universität Hannover (Germany); between 2013 and 2017 he also served as data protection officer and chief information officer of this university. He was appointed as full professor of law at the University of Vienna in October 2017 and has been head of the department of innovation and digitalisation since then. He teaches and consults in all fields of IT law, legal informatics, civil law and legal theory and has been responsible for more than 50 research projects including more than 20 EU research projects personally.